The Big Roads

Books by Earl Swift

Journey on the James: Three Weeks
Through the Heart of Virginia

Where They Lay: Searching for
America's Lost Soldiers

The Tangierman's Lament

The Big Roads: The Untold Story of the Engineers,
Visionaries, and Trailblazers Who
Created the American Superhighways

THE
Big Roads

*The Untold Story of the Engineers,
Visionaries, and Trailblazers Who Created
the American Superhighways*

EARL SWIFT

Houghton Mifflin Harcourt
Boston · New York
2011

For information about permission to reproduce selections from this
book, write to Permissions, Houghton Mifflin Harcourt Publishing
Company, 215 Park Avenue South, New York, New York 10003.

www.hmhbooks.com

Library of Congress Cataloging-in-Publication Data
Swift, Earl, date.
The big roads : the untold story of the engineers, visionaries, and
trailblazers who created the American superhighways / Earl Swift.
p. cm.
Includes bibliographical references and index.
ISBN 978-0-618-81241-7 (hardback)
1. Highway engineering — United States — History — 20th century. 2. Highway engineers —
United States — Biography. 3. Interstate Highway System — History — 20th century. I. Title.
TE23.S95 2011
388.1'22092273 — dc22
2010043624

Book design by Brian Moore
Maps by Kevin Swift

Printed in the United States of America

DOC 10 9 8 7 6 5 4 3 2 1

Excerpts from "The Great American Roadside" by James Agee are from *Fortune* magazine, 9/1/1934 © 1934
Time Inc. Used under license. Excerpts from "The American Way of Death" by Lewis Mumford are used
by permission of the Gina Maccoby Literary Agency. Copyright © 1966 by Elizabeth M. Morss and James
G. Morss. Originally published in *The New York Review of Books*. Excerpts from "Townless Highways
for the Motorist" by Lewis Mumford and Benton MacKaye are used by permission of the Gina Maccoby
Literary Agency. Copyright © 1930 by Elizabeth M. Morss and James G. Morss. Originally published in
Harper's Monthly.

For Amy

Contents

- - - - - - - - - - - -

Introduction

I WAS OVERDUE for a road trip. It had been years since I'd last embraced that most cherished of American freedoms: to slide behind the wheel of a car equipped with a good stereo and comfortable seats, and head out into the country, beholden to no particular route, no timetable; to grow inured to the road, the thrum of the tires, the warbling silence and thuds of a big truck's slipstream, the whistle of hot summer past the windows. To live off the contents of a cooler on the floorboards and whatever sustenance the road happened to offer.

It had to be a long trip, as it might be years more before I got another, so I decided to go west, all the way west, through a thousand towns and across the great sweep of farm and forest and desert and windblown high plain that waited between home and the Pacific. We'd take back roads, I told my daughter, the two-laners of generations past. We'd drive with the windows down so that we could smell the tar of mid-July blacktop, hear the corn's rustle, holler at grazing cows. We'd drive for just a few hours a day, and slow enough to study the sights, immerse ourselves in wherever we were and remember it afterward. We'd make few plans; we'd stop when we were hungry, when we tired, and wherever caught our fancy.

We'd make a circle of the Lower Forty-eight, first on the old Lincoln Highway, America's Main Street, a ribbon of pavement twisting through twelve states, New York at one end, San Francisco at the other, few big cities between. Then we'd hug the California coast to Los Angeles and turn back east through the desert.

"It'll be great," I told her. "A month on the road, seeing the entire country. Just you and me."

Saylor greeted this uncertainly. "Well, I *guess*," she finally replied. "Can I bring a friend?"

So we were three: a single father of forty-seven and two sixth-grade girls in a rented Chrysler minivan, its hatch crammed with tents, sleeping bags, a dozen stuffed animals, and enough T-shirts and shorts for the ladies to execute four wardrobe changes before each day's lunch.

We joined the Lincoln in southern Pennsylvania. Soon after, we came upon a silent gathering of bikers next to the field where a United Airlines jet went down on 9/11, and after paying our respects stumbled into a blinding thunderstorm out of Buckstown. That evening we caught an Independence Day concert in the heart of Ligonier.

We stuck to the old road into Pittsburgh, crawling from one stoplight to the next amid auto-parts stores and no-tell motels and car washes and timeworn bowling alleys, the air dark with diesel smoke. We passed crumbling factories, crossed into Ohio, stayed true to the Lincoln's original path on narrow lanes through Bucyrus and Upper Sandusky, Ada and Delphos.

In Indiana the highway bent northward to shadow the Michigan line; along the way, it cut through South Bend and came within genuflecting range of Touchdown Jesus and the shuttered Studebaker works. It grazed Chicago, close enough to capture traffic but little else of the city. We entered a cornfield near the Mississippi and didn't leave it until Omaha.

The girls passed the hours begging me to stop the minivan to buy them clothes, or candy, or more stuffed animals, and writing notes to each other when I refused. They adopted mock Swedish personas and spoke in what they imagined to be Swedish accents across entire states. They complained that they were bored.

Out in the Great Plains of western Nebraska, I mired the minivan in soft sand and we spent two hours vainly trying to dig it out before a kindhearted local offered a tow. A couple of hours later, stopping for ice cream, we encountered a stranger so odd and menacing that I kept an eye on the rearview for an hour after. We explored Buffalo Bill's ranch in North Platte. Communed with wild horses on a windswept and dusty government preserve. Wandered a Boot Hill studded with the graves of the overly bold.

It was a short way west of there, a week into the drive, a point at which I could recite the lyrics of every song in the Backstreet Boys' repertoire, that I decided we'd no longer stick to the original highway. The Lincoln coincided with U.S. 30 except where a grain elevator or water tower marked a town's approach; there, it usually veered onto narrow blacktop — often as not named "Lincoln Way," straddled by ditches, and the province of sagging pickups and rusted Detroit iron — to dogleg through the settlement's gut. Ages before, the main highway had been shifted to bypass these prairie burgs, and their reliable sameness (Main Street of post office, hardware store, small grocery, consignment shop, long-shuttered bank) came to seem a forgettable delay next to 30's straight-ahead ease and speed.

So we took up the newer Lincoln, the straightened and wider Lincoln, and pressed up the slow-rising prairie toward the Continental Divide. The towns slid by a half mile beyond the shoulder, behind smatterings of low-roofed stores and diners that had moved off Main Street to lure the bypass's passersby.

In places, we could see that we traveled the middle of three parallel highways. The old Lincoln wriggled off to our right, narrow and slow; we drove its bigger and less cluttered offspring; and away to the left, across miles of rolling pastureland, ran U.S. 30's own successor, Interstate 80, four lanes of smooth concrete, its speeding semitrailers unfettered by cross traffic or slowpoke tractors, by blind driveways or train tracks.

It materialized only briefly before the terrain would rise to block our view, but those glimpses made plain that its pilgrims, windshields and chrome flashing in the sunshine, were moving with a speed and purpose that made our own seem puny. On the old Lincoln, we'd tooled along. On U.S. 30, we toured. On I-80, folks were hauling ass.

In Wyoming, 30 and the old Lincoln peeled away from the interstate and struck north as one, trundling across ridges of dinosaur bone and petrified forest into Medicine Bow. The town was a fossil itself, littered with tumbledown filling stations and abandoned motels, their doors agape, roofs staved, parking lots colonized by waist-high weeds — signals, fast fading, that this once was an important wayside on an important way.

We curved with the blacktop back to the south and outside Rawlins found that the Lincoln and 30 fused with the interstate, that the newer road's concrete had been laid right overtop its forebears. For the first time since leaving home, I steered the minivan up an interstate ramp.

The following few hours were downright relaxing. Cruise control set at seventy-five. A couple of fingers on the wheel. Pavement hard and even. Lanes a dozen feet wide, crisply marked and flanked by broad shoulders. Forward visibility of a half mile, minimum, and on most stretches many times that. No grades that required the minivan to downshift. No driveways, no intersections, no roaming cattle, no oncoming cars; after two thousand miles on lesser roads, I-80 seemed well ordered, safe, and so, so easy.

We spent six days in California before turning for home, and it was on interstates — 15, 40, 81, and 64 — that we covered most of the distance. Had we pushed it, and not very hard, we could have gone ocean to ocean in five days.

Back home, I made a surprising discovery as I pored through the digital pictures I'd taken during our month away: I'd snapped hundreds, but only a handful on days we'd traveled by interstate. Wyoming was a blank west of Rawlins, as was Arizona aside from the Grand Canyon. New Mexico? Two pictures of our campsite near Grants. Arkansas was unchronicled; the same went for Tennessee, North Carolina, and Virginia.

What's more, I found that while I could conjure up scores of mental snapshots of minuscule towns and interesting sights from my hours behind the wheel, I'd logged almost all of them while driving back roads. I could recall Franklin Grove, Illinois, and the bridge over the Mississippi in Clinton, Iowa, and the quiltwork of farms east of Lima, Ohio, in great detail. Remembered Nevada, Iowa (which a sign at the city limits proclaimed the "26th best small town in America"), and Cozad, Nebraska (where the Lincoln was spanned by a banner marking the hundredth meridian), and cresting a steep mountain pass at the edge of Austin, Nevada, in the silver-blue early morning, on an empty stretch of U.S. 50 that *Life* magazine nicknamed the "Loneliest Road in America."

I could especially reconstruct our passage over the Great Salt Lake Desert on two hundred miles of narrow gravel — a traverse on which we saw three vehicles coming the other way in two whole days and passed hour on hour surrounded by sagebrush, shimmering salt crystal, bounding antelope, and an eerie silence broken only by the girls' worries that we'd be eaten by mountain lions.

Pennsylvania Dutch barnyards, misty Allegheny hollows, the endless green of corn on the rise — all that came back to me with sharp-edged clarity. But the thousands of miles we'd made on the interstates were a blur of far vaguer impressions. I could not call to mind any specific image of New Mexico, or of west Texas, or of the steamy Mississippi bottomlands. Had we really driven through Little Rock and Nashville? We had, we must have, but I couldn't say much about either. The minivan's windshield became a proscenium through which we watched the countryside pass without actually experiencing it; we were in it, but not of it.

Mind you, that's not a complaint. I knew what we'd get when I turned up the ramp, and the interstates delivered. They carried us without incident, without drama. They offered up food and lodging with minimal fuss. They carved the shortest path all the way home.

And we made very good time.

At nearly forty-seven thousand miles long and at least four lanes wide, the Dwight D. Eisenhower System of Interstate and Defense Highways, as it's formally known, is the greatest public works project in history, dwarfing Egypt's pyramids, the Panama Canal, and China's Great Wall. Its construction saw forests felled, mountains leveled, and rivers bridged, tunneled, or picked up and moved, and it incorporates nearly three hundred million cubic yards of concrete, enough to fill sixty-four Louisiana Superdomes to the rafters.

It has smoothed what was once rough country, enabling us to cruise at a mile a minute across desert and bog, rangeland and Appalachian hollow, to dive eight cars abreast under Baltimore's harbor and drill through the Rockies at more than two miles above sea level—and to do it all with less chance of injury than on any other type of road, in this country and most others.

It is a vast and powerful economic engine that provides millions of jobs, gets goods to Dakota ranchers with the same speed they reach big cities back east, and puts fresh greens on dinner tables a thousand miles from the farms that grow them.

It has its problems. It is so big, and its components so expensive, that maintaining the beast has become a real quandary. It represents a spectacular investment in a mode of transport that will wither without new fuel sources. It is clogged with rush-hour traffic that approaches the tie-ups it was intended, in part, to ease. And it has been blamed, and rightly, for a pox of unforeseen consequences: for hastening the messy sprawl of U.S. cities, carving up neighborhoods, gutting a thousand small-town shopping districts, and fostering an interchange glut of motels and fast-food joints as predictable as the roads themselves.

Like it or not, the interstates "changed the face of America," as Eisenhower would comment after leaving the presidency. They are intrinsic to our everyday life, to the modern American experience, to what defines the physical United States. They form the nation's commercial and cultural grid, binding its regions, bridging its dialects, snaking into every state and every major city in the Lower Forty-eight. They've insinuated themselves into our slang, our perception of time and space, our mental maps.

In fact, they've grown so central to life in a country utterly beholden to the car that they're almost invisible to most of us, one of those features of the landscape that we take for granted even when we're on them. For most of the population, they've always been there—D.C. has always had a Beltway, Los Angeles the 5 and 405, Atlanta its Perimeter, St. Louis a confluence of interstates in the shadow of the Gateway Arch. It's a stretch to imagine Dallas–Fort Worth without its great, dumbbell-shaped array of loops and connectors, or Long Island without the LIE, the Whitestone, the Brooklyn-Queens Expressway.

We've come to so rely on this triumph of engineering — and make no mistake, that's what it is — that to embark cross-country on any lesser road, any Blue Highway, is viewed as nostalgic adventure, or escape, or eccentricity, a journey with an ulterior motive.

Which makes it all the more remarkable that most Americans are oblivious to how this behemoth came to be, and why it was built how and where it was. The conventional wisdom usually figures the system a product of the fifties; the public imagination places it alongside Telstar, coonskin caps, and polio shots. But as our road trip on the Lincoln hinted, that's a myth, like so much of what we think we know about the interstates. They're not nearly as new as we imagine; they are the progeny of older road networks that were, themselves, descended from even older paths, and they from older ones still.

And despite their official name, they didn't spring, fully formed or otherwise, from Ike or his lieutenants. By the time Eisenhower signed the bill that financed the system, in June 1956, most of its physical details were old news. Its routing had been committed to paper for eighteen years. The specifics of its design had been decided for twelve. Franklin Roosevelt had a greater hand in its creation than Eisenhower did, truth be told, and the system's origins go back much further than him.

Its true parents were career technocrats, anonymous outside their fields. If it were to bear the name of the man most responsible for its existence, it would be called the Thomas H. MacDonald System of Interstate and Defense Highways, MacDonald being the man who, with his staff, conceived of the network and proposed its construction before World War II.

Odds are you've heard of neither him nor his quiet and persistent protégé, Frank Turner, who translated that prewar concept into the swooping ramps, mountain cuts, and stacked interchanges that we know today. These guys, more than any others, made it happen. Their supporting cast included auto executives, scientists, inventors, freelance designers and futurists, and no shortage of oddballs. Opponents, too: Lewis Mumford, a respected critic of art and architecture, helped whet the public appetite for superhighways, then morphed into their harshest critic. A quiet family man named Joe Wiles despaired at a highway boring through Baltimore, as did thousands of men and women in dozens of cities, and decided to fight the juggernaut before it destroyed a home and neighborhood he'd worked years to build. Both helped to shape what we got.

But to begin at the beginning, one must go even further back than MacDonald — back to the dawn of the motor age, when America's cross-country roads, where they existed at all, were no more than rutted cart paths.

Back to a horse-drawn America, and a man whose push for interstate highways began on a bicycle.

PART I

Out of the Mud

1

IT STARTED WITH MUD, and manure, and Carl Graham Fisher. Today, that name is virtually unknown outside of a couple of far-flung American cities, and it's not well known in those; but a century ago, Fisher was a regular in the sports and business pages of newspapers from coast to coast and, for a spell before World War I, close to a household name. He was a man of big ideas and the energy to see them through, and one of his inspirations was ancestor to the great network of highways binding the continent. Trace today's interstate highways back to their earliest incarnation, and there stands Fisher, pushing the idea while Dwight Eisenhower was still at West Point, a full forty years before he gained the White House.

When Fisher was born in Greensburg, Indiana, in 1874, the automobile's American debut was still two decades away. Overland travel was the province of the train. Look at any map of Indiana from the period — or any other state, for that matter — and you'll see tangles of thick black lines converging on the major cities; smaller settlements are reduced to dots on those lines, indistinguishable from those marking their neighbors, the size and character of each less important than its status as a station stop. Most of the old maps don't depict a single road.

They were there, but hardly in the form we think of them. The routes out of most any town in America were "wholly unclassable, almost impassable, scarcely jackassable," as folks said then — especially when spring and fall rains transformed the simple dirt tracks into a heavy muck, more glue than earth. In Indiana, as elsewhere, people braved them to the train and back, or to roll their harvest from their farms to the nearest grain elevator. For any trip beyond that, they went by rail.

Such was the world into which Carl Fisher arrived, the son of a hard-drinking country lawyer and his tough, determined wife. The couple separated when Carl was young; Ida Fisher moved her three boys forty miles to Indianapolis, where the boundlessly energetic Carl quit school at twelve and set out to make a fortune. He was bright-eyed, talkative, a natural salesman. And he was disciplined: at fifteen he landed work as a news "butcher," hawking newspapers, books, candy, and tobacco aboard intercity trains; at seventeen, he'd squirreled away $600, a goodly sum at the time, and decided to open his own business.

Choosing a line of work came easily, because for a couple of years Fisher had been caught up in a national craze for bicycles. The streets of Indianapolis, like those of every major city in the country, were busy with "safeties," the forerunners of modern beach cruisers, and with older, far more dangerous "ordinaries," which had enormous front and tiny rear wheels, and saddles perched as high as five feet off the ground. Fisher opened a shop to fix both.

He advertised the business by spending a lot of time on an ordinary himself and developing a reputation as borderline crazy. He'd always been an athletic, daring kid, handy at walking tightropes, able to sprint backward faster than friends could do it face-on, and enthralled by speed, especially by the hell-for-leather, white-knuckle speed of an ordinary, which was essentially brakeless. On steep downhills, the best a rider could do was brace his feet on the handlebars, so that if he crashed, which seemed a good bet — the bike stopped cold, with calamitous results, if that big front wheel encountered an obstacle — he'd at least go flying right-side up.

It didn't much faze Fisher that he was half-blind with astigmatism and had so many wrecks that his friends dubbed him "Crip." Just climbing onto one of the machines gave him a thrill. Racing them was intoxicating. In short order he landed a spot on a traveling race team led by a speed demon named Barney Oldfield and toured county fairs throughout the Midwest. The shop thrived.

By and by, Fisher decided to branch into sales. Impressed with Pope-Toledo bikes, he took the train to Toledo and asked their maker, Col. Albert A. Pope, to make him the brand's Indianapolis distributor — and to help get him started by parting with a boxcar of bikes at cost. Pope agreed, which provided Fisher enough of a profit margin to give away fifty. He had a friend make a thousand toy balloons, then took out newspaper ads announcing that the balloons would be loosed over the city, fifty containing numbered tags that could be exchanged for a new bike. The stunt created a sensation. The sale of Popes spiked across the state.

Fisher was just getting started. He built a bike so big he had to mount it from a second-floor window, then rode it through the city's streets. Indianapolis ate it up. He announced he'd ride a bike across a tightrope strung between a pair of downtown high-rises and, against all reason, actually did it while a crowd watched, breathless, from twelve stories below.

Now a minor celebrity, Fisher put out word that he'd throw a bike off the roof of a downtown building and award a new machine to whoever dragged the wreckage to his shop. This time the police tried to stop him, planting sentries outside the building the morning of the stunt. They were no match for the budding showman; Fisher was already inside and at the appointed hour tossed the bike, then escaped down a back staircase. When the cops showed up at his shop, a telephone call came in. It was Fisher, with word that he was waiting at the precinct house.

As sixth-grade dropouts go, he was doing well. But not well enough to suit him: aiming to have the grandest showroom in Indianapolis, he called on another leading bike maker in Columbus, Ohio. George C. Erland was so charmed by the brash young man that he bankrolled Fisher to the tune of $50,000, a fortune then, and sure enough, Fisher soon had the biggest store in town, with all brands for sale up front and a dozen repairmen working in the back. It became a gathering place for the city's cycling fraternity — members of the local Zig-Zag

Cycle Club, among whom Fisher had several close friends, and of a national organization called the League of American Wheelmen. And on any given day, the conversation came around to cycling's most urgent need: roads on which to ride.

A spin on even a safety bike was likely to be a jarring experience in the 1890s, when city streets were paved, assuming they were paved at all, with cobblestone, brick, or uneven granite block, and snarled with carts, buggies, and horsemen. Outside the business districts, roads dwindled to little more than wagon ruts. In suburban Indianapolis, as out in the sticks, a sprinkling of rain could turn them to bogs; their mud lay deep and loose, could suck the boots off a farmer's feet, prompted travelers to quit the established path for the open fields. Some swallowed horses to their flanks; the unfortunate buggy that ventured down such a muddy lane soon flailed past its axles in the ooze. Even on hard-packed roads, mud formed dark rooster tails behind surreys, spattered long skirts, caked shoes. American business was conducted in mud-soiled suits, as were law, medicine, and church services.

And mixed with the mud was a liberal helping of manure, for city and country alike were dependent on the horse. The situation was grim enough in small towns, where the population might number a few hundred humans and a few dozen animals. It was far nastier in Fisher's Indianapolis, which despite bicycles and electric streetcars was home to a horse for every 14 people, or Kansas City, which had a horse for every 7.4. Boston's Beacon Hill, one observer recalled, had a "rich equine flavor."

Crossing a street could be an unsavory affair. In New York City, by one estimate, horses left behind 2.5 million pounds of manure and sixty thousand gallons of urine *every day*. That amounts to roughly four hundred thousand tons of manure a year — enough to float three *Nimitz*-class nuclear aircraft carriers and a half-dozen navy destroyers. Forget the smell and mess; imagine the flies.

Cyclists thus found their hobby not as pleasant as it could be, to say the least, and the League of American Wheelmen committed to doing something about it. A year after Fisher opened his store, the league launched a magazine, *Good Roads,* that became an influential mouthpiece for road improvement. Its articles were widely reprinted, which attracted members who didn't even own bikes; at the group's peak, Fisher and more than 102,000 others were on the rolls, and the Good Roads Movement was too big for politicians to ignore.

Yes, the demand for roads was pedal-powered, and a national cause even before the first practical American car rolled out of a Chicopee, Massachusetts, shop in 1893. A few months ahead of the Duryea Motor Wagon's debut, Congress authorized the secretary of agriculture to "make inquiry regarding public roads" and to investigate how they might be improved.

So it was that in October 1893, agriculture secretary J. Sterling Morton created the Office of Road Inquiry and appointed to head it one Gen. Roy Stone, a Civil War veteran, civil engineer, and vociferous good roads booster from New York. His appointment was the sort of circular affair — a lobbyist pushing for government action that he winds up leading — that wouldn't fly today but was business as usual in the nineteenth century.

Stone considered it "settled" that Americans "have the worst roads in the civilized world," and that their condition was "a crushing tax on the whole people, a tax the more intolerable in that it yields no revenue." Spending nothing on bad roads cost more than spending money to make them better, he argued, in squandered productivity, spoiled crops, high food prices. A chorus joined in. Prominent magazine editor and opinion shaper Albert Shaw noted that bad roads "are so disastrously expensive that only a very rich country, like the United States, can afford them."

The solution, Stone believed, was a national drive to improve roads financed with "very long loans," so that "a large share of its cost should fall upon its future beneficiaries." He had few resources with which to make this pitch; Stone's staff numbered two, himself included. His budget was $10,000. Still, he was ready with advice and data when the post office inaugurated Rural Free Delivery in 1896, which promised home mail service on roads passable enough to permit it — a mighty popular idea among rural farmers, who until then had viewed good roads and the taxes they required as schemes favoring big-city dandies on their bikes. He launched a program of "object lesson roads" a year later, in which short, scattered pieces of byway were fixed up. Locals reached these good stretches after laboring over unimproved roads, which made their merits all the plainer; their smoothness was broadcast up through a buckboard's plank seat.

All of this was background noise to Carl Fisher, who had a business to run and publicity stunts to plan. The shop survived the economic depression that began with the Panic of 1893, and racing remained popular; his friend Arthur Newby built a quarter-mile wooden oval on the north side of town in 1898 and managed to regularly fill its two thousand seats. But by late in the decade, Fisher was becoming a bit bored with selling safeties. New machines were gaining his attention, carriages and bikes fitted with lightweight gasoline engines. He tinkered with motorcycles, rode them himself, sold a few. And about the time the owners of another popular bike shop, across the Ohio line in Dayton, began to experiment with gliders and propellers, Fisher bought a three-wheeled, French-made horseless carriage, a 2.5-horsepower De Dion-Bouton. It was reputedly the first automobile in Indianapolis.

He was at the vanguard of a new craze. Throughout America, bicycle builders and wagon factories were experimenting with self-propulsion by steam, electricity, small engines. Two years later, in January 1900, Fisher and his old bike-racing buddy, Barney Oldfield, visited the nation's first auto show at New York's old Madison Square Garden. The experience changed both of them. Oldfield would become America's first car-racing star and such a celebrity that his name was part of the lexicon for a full quarter century. A cop's standard greeting to speeding motorists in the teens and twenties was "Who do you think you are, Barney Oldfield?"

As for Fisher, he returned to Indianapolis with a new business model. He closed the bike shop and opened the Fisher Auto Company, among the nation's first car dealerships.

Of Carl Fisher's many adventures, his homecoming from New York gets short shrift from his biographers, because if it went down as advertised, it was a remarkable feat: he's said to have driven back to Indianapolis in a car he bought at the auto show. That would place him among the pioneers of long-distance motoring; though horseless carriages were gaining a small following as pricey diversions for the urban well-to-do, they were fragile, wheezy, and wide open to the elements, and depended on roads that remained barely passable. An afternoon jaunt to the country involved flat tires, breakdowns, and as much digging as driving, and was slow going in even the best of circumstances. The first land speed record, set in 1898, was a hair over thirty-nine miles per hour, and most cars couldn't manage ten.

Horseless carriages were dangerous, to boot — heavy, tippy, slow to stop, and lacking any restraints or padding. It scared a good many people to be anywhere near the unmuffled, backfiring machines, which startled horses, imperiled pedestrians, and belched clouds of blue-gray exhaust.

Driving in the city lent early autoists, as they were called, an exotic, even swashbuckling air. They were dashing. They were nervy. They were almost always rich. Motoring from one city to another, on the other hand, across great stretches of bottomless road, fate tied to a confusion of balky, pot-metal engineering — well, that was a feat apart. That was crazy, Jules Verne stuff. In fact, so few autoists took on long distances before 1903 that it's easy to assemble a list. In 1897, a Cleveland bicycle dealer named Alexander Winton drove to New York to show off the sturdiness of a motorized buggy he'd designed, only to see the trip ignored or dismissed as a tall tale outside of Ohio. Two years later he repeated the stunt, this time accompanied by a reporter for the *Plain Dealer* whose dispatches, distributed to some thirty newspapers, helped popularize the French term *automobile*. A cheering crowd met the pair in New York.

In the summer of 1899, John D. and Louise Hitchcock Davis left New York for San Francisco in a buggy built by the Duryea Motor Wagon Company. Their tiller-steered contraption broke down before they got much beyond earshot of the starting line, and kept doing it; it took them three months to reach Chicago, where they chose to go no farther.

In 1901, Winton attempted a coast-to-coast trip from San Francisco to New York but abandoned the effort when his car burrowed itself into the Nevada desert. That October, automaker Ransom E. Olds commissioned a young test driver, Roy D. Chapin, to pilot one of his new curved-dash Oldsmobile buggies from Detroit to New York. It took Chapin seven and a half days, but it helped make the Olds the first mass-produced American car.

That's about it. Fisher was in a small fraternity, indeed.

It wasn't until July 1903, less than five months before the Wright brothers first flew at Kitty Hawk, that anyone managed a transcontinental passage, and it was greeted with only a little less amazement than the flight. Dr. Horatio Nelson Jackson of Burlington, Vermont, acting on a $50 bet, set out from San Francisco in a stripped-down 1902 Winton with a "mechanician," Sewall K. Crocker, riding shotgun. They cut north into Oregon to end-run the Sierra Nevada, then chugged east across trackless Idaho and Wyoming, acquiring a bull terrier along the way. The goggle-clad dog, "Bud," became a hit in every town they visited.

In Nebraska they followed the Platte River on the remnants of a trail used by the pioneers headed to Oregon and Utah, and the Winton wallowed in mud to the tops of its wheels; they had to muscle it out with block and tackle. But east of the Mississippi was easy going; they reached New York sixty-three days after leaving the Pacific.

Their passage ratified a building sense that the horseless carriage was more than a plaything, that what the press was already calling the Motor Age had begun in earnest — and that sense was only amplified when, two weeks later, a factory-backed Packard pulled in behind Jackson and Crocker, having traversed a far more challenging route from California. Driver Tom Fetch and photojournalist Marius Krarup had churned across the Nevada and Utah deserts and straight over the Colorado Rockies. A few weeks after that, a third team arrived on the East Coast, having made the crossing in a curved-dash Olds. Photos of the car under way in Wyoming depict it crossing rocky, undulating prairie studded with sagebrush, and without a road in sight.

• • •

With such excitement in the air, it's no wonder that auto sales went through the roof. In 1900, eight thousand machines were registered in the United States. In 1903, the count had quadrupled, to nearly thirty-three thousand, and more than doubled again over the next two years. With cars practically selling themselves, the Fisher Auto Company's owner was not long content to simply move product. Early in the new century, he, Oldfield, and their old barnstorming partner, Arthur C. Newby, took up auto racing and toured county fairs much as they had on bikes.

Automobile technology was advancing quickly, now. The spindly, tiller-steered horseless carriage, often steam- or battery-powered, was giving way to beefier models propelled by throaty gasoline engines. Speeds leaped. One of Fisher's favorite schemes was to bet he could outrace a horse in his automobile, over the course of a mile; he let the locals provide the horse and even give it a quarter-mile head start. The horse would tear off to what seemed an insurmountable lead, but without fail, Fisher's car would close the gap late in the race and take the win at the last moment — and Fisher would walk away $250 richer. One season, so the story goes, he earned $20,000.

He became a regular on the track, as well, his favored ride a powerful, long-snouted Mohawk on which he sat high, unstrapped and bare to the wind. The car was deafening, top-heavy, unstoppable, and terrifying to behold. Oldfield likened racing to "being hurled through space. The machine is throbbing under you with its cylinders beating a drummer's tattoo, and the air tears past you in a gale. In its maddening dash through the swirling dust the machine takes on the attributes of a sentient thing."

Failing eyesight be damned, Fisher won races throughout the Midwest and the Ohio Valley. In the summer of 1903, when Oldfield achieved the long-sought grail of covering a mile in a minute, Fisher wasn't far behind; he posted speeds in the mid-fifties and reputedly set a world's record for two miles from a running start at a track outside Chicago — two minutes and two seconds. *Horseless Age* numbered him among "the best-known track racers" in 1904.

It wasn't speed alone for which his racing days would be remembered. In 1903 — the date is usually given as September 9 — Fisher apparently entered a county fair race in Zanesville, Ohio. He brought along two Mohawks, one of which he drove; the other, depending on whom you believe, was piloted by either popular racer Earl Kiser or Fisher's own brother Earle.

As one of these Mohawks roared around the dirt track, its driver — one of the aforementioned three, but beyond that, all bets are off — lost control of the car. It blew through a fence and flipped end over end into the crowd, killing at least one spectator outright and injuring a dozen others.

Early auto racing was as lethal to onlookers as to participants. On the same day in Grosse Point, Michigan, Barney Oldfield's car blew a front tire, veered off the track, sailed fifty feet through the air, and landed on a bystander, who died a few minutes later. Oldfield suffered lacerations and a broken rib, which knocked him out of a race three days later in Milwaukee; a substitute took his car and became the first American driver to die in competition.

Regardless of whether Fisher was at the wheel in Zanesville, he took responsibility for the accident. Asked years later about it, he admitted that he didn't know how many spectators had been killed, as "they were dying for the next two years."

After that, Fisher's racing tapered off in the interest of other business. He wasn't easy to work with — Fisher could be impatient and abrupt, was quick to anger, and regardless of mood cursed in long and imaginative streaks. But his eighteen-hour workdays yielded results. He sold a lot of Packards, Oldsmobiles, and REOs, so many that he outgrew the shop and moved up to a three-story brick showroom on a prominent downtown corner.

In 1904, an inventor named Percy C. Avery approached him for backing on a project he couldn't bring to market himself. Until then, automotive headlights had been lifted, unchanged, from horse-drawn carriages — they relied on kerosene or candles, which blew out at any speed above a horse's trot. Driving was thus a strictly daytime endeavor for all but the foolhardy. Avery had hit on a new and better idea: compressed acetylene was fed to gas lamps from a small tank, producing a hard, white light that outshone anything Fisher had seen. That September he, Avery, and one of Fisher's old cycling friends, James Allison, incorporated as the Concentrated Acetylene Company, better known as Prest-O-Lite, and started making the first practical headlight.

It was revolutionary. The driver turned a valve to start the gas flow, turned it off to kill the lights, and when the tank ran low turned it in for a refill. Prest-O-Lite headlights became original equipment on many American makes, beginning with the 1904 Packard; photos of just about any high-end car taken between 1905 and, say, 1913 depict a tank on the running board. Fisher and Allison became rich beyond their dreams.

Stuffing metal tanks with combustible gas wasn't a safe line of work, however. In August 1907, several Prest-O-Lite workers narrowly missed death when their factory blew up. Another explosion ripped through a company plant in December, killing one worker and badly injuring three others. In June 1908, four distinct blasts ripped through a Prest-O-Lite facility, all but demolishing a firehouse next door and breaking every window in a neighboring hospital. Those were just the Indianapolis explosions. The partners had plants around the country, and in all, fifteen blew; the dangers that Prest-O-Lite posed to surrounding homes and businesses got a lot of ink.

It was only with unflagging effort that Fisher maintained his reputation as a local hero and grand-scale prankster. Among the makes he sold in 1907 was a personal favorite, Stoddard-Dayton, a big, high-end car built in Ohio. In a promotion reminiscent of his bike shop days, he announced he would push a Stoddard-Dayton off the roof of a downtown building to demonstrate its toughness. How he pulled off the trick is a mystery; the car was structurally reinforced and its tires partly deflated to absorb the impact, but getting the huge vehicle to land upright was largely beyond his control. He managed it, however, and in a parting flourish had the car driven from the scene.

His greatest stunt came on October 30, 1908, when he rigged a Stoddard-Dayton roadster to a massive balloon and flew it over Indianapolis, vowing to drive back into town from wherever he landed. In reality, he'd stripped the car of its heavy engine and swapped it on the sly for a matching Stoddard-Dayton driven out to meet him. If the press was wise to the switch, it didn't let on. The city loved him.

Even as Carl Fisher sold increasingly sophisticated cars capable of ever-greater speeds, a good road to drive them on remained hard to find. America's principal overland routes were descended from prehistory — they'd started as game trails, had been commandeered by Native American hunting parties, and later were widened into wagon roads by white settlers. Over decades of use, they'd been cleared of stumps — at least the big ones — but much of their engineering remained the work of buffalo and elk.

Improving on that was no easy matter. A concentration of heavy freight wagons, or "horse trucks," had forced cities to pave their business districts, but the stone used for the purpose was far too expensive for the longer and less-traveled roads of the hinterlands; those were usually built and maintained by county and local governments, which had little discretionary income and could tax their citizens only so much.

Rains continued to turn rural roads into quagmires. No event brought that to light quite so publicly as the great New York to Paris Race of 1908. Six cars — three French, one German, an Italian, and an American — left Times Square on February 12 on a twenty-two-thousand-mile marathon around the planet. As the race was originally conceived, they would traverse the States to San Francisco, travel by ship to Valdez, Alaska, and cross roadless tundra to Nome. From there the racers would drive the frozen Bering Strait to Siberia, then across Mongolia, Russia, and all of Europe to Paris.

It couldn't be done in a modern hovercraft, let alone in one of the enormous, balky racing cars of 1908. The German entry, a three-ton Protos, was nudged forward by an anemic four-cylinder engine of forty horsepower; the French De Dion, even heavier, packed just thirty horses. Mechanical shortcomings were the least of the teams' troubles. Hours after a quarter-million people watched them leave New York, the racers encountered four-foot snowdrifts; by day's end, one of the French cars had quit. Once past the snow, they hit mud, which seemed to worsen with each westward mile.

On day nineteen, one car paused on a steeply crowned Iowa road to ask for directions and "gently and firmly slid off the crest into a small-sized ditch." The mud-spattered Frenchmen in the De Dion "look like Negroes," a *New York Times* headline announced, and were quoted as saying they wouldn't want to live among such roads — surely Alaska's were better. Two days later, the American driver insisted that "people in the East don't know what bad roads are." On reaching Omaha, he compounded the insult: "Never before have I piloted any car through such fields of mud, through such horrible road conditions as have been found in the last two hundred miles."

It didn't help that the drivers were provided few clues as to where, exactly, they wallowed. The same driver, Montague Roberts of Newark, New Jersey, wrote that Iowa had no road signs "except the few at various points which point out to the wayfarer that he can save money by purchasing his socks or tea at Podger's Universal Store. A hand points to the direction in which the economical traveler should go, but it does not state whether Podger's Store is located in Cedar Rapids or Sacramento."

Much of the Midwest was no better, and even the best country road of the early twentieth century was primitive. The most common "improvement" was simply to grade a dirt road's surface, in an attempt to smooth its bumps and fill its ruts. A step up was sand-clay construction, for which a mix of the two soils would be imported and spread on an earthen bed; the result, at least in theory, was a surface that drained well and with traffic achieved a smooth hardness. It also broke down quickly under heavy loads.

A little better was the gravel road, on which river rock or broken stone was spread on a graded bed; it held up better than dirt, especially to horse traffic, but had to be dressed regularly to keep the gravel from scattering, and it was stripped bare by the skinny tires and higher speeds of cars and trucks.

The most popular solution to that dilemma was macadam. It predated the automobile by nearly eighty years: Scottish road builder John Loudon MacAdam noticed that gravel highways didn't become smooth and durable until a lot of traffic had compressed their stone into a unified, interlocking mass, so on an 1816 turnpike job he covered a firm, smooth dirt bed with a ten-inch layer of stone broken especially for the purpose by workers armed with small hammers, then passed over the rock with a heavy, horse-drawn roller. The sharp-edged stones knitted into a tight bond.

American road builders refined his system by spreading a thick layer of large broken stone onto graded earth, rolling it, covering it with a second layer of much smaller stone, and rolling it again. They then sprinkled the surface with rock dust, hosed the whole business down with water, and rolled it a third time.

"Water-bound macadam," this was called, and it performed well under normal loads and low speeds. To keep dust down, some highway workers topped it with a thin layer of asphalt, a black, sticky, molasses-like petroleum goop that occurs in natural deposits around the world. Soon enough, engineers realized that asphalt or its coal-derived substitute, tar, also kept the rock in place, and began using it even where dust wasn't an issue. The bituminous macadam road, or tarmac, was born.

In the years since, non-engineers have lazily dropped the "bituminous," and "macadam" has evolved into a synonym for blacktop. In truth, it's one of several kinds, the most common of which — and the sort usually laid today — is asphaltic concrete, also known as flexible concrete, also known as scrimshaw, a blend of asphalt or tar and an aggregate, or filler, most commonly broken rock or gravel.

The highest type of road construction, the darling of engineers everywhere, was Portland cement concrete, but it was still in its infancy as a road material. A few cities had experimented with it on small jobs, and the French were singing its praises, but its first real American test was just then getting under way in Wayne County, Michigan, outside Detroit.

At the end of 1909 the country had 2.2 million miles of state and county road. Just 8 percent, or 190,400 miles, was improved in any way; more than half of that good road was gravel. Concrete accounted for all of 9 miles.

Carl Fisher had grown rich by recognizing trends ahead of the next guy, and though he was now enjoying a full-on boom in auto sales, it was plain that it couldn't last. The industry would achieve its full potential only if the country's sad road situation were fixed — and only if, in the meantime, cars improved to better navigate roads as they were.

Every year, America's more than 250 automakers achieved new advances in safety and practicality — their products were sturdier, faster-stopping, more reliably free of catastrophic flaw. But they didn't measure up to their European kin, a fact underscored whenever they raced. Fisher came away from one such contest with the seed of an idea, that what the country needed was a big, high-speed proving ground where new cars and ideas could be put through their paces, a place where reliability, speed, and strength could be tested. "It seems to me," he wrote to *Motor Age* magazine, that "a five-mile track, properly laid out, without fences to endanger drivers, with proper grandstands, supply stores for gasoline and oil, and other accommodations would net for one meet . . . a sufficient amount to pay half of the entire cost of the track." He was convinced, too, that Indianapolis, which at the time vied with Detroit as an automotive center, was a logical place for it.

In the fall of 1908, he bought a farm northwest of the city and the following February incorporated the Indianapolis Motor Speedway Company with James Allison and two other old friends: Arthur Newby, his bike and car barnstorming partner, who'd gone on to create the National brand of motorcar; and Frank H. Wheeler, the head of a carburetor company. The four hired a New York engineer to design a 2.5-mile rectangular track with steeply banked corners. Having judged concrete or brick too expensive, they decided on a driving surface of crushed stone and asphalt, laid over clay.

The plans drew ridicule from many in town, who pointed out that attending a race would require a long buggy ride. But in June 1909, the twelve-thousand-seat grandstand was up, along with wooden garages, viewing stands, and a hospital, and by early July the track was

far enough along that Barney Oldfield was able to take a spin and pro-
nounce its turns "so perfectly graded that two miles a minute can be
made with no greater danger to the driver than on the flat."

That was even before Fisher's crews completed the track's layer-cake
surfacing, a variation on bituminous macadam. The finished track was
"said to be the fastest automobile racecourse in the world," the *New
York Times* advised. "Expense has not been spared in the effort to give
the public the best that can be had in the racing line."

Ah, but forgoing a hard surface turned out to be a false economy,
and a caution for road builders everywhere. Even bituminous macadam, sturdy and long-lasting as it had proved to be under slow-
turning wheels, was no match for fast-spinning rubber tires. The first
hint of trouble came when motorcycle racers showed up for the track's
warm-up weekend and immediately complained about loose rock.
Only six of forty entrants agreed to actually race. Two of them were
injured. The program ended early.

A three-day extravaganza of auto racing loomed, and as the arriv-
ing competitors started to practice — among them Oldfield and Louis
Chevrolet, a Frenchman who'd soon lend his name to a division of
just-created General Motors — the track's asphalt lost its tenuous grip
on the gravel beneath. Deep gouges opened in the turns. Tires kicked
up clouds of dust and stone. By the first day of auto racing at America's
first speedway — Thursday, August 19, 1909 — the track was wildly
dangerous, its surface shredded, the air filled with shrapnel. Just past
halfway in a 250-mile race, Chevrolet caught a rock in his goggles that
sent glass into his eye, and had to be walked to the hospital. Minutes
later, the car carrying Wilfred Bourque and his mechanician, Harry
Holcomb, veered off the track, nosed into a ditch, and flipped, sling-
ing Holcomb into a fence post that "laid bare his brain," as the *Times*
put it, and trapping Bourque beneath his machine. "The accident was
witnessed by nearly 10,000 persons," the newspaper reported, "and
women fainted and the faces of men blanched as they saw the car leave
the track and turn over upon the daring occupants, crushing out their
lives."

The American Automobile Association, which sanctioned early

races, threatened to withdraw if the track wasn't overhauled by the next day. Fisher vowed that it would be, and indeed, things went better on Friday; the speedway's surface, patched overnight by an army of workers and mules, held together. But in the last event of the meet's third and final day, the right front tire on a car driven by local boy Charles Merz exploded as he rounded the first turn. His big National rocketed off the track, through a fence, and into a group of spectators. "The machine was in the midst of the crowd almost before its coming was realized," the *Times* said, "and a panic immediately followed." When it calmed, two spectators and the car's riding mechanician were found dead in the dirt.

A few days later, the county coroner blamed Fisher and his partners for the deaths of Bourque and Holcomb, charging that the trackside ditch likely had made a survivable wreck fatal. At a separate inquest, the coroner found that Merz's blowout was caused by "the unfinished track, and that the Indianapolis Speedway Company put on the races before the track was completed and safe." Out-of-town criticism was even harder on the partners. The Cincinnati Automobile Club passed resolutions branding the races "hazardous and detrimental to the advancement of the automobile." In New York, the *Times* denounced the entire sport as "useless and barbarous" and "an amusement congenial only to savages."

Word reached Fisher that the AAA was thinking about washing its hands of the speedway for good. He persuaded Newby to underwrite paving the entire track with ten-pound bricks, then went to the papers. "We are ready to spend $100,000 or more, if necessary, to make the speedway safe for spectators as well as drivers," he announced. "When the job is completed, we definitely will have the world's finest and safest race course; and I'm sure everyone connected with racing will want to return to Indianapolis at the earliest opportunity."

Crews laid down 3.2 million bricks over the next two months. Turns were rimmed with concrete walls. The Brickyard was born. The first Indianapolis 500 took place two springs later, and eighty thousand fans showed up. Carl Fisher drove the pace car.

• • •

Fisher was as busy as ever after the speedway's opening. He married a teenaged admirer, Jane Watts; with several partners, he founded his own car company, Empire, and produced a middling couple of models; he started an aeronautics firm that didn't amount to much; he, Allison, and Wheeler built lavish estates on adjoining properties on Indianapolis's north side. He weathered another Prest-O-Lite tragedy, this one the costliest of all — the deaths of ten men in a construction accident at a new plant. And somehow he found time to drive, and to grow increasingly frustrated behind the wheel.

Most of the roads in and around Indianapolis, as everywhere else, remained bare-dirt scars flanked by deep and weedy ditches. The newer ones had high crowns, their edges sloping downhill from their centers to drain water, but it wasn't long before they were mashed into concavity and diabolically rutted. Some highways were dragged, meaning that after a rain a neighboring landowner would hitch a horse to a rig of split logs and pull it over the ruts to flatten them out. Rebuilding a road consisted of shoveling dirt from its sides into the middle, then tamping it down. Grading with a horse-drawn blade was a cause for local celebration. But even well-built and well-maintained roads dog-legged to nowhere or jogged along section lines surveyed a century before. Theoretically, 382 miles of local road had been improved, but you wouldn't know it; outside of the city proper, the area's only modern, reliable stretch of pavement was on the way to the speedway, and Fisher and his partners had built it.

Even a short journey threw up obstacles, as Fisher recalled years later:

> Three of us drove out nine miles from Indianapolis and being delayed, were overtaken by darkness on the return trip. To complicate matters, it began to rain pretty hard, and you know automobiles didn't have any tops on them in those days, so we all three got pretty wet.
>
> We guessed our way along as well as we could, until we came to a place where the road forked three ways. It was black as the inside of your pocket. We couldn't see any light from the city, and none of us

could remember which of the three roads we had followed in driving out; if, indeed, we had come that way at all.

So we stopped and held a consultation. Presently, by the light of our headlamps, reflected up in the rain, one of us thought he saw a sign on a pole. It was too high up to read and we had no means of throwing a light on it, so there was nothing to be done but climb the pole in the wet and darkness to see if we could make out some road direction on the sign.

We matched to see who should climb. I lost. I was halfway up the pole when I remembered that my matches were inside my overcoat and I couldn't reach them. So down I had to come, dig out the matches, put them in my hat, and climb up again.

Eventually, by hard climbing, I got up to the sign. I scratched a match and before the wind blew it out I read the sign. It said: "Chew Battle-Ax Plug."

The cars kept flying out of Fisher's dealership. Motoring filled magazines and the lyrics of popular songs and new, fat sections of the Sunday papers. Americans who'd shied away from the noisy machines in their early days had since become, or planned to become, purchasers themselves — especially after Henry Ford introduced a stiff-backed little runabout in 1908 that could be serviced with simple hand tools and tough out even the goopiest farm road, and after the electric starter spelled the end of hand-cranking engines to life, an advance that boosted motoring's appeal to women. Nationwide, vehicle registrations were on the brink of topping a million in 1912, having doubled in two years, tripled in three, quadrupled in four.

The machines promised a freedom previously unknown: to truly roam, independent of rails or stage routes; to venture into the country without a care about schedule; to throw off the shackles of the horse. And you can bet those shackles weighed heavily. For one thing, horses were slow; movie westerns have filled our heads with images of cowboys on horseback galloping across the prairie, but real horses can't keep that up for long and need frequent rest, food, water. Even the most spartan automobiles of 1912 made better time across long distances.

Alongside passenger cars came the first trucks. Production in 1911 amounted to 13,319 vehicles, more than in all the previous years combined, and the 56,000 turned out two years later were again more than all those built to that point. Such geometric growth, impressive as it was, marked just the beginning of a tectonic shift in urban commerce. "Manufacturers of trucks," the *Times* observed, "are just now looking into the future of the use of commercial vehicles on a scale that would startle the general public if the plans were made known."

The horse was in its twilight. In the fifteen years since the first American auto sale, in the ten years since the first transcontinental road trip, the automobile had "changed conditions of life in every phase," the *Times* marveled. "We move faster, get our mail and freight more quickly, buy and sell our products more surely, and we even scorn the handicaps that once were put upon our business or pleasure travel by storm and snowdrift."

It may seem counterintuitive, but part of the motorcar's appeal came down to money, because while buggies might be cheaper to buy, their drive trains were mighty expensive to maintain. Horses required stabling, feed, and health care, which nationally amounted to $2 billion a year, or as much as it cost to maintain all of America's railroads. Feeding the typical horse consumed five acres of tillable land per annum; devoted to food for people, the nation's feed-producing cropland could support millions.

Then there was the question of health, especially in the cities. "All wars together have not caused half the deaths that may be traced to the horse," one motoring advocate claimed. "Business, humanity and public health demand that the horse be eliminated from urban civilization." Motor vehicles, said the industry's boosters, polluted far less noxiously.

City and country alike were changing to accommodate the new technology — filling stations now dotted the roadside by the thousands — except in a key respect: the roads themselves. "Hard roads, smooth roads, and, above all, lasting roads," the *Times* reported, "are now the cry from every section of the country."

No one cried louder than Fisher. He had little faith that government would fill the need; the feds were building scattered demonstration roads but left the real work to states and localities, most of which, it seemed to him, didn't know what they were doing. "The highways of America are built chiefly of politics," he wrote to a friend, "whereas the proper material is crushed rock or concrete."

It was up to the industry to get things started, to provide an example of what could be accomplished with imagination and will, to inspire others. So in the late summer of 1912, Carl Fisher began talking up a new project, a transcontinental highway, a rock road stretching across a dozen states or more, from New York to California. A highway built to a standard unseen in the United States — dry, smooth, safe, not just passable but comfortable in the rainy seasons. A road built for the automobile. For the future.

2

....

CARL FISHER WAS NOT alone in calling for a big interstate highway. Even as he refined his proposal, others were going public with similar visions. Earlier in the year, good roads advocates meeting in Kansas City had created the National Old Trails Road Association, backing an auto road from Washington, D.C., to Los Angeles. In June, *Scientific American* carried a letter from C. Francis Jenkins, an inventor and motorist, arguing that an ocean-to-ocean highway would open the West to economic development.

But Fisher brought a unique blend of traits and skills to the proposition. Through Prest-O-Lite, he'd become close friends with the chiefs of the auto industry, men with money and smarts and influence unequaled outside the White House. He was tight with the press; few men could excite newspaper reporters like Fisher, a walking quote machine whose every deed made good copy. Not least, the Hoosier had energy to burn.

So with Allison's help, he studied the cost of building such a road and devised a plan to raise the cash. He laid out their findings in a September 6, 1912, letter to Henry Ford. The highway would follow existing roads for most of its length, new construction fusing just those stretches that failed to connect. Over time, the daisy chain of existing and new roads would be upgraded to a uniform standard, broadened and straightened and beautified to meet the rising demands of traffic.

They proposed that the industry supply the materials for the job, and the public the muscle. The manufacturers and dealers of cars and accessories would kick in a small fraction of their gross receipts (one-third of 1 percent for three years, or one-fifth of 1 percent for five) toward the purchase of rock, cement, and asphalt, to the tune of $5,000 per mile; volunteers and governments along the route would actually do the necessary work.

Four nights later, he and Allison unveiled their proposal at a dinner in Indianapolis for fifty-odd industry leaders. Fisher urged that work start without delay so that the "Coast-to-Coast Rock Highway," as he called it, would be finished by May 1, 1915; a convoy of twenty-five thousand automobiles would then take it to a world's fair planned for that summer in San Francisco. "It can be done," Fisher cried. "Let's build it before we are too old to enjoy it."

By evening's end, pledges were rolling in. Goodyear president Frank Seiberling promised $300,000 without consulting his company's directors, calling the pledge "a movement on which we will expect to realize dividends." Over the next few days, Fisher received commitments totaling twice again as much.

Ford showed no interest, despite Fisher's persistent entreaties — believing, as one of the automaker's lieutenants explained, that "as long as private interests are willing to build good roads for the general public, the general public will not be very interested in building good roads for itself." But he was a rare holdout. Roy Chapin, the former Oldsmobile test driver, now had his own company, Hudson, and backed the highway with time and money. Fellow automaker John D. Willys and cement magnate A. Y. Gowen did likewise, and Packard president Henry B. Joy emerged as the most impassioned cheerleader of all.

With the project gathering momentum, Fisher now did something out of character for a showman: he abdicated his starring role. He worried, he said, over "the idea that this road plan is mine," and that "if any particular noise is made for any particular person or small clique of persons, this plan is going to suffer."

He remained a guiding influence but passed the top post to Joy, whom he'd known since Prest-O-Lite headlights had become standard equipment on Packards in 1904. Joy proved an inspired choice.

A Detroit native, Yale graduate, and navy veteran of the Spanish-American War, he'd organized a takeover of Packard after driving one of its early runabouts and had turned it into the country's foremost luxury brand. Its motto reflected his cool confidence: "Ask the man who owns one."

Joy brought field expertise along with his business acumen. He'd sent his cars on annual overland expeditions since 1903 and had completed eleven transcontinental trips himself; when he wrote in a magazine piece that "a 'good' road here would, as a rule, be a disgrace in a foreign country," it wasn't just rhetoric.

He also boasted an interesting family history. His father, a railroad lawyer, had been close to Abraham Lincoln, and Joy inherited a fierce admiration for the late president. Even before Fisher handed over the reins, Joy observed that a highway was a more fitting monument than the Lincoln Memorial then contemplated in Washington. No surprise, then, that not far into 1913, the Coast-to-Coast Rock Highway acquired a new name.

The Lincoln Highway Association incorporated in June 1913, with its offices in Detroit, Joy as its president, and Fisher as a vice president. Joy wasn't in town when the papers were filed; he was headed west to reconnoiter possible routes. His Packard took him across the Midwest and into Nebraska and Wyoming. He cut to the southwest from Salt Lake City, following the old Pony Express trail south of the Great Salt Lake and across the alkali wastes of the Utah desert, and crossed central Nevada from Ely to Carson City. The 2,753-mile trek took 15½ days.

The going wasn't much improved from Joy's first long road trip a decade before, on which he'd asked a Packard agent in Omaha how to get to the road west and was told there wasn't one; the agent had led him out of town to a wire fence and told him to take it down and drive on, and at the next fence do the same, and likewise at the next. Soon enough, the fences had given way to open prairie, and Joy had found himself surrounded by broken planks and rusting bits of iron, fossils of the previous century's wagon trains.

In 1913, Nebraska's chief east-west highway remained a simple dirt track, the sort you might find created by tractors at the fringe of a modern-day cornfield. Even so, Joy predicted that by 1915, "motorists should have no difficulty in making the trip from New York to San Francisco in eleven days. By that time many miles of good roads will have been completed and good sign posts will mark the transcontinental route."

While Joy was on the road, Fisher was in Indianapolis, getting up a tour of his own: a convoy of seventeen Indiana-built cars and two supply trucks, bound for San Francisco via a more southerly route — through St. Louis, Kansas City, Colorado Springs, and Denver, over the Rockies to Glenwood Springs and Grand Junction, and on to Salt Lake City. The Hoosier Trailblazers, as this seventy-member expedition called itself, included reporters, photographers, telegraph operators, an AAA rep, factory drivers, speedway veterans, and passengers handpicked for their strength and fortitude. All had to pass a physical, and each car was loaded with survival gear — water bags, block and tackle, six hundred feet of rope. Their preparations aroused tremendous excitement in the newspapers, and even more among western city and state officials who assumed their route marked the future Lincoln Highway — and who knew that (a) a place on such a main route was a ticket to prosperity, while (b) the Plains were dotted with the ruins of once-promising towns that had withered after railroads passed them by. Hundreds of telegrams rained on Fisher and his associates, pitching the benefits of running the highway through one town or other. Delegations turned up from a thousand miles off to plead their cases. New road was laid and bridges were built to entice them. Colorado remade the winding path through Berthoud Pass, west of Denver; Nevada's legislators passed an emergency appropriation to fix a trail spanning the entire state.

Under way, Fisher enjoyed royal treatment wherever he went. Kansas governor George H. Hodges met him at the Missouri line and traveled with the convoy clear to Colorado, and his colleagues to the west rode along, too. California governor Hiram Johnson promised that his state would finance every foot of the Lincoln within its borders. The travelers were feted by crowds, brass bands, and automobile escorts by day and treated to lavish dinners at night. Weary, sunburned, and overfed, they reached San Francisco after thirty-four days, then drove south to Los Angeles, finishing the trip without the loss of a single car — without any mechanical trouble, really, except blown tires.

All of America was now talking about the Lincoln Highway. In terms of publicity, the Hoosier tour could scarcely have gone better. For all of that, Fisher had to confront some hard realities on his return to Indianapolis. After a fast start, pledges had dwindled; they didn't amount to even half the association's goal. Second, there now waited the touchy business of settling on the highway's route.

East of Chicago, it was fairly straightforward. The Lincoln would cross New Jersey on a plank road first cut by Dutch colonists of the seventeenth century, and much of Pennsylvania on the descendant of a British trail dating to the French and Indian War. It would pass through Pittsburgh, span Ohio's middle, and curve across Indiana to the Chicago suburbs, all on well-established, commonsense paths. West of the Mississippi, however, the going was less certain. The highway might follow three general paths, each offering advantages: southwest from Missouri to Arizona, and on to Southern California; the Hoosier tour's route west through the Colorado Rockies; or to San Francisco via Wyoming and Salt Lake City.

The last seemed the most fitting to Joy, who had a single criterion for the highway's path: it had to be the most direct possible. He was backed up by a Packard colleague, Sidney D. Waldon, who analyzed the corridors according to which was available, weather-wise, to the greatest number of users for the greatest part of the year. "There are no two questions in my mind about the Omaha-Cheyenne-Salt Lake City route being the shortest and offering the least possible trouble to the tourist," he concluded. "All parts of the line will be in condition for travel at about the same time."

And so the Lincoln followed the Platte River across Nebraska, skirting Buffalo Bill's ranch and the Sand Hills; crossed the Continental Divide just east of Laramie; thumped over single-track through Medicine Bow, Rawlins, and Green River; and traversed the Wasatch

Mountains into Salt Lake City. And so it took the Pony Express trail across the Great Salt Lake Desert, dusty, empty, and sun-bleached, to Nevada.

If the association took care in unveiling the route, it might well prompt enough excitement to solve the money shortage. And Fisher believed an opportunity now loomed to accomplish this second objective. A governors' conference was scheduled for late that summer in Colorado Springs, and Fisher told his fellow directors that if they revealed the Lincoln's path there, they might convince the affected state executives to get "three or four million dollars spent next year."

Off went Fisher and Joy to Colorado Springs, and there they announced the Lincoln's route on August 26, 1913. The governors embraced it with gusto, save for Hodges of Kansas and E. M. Ammons of Colorado; both had assumed that the Hoosier Tour had taken the chosen path.

Their heated reactions aside, the visit was a huge success. On the train ride back east, the Lincoln men prepared a public proclamation for the papers in which they made clear what they expected of their fellow citizens: "*Upon all the people*, and especially upon the officials of each state and county and upon the inhabitants thereof . . . does rest the patriotic burden of *establishing, broadening, straightening, maintaining, and beautifying* such highway to the end that it may become an appropriate memorial to the Great Martyred Patriot whose name it bears." The emphasis is theirs.

That launched a publicity offensive. The association mailed posters bearing the proclamation to politicians, business leaders, and auto dealerships in the states the highway would cross, a gesture that required a corps of one hundred stenographers to address the mailing tubes. It issued an "Appeal to Patriots," urging Americans to "See America First" on the Lincoln, rather than vacation in Europe.

And on Halloween it formally dedicated this "lasting monument to the automobile industry, and one of the greatest developments ever made in this country," in the words of the *San Francisco Examiner,* with fireworks and parades, dances and speeches in "every city, town and hamlet" along the route.

One such town was Jefferson, Iowa, where the speakers included a stiff, serious young state highway engineer by the name of Thomas Harris MacDonald. The Lincoln Highway would be a fine asset, MacDonald said, but its greatest value lay in its status as a starting point, as "the first outlet for the road-building energies of this community." After the Lincoln, he predicted, would come a system of connected radials branching from the cities through which it passed, and in time, "great transcontinental highways."

If the national clamor over Fisher's coast-to-coast dream seems a bit over the top today, bear in mind that it was, at least in theory, the sort of long-distance touring road that thousands of autoists coveted but had seen little sign of becoming reality. Just about every state was desperate for better roads but exasperated by its inability to provide them. The cost of bringing highways up to even minimal "surfaced" standards was beyond the means of most, and the technical capabilities of many; only a few states had full-fledged highway departments.

The federal government's Office of Public Roads, the successor to General Stone's Office of Road Inquiry, was stymied, as well. It had built 410 short "object lesson" roads using local materials over the past decade and talked itself hoarse about the benefits of new construction: Rural school attendance averaged 57 percent before road improvement; after, it jumped twenty points. The costs of moving a ton of freight stood at 21 to 23 cents a mile on an unimproved road; with surfacing, the rate averaged about 12 cents, raising the profit margin on farm and industrial products and lowering prices to everyone. Road work also promised to "materially raise the value of farm property," the top federal roads man, Logan Waller Page, wrote in a 1915 memo, and "lighten the labors of American horses, save wear and tear on harnesses and wagons, and add to the comfort and happiness of all rural residents."

Recognizing their merits didn't get roads built, however. No consensus had emerged among politicians on exactly how to apply federal money and muscle to the situation. Drivers — voters — were growing impatient. Something had to be done. But what? Page, a former geologist who'd led Public Roads since 1905, favored a strong Washington role in road building, and he wasn't bashful about it. He and his lobbyists pushed a financing scheme called "Federal Aid," under which the states would develop road projects to suit their needs, the feds would lend them technical support, and both sides would share construction costs. This bottom-up approach left most decisions about how and where to build roads to the experts, the people who would actually use them.

To a vocal group of taxpayers and highway officials, however, Federal Aid seemed fatally complex, involving too many players, too many levels of government, too much opportunity for local politicking, and far too much delay in addressing already critical needs; how much simpler it would be to have the feds build a network of highways directly, without the nettlesome involvement of states and counties unprepared for the job. Washington would own the network outright, ensuring that standards of design, construction, and maintenance did not vary across state lines.

This approach had precedent. A century before, Congress had devoted more than $6.8 million, a mint at the time, to the construction of an unpaved toll road from Cumberland, Maryland, to St. Louis. Construction had reached Vandalia, Illinois, when the feds abandoned the project in the 1840s with the advent of railroads. Over the next several decades, Washington invested its transportation energies in train travel. States, cities, and towns did likewise, and rails snaked their way to every corner of the continent. In 1840, the United States had 162 miles of main line track per one million inhabitants. Fifty years later, despite a fivefold increase in population, it had 2,600. Meanwhile, the turnpike out of Cumberland reverted to weeds. Roads, as Page put it, had been "relegated to the background as a purely local affair."

The competing approaches to resurrecting federal involvement turned on a question that at first glance seems semantic: Should America have a national system of highways, as Page and his allies urged, or a system of national highways? A related decision divided roads advocates, as well: For whom should such a system, of whatever type, be built — the farmer, who would use it to get his produce to town, or the commercial and recreational driver who sought travel between cities? Page consistently stressed that getting farmers "out of the mud" with farm-to-market roads was his first priority. Many East Coast highway men facing greater demand for urban and intercity connections differed with him; so did auto executives, motor tourists, and leaders of the AAA, all of whom favored long-distance highways.

In the months before Carl Fisher unveiled his proposal for the Lincoln Highway, Capitol Hill had witnessed the introduction of sixty separate bills proposing solutions of great variety — for Federal Aid, for federal construction of post roads, for a web of hard interstate roads, for replacing Page's agency with a federal highway commission. In 1912, Congress authorized an experiment in federal assistance, po- nying up $500,000 for upgrading roads used in rural mail delivery. The program was cumbersome and beyond the means of most local governments, however; it saw only 450-odd miles of road improved and quelled neither the public pressure for action nor the flood of new roads legislation. The following year, fifty-odd bills were pending in the Capitol.

Among the backers of a federally owned and managed system was Virginia's recently appointed highway commissioner, George P. Cole- man. Like many of his eastern colleagues, Coleman oversaw an es- tablished state roads network, though that term is strictly relative; in wet weather, Virginia's highways were as mired as those in Indiana, Iowa, or anywhere else. He viewed Page's farm-to-market roads as go- ing from nowhere to nowhere, and of little benefit to motorists at large.

Coleman had limited opportunity to confer with others of like mind. The existing highway organizations were peopled not only by the state engineers actually pressed to solve America's road problem, but by representatives of the automakers, construction trades, and materials industries. "None of the associations," Coleman wrote years later, "seemed to a small group of engineers here in the East and South to meet the requirements of the fast-developing highway movement."

The solution was simple enough: he would create his own associa- tion and limit membership to engineers and state highway commissioners. Coleman floated the idea in letters to several colleagues, and when state engineers met at a big American Road Congress in Atlanta in November 1914, a group of them adopted a resolution calling on "all State highway commissions or departments to send a representative with power to act to a meeting" in Washington. With that, representatives of seventeen state highway departments, along with Page and other federal reps, convened at the Raleigh Hotel on December 12, 1914, to create the American Association of State Highway Officials.

It was a turning point, though it went largely unheralded at the time. With AASHO was created the first key ingredient of government's involvement in the interstate highways to come. Named to the group's executive committee was the tense, unsmiling Iowa engineer who'd spoken at the Lincoln's dedication: Thomas MacDonald.

By its first anniversary, the Lincoln Highway's secretary, A. R. Pardington, boasted that it was "the longest road in the world," and "the most traveled road in the world," and "the one road on which more has already been spent, on which more is now being spent, and on which, during the years to come, more money and effort will be expended, than on any other single road known."

Its path through New Jersey was being remade in brick and concrete. Counties in Ohio and Indiana had committed to improving the stretches of the Lincoln within their borders. One day in April 1914, thousands of businessmen and children wielded picks and shovels on the highway in Illinois; each received a check for a penny and honorary membership in the American Federation of Labor. Throughout the East, improving the highway had become a point of local pride.

The going remained rough west of the Mississippi. Though Pardington claimed that in Iowa, "there remains but one bridge or culvert to be replaced by concrete," and that the Lincoln was "being resurveyed, straightened and broadened," travel in the Midwest remained a function of the weather. Farther west, little had changed from the days when Mark Twain had ventured to Nevada's gold fields by stagecoach and in Utah crossed "a vast, waveless ocean stricken dead and turned to ashes," under a sun of "dead, blistering, relentless malignity," while breathing alkali dust that "cut through our lips" and "persecuted our eyes" and "ate through the delicate membranes and made our noses bleed and *kept* them bleeding."

That was the nature of the West, however, and much of its appeal. In an automobile, the adventurous might explore territory forsaken by trains and unimagined by the city-bound. By 1915, the highway's cheerleaders insisted that a coast-to-coast drive was more exciting than it was arduous. The first official Lincoln guidebook, published that year, jauntily acknowledged that it was "still something of a sporting trip, and one must expect and put up cheerfully with some unpleasantness, just as you would on a shooting trip into the Maine woods for example." Those who expected otherwise "should take a de luxe train."

A. L. Westgard, the AAA's field agent, pooh-poohed any "fear of danger, insurmountable obstacles or serious discomforts," assuring the readers of *Motor* magazine that "they no longer exist." Joy figured that as long as the weather was fair, a coast-to-coast drive was easy "every foot of the way," and marveled at the burgeoning traffic he encountered on his annual drive to California in 1915: "Two years ago, when I made this same trip, I was doing something out of the ordinary, one perhaps of fifty tourists who took the same journey. This spring I do not believe it is an exaggeration to state that I was but one out of five thousand."

Informal counts bore him out. The Lincoln carried more than double the traffic through Ely, Nevada, in 1915 than it had a year earlier. The mid-desert oasis of Fish Springs, Utah, logged 225 cars in June 1915, up from 52 two years before. And the trend promised to continue. In 1916, a casual motorist drove the highway in six days, ten hours, and fifty-nine minutes, prompting the association to boast it promoted "a real road which will permit a traveler to average twenty miles per hour each of the twenty-four."

If the highway's chief promoter was uncharacteristically quiet through these first seasons of success, it was because Carl Fisher was already busy with a new project. A few years before, charmed by a visit to Miami, Fisher and Jane had bought a winter home there and taken up speedboat racing. Their place overlooked Biscayne Bay to a low, mangrove-laced sandbar that protected the city from the open Atlantic; ferries rounded its tip every day to deliver sun worshipers to the lovely white sand beaches and arcing coconut palms on its ocean side.

Others had attempted to develop the sandbar, on and off, as a coconut plantation, an avocado farm, a beach resort. All had limped along, at best. Development was foiled not only by access to the spit but by the jungly swamp that consumed its west side and interior, a thicket so well rooted, so dense and dark and twisted, that clearing the property seemed beyond hope. The latest scheme, involving the construction of a two-and-a-half-mile wooden bridge across the bay, had run out of steam, like so many before it. The bridge stood half-finished when Fisher decided that the sandbar might make an interesting investment.

He gave the old-timer who owned the bridge the money to complete it and in exchange took possession of 200 acres of sand. He also loaned money to an outfit trying to develop housing on the bar, and for his troubles earned not only 8 percent interest but another 105 acres. He ripped out the mangroves with tractors, filled in the swamp with sand and mud dredged from the bay, bulkheaded the shoreline, and started to build a city. We know it today as Miami Beach.

Money was no worry; Fisher and Allison had agreed to sell Prest-O-Lite to Union Carbide and wound up splitting $17 million. Fisher spent his share in Florida. Once he'd tamed the sandbar, he laid down a main drag, which he called Lincoln Road, and opened a land-sales office on it. He built an enormous house, the biggest on the spit. He began planning a modest, thirty-five-room hotel, named, again, for Lincoln. And he envisioned an artery to supply his venture with auto tourists, a tributary of the Lincoln Highway that would connect the industrial Midwest with Miami Beach. He initially called it the "Hoosier Land to Dixie Highway," envisioned it starting in Indianapolis and following existing roads, just as the Lincoln did, down through the Ohio River country and across Kentucky and Tennessee and over mountains as uncharted and fearsome as those out west.

He stood to gain from the highway's success — this was far less selfless a mission than his first road venture had been. Even so, it was overdue. "The biggest part of the South might just as well be a foreign country as far as the automobile is concerned," Fisher correctly observed. "The average automobile is almost a wreck by the time it gets over the Cumberlands."

In early 1915, he organized a summit in Chattanooga that drew thousands of delegates and hangers-on. Equal parts convention, circus, and utter chaos, the blur of shouts and arguments, florid speech, and brass bands managed, somehow, to birth a corporate entity called the Dixie Highway Association, modeled closely on the Lincoln.

Cities, towns, and states so shrieked for inclusion that Fisher suggested two roughly parallel Dixie Highway branches, an eastern from Detroit through Cincinnati and Knoxville, and a western from Chicago through Indianapolis and Nashville. The two were connected in every state through which they passed by perpendicular rungs; all told, the Dixie covered nearly four thousand miles. Over the next few years it grew even more inclusive, stretching north to Michigan's Upper Peninsula and east to Savannah, and wandering so indirectly, in spots, that it seemed little more than a vague southward inclination. Even so, it was celebrated as the first major highway between the Deep South and the industrial North, as a conduit for Yankee dollars, and as a gateway to romanticized, almost mystical, country. The *Atlanta Constitution* ranked its importance with the roads of ancient Rome.

Other newspapers, both Yankee and southern, devoted pots of ink to the Dixie, too, especially when Fisher and an "official" inspection party of autoists embarked on a Dixie Highway Pathfinding Tour reminiscent of his Lincoln expedition. The pathfinders inspired the highway-minded all over the country. Private "auto trail" associations materialized by the dozens, each promoting its route as the straightest, or fastest, or most scenic, or safest way to travel between far-flung points, and the few highway groups already doing business kicked their efforts up a gear.

Soon the Yellowstone Trail was mapped from Plymouth Rock to Puget Sound. The Jefferson Davis Highway, a pet project of the United Daughters of the Confederacy, theoretically stretched from D.C. to San Francisco via New Orleans. The 3,568-mile Midland Trail coincided with the Lincoln from New York to Pittsburgh, with the Old Trails Road to Kansas City, then veered alone through the Rockies and into Utah, where it again joined the Lincoln through the desert before cutting south at Ely, Nevada. The Lakes to Gulf Highway linked Duluth, Minnesota, to Galveston, Texas, and lent a nickname to its headquarters town of Chillicothe, Missouri — "The Highway City" — that was popular in Chillicothe, if nowhere else.

Like the Lincoln and Dixie, most of the new trails followed existing roads and relied on a mix of private subscription and local government labor. Many were more abstractions than fact, outlets for sloganeering and self-promotion rather than any real road building. For all that, the forty-eight states soon were crisscrossed with colorfully named highways, real and imagined. Primitive though it was, America had its first interstate road network.

Regardless of what labels they went by, the country's highways were dependent on government for their construction and maintenance, so AASHO's first order of business was to draft a federal highways bill to propose to Congress. Meeting frequently, and usually in the East, its executive committee drafted a measure advocating a network of federally owned highways, then offered it to Congress before much of the association had seen it. Several members in the Midwest immediately objected that they'd been blind-sided; since when had AASHO discussed, let alone agreed to, a system owned by the feds?

With a sizable piece of the membership in revolt, AASHO's bosses thought it wise to take a second crack at the bill. A gathering of automotive interests, the Pan-American Road Congress, was already scheduled for mid-September 1915 in Oakland; the association piggy-backed on the congress with a special meeting on September 11.

Eighteen departments were represented, including Iowa's. That odd, uncomfortable engineer, MacDonald, took command of editing the measure and, despite his quiet manner and the strong personalities with whom he shared the room, managed to turn the thing on its head. The bill became a call for Federal Aid; it favored rural projects and required federal and state governments to share the costs of construction, dollar for dollar. More than a million miles of public road would be eligible for improvement — any country lane on which the mails were, or might be, carried. Because some of the most urgent needs were felt in big states with small populations, the group devised a formula for doling out the federal money that combined square mileage, population, and mail route mileage. In no case would the feds pay more than $10,000 per mile, and there would be no money for toll roads.

Perhaps most important, the bill reserved most big decisions for the states. They'd initiate the projects, choose routes, and do the actual building. They'd develop their own standards, too, though they'd need Washington to review and approve their plans before they'd get any of its money. Maintenance was solely a state responsibility, subject to federal inspection and penalties. In what was perhaps its most lasting provision, the bill required that each participating state have a bona fide highway department. When Page's staff later undertook an "exhaustive examination of state laws" to ascertain which met the bill's definitions, it found that eleven states were without "departments in the sense contemplated," and that "the highway departments of five other states might be considered as in the doubtful class." All told, "few of the states were in position . . . to begin immediate cooperation." MacDonald's bill would force them to modernize — in effect, to develop the expertise they would need to partner with the Office of Public Roads.

The Oakland meeting thus ended with AASHO's position reversed. Three months later, the membership ratified the new bill and passed it along to the U.S. Senate, where it was approved with a smattering of amendments. President Woodrow Wilson signed the Federal Aid Road Act of 1916 into law that July.

It marked the beginning of a federal-state partnership in highway work, still in place today, that was the second vital ingredient of the modern highway network.

Shortly after the Federal Aid Road Act became law, Logan Waller Page called a meeting of state highway officials to craft regulations governing the new partnership's everyday business. Thirty-five states sent representatives, Carl Fisher among them. They debated whether there should be a minimum width for Federal Aid roads (no, seemed to be the majority view), whether right-of-way purchases should be included in a road's shared cost ("I think it better for the work if the government does not spend any money in the purchase of property to which the government gets no title whatever," Page argued), and the pros and cons of various paving types.

Among the most interesting exchanges was one that came late in the meeting, when Arthur Crownover, chairman of the Tennessee Highway Department, took the floor. "I would like to make a motion," he said, "that the money be expended on interstate highways as far as possible, instead of local roads."

Page replied that the act gave the feds no authority to dictate which roads might be improved. Crownover replied that Tennessee wanted long-distance highways. "If we build roads along that line," he said, "and the people in Alabama, or the people in Kentucky . . . did not take to it, or the people in West Virginia, a great deal of our labor would be in vain.

"We ought to have cooperation between states, and these national highways that we have ought to be looked to."

The discussion ended there, but Crownover had struck on a shortcoming of the 1916 law: though it united federal and state governments in a cooperative effort, it provided them with no sharp goal beyond a vague aim to better the nation's roads. States were free to scatter improvements within their borders, without having those better roads connect to others in neighboring states, or in the same state, or even to other stretches of the same highway. The act did not build a *system*.

For that, the motoring public would still rely on the anarchic jumble of auto trails — each of which was almost wholly dependent on state engineers who might, depending on local needs, improve one stretch of the trail's mileage but not another. Across a single state, let alone the continent, none boasted a consistently smooth ride. Even the Lincoln remained a necklace of dirt, gravel, and mud; pavement covered just seven miles of its more than nine hundred in Nevada and Wyoming.

And while its people might gush about the ease and fun of a long-distance drive, the association's engineer, F. H. Trego, recommended that motorists pack an ax, shovel, and four-foot hardwood plank, fifty feet of heavy rope and sixteen of cable, an extra engine valve, two jacks, two spares, three gallons of oil, and a pile of cooking and camping gear — and "possibly a small pistol of some sort."

A State Department survey judged U.S. road conditions to be "far worse than any other major nation except Russia and China." This, as America became more motorized by the hour: some 3.37 million automobiles were in use in 1916, double the number of two years before. Within a year, there would be a car on the road for every fifth family. In three years, the number of motor vehicles would double yet again. A dozen years before, France had been the world's leading automotive producer and user. Now, close to eight in ten of the world's cars operated in the United States.

State highway officials were eager to get busy. By January 1917, legislators in Indiana, South Carolina, and Texas introduced bills to establish highway departments, and those in at least a dozen others bolstered or revamped their existing departments to meet the law's demands. New departments hired engineers and scrambled to acquire the expertise they needed to propose, design, and build the projects they would bring to the feds.

Page was confident they would find the effort worthwhile, as "the tendency of the Act will be to greatly strengthen and amplify the policy of state participation in road work." It was a slow and often trying process, though, made more so by Page himself. He and his people cast a picky eye on state paperwork, demanded numerous revisions, were thorough to the point of meddling — behaved, in short, more as supervisors than equal partners.

The two sides might have smoothed over these snags in time, but as it happened, that was one thing they lacked. In April 1917, when only a handful of projects were ready for contracts, the United States entered World War I, and practically overnight, road construction became a low federal priority except on the odd section of highway deemed vital to national defense. Before long, the Wilson administration suspended any rail shipments of road-building materials. Every road-related company and agency saw its employees called up for service; Page lost 35 percent of his staff. Construction and maintenance stopped cold.

The roads of the day wouldn't have fared well without regular care under any circumstances, but added to the growing millions of automobiles using them were, for the first time, heavy motor trucks, heretofore relegated to service on city streets of cobblestone, brick, and concrete, the only surfaces that could hold up under their weight and skinny, solid-rubber tires.

Their shift to the open road was an army idea. In December 1917, a military convoy of thirty Packard trucks set out from Detroit for the piers in Baltimore, and ultimately the Western Front, in what the respected journal *Engineering News-Record* called a "daring adventure." Loaded with spare parts, the trucks bogged down on muddy roads, met heavy snow in the Alleghenies, and took three weeks to cover the 540-odd miles — but all but one of them made it, and over the next several months, thirty thousand trucks followed, a feat inconceivable before the war began and the bellwether of a new era in freight hauling.

But as Carl Fisher had learned in the opening races at Indy a decade before, all but bona fide pavement was unequal to the demands of motor traffic; macadam didn't stand a chance against the weight of the trucks, their four-wheel-drive transmissions, and tires that concentrated tremendous weight on tiny footprints. State highway bosses found themselves the caretakers of shredded roads that they lacked the manpower and material to repair.

At the war's end, some 572 Federal Aid projects had been approved for construction, but only 5 had been finished. More than two years of federal-state partnership had netted 17.6 miles of road. Page did his best to put things in a positive light, arguing that completed mileage wasn't nearly so important as the progress states had made in setting up their departments. Disenchanted state officials were having none of it. They needed relief. They needed trunk highways that could withstand the battering effects of ever-heavier traffic. They wanted to streamline the process of getting them.

A federal highway network, built by a federal highway commission, seemed the answer. A matter thought settled — the old argument over whether to build a national system of highways or a system of national highways — returned to the fore.

A month after the Armistice, a showdown over the question loomed in Chicago, at a five-day joint congress of AASHO and an alliance of state engineers, automakers, and building suppliers called the Highway Industries Association. Page arrived with proposals that promised to snip away a lot of the red tape the states endured in their dealings with the feds, and promised a huge boost in federal roads spending in the coming four years.

It wasn't enough to quell agitation for federal highways, however. Put Washington in charge of the interstate highways, have a presidential commission decide where they should go and oversee their construction, and the country would be done with all the parochial dithering the states introduced to the process — so said Coleman and other national roads proponents. A federal commission would make highway routing decisions based on America's needs, not the individual wants of forty-eight feuding fiefdoms. There would be no question about a highway in one state connecting to another; it would be decreed. If the host states didn't like it, too bad. As for accountability, it would rest with the handful of people on the commission. Credit and blame would be easily assigned. The American people would know the names and faces of those to whom they'd entrusted their tax dollars and expectations for a great cross-country road system.

Page and like-minded state highway officials countered that for all their flaws, state-based highways benefited everyone who used them, locals as well as long-distance travelers. If you routed a highway so that it best answered local needs, and connected it to other highways that did the same, and they to others, you'd end up with a cross-state highway; and if you linked that highway to those developed in the same way in adjoining states, why, you'd soon enough have a highway across the entire country—and it wouldn't be an arbitrary slash of pavement, serving only "through" traffic, but a road woven into the communities through which it passed.

Besides, the Federal Aid advocates believed national highways would actually take longer to build. States would no longer match every federal dollar, meaning the feds would have to double their spending to achieve the same mileage of improved road—which nobody believed would happen—or double the time it took to do the job.

The debate was settled without Page. On the first of the congress's five days, the forty-eight-year-old bureau chief fell ill at dinner, retired to his room, and was found dead there later that night. AASHO gathered the next morning with the membership in shock and the Federal Aid side now lacking its chief advocate. Into the void stepped that same glowering fellow from Iowa, Thomas MacDonald, and when a vote came on the creation of a national highway commission, it was a deadlock, 20 to 20. A recount came out the same way. A single additional vote for a national highway commission, and American roads might have developed along a profoundly different, and presumably far less successful, course.

Having twice arrived at a stalemate, the membership decided to drop the matter. Though it later approved a resolution calling for "a Federal body or officer with adequate power or funds to administer all Federal and Federal-aid highway laws," a critical passage added that the states remained the initiators, builders, and owners of the roads; any "federal highway system" the resolution advocated was simply another label for the state roads granted Federal Aid.

There now loomed the question of who should succeed Logan Waller Page. In the weeks following the Chicago convention, David F. Houston, the secretary of agriculture, narrowed the search to two state engineers. One earned $10,000 a year, which Houston couldn't match. The other was the quiet, all-business engineer from Iowa, MacDonald.

No highway man enjoyed a better reputation. In nearly fifteen years on the job, he'd painstakingly built a web of intercounty roads, gravel-topped in places and well engineered throughout, with concrete bridges and culverts, drained surfaces, shiftless beds, and few sharp curves or steep grades. "The hills are being cut off and dumped into the valleys," the Lincoln Highway's Henry Joy said of the work. "Oftentimes the cuts are thirty feet deep."

He'd accomplished this with next to nothing. For most of his tenure in Iowa, the highway commission's entire staff had consisted of three full-time and two part-time employees, and as late as 1913, the state roads budget was just $10,000. Next door, in Illinois, it was ten times as much, and in Minnesota, commissioners had $150,000 for engineering alone.

He'd survived Iowa's lunatic politicians, too. The legislature had balked at the fifty-fifty spending imposed by Federal Aid's passage in 1916 — or, rather, at raising the state's share; bond issues for roads had become central to Iowa elections that year, especially the race for governor. In a state that was home to an automobile for every seven residents, among the highest ownership rates in the country, it was the "mud roads" candidate, Republican lieutenant governor William L. Harding, who prevailed.

Harding is still remembered nearly a century later for all the wrong reasons — most infamously, his wartime edict outlawing the public use of any language but English, which the governor persistently referred to as "American." The so-called Babel Proclamation was interpreted to include any conversation involving two or more people, even on the phone, and if he'd been able to take it further, Harding might have. He insisted, for the record, that God didn't hear prayers uttered in foreign tongues. At his instigation the General Assembly had taken up a vote on whether to junk the highway commission and disband its entire roads effort. It came to a 54-to-54 vote five times before the matter was dropped.

If MacDonald could survive that, he might do all right in Washington. The offer came just after the new year, when Houston called MacDonald to D.C. "and took up with me the proposition of Mr. Page's successor," MacDonald recalled later. "When he asked me if I would consider such an appointment, I was entirely unprepared, as I had never considered myself fitted for this place."

MacDonald initially turned Houston down, citing the position's salary — it amounted to a pay cut. The secretary took more than two months doing it, but he met the engineer's asking price. "Tender you the position," he wired MacDonald, "and hope that you can come in a very short time."

MacDonald accepted the job on March 20, 1919. A third ingredient of America's highway future fell into place.

3

THOMAS HARRIS MACDONALD earned his place in history less as a visionary than as a relentless refiner of the existing. He was an engineer's engineer, a man gifted at recognizing a problem and developing a methodical plan for fixing it. He did nothing "on spec," took no gambles; his decisions were founded on careful research, overlaid arguments, numbers — and accompanied by charts, measurements, cost figures, traffic counts. All of which made him the perfect man for the nation's top roads job in 1919, because the American highway system was a chaos of overlapping auto trails, disconnected state highways, dead ends, and doglegs, and MacDonald was order personified.

He didn't much discuss his past, but it's known that he was born in a log cabin in Twin Lakes, Colorado, thirty miles southwest of Leadville, in July 1881. That his father, a Canadian carpenter by the name of John MacDonald Jr., had crossed the border with his father and brothers ten years before to rebuild Chicago after the great fire, and had moved on to a new town, Montezuma, springing from the Iowa prairie. That John had met Sarah Elizabeth Harris, whose family owned Montezuma's dominant grain and lumber business. That the couple had married and ventured to Colorado during the silver rush of the 1870s, and that young Thomas was three when they returned to Montezuma to stay.

He'd grown up in the embrace of a slew of relatives, in a family enterprise that included grain elevators, offices, ranches, warehouses, and lumberyards, in a bustling little county seat of 1,300. MacDonald had been a typical Iowa teenager of the 1890s, in some respects. He was one of eleven in his class at the town's four-room high school, which had electric lights but outdoor plumbing. He enjoyed debate and was thought good at it. He earned pocket money by driving a grocery wagon, hunted the woods outside town for hickory nuts, endured long Presbyterian sermons and Sunday afternoons on which the Scriptures forbade fun.

But from early on, MacDonald showed himself an odd kid, too —distant, unnaturally formal, compelled to keep his emotions in check. His typical expression was tight, even grim; family photographs depict him erect and glowering, his neck braced by a high paper collar and bow tie. By his teens, he had four younger siblings. He insisted that they address him as "sir."

Montezuma was a self-contained place, with its own opera house, two newspapers, two hotels. It had to be: mud was a complaint all over America; in Iowa, where it took the form of a black paste called "gumbo," it was paralyzing. For weeks, sometimes months at a time, it marooned the farming families outside town and every spring and fall forced MacDonald's father to all but suspend his business.

Iowans had come to view gumbo as inevitable, as much a part of the calendar as full moons, and a small price to pay for a greater gift: the goo that snared their wagons also grew the finest crops in the world. If MacDonald felt differently, he kept it to himself. In 1899, when it was time to choose a college, he let his mother and grandfather talk him into the Iowa State Normal School in Cedar Falls.

The campus, today's University of Northern Iowa, turned out teachers. MacDonald was miserable there, both in and out of class, and decided to decamp for the Iowa State College of Agriculture and Mechanical Arts in Ames, where the instruction promised to better square with his exactitude, his comfort in mathematical certainty. He had months to kill before the new school year started. He spent them in Nebraska, where he punched cattle on his grandfather Harris's ranch in the Sand Hills.

Examine just about any photograph ever taken of MacDonald, and it's hard to picture him as a cowboy. At nineteen, he stood five foot seven.

He wore his dark hair short, parted down the middle and shellacked to his skull, which accentuated his very large and slightly pointed ears. His pale blue eyes, drilled deep under beetle brows, were almost comical in their intensity. He was sure to have looked ridiculous in a Stetson.

It turned out, though, that he was at home on the range. He reveled in riding fence and branding cattle, the austere beauty of the country, and, not least, his solitude in it—he passed his nights in a sod house with a single book, Booth Tarkington's *Monsieur Beaucaire,* on which he later claimed to be the world's foremost expert. He found that the ranch's quiet, its absence of idle talk, of chitchat, of distraction, enabled him to think, to recharge.

He arrived at Iowa State in the fall of 1900 ready to work, and demonstrated as much with a heavy load of math, library and military science, drawing, and lettering. He did well, excelled in a couple of summer internships, continued to impress when, in his junior year, the curriculum veered to railroad engineering and mechanics. And if it didn't happen sooner, it was probably at this point that he drew the notice of the college's senior engineering professor.

Still in his thirties, Anson Marston already enjoyed a formidable reputation as a pioneer designer of water, sewage, and flood-control systems and was forming some of the foundational theories of culvert and underground pipe design. Most important, in terms of his influence on young MacDonald, the professor was a classic product of the Progressive Era. He viewed technical expertise as the keystone to addressing the world's problems, experimentation and fact gathering as vital to social progress; not only did they offer apolitical solutions to complex ills, but they encouraged new questions and untried answers.

Marston called MacDonald into his office to suggest a subject for his senior thesis. Why not devote it to a new and virtually unstudied problem—namely, Iowa's roads? Everyone knew that they were a mess; gumbo was infamous hundreds of miles beyond the state's borders. But little research existed on the cost of a bad road versus a good one, or on the needs and desires of road users.

They agreed on a two-pronged assignment. MacDonald and another senior would "determine and report the pull or force a team must exert to move a wagon of varying weight over a road of varying condition" and "study and report the needs of the farmers of the county for good roads and the actual value thereof to the farmer in the way of taxes to be paid." With that, MacDonald and Laurence Timmerman Gaylord, an easygoing six-footer, toured the state, interviewing farmers; nearly all identified drainage as the chief trouble with their local roads. The students attached a simple dynamometer to teams pulling wagonloads of sand over roads in Ames and Cedar Rapids. Their data showed that horses had to work seven times as hard on a dirt road as on a hard, smooth rock surface, and that asphalt and brick offered even easier going.

By his 1904 graduation, MacDonald had inherited Marston's near-religious faith in the power of science, of technical expertise, to right the world's problems, and in research as a building block of rational decision making, an "administrative tool of first importance," as he later put it. He continued to learn from his mentor after receiving his diploma. That spring, Iowa legislators decreed that the college would serve as a state highway commission, which until then didn't exist; at the same time, the college created a full-fledged division of engineering, with Marston as its dean. The professor invited him to work for both.

It was an interesting, if not long-term, proposition. Iowa was home to all of 931 automobiles, and it was by no means certain that the machines were anything but a fad. The state was entirely unpaved. Besides that, the legislature had authorized a budget for the new commission of just $3,500; for an engineer, the money was elsewhere.

Marston must have been persuasive. Thirty-five years later, MacDonald credited the professor with setting his life's course. "Had it not been for his vision into the future," he wrote, "I would undoubtedly have chosen some of the more firmly established fields which seemed at the moment to offer greater possibilities."

His highway career started on horseback. MacDonald spread the gospel of good roads in lectures and demonstrations around the state. He visited road construction jobs, where he found waste and shoddy work in abundance; localities often got about a dime's worth of road for every dollar they spent. He eventually turned his attention to bridges, which tended to be wooden and badly built by design; contractors had carved the state among themselves so that each would be assured all the bridge work in a particular territory, an arrangement that cost taxpayers twice — in contracts that were wildly overpriced, and in bridges that demanded frequent replacement.

Quietly, patiently, the straight-arrow MacDonald dismantled the racket and saw to it that one contractor reimbursed the state for inflated charges and sloppy work. More important, he rode back and forth across the state to demonstrate the principles of concrete and steel bridge construction to Iowa's county engineers, showing them — in the midsummer heat, while wearing a suit, his necktie knotted high and tight — how to mix the cement, how to build forms and foundations, how to use corrugated metal or concrete pipe for culverts.

In March 1907, MacDonald married Elizabeth "Bess" Dunham, a former schoolteacher from Ames whom he met while she worked as Dean Marston's secretary, and whom he courted through her subsequent service as right hand to the college president. The wedding made the front page of both local papers. The *Ames Times* noted they "quietly married" on a Thursday night at the home of the bride's parents, in the presence of immediate family and three friends. The *Ames Intelligencer* offered a more imaginative telling of the event, explaining it as the work of a charmed silver chain, a "wonderful instrument of Cupid," handed down from one secretary to another and bringing love to each. Records at the county courthouse hint at a more earthbound impetus for the union: the couple's first child, Thomas Jr., was born eight months, fourteen days later.

Charmed or not, the MacDonalds set up house a few minutes' walk from the commission's office. It was a comfortable existence in a progressive little city. They were an easy stroll from restaurants, libraries, and the railway linking Iowa State with the business district. A campanile's melodies drifted over sheep grazing on the campus lawns. And years before he made his mark in AASHO, MacDonald began to build a reputation. He was a perfunctory writer but became a font of magazine articles on the hot topics of highways and automobiles. He was a simply awful public speaker — stiff, unsmiling, a reader who made rare eye contact with his audience and whose delivery forsook anything in the way of inflection or drama — yet he found himself giving one dinner speech after another.

His audiences were eager to learn how he proposed to meet the seemingly insatiable demand for his product. In his first ten years on the job, the state's 931 registered autos ballooned to more than 110,000; motorcars rivaled horse-drawn vehicles not only in Des Moines and other big cities, but in Ames, Montezuma, even the remotest farming crossroads. All of their owners cried for better roads — farmers anticipating the bounty of shopping, schools, churches, and entertainment waiting a few miles away, and urban autoists eager to range farther from home, to *tour*.

Over time, MacDonald arrived at a solution. If Iowa were to try to improve all of its highways at once, it would have so little to spend on each that it might as well do nothing at all; anything but the most rudimentary maintenance would be out of reach. Real progress demanded hard choices — classifying the state's roads by importance, spending the state's money only on those deemed primary roads, and leaving secondary roads to the counties and townships to worry about.

How would Iowans decide which roads were primary? The answer, on a highway commission led by Anson Marston, was obvious: by the traffic they carried. A simple, scientific approach would not only accelerate improvement of the chosen roads, it would keep highway financing beyond the reach of politics. "Iowa has an estimated mileage of 102,000 miles of public highway, but the primary system of roads would probably not exceed ten to fifteen percent of this amount," he wrote in a 1912 article, explaining that with 10,000 to 15,000 miles, "it is estimated that every trading point in the state would be reached from at least two directions by main traveled roads."

He carried this idea an important step further by noting that "the cross-county roads which would form the primary system of any one county could be so determined as to join with the primary system of the bordering counties" to form "the great trans-state roads" he mentioned at the Lincoln Highway dedication.

When Iowa reorganized its highway commission in 1913, Mac-

Donald, now the state highway engineer, started to assemble the system of primary roads he'd envisioned. He left the actual choice of the routes through each county to officials there; these were, first and foremost, local roads, carrying local traffic, and wouldn't be much use to anyone if they didn't answer local needs. The state's role would be to ensure that the roads were worthy of attention from a traffic standpoint, that they connected to the overall network in an agreeable fashion, and that they met uniform standards for construction and maintenance.

"We are not attempting to build up a large central department," as he explained it, "but are leaving as much of the detail work as possible to the district engineers and the county organizations." The result was "a fine organization in which harmony prevails."

By the time MacDonald accepted the secretary's offer, his collaborative, bottom-up approach to choosing and improving primary roads had won over the state. The General Assembly was about to approve a 6,400-mile primary system that connected every town of more than a thousand residents. Iowa had just 21 miles of rural concrete road, but thanks to MacDonald's long concentration on foundation work — on good drainage, gentle grades, and straight alignments — much of the primary system was already in place and ready for surfacing, an improvement that even the infamous Governor Harding favored. "Seldom has there been such a swing of opinion away from earth roads as exists in Iowa today," marveled *Engineering News-Record*. "The Governor has turned around completely, and is now an ardent advocate for hard surfaces." MacDonald was as surprised as anyone. "Six months ago," he wrote, "I would not have believed it possible for public sentiment in the state to change as it has."

The *Des Moines Capital* met the news of his federal appointment with the sort of editorial most bureaucrats only fantasize about. "It would be difficult to enumerate the patient faithfulness of Engineer MacDonald," it read. "In all his works he has obscured himself. He has never carried an advertising ear. His only consolation has been in duty well done. It has been known in the state for some time that Mr. MacDonald would be tendered the place which he has now accepted, but Iowa men have hoped that he might not accept."

He spent his free moments that spring of 1919 exchanging letters with well-wishers. One theme is plain in these notes: he was a true believer in the federal-state partnership. "I know it is not necessary for me to say that I have only one thought — that of placing the Federal work on a cordial co-operative basis with each state department," he wrote to one state highway engineer. The nation's highways, he wrote another, "have reached far beyond the possibilities of any one organization," and only "the cooperation and combined efforts of the States and the Federal Government . . . will produce the results which are demanded."

Among the warmest letters was Henry Joy's. "You have had a hard fight in Iowa," the Packard chief wrote on April 2, "but the fruits of your efforts will be coming to the people of Iowa during generations to come." The second half of his note was devoted to an aside about the Lincoln Highway. "You may be amused that I am trying to bring about a trip to the Pacific coast of an Army Truck Train," he wrote, justifying an obvious publicity stunt with the argument that it "would be important for the military 'brass hats' to know" whether they could drive supplies to West Coast ports, as they had to the Atlantic during the war.

"If the Army would start three loaded truck trains across the country," he wrote, "one for the northwest country, Washington and Oregon; one for the San Francisco Bay area; and one for the Los Angeles and Southern California area; and make the reports public our people as a whole would have a reliable picture." He closed the letter: "More Power to you."

MacDonald replied that he looked forward to working with Joy and was "much interested" in the truck project. "In fact," he added, "if it seemed possible to spend the time necessary, I would feel better prepared to undertake the work at Washington after just such a trip."

As it happened, Joy was persuasive — the army did send a convoy of its trucks across the country, from Washington to San Francisco, on the Lincoln Highway that summer. Among the officers assigned to the mission was a young lieutenant colonel named Eisenhower.

PART II

Connecting the Dots

4

········

DWIGHT EISENHOWER ENJOYED little promise of a great military future when, in the first days of July 1919, he heard that the army would attempt to drive a train of heavy trucks from the Atlantic to the Pacific; he volunteered to go along as a Tank Corps observer because he had nothing better to do.

He had missed the war. While his West Point classmates earned battlefield reputations in Europe, Eisenhower had overseen a training camp erected on the battlefield at Gettysburg. When he'd finally won orders to lead troops overseas, the Armistice had intervened. Depressed, angry, and convinced that he would be little more than a desk-bound functionary for the rest of his career, he'd seriously considered resigning his commission.

But he was unaccustomed neither to setbacks nor to overcoming them. Eisenhower's affable, smiling, upbeat manner masked a stoic core. Raised in Abilene, Kansas, squeezed into an 818-square-foot house with his parents and five siblings, the young Dwight had devoured military histories and thrown himself into sports; he'd sought an appointment to West Point more for a place on its football and baseball teams than out of a thirst for martial glory. After lettering in football his first season at the academy, he'd injured a leg, snuffing his athletic career — a blow that robbed him of ambition until he was encouraged to coach the junior varsity squad. His football players responded to his leadership style. It was his first command, and it went well.

After graduation he'd been stationed at Fort Sam Houston, Texas, where he coached a local military school team and met Mamie Doud. They'd married in 1916 and had bounced among stateside postings since — an increasingly frustrating period during which Ike strove, he said, "to perform every duty given me in the Army to the best of my ability and to do the best I could do to make a creditable record, no matter what the nature of the duty."

A road trip would be, if nothing else, a break from the slow, stultifying routine of Camp Meade, Maryland, so on the afternoon of July 7, the twenty-eight-year-old Ike left the base to join the motor truck train at its first encampment, forty-six miles into its journey. Seventy-two vehicles made up the caravan, sixty-five of them trucks, bearing two companies of army truckers, units of mechanics, engineers, and medics, and fifteen military observers — in all, 260 soldiers and 35 officers. They aimed, their commanders said, to test the army's equipment, collect data that might be useful in the future training of its Motor Transport Corps, and investigate the viability of long-distance trucking. They hoped to excite the Good Roads Movement. They might pick up some recruits along the way.

They were also engaged in a risky bit of on-the-job training, because most of the enlisted men were raw recruits with virtually no experience driving heavy machines, which at the time required even more skill than it does today: some of the beasts were giants, the biggest weighing eleven tons empty, with touchy gearboxes and springs overmatched by washboard roads.

The trucks had trundled out of Washington after a late-morning ceremony on the Ellipse, just south of the White House and a few blocks from Thomas MacDonald's new office, accompanied by a flock of civilian hangers-on. It took seven hours to reach Frederick, where Eisenhower reported for duty, ready, he admitted later, for a summertime lark. Instead he got "a genuine adventure."

The convoy joined the Lincoln Highway in Gettysburg and grunted up its twisting, steeply graded path over the Alleghenies. The greenhorn drivers took the Midwest's rough roads too fast, stripped gears, gunned engines until their radiators boiled over. Breakdowns were frequent. The trucks crushed scores of bridges — fourteen in one day, by Eisenhower's count — which trailing soldiers scrambled to rebuild. But the expedition encountered nothing truly unexpected, and though long hours and summer heat and seemingly unending repairs wore on the men, that held true until the convoy reached the desert southwest of Salt Lake City.

Headed out of town, the Lincoln hugged the southern shore of the Great Salt Lake, then turned south into sparsely populated Tooele County. The turn marked the end of civilization, as it existed in 1919; here began the highway's rough passage across mountain and desert on the old Pony Express trail, for two-hundred-odd miles little more than a pair of grooves worn into sun-seared and shadeless hardpan. The Lincoln end-ran the desert's salt flats — a vast, shimmering plain of dirty white crystal that hid, below its brittle crust, a briny sludge as deep, sticky, and black as the worst of Iowa's gumbo — but its more sure-footed route had a downside: it added miles to the desert crossing, miles that translated to hours spent under a broiling, potentially lethal sun.

So the Lincoln Highway Association had committed to trimming the route. In November 1916, Carl Fisher had donated $25,000 of his own money toward a shortcut through a narrow mountain pass west of the town of Tooele, and in 1918, Goodyear's Frank Seiberling, having succeeded Henry Joy as the association's president, had convinced his company to pony up $100,000 for a seventeen-mile causeway across the salt. This straight shot was to be elevated on a rock and earthen grade, much like a railroad track. The association signed a contract with Utah officials to build what it called the Seiberling Cutoff in March 1918, specifying a completion date of July 1, 1919.

Once the convoy had become a sure thing, the association had discussed scheduling a dedication ceremony to coincide with the trucks' arrival but couldn't pin down a date that worked for everyone. Just as well. The road over the pass, now named for Fisher, was finished with time to spare, but not so the causeway. Only seven miles had been surfaced with gravel; its eastern end was a berm of loose dirt.

On the morning of August 20, 1919, the truck train crawled over

Fisher Pass without incident, only to flounder in hip-deep dust on the downhill; no rain had fallen for eighteen weeks, and one vehicle after another spun its tires until its frame bottomed out. It took all day and most of the night to jack up the trucks, stuff the holes beneath their tires with sagebrush, and ease them on their way—after which they all too often restuck themselves. That was mere prelude to August 21. The convoy broke camp early, its soldiers eager to get the desert behind them—and, finding the Seiberling Cutoff impassable, set off across the salt.

This would have been a risky move in a light runabout. In a giant cargo hauler, the consequences were inevitable. Every truck that ventured onto the flats broke through and became helplessly mired; even a caterpillar tractor failed to achieve any traction in the stinking goop that lurked beneath the crystal. The convoy's commanders had but one option: they harnessed up teams of soldiers, as many as one hundred, and, in a torturously slow and difficult feat of muscle and will, had them tow the stranded vehicles over the desert by hand.

Darkness came with hundreds of men marooned on the flats. Cooking fuel couldn't reach them, so those lucky enough to get supper had to settle for cold beans and hard bread. Water was in such short supply that the convoy's commander posted guards around the tanker truck. So the night passed on the best long-distance road in the country.

After that misery, the rest of the trip seemed a glide. The convoy pulled into San Francisco sixty-two days and 3,242 miles from Washington. Eisenhower's after-action report, submitted to his bosses several weeks later, understated the perils of the desert crossing. "In western Utah, on the Salt Lake Desert, the road becomes almost impassable to heavy vehicles," he wrote. "From Orr's Ranch, Utah, to Carson City, Nevada, the road is one succession of dust, ruts, pits, and holes. This stretch was not improved in any way, and consisted only of a track across the desert. At many points on the road, water is twenty miles distant, and parts of the road are ninety miles from the nearest railroad."

Some of his colleagues came away with strong opinions about how to fix the situation. Army first lieutenant Elwell R. Jackson reported that he and his fellow officers "were thoroughly convinced that all transcontinental highways should be constructed and maintained by the Federal Government" and helpfully pointed out that a bill then before Congress "provides for just such an undertaking under a Federal Highway Commission." He "earnestly hoped," Jackson wrote, "that this measure may be favorably acted upon at an early date."

Back in the capital, Thomas MacDonald was imbuing his new office with the old-fashioned formality that had long been his style. The grave, soft-spoken engineer was invariably "Mr. MacDonald" or "Chief," even to his closest friends — even, it was said, to his wife. He was more severe-looking, more unsmilingly intense than ever; photographs depict him glaring at the camera with an evident mix of discomfort and impatience, cadaver-stiff, fists clenched, his expression shouting: *Take the damn picture.*

He did not make chitchat. He did not cajole or cheerlead. He often seemed lost in thought; it was best not to speak to him at such moments. In time, his people learned, it was best not to talk to him at all unless he spoke first. Hair thinning, waistline expanding, his suits increasingly snug around the belly, he looked older than his thirty-eight years, which only reinforced the impression that this was not a man with whom one joshed.

But then, there was little cause for levity in the bureau's offices. In the first months of peace, road projects were hamstrung by a national dearth of railroad cars and a consequent shortage of sand, gravel, and broken stone; by an absence of qualified workers; by leaping prices. States were eager to build and repair roads, but little work was under way.

So once again, a federal highway system was back in vogue, this time in the form of the bill to which the young army lieutenant referred — a bill introduced to much fanfare by Sen. Charles E. Townsend, a Michigan Republican and chairman of the Senate's Committee on Post Offices and Post Roads. The Townsend bill called for at least two highways through each state, linking to a web of such roads stretching the length and breadth of the country. A five-member commission appointed by the president would oversee the system and take over the federal government's other road-building duties. The Bureau of Public Roads would cease to exist.

Good riddance to it. As Townsend would explain, "Under the state aid system, as we have it now, there is very little system," just "little patches of roads here and there all over a state, beginning nowhere, leading nowhere, having no system in view." Stick with the current setup, and it "would take a hundred years to get these roads into a system which began and ended somewhere."

Support for the senator's measure came fast and loud — from the automotive press, automakers, and, not least, from rank-and-file autoists. The American people were impatient for modern highways, and every time they got behind the wheel, they were convinced anew that the existing arrangement had failed to provide them. Never mind that just three years had passed since most states took up scientific road building; never mind that the war had diverted money and material from the industry. They wanted to drive, and to do it at once. If a commission could deliver decent roads, bring it on; if a system of national highways was the fastest solution, by all means, build it.

The Bureau of Public Roads offered little reason to think otherwise. Its district engineers spent far too much time in the office getting far too little done, and their underlings weren't pictures of industry, either. J. M. Goodell, a former *Engineering News-Record* editor now working as a bureau consulting engineer, warned MacDonald that the outfit was "notoriously one of the most slack" in government, full of "dry rot and mild faking," of "old hands who have not done a day's work a week these many years."

But the new boss was up for a fight. Twenty years before, MacDonald had stepped off a train in Seneca, Nebraska, to find that his grandfather's cattle ranch was fourteen miles away. A man in a nearby store told him he could use the gray pony outside for 50 cents, provided he could catch it. So the teenager had walked into the pasture, rope in hand, and backed the pony into a corner. It stood calmly as he stroked its neck. The instant he tried to slip the rope over its head, it tore off.

MacDonald cornered it again. The pony ducked the rope, fleeing side by side with a bay mare that shared its enclosure. MacDonald cornered the pair again. Once more, both horses bolted. Thirty-one times, as MacDonald would recount it, the sequence played out until, exasperated, he cornered both horses and tied their tails together, then showed them the rope. They took off, tripped on each other's legs, hit the ground. MacDonald threw the rope around the pony's neck and rode to work.

His first memo to bureau staff read like that of a man confident about the days ahead. "This is an all-American job," he wrote. "Through enthusiastic endeavor we will try to justify the confidence that has been reposed in us by Congress.

"There is no work more worthwhile. I have yet to know any man who has devoted a considerable period of his life to the building of roads who is not conscious of having accomplished results whose returns to the public in service can scarcely be measured."

MacDonald's differences with the Townsend bill went beyond his own job security. He was positive that the federal government could not afford to build a system of long-distance highways and, from the same tight treasury, provide for state roads that would serve local populations. The latter were more important, on a daily basis: roads were, first and foremost, economic tools, as he told AASHO in December 1919, the first of the group's meetings that he attended as the bureau's boss. Those that filled no economic need were unnecessary, while those "laid out along sane and sound economic lines," he said, would "eventually produce systems of highways suited to the special needs of each locality, and yet be entirely adequate to meet" the demands of long-distance travelers.

The trick to fostering such networks was taking the same "basic and fundamental" step he'd advocated since early in his Iowa tenure: classification. Primary routes would be those that eventually joined to form what he'd called the "great trans-state roads" back then; secondary would link farms to markets, a county's small towns to one another, and other strictly local destinations.

Most states' primary highways would account for "in the neighbor-hood of five to seven percent of their total mileage," he estimated — a refinement of his thinking in 1912. "The step which seems necessary now is a definite plan of cooperation between the states and the federal government, which will insure that the primary systems of each state are connected up with the primary systems of the adjoining states."

How he arrived at the "five to seven percent" figure has never been fully explained. Competing theories hold that it originated with a pair of U.S. senators trying to work out what percentage would guaran-tee their western states a major highway in each direction, or with MacDonald's own experience in Iowa.

Other speeches followed, dozens of them; with both Townsend and Federal Aid getting a lot of attention from the press, MacDonald was much in demand. Traffic's overwhelmingly local nature, he told the pro-Townsend U.S. Chamber of Commerce, had been confirmed "by scientific study of the character, origin and destination of highway travel." The small percentage engaged in the long haul certainly had to be accommodated, "but it is not necessary to build an especially chosen national system to reach this desired end."

The importance of his topic usually trumped the failings of his de-livery, and a good thing. As he had in Iowa, he tended to read his care-fully typed speeches in a flat-line drone, lifting his eyes from the script only to insert the odd parenthetical remark that often spun into a long and complicated tangent; sometimes, like a comet returning on its ec-centric orbit, he found his way back to the main narrative, but with painful regularity he did not and skidded into an oratory dead end. Those moments of tension were public service, really, because staying awake in the stuffy, smoky banquet rooms of the day must have been hell.

He spent hours talking on the phone, meeting congressmen, and dictating letters aimed at creating consensus among state commis-sioners. When he broke for lunch, it was usually at the Cosmos Club, an exclusive, all-male fraternity of political and industry leaders on Lafayette Square, where he continued his quiet, persistent lobbying amid cigar smoke and wood paneling.

The matching state money required by Federal Aid doubled every dollar that Washington spent on roads, he stressed. The answer wasn't to cut the states out of the national highway scheme, but to better focus the combined spending.

After two long and anxious years, his campaign paid off.

Had the Townsend bill come to a vote in 1919, at the postwar highway program's darkest moment, it almost surely would have passed. But Townsend failed to get his bill out of the headlines and onto the Senate floor. He fiddled with it continuously, held a seemingly endless parade of hearings on each new version, and in the meantime, the country's highway program made a U-turn. The wartime paralysis, the postwar supply problems, all passed; by 1921, a million men labored on the nation's streets and roads. "Picture a pile of gravel and stone twice as high as the Washington monument and of equal length and breadth, and you will have a fairly accurate notion of the quantity of material required for the Federal aid roads under construction and completed" that year, MacDonald wrote in an uncharacteristically vivid magazine essay. "To haul that material from the quarry or pit to the road requires a million freight cars. Now place alongside of your stone pile another pile four hundred feet high and a little more than four hundred feet in width and breadth and you will have some idea of the amount of Portland cement required for the same roads."

With the turnaround, MacDonald could claim that Washington had appropriated more in five years of Federal Aid than it spent on the Panama Canal, the standard for monumental work — and the outlay in Panama had been spread over a full decade. The state-federal partnership looked good again, and it got another boost when AASHO's executive committee drafted a highway bill of its own in 1921. It was pure MacDonald: Each state was to designate a system of roads on which all Federal Aid would be spent, and which did not exceed 7 percent of its total highway mileage. The state was to classify its Federal Aid highways as primary or secondary, the former being roads of an interstate nature, the latter connecting county seats — and the wording was such that the bulk of each state's federally subsidized system would comprise these strictly local roads.

The House approved the AASHO bill and delivered it to the Senate, where the nature of highway building, the question of top-down versus bottom-up planning, and Thomas MacDonald's fate all at last came to a decisive vote. The Senate wasted little time. On August 19, 1921, it backed the Chief. As *Engineering News-Record* observed, it was "an overwhelming vote of confidence for the U.S. Bureau of Public Roads."

The Federal Highway Act of 1921, signed into law that November 9, was the foundation for modern highway building in the United States; it remains the single most important piece of legislation in the creation of a national network — far more so than the later interstate highway bill, which would not have been possible, or necessary, without it. Until its passage, America had no grand plan for its roads, and the federal government no legal interest in what the act termed "an adequate and connected system of highways, interstate in character." It brought into being what until then was a fantasy: an improved route into every county seat in the country and every town of decent size, connected to other improved roads, and they to others, enabling a motorist virtually anywhere in the United States to reach any other place of even minor importance without getting mud on his fenders.

The act preserved the best parts of its 1916 predecessor. The states remained the source of highway plans, and the federal government the enforcer of design, construction, and maintenance standards. It called on the states to choose the "seven-percent" highways but gave the secretary of agriculture final approval of those choices, as well as the type of construction to be used. Once the individual states and feds agreed on the routes, and no later than November 1923, the Department of Agriculture would publish a map of the whole network, and on those roads and only those roads would the federal government's money be spent. America would at last have a highway system.

This wasn't necessarily recognized as momentous at the time. The *New York Times* devoted five lines of type, deep inside the paper, to the House's approval of the conference bill. President Warren G. Harding's signature earned a paragraph at the bottom of page 21. MacDonald, however, saw the new law for what it was. "Those who are a part of these organizations have the good fortune to be engaged in their chosen field when the greatest development that can ever come is taking place," he told AASHO members at their annual meeting in Omaha a few weeks later. "This body of individuals and their associates will determine the efficiency of the highway systems of the future."

Choosing the participating roads was the most serious responsibility they would ever have, he told the state engineers. "Here is an opportunity to do a big, basic work, such as comes to few in the course of a lifetime," he said. "The individual who fails to vision the importance of the task has no moral right to hold a position of authority in its performance."

5

N OW CAME THE TASK of choosing the Federal Aid highways and ensuring that all of the far-flung pieces connected into a coherent system. The first step of the process was already completed; while the tussle was still on over the Townsend bill, MacDonald had met with the army so that he could incorporate its needs into any future bureau decisions about which roads got top federal priority.

From the start, he and the generals had agreed on a few guiding principles, the foremost being that civilian roads and military should, with rare exception, be one and the same; neither favored a segregated highway network for troops. Nor did they see much value in a "transcontinental road which merely crosses the continent," as the army put it; better were "roads connecting all our important depots, mobilization and industrial centers, which, as thus connected, will give us a transcontinental route."

Once they'd dispensed with these basics, MacDonald had ordered the preparation of detailed state highway maps on which military leaders could identify the routes they considered most vital to their needs. The army had used them to produce what became known as the "Pershing Map," which identified better than seventy-five thousand miles of road as strategically important, emphasizing coastal and border defense and links to major munitions plants. It had some curious omissions. The Deep South was largely ignored and southern Florida left a blank; in the army's eyes, it was too swampy for any foreigners to invade.

But if nothing else, the process had produced those forty-eight state maps, which the bureau now distributed to the various highway departments so that they could ink in their candidates for primary and secondary Federal Aid highways. MacDonald wasn't content to wait on the states; he figured that the bureau ought to have its own model for what a 7 percent system should look like, so that it could better judge the states' selections and, one hoped, encourage a stronger, more rational grid. A small committee led by engineer Edwin W. James was assigned the task of mapping the model.

James was to be one of a handful of associates on whom the Chief would heavily rely over the next three decades. Born in Ossining, New York, educated at Phillips Exeter Academy, Harvard, and the Massachusetts Institute of Technology, he'd joined the bureau in 1910, after engineering stints in the Philippines and with the Army Corps of Engineers. MacDonald had come to value his clear head, engineering skill, and, not least, his diplomacy. It was James whom the Chief had dispatched to Little Rock early in 1921 to sort out a messy highway financing scandal there, and whose report had prompted the bureau to briefly suspend Federal Aid to Arkansas. It was James whom the chief had deployed later in the year, again to Arkansas, to account for more than $2 million in missing road-building equipment that had been donated to the state as part of a postwar military giveaway; when James asked the state highway boss where the gear was, the man had taken a sparkplug and a wheel lock from his desk drawer and told him that was it — which had led to Arkansas' suspension from *that* program.

Now James and two other bureau engineers rounded up population figures for every county in the forty-eight states, along with four key economic indicators from the census for each — agricultural production, manufacturing output, mineral yields, income from forest products. They assigned a value of 100 to each state's total population, and a number to each county based on its percentage of the statewide whole. They repeated the process for each of the economic statistics. The result was a quick-and-dirty gauge of county wealth and importance.

James and his coworkers next took the bureau's new state maps and attached a square to each county, those with big numbers earning a big square, poor and unproductive ones a small. Once the squares were blackened in, "we had a series of emblems through which diagrammatic routes could be laid out," James recalled decades later. "Routes through the heaviest emblems were routes through the generally wealthiest and all around most important county areas. Road locations could be made catching obvious local control points along these diagrammatic lines, and you had a selection from best to poorest almost staring you in the face."

The states had until late January 1922 to submit their choices. They corresponded closely with James's routes. As finally laid out, the Federal Aid system totaled 168,881 miles, or only about 5.9 percent of the total road mileage—and as the Chief noted, it reached 90 percent of the nation's population and included "not one, or two, or three transcontinental roads but dozens of them crossing the country from the East to the West and from Canada to the Gulf and the Mexican border.

"Through practically every feasible pass in the Western mountains," he said, "one of these roads will be open to the traveler."

Drawing the system did spark one controversy, centering on a familiar stretch of road: the arid, salt-crusted route through the western Utah desert on which the army convoy had bogged down. Folks in western Utah had been complaining for years about the Lincoln's desert routing. "This Roda serves absolutely No good Purpose, or Parties," one Joseph Conley had informed Logan Waller Page in August 1918, in a letter he evidently typed himself. "Serves No Producers, Not even Tourists and is located more than 50 Miles from any parallel Rail Road and is of absolutely no Military Value, and is absolutely a Eseless and Brazen expenditure."

The more sensible route for a road to California, Conley had advised, was straight west from Salt Lake City alongside the Union Pacific's tracks to Wendover, a town on the Nevada line, and westward along the Humboldt River to Reno. No such road then existed, and building one would be a job; about forty miles of salt flat stood in the way. Still, Conley's was not a lone voice in the proverbial desert. The following year, Dwight Eisenhower had noted a sharpening dispute "between the Lincoln Highway Association and some of the people in the section west of Salt Lake City" in his after-action report.

If the bureau paid any notice to such talk, it was passing. Decisions on location and routing belonged to the states; only a flagrantly un-sound choice would provoke MacDonald's intercession. The Lincoln Highway Association didn't seem overly worried about the grousing, either, perhaps because its existing route had been suggested by Utah's own governor in 1913, and because, after all, Fisher and Goodyear to-gether had donated $125,000 toward its completion — money that the state had accepted with a contract to complete the road. In so doing, it seemed, Utah had guaranteed that the way west would stay where it was.

But in September 1919, less than a month after the convoy's debacle on the salt flats, Utah officials halted work on the Seiberling Cutoff. They'd run into equipment troubles, they explained. The following January, they pleaded poverty. In March 1920, their story again shifted. Now they weren't sure they'd ever get around to finishing the job.

To the Lincoln's directors this represented a breach of honor, as well as contract. Seiberling fired off a series of increasingly outraged letters but failed to budge the folks in Utah — who, despite their supposedly empty pockets, quietly launched work on a Wendover Road. When the state submitted its proposed Federal Aid road system to the bureau in the fall of 1921, it did not include the Lincoln west of Salt Lake, in any form. Not as a primary road. Not as part of the state's secondary system. Every foot of Carl Fisher's highway, from the Atlantic to the Pacific, was nominated for Federal Aid, save for that stretch in western Utah. In its place, the state nominated what was, by and large, a still theoretical northern route.

Newspapers throughout the West condemned the move as a sleazy cash grab by power brokers in Salt Lake, reasoning that Lincoln mo-torists bound for both northern and southern California traveled together until they reached Ely, Nevada, where those headed to Los

Angeles peeled off on the Midland Trail; by abandoning the Lincoln and rerouting traffic to Wendover, Utah would force travelers to make their southern turn at Salt Lake, onto the Arrowhead Trail, which ran south the entire length of Utah. "Now do you get the picture?" asked the *Ely Daily Times*. "If Utah can force tourist travel to her play grounds she will add immensely to her revenue by keeping the traveler longer in her boundaries." Salt Lake City, a Placerville, California, paper raged, was home to "some of the biggest hypocrites that ever held public office."

Hoping that the Lincoln's position might play better in Washington, Henry Joy prepared a "brief" on the dispute for agriculture secretary Henry Wallace, 172 pages long and appended by a 26-page letter. Wallace asked the Chief to investigate. The bureau was already on it. It studied both routes, assessing the relative populations of each, the value of roadside property, the traffic, water sources, and supply points, the rigors of the terrain. In most respects the comparison favored Wendover; a road there crossed more valuable land, required fewer curves, and rose and fell less than half as much as the Lincoln. The "one outstanding barrier," the bureau found — and it was daunting — was the salt flats. But with care and money, that could be overcome, and the result would be a more direct, more economically sound, and probably safer road, regardless of the "very strong pride of opinion" that might say otherwise.

In a May 1923 letter to MacDonald, Wallace announced that the Wendover route was "a public necessity" and wrote Joy that he could "be most helpful in bringing a satisfactory conclusion to the situation" by rerouting the Lincoln to follow the new road. Joy and the rest of the association were in no mood to cooperate. A few months later he informed Wallace that they'd formally rejected his suggestion. "We do not desire to differ," he explained. "Facts compel it."

With that, the Lincoln Highway hewed to a line that doomed it. For the first time in its history, the association had chosen a route that was bound to be eclipsed in its engineering, its maintenance, its ability to meet the demands of increasing traffic; no private auto trail could possibly match Federal Aid's manpower and money. And as the quality of the Wendover Road outpaced that of the Lincoln, it was destined to sap the older road of its traffic until none remained. No matter how righteous its position, the association would be out of business.

Carl Fisher was too busy in Miami Beach to pay much mind to the dispute. He opened a new hotel, the Flamingo, overlooking Biscayne Bay, and imported a herd of Guernsey cows to supply its guests with fresh dairy. He built a popular beachfront swimming pool and casino, encouraged a new style of women's swimwear that showed shocking expanses of bare leg, and imported a baby elephant, "Rosie," to walk the beach and pose for photographers. Tourism exploded.

Fisher hungered for more. He was after a winter home for the nation's wealthy and beautiful, a resort of expansive mansions and palm trees and full-time play. So he built a top-of-the-line harbor for wealthy yachtsmen, hosted speedboat races on the bay, and opened polo fields and stables the equal of any in the country. He smuggled in large stores of outlawed liquor.

In January 1921, president-elect Warren G. Harding vacationed in Miami Beach, fished on Fisher's yacht, and golfed with Rosie caddying. The visit helped fuel a Florida land boom; Fisher's sales leaped into the millions, then the tens of millions. Even by his standards, he was stinking rich.

The desert unpleasantness aside, the 1921 act ushered in what the highway industry would come to see as a golden age of road building. More than ten thousand miles of Federal Aid highways were laid down in 1922, three times the total finished since the start of the program in 1916. Two years later, more than that amount was built of concrete alone, and the pace was accelerating.

Roads ballooned into a huge employer, providing jobs not only for those actually building them, who numbered in the hundreds of thousands, but also for an army of men who made road-laying gear and provided the raw materials. More than 200 American companies made cement, 127 made paving brick, and 42, asphalt; another 380 provided crushed stone, and 340 shipped sand and gravel. The various public officials involved in roads numbered eighty thousand. In 1923, the Chief noted that America's highways were undergoing improvement at the rate of forty thousand miles a year. "At his nod, millions move from the United States Treasury," *Motor Life* magazine said of MacDonald, crowing that neither "Morgan nor Rockefeller nor Carnegie nor the First Families of Croesus ever had the spending of so much money in so small a time."*

The new Federal Aid roads transformed the country through which they passed. Farm products were cheaper to transport, reducing prices at the nation's grocery stores. School buses were transporting millions of rural children to consolidated schools, huge improvements over meager one-room schoolhouses. Shoppers in towns overlooked by the railroads were starting to see more than staples at the local dry-goods merchant. Before long, the Department of Agriculture could boast that one could travel from Seattle to San Diego on paved highway.

What form pavement took, on that West Coast highway and any other, varied from state to state, project to project, even engineer to engineer, for consensus was just beginning to gel on the traits of an ideal highway; the experts differed on the appropriate size and surface and overall form of a cross-country road, on the arc of its curves, its lighting, its capacity.

The first tentative step toward building some unity of thought came not from AASHO or the bureau, but from the Lincoln Highway Association. While debate over the Townsend bill was still going strong, the Lincoln's leaders decided to build a section of ideal road — a combination of the best available design and construction, a money's-no-object example for the nation and world. In April 1920, the group mailed a questionnaire to 4,600 engineers, seeking their thoughts on the perfect highway, then assembled a panel of engineering luminaries to sift through the suggestions and come up with a model.

As it happened, the responses offered little guidance, even on such

---

* He was enough of a personage that when little Blackwell, Oklahoma, learned it had the nation's top roads man in its company, the town fathers treated him to meals and a hotel room, gave him a tour of county highways, and cashed several of his personal checks. Their visitor was long gone before they learned he was a fake.

a road's basic form. Most responses fell into three categories: they favored a paved, two-lane highway that could be expanded with the addition of a parallel road a mile or two away; two paved lanes in each direction; or two lanes in each direction, separated in some manner. Variations included segregating trucks from cars and slow from fast traffic. One engineer suggested lanes for horse-drawn vehicles.

At the committee's first meeting, just before Christmas 1920, members disagreed over whether highways should be lighted, one saying that in his experience "on the lighted highway practically no one used their headlights. On the unlighted sections they had big headlights that made it almost impossible to meet them and proceed with safety." Similar debates ensued on traffic capacity and general design. But over the course of two additional meetings, the members hammered out a common vision of the ideal highway of 1921. It would have a right of way at least one hundred feet wide and a paved width of forty feet, enough for two, ten-foot-wide lanes in each direction. It would be flanked by five-foot grass shoulders and gravel sidewalks. Curves would be kept to a minimum; those that were unavoidable would be banked and have a radius of no less than a thousand feet, enabling cars to safely round them at thirty-five miles per hour and trucks at ten. It would have no roadside ditches and no advertising signs.

Finally, its surface would be made of reinforced concrete ten inches thick, a decision that prompted Thomas MacDonald, who'd agreed to serve on the committee and was courted to lead it, to boycott the proceedings. The attention of such a panel, he wrote, "should be attracted not to the character of the surfacing material used but to the design of the highway," for recent history had "amply demonstrated that a considerable number of materials will carry traffic satisfactorily."

That might seem a strange objection nowadays, what with concrete being ubiquitous, the most-used construction material on Earth, a literal foundation of modern life. More than a ton of it is produced each year for every man, woman, and child on the planet, and its advantages are obvious. It spills to the ground a suggestible ooze, ready for any shape, many tasks, and within hours stiffens into a hardy mass that resists fire and insects, endures the extremes of weather, and shoulders tremendous loads. It is liquid rock, the dust of fallen mountains reconstituted, made of all-natural, abundant ingredients.

But the Chief had long preached spending only as much on a highway as its traffic and loads warranted; to overbuild a road was every bit as stupid and wasteful as leaving it in the mud. An "Ideal Section," as the Lincoln people called their project, did not necessarily mean paved, to MacDonald's thinking — it meant constructed to suit its purpose and economy. Might be macadam. Might be graded dirt. Could still be ideal.

Not only that, but concrete was still relatively untested as a road surface. America's earliest concrete paving, surrounding the courthouse in Bellefontaine, Ohio, had been poured just thirty years before. The first substantial concrete road building, 250 miles' worth scattered among several states, hadn't occurred until 1912. And there was this: concrete's modern recipe was just two years old.

The stuff itself was hardly new. The ancient Greeks had used some form of concrete nearly four thousand years before. In Rome, the famed Trevi Fountain was supplied by a concrete aqueduct that had been standing when Christ was born, and the Coliseum, nearly two thousand years old, had a concrete foundation and superstructure; its stone was mere cladding.*

Like modern concrete, the Roman variety consisted of cement, water, and filler. Mixed, the first two ingredients form a binding paste; the filler, usually sand, gravel, or shale, is added for volume. The only complex part of the mix is the cement, which is derived, in part, from calcium carbonate, a compound found the world over in limestone; heating it in a kiln burns away the compound's carbon and much of its oxygen, leaving behind calcium oxide, also known as quicklime.

Adding quicklime to water sparks a chemical reaction — heat, gas, and a sticky gunk called slaked lime, which the Romans stored wet, in jars, until they were ready to mix it with sand to create mortar. If the

---

* What's more, recent scientific papers suggest that Egypt's great pyramids might be made not of carved blocks of stone, as long thought, but of limestone-rich concrete cast in place.

job called for a denser, harder, less porous material, they held back on the sand and substituted pozzolan, or volcanic ash, which they possessed in abundance; the result was a gray concrete of such exceptional strength and durability that it wasn't matched until modern times.

Over centuries of trial and error, the Romans came to understand that concrete has great compressive strength, meaning it can bear weight placed on top of it, but little tensile strength — it can't be pulled or twisted. They learned that it is susceptible to cracking because it shrinks as it hardens, and does so faster near its surface than in its depths, and that cracks exposed to the elements can spell its end; water seeping into a fissure expands when it freezes, scouring the crack, forcing it open, and over time reducing the concrete to rubble.

Ancient engineers found that by adding horsehair to the mix they could better regulate its shrinkage, and that a dab of blood or animal fat helped it weather the freeze-thaw cycle; combined with calcium oxide, the fats created a primitive soap, and its bubbles formed microscopic air pockets that enabled the mass to withstand temperature shifts. The ancients used their expertise to build monuments, libraries and public baths, shops and houses, and roads and aqueducts traversing leagues of rolling countryside.

Then the empire collapsed. For thirteen centuries, the world went without. Roads devolved to mud. Cities were tinderboxes of wood and thatch. The only structures built to last were castles and stone churches, and they could take generations to complete. It wasn't until 1756 that England's John Smeaton, the first person to call himself a civil engineer, mixed lime with Italian pozzolan to create what he called "Roman cement," then used it in the stone-block Eddystone Lighthouse, built between tides on a treacherous rock off England's southern coast. Two lights had already failed at the spot. Smeaton's proved equal to anything nature threw at it, and made his a household name.

Englishmen patented a succession of cements over the following sixty-odd years, each with a slightly different recipe, each claiming a new peak of strength and convenience, until, in 1824, a Yorkshireman named Joseph Aspdin patented an artificial stone "for stuccoing buildings, waterworks, cisterns or any other purpose to which it may be applicable." He named his cement after the finest building stone around: Portland.

What set it apart from the competition was its mixture of slaked lime and clay — the latter replaced the Roman pozzolan — which together were fired in a kiln, then ground into a powder. Mixed with water, it proved fast-setting and strong. Years later, Aspdin's son William used more limestone in the mix and cooked it in much hotter ovens. This yielded hard, dry nodules called "clinker," which he then ground. The resulting powder was what goes by the Portland name today.

By the close of the nineteenth century, concrete was in use around the world. Spurred by demand for fireproof buildings and a cheap alternative to stone and brick, reinforced concrete — poured around steel dowels, or "rebar," to increase its tensile strength — had been fashioned into thousands of hotels, offices, and factories. But much was still unknown about the stuff. Engineers understood that adding filler to the mix in the form of aggregate — crushed rock, gravel, whatever — didn't compromise strength. That because aggregate was cheaper than cement, it made sense to add a lot of it. But the specifics were sketchy. Was coarse aggregate stronger than fine? What made the stronger mix — more cement or less water? Should cement be measured by weight or volume? Measuring its strength eluded them, too. Concrete wasn't rated by its finished characteristics, as it is today, but by how much cement it contained per cubic yard. A batch might be described as a five- or six-sack mix, for instance; the latter was presumed stronger, but how much stronger was hard to say.

The ancients had held the advantage until a Chicago researcher named Duff Abrams published a 1918 paper sharing insights he'd gleaned from "about fifty thousand tests" on concrete mixtures. The most important: water, more than any other ingredient, determined concrete's strength. "One pint more water than necessary," he wrote, ". . . reduces the strength to the same extent as if we should omit two to three pounds of cement from a one-bag batch." He concluded that "the following rule is a safe one to follow: Use the smallest quantity of water that will produce a plastic or workable concrete."

This was still very fresh news when, two years later, the Lincoln Highway Association approached the Chief about serving on its committee. Which is to say that the roads on which American motorists traveled — or some of them, at least — were as newfangled and fast-evolving as the vehicles being driven.

6

I N 1922, ESSEX, a division of Hudson, introduced an affordable, completely enclosed car — the first for the masses sealed against the weather, with glass windows and a hard roof — and motoring, until then an unpleasant undertaking in rain and cold, became a year-round endeavor in the harshest climes. The following year, American factories produced 3.9 million cars and trucks and registrations topped 15 million, so many that economists predicted the industry's growth couldn't continue. Most of the white male heads of households who wanted and could afford a car already had one. Most poor whites, minorities, and women wouldn't be buying. Market saturation was at hand.

It turned out that current owners nursed a hunger for bigger and better cars, and replacement sales flourished. Buyers demonstrated an eagerness to assume debt, as well; thousands were lured behind the wheel by easy credit terms — down payments slashed, installments stretched to twenty-four months. In mid-1925, registrations reached 17.5 million, a car for every 6.5 Americans. A year later, they stood at 19.7 million. And the industry's growth only accelerated. By the end of 1928, another 7 million vehicles were in use. Never before in the history of industry had a product gone from its first appearance to complete societal dominance in so short a time. In thirty years, America had become a nation on rubber wheels.

The invention's costs grew apace. In 1925, automobiles killed more people in Illinois than diphtheria, measles, scarlet fever, typhoid, and whooping cough combined, in an age when those diseases remained scourges. The same year, 932 people died in auto accidents just in New York City, more than a third of them children, double the rate of five years before. Manhattan's streets, the City Club of New York cried, were host to "Municipal Murder," a daily "Dance of Death."

It only got worse. In 1928, the rate of death by motor vehicle was five times that of fifteen years before. In 1929, when a new automobile rolled off an assembly line every six seconds, a life was lost to one of the machines every sixteen minutes.

Danger could not cool the nation's ardor for its cars, however. Neither could burgeoning traffic. By the late twenties, traffic congestion had grown into one of the greatest vexations of everyday life in all of big-city America. As fast as new pavement was laid, it seemed to fill with cars and trucks. In Chicago, the number of weekday auto commuters jumped by nearly a fifth between 1926 and 1928, despite congestion so stultifying that the city outlawed left turns and weekday parking at its downtown curbs.

"Our street systems will soon be strangled," the *American City* worried. "Neither the sidewalks nor the roadways of the streets will be able to accommodate the traffic that will be produced. The city's fire protection machinery will not be able to function, and consequently the fire hazards will be greatly increased. The public health will be jeopardized and the congestion problems of all kinds that are developed will soon become a public menace."

People lamented the death toll even as they piled into their cars. They complained about the traffic as they became part of the problem. They spent ever-growing chunks of their incomes and free time on the automotive habit; in most states, road-hungry consumers welcomed new taxes on gasoline.*

No wonder cars came to be seen in the same light as older vices. "The number of persons who devote their spare time to study has dropped

---

* Not only did gas taxes seem puny next to the progress they bankrolled, but their arrival coincided with drops in fuel prices. A gallon fell from almost 30 cents in 1920, on average, to less than 21 cents in 1924, and kept dropping; during the Depression, it would dip below 17.

materially," claimed a visiting member of the German Reichstag in a damning portrait of auto-obsessed America. "There are also many complaints about the increasing superficiality of intellectual life. The common answer is that formerly alcohol injured the people's culture, and that motor driving is a sort of substitute for liquor."

Their highways improving by the day, their cars increasingly sturdy and comfortable, their prosperity leaping in the burgeoning economy of the mid-twenties, Americans took to the road. Long-distance touring was no longer reserved for well-heeled adventurers, no longer required goggles and a pistol; it became popular recreation for couples and families, who struck out from the cities in search of elbow room, fresh air, a closer acquaintance with nature.

Popular culture rode shotgun. New characters became standards of jokes, books, movies — the traveling salesman, car broken down just up the road from the farm where he asks to spend the night; and the young woman stopped on the shoulder, staring incomprehending at the confusion of metal and rubber under her roadster's raised hood. And with this nomadic yen appeared new industries catering to the explorer's needs. Filling stations and repair shops multiplied. Eateries sprang up. And most notably, the pavement was soon straddled by places offering beds for the night.

They started simply. As hotels varied in quality and didn't readily cater to motorists — reaching them could require a battle with traffic, and parking was tight — enterprising towns opened public campgrounds at their edges, often no more than a cluster of tent sites equipped with fire rings, trash cans, and parking spots, the more lavish efforts including restrooms or picnic shelters, central kitchens, even free telephones. They became immensely popular in the early twenties.

But they also attracted riffraff who stayed long past their welcome, so many municipal camps introduced fees. The moment they did, they found themselves facing private-sector competition, and it wasn't long before City Hall was driven from the campground business. Then the for-profit campground operators squared off, undercutting each other's rates and boosting their offerings; some built little cabins, angling for travelers who didn't care for tents, and the idea took hold — pretty soon the auto cabin camps, as they were called, were roadside fixtures from coast to coast, some bare-bones (a bucket for water, communal showers and cooking), others quite comfortable.

Within a few years these mostly mom-and-pop operations were biting into the traditional hotel trade, a development that *Fortune's* James Agee, judging them "both a sound invention and a new way of life," didn't find at all surprising:

> It is six in the afternoon and you are still on the road, worn and weary from three hundred miles of driving. Past you flashes a sign DE LUXE CABINS ONE MILE. Over the next hill you catch the vista of a city, smack in your path, sprawling with all its ten thousand impediments to motion — its unmarked routes, its trolley cars, its stop and go signs, its No Parking markers. Somewhere in the middle of it is a second-class commercial hotel, whose drab lobby and whose cheerless rooms you can see with your eyes closed. Beyond, around the corner, eyes still closed, you see the local Ritz with its doormen and its bellboys stretching away in one unbroken greedy grin. You see the unloading of your car as you stand tired and cross, wondering where you can find the nearest garage. Your wife is in a rage because she has an aversion to appearing in public with her face smudged, her hair disarranged and her dress crumpled. All these things and more you see with your eyes closed in two seconds flat. Then you open them. And around the next bend, set back amid a grove of cool trees you see the little semicircle of cabins which the sign warned you of.

The auto cabin camp traded on speed, thrift, and simplicity. You paid maybe a dollar a head for a small, clean room with a double bed — "a sign may have told you it is a Simmons, with Beautyrest mattress" — and a dinette, washbasin, toilet. Your parked car was a few feet from the door. "And in the morning you will leave without ceremony," *Fortune* advised, "resume the motion you left off the day before without delay." In some parts of the country, particularly California, the cabins weren't so unassuming. Some asked eight bucks a night, which would have been unthinkable in the Midwest. Some were giants, like Long Beach's two-hundred-room Venetian Court. Some dropped the "Cabins" from their name for "Motor Court" or even — get this — "Mo-Tel."

Touring by auto remained, despite such improvements, a journey of faith, one best undertaken with a trunkful of tools and a head full of mechanical know-how. Consider the travails of a young family man driving from Texas to California, who described his journey in a letter to his parents: Outside of El Paso, his ignition failed; he spent "a couple of hours discovering where the trouble was" and three more "walking into town, waiting on mechanics to eat dinner, and other delays." Farther west, in Holbrook, Arizona, the oil lines clogged. "I took the whole overhead valve system off the car and took it inside and cleaned it up, finishing about midnight," he wrote. "Naturally my flashlight burned out just when I needed it, so I had to go to bed and wait until morning to put the thing back on the car." In the meantime, the temperature dipped to ten below zero, "and the car froze up so tight a Cadillac wrecker with chains on couldn't pull me to get started." Back on the road, he encountered bone-crunching cold again the following night, "but drained the car and heated the water on the stove the next morning."

It didn't hurt to have a good sense of direction, either, because even as the states and federal government rolled out new highway mileage, the tools available to chart one's course on it were few. In 1924, the Bureau of Public Roads published its map of the Federal Aid system, making it available for general consumption as a hardcover portfolio of eighteen oversized sections. But big as it was, the hard-spined portfolio was useless on the road, and Rand McNally didn't produce its first road atlas until 1926. Directional road signs were meager and, often as not, inaccurate.

The surest source of navigational insight was the *Official Automobile Blue Book,* which since its first edition in 1901 had served as a low-tech forerunner of today's Mapquest, using odometer readings and landmarks to guide motorists from point A to point B. At mile 51.5, it might say, take the left fork past an unpainted Methodist church. At mile 82, stay to the right to avoid a bottomless mud wallow.

Even with a *Blue Book*, the correct path could be difficult to discern, because by now the Lincoln and Dixie highways had scores of imitators; the States were crisscrossed by at least 250 named trails — the Victory Highway, the Jefferson, the Roosevelt, the Apache Trail and the Bee Line, the Red Star, Red Ball, and Red X, each boasting that it was the best way to wherever. More than forty of them crossed Indiana. Sixty-four were registered in Iowa. The trails were blazed with shingles tacked to trees, fences, and barns, and with rings painted on telephone poles; each trail had signature colors — the Lincoln's being red, white, and blue, with a black capital *L* on the white stripe — so staying on track theoretically meant just following the colored blazes from one pole to the next.

Trouble was, the trails overlapped. "One well-known route 1,500 miles long overlaps other routes for seventy percent of its length," the *Times* reported. "Ten different routes are involved in this overlapping and in places two or three of them coincide for many miles." In places, a single road could go by a half-dozen names, and telephone poles were encircled by so many rings that picking out where one blaze ended and the next began was a confusing and dangerous distraction.

Meanwhile, state highway officials struggled to find sensible labels for the Federal Aid roads in their inventories. Wisconsin was the first state to attempt replacing names with numbers, and a straggle of states followed its example, but the trail associations kept pushing their products with enough zeal that the old names stuck. The cure, highway officials were coming to see, was to strip private entities of their power to name roads.

Utah's Wendover Road controversy had brought home that trail associations, helpful though they'd often been in automobiling's early days, had become unnecessary, time-consuming, and meddlesome third parties in road-building decisions. In November 1924, during AASHO's annual meeting in San Francisco, the subject of confusing highway names came up in a subcommittee led by Edwin W. James. It recommended that the full association ask the secretary of agriculture to work with the states to fix the problem.

AASHO followed the recommendation, calling for "the selection and designation of a comprehensive system of through interstate routes" and a "uniform scheme for designating such routes." The aim wasn't to alter the Federal Aid network, which would remain intact; the states merely sought new labels for the most important Federal Aid roads. AASHO asked the secretary to appoint a joint board of state and federal highway men to handle the task, which he did. James was named its secretary; the Chief, its chair.

At the joint board's first meeting in April 1925, the members reached speedy agreement on numbering the nation's principal roads, rather than naming them, and chose to select the routes to be included in the system before trying to apply the numbers. They also decided that a marker of uniform shape and style should identify the chosen routes, prompting an Ohio engineer, Leo Boulay, to remark that the United States shield, which appears on the front of the dollar bill and was a de facto logo for the *Official Automobile Blue Book,* would fit the bill. Decades on, James recalled that Frank Rogers of Michigan passed him a doodled shield. James redrew it, including a small "U.S." over a large route number, and the name of a state across the shield's pointed crown. The other members approved the design on the spot.

That May and June the joint board held a series of regional meetings to gather input on what routes to include in a numbered system. Reconvened at the bureau's offices in August, the group settled on a network of 50,100 miles to submit to the states. Its members took up three other matters that day that left a lasting imprint on the continent. They formally approved James's shield design as the marker for the U.S. highway system. They adopted the modern red-yellow-green traffic light sequence, and road sign designs for use throughout the United States that included the octagonal stop sign — painted black on yellow at the time, because a sufficiently durable red paint wasn't yet available (and wouldn't be until the mid-fifties). Finally, the joint board delegated the actual numbering of the new system to a committee, with James in charge.

The assignment was a tough one. Numbers would have to be user-friendly, instinctively sound, and flexible enough to permit future additions to the grid. James would later recall that he was told to confer with A. B. Fletcher, a former California highway chief who was serving as a consulting engineer to the bureau, and who apparently had thoughts on how the numbering might work. Fletcher's "big idea," James recalled, was a highway stretching from "away up in the north west, to Key West below the tip of Florida," which he figured would "be the greatest road in the world" and would make a fitting Highway 1.

James wasn't so sure. "As I listened and looked, I first wondered where No. 2 road would be laid, and where Nos. 5, 10, 50 and 100?" he remembered. Convinced that Fletcher's idea would invite chaos, he studied the map himself, and in very little time, a pattern suggested itself. "It stares one in the face, it is so simple and so adjustable," he said. He would assign even numbers to all of the east-west highways, and odd numbers to those running north-south. The numbering would be lowest in both directions in the northeast corner of the country, up at Maine's border with Canada, and would climb as one moved south and west — in other words, the east-west highways with the lowest numbers would run through the nation's northernmost states, and those with the highest, along the Gulf Coast and Mexican border; north-south highways would bear the lowest numbers on the Atlantic coast and the highest on the Pacific.

One- or two-digit numbers would denote principal highways. A three-digit number would mark a spur or variant of a main route and usually would connect with the parent road at some point.* The arrangement created a simple geographic weave. With the lowest east-west number at 2 and the highest at 98 (zero and 100 weren't used), U.S. 50 was sure to run somewhere near the country's waist; likewise, the intersection of U.S. routes 25 and 60 would be quite a ways east and just a little south of center.

James and his committee struck on one more detail. The most important of the east-west routes, including all the transcontinental highways, would have numbers ending in zero — 10, 20, 30, and so

---

* An exception to the rule is U.S. 101 in California, which is considered a two-digit highway.

on. The most important north-south highways would end in 1. James considered it "simple, systematic, complete."

Looking to drum up support among his state colleagues, James called on Paul Sargent, chief engineer of the Maine State Highway Commission, to whom he pointed out that U.S. 1 would run from Sargent's own state to Miami. For most of its length, he added, it would follow the eastern seaboard's "Fall Line," along which the Piedmont gives way to coastal plain and the falls of the middle Atlantic's big rivers lay — of the Delaware River at Trenton, the Potomac near Washington, the James at Richmond. The route had been used since colonial times, which appealed to the Maine engineer: as soon as he mentioned it, James later wrote, "Sargent said he was with the whole idea."

His next stop was Detroit, and the offices of the Lincoln Highway Association, where he "laid [his] scheme before them, very frankly telling them that it would mean the end of the Lincoln Highway Association, the Dixie, and all others." Privately, the association's leaders weren't thrilled with the idea. "In the factory, a motor car model might be Model 'N' or 'X,' or some designated number; but it's known to the trade by a name — never a number!" Henry Joy later complained. "Why can't the Bureau, in the name of common sense, adopt industrial practice?"

But officially, the association posted no vigorous objections. "They understood it all; said they were for a big plan for roads across the U.S.; would be with my scheme if I would give the Lincoln Highway recognition so far as possible in the No. 30," James wrote. "I agreed to do all I could to put it across, and so had their support toward washing out all the named routes.

"They were the strongest of all the Associations and with them with us, who could be against us?"

Everybody and his brother, as it turned out. When the secretary of agriculture signed off on the plan in November 1925, all hell broke loose. The Lincoln's fellow trail associations denounced the numbers their routes had been assigned, or the board's failure to include their routes, or their looming obsolescence. Eastern highway officials railed that midwestern states had far more mileage than their populations justified. And the governor of Kentucky, William J. Fields, charged that "Chicago influence" was "written all over the map," citing as evidence a curious exception to James's numbering system: U.S. 60 did not run from the East Coast to the West, as one might have supposed, but started in Chicago and cut a long southwestern arc to Los Angeles, passing through St. Louis, Tulsa, and Albuquerque on the way. Its numbering irked Fields for two reasons. First, U.S. 50 missed Kentucky to the north and U.S. 70 missed it to the south; logically, U.S. 60 should have passed right through his state, but Kentucky had been left without a zero-ending east-west highway — and a state so important should have one. Second, three members of James's committee lived in states through which the proposed U.S. 60 passed. One of them, Cyrus Avery of Oklahoma, had proposed the route.

This was by no means the only anomaly in the numbering sequence. U.S. 1 strayed inland while following the Fall Line, so several routes with higher numbers ran east of it. Highways braided, too, so that they might be in proper sequence at some points, but not others; U.S. 11, for instance, curved so much at its southern end that it wound up west of U.S. 49. Even so, the proposed U.S. 60 stuck in the Kentucky governor's craw. He took his beef to AASHO's Executive Committee, which elected to leave the number unchanged but to designate a route from Newport News, Virginia, to Springfield, Missouri — and through Kentucky — U.S. 62. The governor was not mollified. In late January 1926, he and a delegation of his state's congressmen took their case to the Chief.

MacDonald was won over. Fields used logic and a map of the system to make "an argument that could not be fairly met," and the bureau came down on the side of numbering the Chicago-to-L.A. route 62, and the Newport News–to-Springfield road 60, pending agreement from the other affected states. Now it was Avery's turn to steam, which he did with passion for nearly three months.

There were other disputes over the joint board's work. The network almost doubled in size in the process of state review, to 96,626 miles, and routing and numbering caused dozens of minor squabbles. But the

Kentucky disagreement was by far the toughest, and the longest-lasting. It ended, finally, on April 30, 1926. Having learned from his state's chief highway engineer that the number 66 did not appear on the proposed system, Avery and his Missouri counterpart telegrammed the Chief: "We prefer sixty six to sixty two." MacDonald gave the label his blessing, as did Governor Fields. AASHO adopted the whole system late that year. So was born Route 66, the "Mother Road" made famous by John Steinbeck in *The Grapes of Wrath*.

And so began the end of the auto trails, America's first stab at an interstate network. It was inevitable that the old names would fall out of favor, for the numbering scheme took pains to avoid corresponding to them. The Lee Highway became routes 1, 11, 29, 45, 54, 60, 64, 70, and 72, at one point or another, and a few others besides; the Midland Trail became 6, 40, 50, 60, and 95. The Dixie Highway's branches bore dozens of numbers, and the Lincoln went by 30 only from Pennsylvania to Wyoming, carrying a half-dozen other numbers toward its ends. Henry Joy joked with some bitterness that it should be identified as "a memorial to the martyred Lincoln now known by the grace of God and the authority of the Government of the United States as Federal Route 30, Federal Route 52, Federal Route 29."

The trepidation that the new system caused the trail boosters turned out to be well placed. For every burg that thrived alongside the new numbered highways, for every business that earned its keep from their burgeoning traffic, there was another that had been bypassed by the grid and left to wither on now-unimportant lanes that were no longer on the way to anyplace of mention.

They're sprinkled all over the American West — towns like Lida, Nevada, which seemed a charmed place in the early years of the Motor Age. When the coast-to-coast Midland Trail was blazed in the teens, it was routed right through Lida. When the army drew its Pershing Map of principal military routes, Lida was on it. When the states selected the Federal Aid network in 1921, again, Lida was on a main line.

Named for a prospector's wife, built on the site of an old Shoshone camp, brought to life in a rush for silver, and swelled by another for gold, Lida had spawned newspapers, hotels, stores, and saloons; the town even stamped its own coins when cash ran low. Attracted trouble, too: In one affray, a self-styled gunslinger named George Chiles worked the nerves of card players in a Lida saloon until one clocked him. Chiles hit the floor and came up shooting, his aim wild, and wounded two innocents at the bar. Both men bled to death as others in the room rushed Chiles and killed him, too.

Then the numbered U.S. highways came — or, rather, didn't come. U.S. 95 passed nineteen miles east of town, and U.S. 6 was more than an hour to the north, and suddenly nobody took the Midland Trail anymore. Today it's a two-lane road to nowhere. In one direction is Death Valley; in the other lies the great cartographic blank of the Nellis Air Force Range Complex, the mysterious Area 51.

Minus traffic, Lida emptied, businesses moved out, the post office closed in 1932. When I pulled into town seventy-four years later, it was down to two year-round residents, an older couple whose declining health was about to force their flight. What little remained of the settlement rose rusted and wind-scraped from the sagebrush: a handful of sagging shacks and the ruins of a half-dozen more; a small graveyard fenced in barbed wire and steel pipe, ground littered with toppled wooden crosses; forever busted pickups sandblasted down to their bones. Mining gear decayed among clumps of buckwheat and scorpion weed.

In the sun, the wind, the desiccated Nevada air, colors had leached from wood and metal. An old Coca-Cola truck, windshield gunned out, was bubblegum pink; on the houses, paint had cracked and curled from clapboard and tin roof, revealing a spectrum of browns beneath. With each passing year, Lida moved a little closer to matching the coarse desert floor, the bare palisades that form the northern rim of its valley, a little closer to vanishing altogether.

The Lincoln Highway's end came just a year after the new numbers became official. Traffic crossing the desert was shifting more every year to the Wendover Road, now marked U.S. 40; elsewhere, the Lincoln was undergoing steady improvement. Not much remained for the association to do, it seemed to Henry Joy, especially with shields popping up all along the highway's shoulder, so in October 1927, he urged his fellow officers to pack it in — and, as a last act, to adopt the hated northern route out of Salt Lake City, now the most direct way west. "We have exerted every possible effort to prevent this change of route," he wrote, "but it has been done."

His fellow directors balked at the latter suggestion, choosing instead to support a hybrid route. The Lincoln would abandon the Seiberling Cutoff to follow U.S. 40 to Wendover, cut south on a new Federal Aid highway to Ely, and there resume its original course across Nevada on what was now U.S. 50. They agreed, however, with Joy's suggestion that they "cease active and aggressive operations" and voted to spend the association's remaining money on three thousand concrete markers, which the Boy Scouts would help plant on the Lincoln's shoulder.

Everyone seemed content with the highway's modified route out of Salt Lake but Joy, who argued that it made far more sense to follow U.S. 40 all the way to California. In a spate of letter writing, he complained that the association had "for the first time in its history approved a lengthening instead of a shortening of the road," thereby betraying its "very foundation principles." He worried to Sidney Waldon, his old Packard colleague, "that we have made a most disastrous move" and promised that if "we, with our great intelligence, are to put on the map of the United States a Lincoln Highway with such a 'broken back' in the middle of it, then I will regret all my life that I ever started the work, or ever had anything to do with it, as I feel that it is a total discredit to us all."

He wrote more, a lot more, but it didn't sway the others to revisit the decision. With the new year, the Lincoln Highway Association closed its Detroit office and assigned Gael Hoag, its field secretary, the task of distributing the concrete markers, each adorned with the highway's tricolor blaze and a bronze medallion of Abraham Lincoln's profile. At 1 P.M. on September 1, 1928, Scouts dropped the waist-high posts in place. It was the association's last official act.

Even as Scouts tamped flat the soil at the markers' feet, the old highway, now existing solely in the abstract, as a nostalgic recollection, was undergoing a very modern upgrade. At a busy intersection in Woodbridge, New Jersey, crews were building a novel type of grade separation that enabled motorists on either road to turn right or left onto the other without having to stop. Those on the Lincoln could turn right onto Amboy Avenue by veering onto a ramp that cut the corner on a descending diagonal. They turned left by crossing over Amboy, then veering right onto a descending ramp that curved 270 degrees and sent traffic under the overpass.

This arrangement had been patented a dozen years before by a Maryland engineer named Arthur Hale but hadn't been tried in the United States — not until an engineer on the Lincoln job saw a magazine cover depicting an Argentinian highway that put Hale's invention to use. The Woodbridge intersection took its name from the shape formed by its four curving left-turn ramps: a cloverleaf.

Carl Fisher was represented by proxy as the Lincoln entered its final days. He'd been busy, as always. He built three new hotels in three years as Miami Beach boomed around him, palled around with Will Rogers and other celebrities, threw lavish parties at his enormous mansion. And he wrestled with a succession of personal tragedies. His parents died. His young son succumbed to scarlet fever. Always a neglectful husband, he became so withdrawn after the boy's death that his marriage splintered. His longtime mistress — probably not a boon to the marriage, either — quit their affair to marry a preacher.

He took to drink. His hard-muscled body turned to fat, and his face grew bloated and splotchy. His cursing became so wall-to-wall that with every sentence he approached self-parody. He angered instantly, spun into loud, crazy fits.

For all that, he retained the entrepreneurial vision that had served him so well. In September 1925, enchanted by the windswept solitude of Long Island's eastern tip, he and a few partners bought 9,632 acres at Montauk Point, envisioning a summer retreat to bookend Fisher's winter playground in Florida. He promised tennis courts, stables, grand hotels, lavish homes, a saltwater yacht basin, and railroad service from New York City by "the finest club car trains."

In February 1926, Fisher took title to nine parcels covering virtually all of the point, including fifteen miles of rugged shoreline, an "eagle's beak" of surf-pounded bluffs that once had inspired Walt Whitman. He might have bought more, had it not been for the Long Island State Park Commission, which as he negotiated the purchase snatched up 1,750 acres at the point's western end, an area called Hither Hills. Fisher figured the grab was illegal and decided to fight it.

But his opponent was formidable. The commission's young president was a New Yorker named Robert Moses, who envisioned his own great project on Long Island, a system of parks and public beaches linked by landscaped motor parkways. Over a career that stretched into the late sixties, Moses would prove himself a brilliant politician, a bold and creative builder of highways, parks, all of New York's great twentieth-century bridges, and acre on acre of housing — and an artful manipulator who consolidated and wielded enormous power beyond interference from a procession of mayors and governors. In 1926 he was still gathering his tools, but already he was acquiring land for the future Southern State Parkway, the Cross-Island Parkway, and the promenades, parking lots, and bathhouses at Jones Beach. He'd been talking to property owners out at Montauk for a couple of years.

Fisher lost the skirmish. Hither Hills became a state park, as did a twenty-two-acre piece of property at the peninsula's tip. But aside from a small plot on which a government lighthouse stood, Fisher owned the rest, and he put a brigade of men to work there. Within a few months, the harbor was taking shape, a seven-story office building was open for business, and work was under way on a golf course and polo fields, the two-hundred-room, Tudor-style Montauk Manor, and sixty-three miles of roads. Fisher imported a thousand sheep to graze the property and predicted that within four years, Montauk would have a year-round population of fifty thousand, a summertime head count three times as big.

Ah, but then came September 17, 1926. Miami Beach woke to a breeze that by late morning ratcheted into a howl, and that night a hurricane smacked the resort square in the chops. For eight hours it blasted the spit with 130-mile-per-hour winds, easing at dawn just long enough to coax punch-drunk residents onto the debris-strewn streets — at which point the gale abruptly returned. Giant waves swamped the city. Yachts and a navy destroyer were beached among shattered houses. "The ocean-side hotels were battered, walls smashed, windows broken and the lower floors flooded," the *Times* reported, and "casinos, small apartments and bath houses along the beach were swept away or irreparably damaged."

Fisher hired a train for Florida. "As soon as the homeless are cared for the work of reconstructing Miami Beach will begin at once," he promised. "Miami Beach was built from a mangrove swamp to an artist's picture of reality. What was once done can be done again." So it was; most of his properties were repaired by the season's start. But tourists didn't flock to Miami Beach as they had in past years, and some property owners quit their payments. Fisher's income dried up, and with it his ability to bankroll cash-gobbling Montauk.

Scrambling to raise money, he sold his stake in the Indianapolis Motor Speedway to auto racer and air ace Eddie Rickenbacker. It wasn't enough. Soon both of Carl Fisher's empires were in trouble. He'd lose what he had left in the stock market crash — his houses, his hotels, the land, his great dreams for Long Island. In years to come, he'd be forced to work for friends he once entertained on his oceangoing yacht.

The tycoon of Prest-O-Lite, creator of Indy and Miami Beach and the resort lifestyle, the millionaire, philanthropist, and visionary, the pioneer car buff who'd started America's first interstate auto roads when all about was mud and manure, slipped from the front page. In a very little while, he vanished from any page at all.

7

SLAPPING NUMBERS ON old roads made them easier to follow, sure enough, but old roads they remained — meandering and ditch-lined and, when they approached a city or town, totally inadequate for the traffic that snarled their narrow lanes. By the Depression's onset, two strategies had come into favor for addressing urban congestion, the first based on the assumption that a large share of it was caused by out-of-towners merely passing through. The new U.S. 30, for instance, drilled straight through the heart of most towns it encountered, following the Lincoln Highway's lead. At Gettysburg, Pennsylvania, it met U.S. 15 in the town square; at Pittsburgh it twisted and turned through the central business district and did the same in Fort Wayne and Ames, Omaha, and Carson City. Divert this over-the-road "through" traffic, the theory went, and you'd eliminate jams.

Lo, the bypass movement was born. In 1924, the First National Conference on Street and Highway Safety, chaired by secretary of commerce Herbert Hoover — and including the Chief and Edwin W. James — urged localities to consider "by-pass highways and belt highways which will permit through traffic, especially trucks, to avoid congested districts or even any built-up portions of the city or town." Five years later, the *American City* reported that bypasses had proved "a real benefit to the community, and this fact is becoming very generally recognized."

The benefit didn't last. Bypasses failed to ease congestion in most towns for long, and a glance at the country's shifting demographics spelled out one reason why. Between 1880 and 1920, the American people had more than doubled in number, and the overwhelming majority of the newcomers now lived in the cities. The influx was sure to continue, along with a concomitant rise in the number of vehicles struggling to negotiate overloaded streets, because traffic wasn't going *through* cities, it was traveling from point to point *within* them. You could siphon off every bit of through traffic, and the typical American downtown would still slow to a honking standstill at rush hour.

Bypasses fell short for a second reason, perhaps even more important. They soon attracted businesses to their own flanks — which generated their own traffic, so that after a few years the bypasses needed bypasses. The Chief observed that the typical bypass was good "for perhaps five years. Then we will have more traffic on the bypass, and more congestion of new industrial establishments and other occupations of the land than upon the main streets that we are designing to bypass completely."

Desperate, city planners deployed a second weapon: the "superhighway," which as originally conceived was something like a modern-day boulevard — a surface street, often divided by a concrete hump or some such barrier, with at least two lanes in each direction and an emphasis on smooth but relatively slow travel. Through the late twenties, planners talked of building superhighways to move traffic from the fast-expanding suburbs to city centers. The best-known was Woodward Avenue in and near Detroit, which boasted four lanes each way astride an electric railway.

But these arterial streets were simply bigger versions of the roads they replaced, and they suffered the same fate as bypasses. Even the biggest and best of them bogged down as stores and cafés rose along their edges,* and cross-street tributaries emptied their traffic into the larger stream. You can get a taste of the problem with a spin on any "business route" or urban leg of a numbered U.S. highway today. Take

---

* And especially "hot-dog stands," which, if you believe the literature of the day, must have occupied a tremendous share of the roadside; virtually every contemporary article on the problem cited the lowly hot-dog stand as a particularly foul menace.

U.S. 13, the old Ocean Highway, through Delaware. Between Dover and the New Jersey line, daytime movement on the highway is so hobbled by traffic lights, so gluey with the sheer number of vehicles squeezed onto its lanes, so crowded by the furniture stores and gas stations and pancake houses pressing its flanks, that you measure your progress in obscenities more than miles. Farther south in Norfolk, Virginia, and its suburbs, 13 crawls through a gantlet of fast-food joints and cinder-block motels, nail salons, discount mattress warehouses, cars for sale or rent, big-box hardware and army-navy surplus, all advertised with words and light of every size, color, intensity. Jesus, it's ugly, and slow and dangerous, besides — all those businesses pump more cars into the already thickened flow, launch others across the near lanes for left turns into the far.

It didn't occur to city planners that they might address the predictable obsolescence of even the biggest "superhighway" only by controlling the roadside. Even a 1929 proposal for "a national system of express motor-ways" — a resurrection, yet again, of the old federal commission idea — didn't call for expressways as we know them today.

But the idea came to them soon enough, and from several directions at once. As a starting date for the modern highway — a starting season, anyway — the early spring of 1930 is a fair choice; that's when a flurry of magazine pieces advocated a new approach to highway building, chief among them an expansive article in the *New Republic* by New England conservationist Benton MacKaye.

A tall, rawboned Yankee, MacKaye had turned an idea about a mountaintop hiking path into a magazine article a few years before and had thus sired the famed Appalachian Trail. He belonged to a circle of farsighted friends — architects and planners, landscapers and writers — who in the early twenties had formed the Regional Planning Association of America (RPAA), a grand title for what was actually a casually organized group that got together on weekends to mull the sprawl and overcrowding of America's cities.

The modern metropolis, as MacKaye and his friends saw it, had grown too big to fulfill its function as a setting for and facilitator of personal interaction. A few generations before, when personal speed topped out at a horse's pace, American towns had tended to be compact, tightly settled, and, barring such obstacles as rivers and hills, roughly circular in layout. Streetcars, far faster than carriages, had lengthened the distance workers could cover on their morning and evening commutes; soon suburbs had sprung up within a short walk of the radiating streetcar lines, so that the settlement resembled the spokes of a wheel. Now the automobile was further pushing the boundaries of settlement. And as the city spread like a stain, it lost its human scale and thus its capacity to enrich. Its shopping and jobs were concentrated in a center that was increasingly taxing to reach. Its homes were overcrowded warehouses stripped of privacy, or suburban cottages metastasizing in the green fringe that had just yesterday represented out-of-town escape. With each passing month, the countryside receded as the metropolis oozed outward, spilling suburb into farm field and city into suburb.

What was needed, MacKaye and his friends believed, was an altogether new model of urban living — a regional city. The excess population of the bloated metropolis should be skimmed off and relocated to satellite cities, which would be surrounded by greenbelts of parks, farms, and forests. These smaller cities would host the jobs held by their residents, thus eliminating much of the central city's rush-hour madness. And each satellite would have unique amenities necessary to the well-being of the whole region — one might be home to the opera house; another, the ballpark; a third, the best shopping — thus decentralizing metropolitan culture, as well as population.

Theirs wasn't a vision of today's suburbia. The greenbelts would be inviolate, giving definite edges to the central city and its satellites, limiting their population and physical growth; aimless, amebic sprawl was precisely what the regional city sought to avoid. And ironically, members of the RPAA believed the auto could help usher in this less frenzied, less congested life; properly harnessed, the car could help decentralize overstuffed cities, could foster the wise and efficient use of the surrounding country, could help relocate workers and industries to new settlements "where," as one member put it, "the human opportunities for living are best."

In 1924, MacKaye and company attempted to turn their talk into bricks and mortar. They couldn't scare up enough cash to build a full-scale regional city, so they opted for a more modest experiment on a weedy chunk of industrial wasteland in Queens: Sunnyside Gardens, a mix of co-op apartments, small houses, duplexes, and triplexes that incorporated the association's theories. Its two-story brick buildings were clustered around playgrounds, greens, and courtyards sequestered from the city's bustle and noise. The target buyers were working people, members of the lower middle class. A small, one-family house went for $883 down and $66.78 a month — "easy for people with average incomes," as the corporation's advertising promised.

With the success of Sunnyside Gardens, the group got more ambitious. It bought a two-mile-square piece of Bergen County, New Jersey, and set to work building Radburn, the first-ever "town for the motor age" — a regional neighborhood more than a city proper, but incorporating a slew of novel controls on the automobile and its everyday impact. Radburn was built in residential superblocks, at the center of which were open parks. No roads penetrated these superblocks; cars were kept at their periphery on curving streets that branched into short cul-de-sacs, each of which serviced the attached garages of a few homes. The living and sleeping areas of each house faced garden, rather than concrete; both cars and streets were invisible during most of one's day. At those points where a sidewalk crossed a road dividing one superblock from another, it did so via a bridge or underpass. As the *American City* observed, "Children going to and from school will simply leave their homes by the garden door, pass through to the pedestrian path and thus into the park to school without the necessity of crossing a single traffic street."

So segregated was foot and motor traffic that standing on the greens, one felt transported to an old country village, an effect heightened by the colonial revival shutters and gable roofs assigned to Radburn's houses, townhomes, duplexes, and apartments. In April 1929 the first were ready for occupancy, and plans were afoot to grow the place into a community of twenty-five thousand. The stock market crash intervened; just two superblocks, room for about a thousand people, were completed.

Regardless, Radburn had a dramatic effect on the pattern of American life. It popularized such suburban staples as the cul-de-sac and subdivisions of sinuous back streets. And it got Benton MacKaye wondering whether the village's charms could be turned upside-down. If it was possible to build a roadless town, MacKaye thought, why not the reverse?

MacKaye's *New Republic* piece, "The Townless Highway," opened by identifying the crux of the problem facing the country's highway planners: "Even our most modern roads, modern in the sense that they have solid foundations and concrete surfaces and banks at the sharp turns, are conceived as mere extensions and widenings of the old-fashioned highway designed for horse-drawn vehicles."

Naturally, they were deficient — how could they be otherwise? Not only were they built on old buggy trails, their flanks were crowded with food stands and souvenir shops and billboards, each an eyesore, and with parking lots and driveways, each a potential hazard. MacKaye called such roadside development the "motor slum" and damned it as "as massive a piece of defilement as the worst of the old-fashioned urban industrial slums."

A break from America's equine past, MacKaye wrote, required "a highway completely free of horses, carriages, pedestrians, town, grade crossings; a highway built for the motorist and kept free from every encroachment, except the filling stations and restaurants necessary for his convenience."

"We must provide for properly guarded approaches to, and crossings of, the main motor highways at proper intervals," he wrote, and "must take possession of the surrounding right-of-way, keeping it free from haphazard commercial development and obtaining for the benefit of the motorist the pleasant views and aspects of the country, unsullied by the rowdy clamor of billboard advertising."

What MacKaye was advocating, of course, was a grade-separated, limited-access highway with occasional rest stops, a conceptual quantum leap beyond the so-called superhighways envisioned by most of his contemporaries. It's ironic that the man who proposed the Appalachian Trail was also among the conceptual fathers of the modern expressway, but there it is.

The article found a receptive audience, because millions of urban Americans could no longer reach the untrammeled outdoors on a day trip; not only was the city's blot spreading ever larger on the land, but the highways themselves had bred a glut of development. When journalist Walter Prichard Eaton drove into the countryside on the road once galloped by Paul Revere, he found it "a swiftly moving steel and rubber river between banks of 'hot-dog' kennels, fried-clam stands, filling stations, and other odoriferous and ugly reminders of this progressive age." The roadside clutter was "like having a cinder in your eye," as interior secretary Ray Lyman Wilbur said. Billboards, especially, were a pox; regulated only in Nevada, they'd multiplied elsewhere to blot out a traveler's view from the road, compromise national landmarks, become a community's disgrace. "They are not needed by the public," MacDonald understated, "and are of doubtful value to advertisers."

MacKaye's despair over the motor slum mirrored that of Raymond Unwin, a British planner and critic of "ribbon development" who concluded that "frontage development can no longer be regarded as compatible with . . . traffic highways." It also coincided with a short February 1930 article in the *American City* by New York lawyer Edward M. Bassett, who observed that an improved highway stayed that way only a short while: "Even if important grade crossings are eliminated, the driveways, gasoline stations, garages, stores and parked cars cause a great limitation."

America, Bassett wrote, needed "a new kind of thoroughfare — one which will be like a highway for both pleasure and business vehicles, but which will be like a parkway in preventing the cluttering-up of its edges." No name existed for such a highway, he added, as no such highway existed. With that, Bassett proposed a name: "freeway." He judged it "short and good Anglo-Saxon" that connoted "freedom from grade intersections and from private entrance ways, stores and factories."

"The Townless Highway" dovetailed with the work of two prominent traffic engineers who share the parentage of the modern expressway. While MacKaye labored on his article, an Austrian expatriate named Fritz Malcher was conceiving his "Steadyflow System," in which major city streets would take the form of divided boulevards, their broad medians crossed here and there by looping turnaround lanes. These boulevards would meet at traffic circles — actually, they were more like diamonds — and the theory was that once in motion, a driver need not come to a stop until he reached his destination. He could reach any address via diamond, boulevard, or turnaround without encountering a traditional intersection.

Pedestrians would be kept out of the way on grade-separated sidewalks, and houses were clustered around Radburn-style superblocks. "Imagine a city," Malcher wrote, "where the street system permits vehicles to move without obstructions, traffic lights or officers, with automatic regulation of speed and capacity; where pedestrians can walk continuously through the whole city area — no matter whether this be in the outskirts or in the center — without any fear and danger of vehicular traffic . . . Such a city ideal we can make come true."

Malcher set out to fuse his urban Steadyflow to cross-country expressways, so that traffic had a means of leaving his free-flowing city to go elsewhere, and he spent great energy devising high-speed interchanges between the two, most of which were variations on the cloverleaf debuted at Woodbridge, and still look modern today.

Another visionary was Harvard-educated Miller McClintock, reputedly the first person ever awarded a doctorate in traffic. As head of an auto industry–backed research lab at his alma mater in the midtwenties, McClintock had counseled several cities on how to cure their congestion headaches, among them Los Angeles, where he'd helped outlaw jaywalking, and Chicago, where, while studying accidents and rush-hour snarls, he'd hit on his "friction theory."

McClintock had come to see roads as rivers or veins, and traffic as the fluid coursing within them — racing smoothly in some places, slowing to a viscous dribble in others, dammed by obstacles or churning through rapids elsewhere still — its flow determined by the degree to which it was subjected to four "frictions." One or more of these frictions also happened to be the cause of every traffic accident he investigated.

Street crossings produced intersectional friction, which caused the worst traffic backups and nearly one in five accidents, including the often-deadly T-bone. Medial friction involved opposing flows—a head-on smash-up was one example—and accounted for 17 percent of accidents. Internal-stream friction erupted between cars traveling in the same direction and caused sideswipes, rear-enders, lane-change mishaps; it was the most common source of accidents, at 44 percent. And marginal friction, the cause of one in five smash-ups, happened on or beyond the road's edge, where lurked such potential hazards as boulders and buildings, guardrails, gulleys and bridge abutments, signposts and unlucky pedestrians.

Eliminating the frictions called for a wholesale redesign of the American road, so that it might better control the speeds it invited. McClintock called his answer a "limited way," with four attributes that would prevent every accident he'd encountered. A dividing island or median strip at least ten feet across would erase medial friction. Grade separations at all crossroads would end intersectional. Closing off access to the road except at occasional ramps, and offering a straight, broad alignment, would knock off marginal; and providing acceleration and braking lanes at those access points would do much to counter internal-stream.

Other thinkers offered variations on these ideas—each month's science and mechanics magazines seemed to offer something new. Right behind McClintock, in August 1931, a New York planner named Robert Whitten suggested in the *American City* that a highway need not be townless to work properly; in fact, a limited-access expressway could run right through a city, and do it with less noise and danger to its residential neighbors than the typical arterial surface street. For that to happen, it had to be "so designed and planted," Whitten wrote, "that much of the noise incident to heavy traffic will be dissipated or absorbed before reaching the abutting residential frontages." His recommended tool for minimizing a highway's negative effects: depress the roadway in a broad ditch or put it on an embankment, well above street level. Either would "prove helpful in promoting traffic efficiency, noise reduction, beauty and amenity."

The same month, MacKaye brought the discussion full circle with a refinement of his earlier article, this one in *Harper's Monthly* and produced with a coauthor — Lewis Mumford, a New York writer, author, social critic, and fellow member of the RPAA's inner circle. It was an infinitely more elegant work than the original, starting with the observations that on America's overcrowded and underbuilt roads, "a spavined horse could often travel as fast as a 120 h.p. car," and "the only point where the automobile is permitted to come within sight of its potential efficiency is in the factory."

"Having achieved thousands of miles of wide, concrete-paved highways, having projected many thousands more on almost exactly the same pattern, we lean back complacently in our chairs and fancy we have solved the problems of motor transportation," the essay read, " — although our jammed city streets, our run-down suburbs, our spoiled villages, our devastated tracts of countryside, our country homes that are as quiet and peaceful as boilerworks are all large and ironic commentaries upon our pretensions."

The pair made a more explicit pitch for two principles of the townless highway: that it always remain outside of large communities and connect to them via spur highways; and that it "be provided with enough land on both sides of the road to insulate it from the surrounding area."

And they included a melancholy passage that underlined why highways and people made uncomfortable neighbors. "In the days of the horse and buggy the high-road served as company," it read. "As the cart or carriage joggled by, the farmer in the field or the housewife on her porch could hail it; the horse would stop almost of his own accord, and a chat would follow.

"But once the country road becomes a main highway, filled with fast traffic a good part of the day and even of the night, when the cars themselves are driven mostly by strangers, not neighbors, the whole situation is changed: the road ceases to be a symbol of sociability; it becomes very largely a curse."

Thomas MacDonald was beginning to sharpen his own thoughts on the roads of the future. He did it in his usual methodical fashion, for the Chief was not an impetuous man. Meetings in his office often fell silent for long minutes while he weighed a decision, sitting wordless at the conference table, eyes closed, head lowered, pinching the bridge of his nose, deep in thought as his people watched and waited, none daring to intrude. MacDonald believed that small decisions made well would, over time, build unassailable policy, sure direction. And he believed that the essential elements of any good decision were facts.

The Bureau of Public Roads had been enthusiastic about research from its earliest days. It opened its own testing lab in 1900. A few years later, it set up an experiment station in Arlington, Virginia, where it experimented with various road surfaces and where, after World War I, its tests demonstrated that worn, solid-rubber truck tires were devastating to just about any road, thereby helping to spur the development of heavy-duty pneumatic tires. The bureau had participated in road tests at Bates, Illinois, that proved concrete pavement should be thickest at a road's outside edges, reversing the standard practice of many states and contractors. MacDonald had been among the founders of the Highway Research Board, which would become the country's foremost clearinghouse for transportation study. His old professor, Anson Marston, was the board's first chairman, and MacDonald, a member of its executive committee.

In the wake of his victory over the Townsend bill, MacDonald had hinted at a new subject of research: "to study the existing highway traffic and probable changes and developments with a view to adjusting the location, type and width of the roads." Surveying the "points of origin and destination of pleasure traffic," he'd written, would make it "possible to define with sufficient accuracy the natural lines of traffic, and prescribe the type and width" of the roads it justified.

The first such studies had come in the mid-twenties, in the form of driver surveys and traffic counts. In New England, California, and a handful of other places, investigators had stopped motorists at roadblocks to inquire as to the origin and destination of their trips; others, counting by hand or with machines, had monitored roads to determine favored routes. Those early surveys had revealed a few basic truths about American drivers: that given a choice, they followed the better road; that they crowded an area's roads in proportion to the area's total population; and most significant, that they traveled in greatest numbers between and adjacent to big cities.

The Chief entrusted this fact gathering to a personality even more hungry for information than he: Herbert Sinclair Fairbank, a lifelong bachelor who commuted to the bureau's offices from Baltimore. Thin, bespectacled, and scholarly, Fairbank was both a man of letters and an accomplished engineer — a voracious student of the classics and of history, a graceful writer, and a champion of research as the primary foundation of road building.

A Cornell man, class of 1910, Fairbank had spent a short while with the federal Bureau of Mines before coming to work for Logan Waller Page as a student engineer aboard Good Roads Trains — a whistle-stop publicity venture popular early in the century, in which trains would roam the country for weeks at a time, stopping at cities and towns to deliver the gospel of road improvement and how it might be accomplished with whatever materials happened to be at hand. In time, Fairbank had been recognized for his strong gifts as a writer. He was put in charge of *Public Roads,* the bureau's magazine, a role that required not only skill as an editor but an ability to vet technical papers submitted for publication. By the late twenties he'd become the Chief's intellectual right hand and exerted a growing but anonymous influence on bureau policy. Together, they'd elevated the bureau's spirit of inquiry to an institutional obsession.

Now, while MacKaye and Mumford, McClintock and Malcher offered up their visions of the ideal highway, the Depression was pushing the bureau into research that would yield an ever-clearer picture of how, and where, to build what we now know as modern expressways. The economic crisis reordered the nation's road-building priorities. The goal was no longer perfecting a system of national highways, but putting men to work. The rate at which the money gushed out of Washington was unprecedented. In 1931, more than 1.1 million people had jobs on Federal Aid and emergency road projects, and federal dollars poured into not only primary roads, but city streets and farming lanes.

MacDonald was exasperated by the unfocused nature of the make-work approach. Money was squandered on minor roads that served few users; meanwhile, many of the important roads built since 1921 were going to hell from lack of maintenance, and a tremendous number were already obsolete. Pavements were narrow — in many states, the standard width of two-lane primary roads was just eighteen feet, and some weren't even that. The cars using these skinny lanes were bigger than their predecessors, and a lot more powerful; the new ones could hit eighty-five miles per hour and needed roomier lanes, wider curves. Their drivers had to have unobstructed views of what lay ahead, to give them time to react to trouble.

What was needed, in a system that already measured three million miles, was not work for its own sake, but a better sense of priorities — a firmer grip on where money should be spent first, on where motorists went and how and why they chose their routes. The bureau needed such insight, to be sure, but so did Congress, the states, and the president. So the Chief and Fairbank conceived of a study that would identify the most important of the most important roads, and thus which should be improved, to what degree, and in what order. They got the go-ahead in 1934, with the passage of that year's Federal Aid highway bill. Sponsored by Sen. Carl Hayden of Arizona and Rep. Wilburn Cartwright of Oklahoma, it contained a provision that set aside up to 1.5 percent of each state's Federal Aid apportionment for highway planning and research.

The earmark was used to finance a years-long campaign of highway surveys that MacDonald would describe as "the most comprehensive research study ever undertaken," and which produced insights "of such fundamental character and rich content" that they propelled highway planning "from guess work and opinion to full professional stature." They were the scholarship behind Washington's highway thinking for decades, not least the interstate highway system.

The surveys involved 240 bureau employees and about 5,000 hired hands from forty-six states. They mapped and conducted a detailed inventory of every mile of road in the country, pinpointing tight curves, drop-away shoulders, deep ditches, exposed culverts, narrow bridges — the hazards that became more dangerous with each new year's speedier cars. Seeking road designs that would keep up with the models and traffic to come, they launched "vehicle-performance studies" that yielded a catalog of typical driver responses to a wide range of road conditions — the way motorists adjusted their speed to account for lanes of a particular width, for instance, or for curves and grades of varying severity; how they hugged the center stripe when a ditch or bridge abutment lay hard against the shoulder.

Companion studies tested how well trucks and buses climbed hills pulling different loads; the data would prove useful in identifying too-steep grades, as well as stretches of highway demanding additional lanes for slow-moving heavy haulers. To measure traffic and its characteristics, the bureau used an assortment of counting machines, some of them permanent, others portable, several of which its engineers invented. One, installed nearly five hundred times over, used photo-electric cells and light beams; others used electric strips or pneumatic tubes laid across the road.

The level of detail these machines produced bordered on the microscopic. In studying the physics of passing on a two-lane road, the tests measured the speeds of the passing and passed vehicles before, during, and after the pass; the specific points at which any changes in speed occurred; the distance the passing vehicle traveled in the oncoming lane; the time and distance it straddled the center line; and the actions of both vehicles in response to traffic approaching from the other direction.

What did the bureau glean from this? For one thing, how much room it took to pass safely at various speeds and in a range of circumstances, and how far ahead a would-be passer needed to see before he swung into the opposing lane. Beyond that, though, it learned that if passing were difficult on a particular stretch of blacktop, traffic would stack up behind slower-moving vehicles and the capacity of the road would be reduced. With changes to its geometry, the road's flow might be eased, its capacity boosted, its useful life extended.

The surveys also fulfilled their first mission. They instructed the bureau and the states as to where the public's money was most intelligently spent. In a word, the answer was: cities. The data showed, in Fairbank's words, "traffic that moves in great volume into and out of cities, but dwindles to much smaller proportions as cities are left behind."

In fact, the surveys showed that there was precious little demand for the open roads that politicians and automakers had pushed for since the Lincoln Highway's debut. Americans seldom drove long distances; journeys of 29.9 miles and less accounted for 88 percent of all trips. Those of more than 500 miles, on the other hand, made up less than one-tenth of 1 percent of the total.

The bureau's philosophy began to shift to meet the new data. Far from being townless, the new thinking held, highways should mostly serve towns. The Chief would come to advocate "free-flowing highways" in the cities, and even extending them "well into the country," and to allow that in a few corners of the forty-eight states, it made sense to further extend them "until they connect with those radiating from other large centers of population to form continuous routes wholly disconnected from our present system of highways."

But such places were the exception, MacDonald believed. Ironically, the man who would be most responsible for building America's modern highway network reckoned that a uniform grid of expressways crisscrossing the nation would be a huge waste of money.

8

IT WAS WHILE his bureau was immersed in the surveys that MacDonald lost his wife. Bess fell ill with ovarian cancer, and on August 6, 1935, after two years in decline, she suffered a pulmonary embolism. Always one for long days at the office, the widowed MacDonald now passed the bulk of his waking hours there.

He became more a loner than ever, an unsmiling enigma to most of his coworkers. Few could claim to know him, and even fewer dared to describe him as a friend. MacDonald's circle of adult confidants had just three members. Besides Fairbank, there was Charles D. "Cap" Curtiss, well educated and six years younger than the Chief, who had worked for MacDonald in Iowa before joining the army, making captain, and acquiring a nickname for life. Curtiss was among the few visitors to the MacDonalds' Chevy Chase home on weekends, who could speak firsthand of the Chief's prowess at his backyard grill, and who accompanied the family on Sunday drives into the country. Even so, MacDonald never strayed from addressing him as "Mr. Curtiss" or "Captain Curtiss."

And there was Caroline L. Fuller, MacDonald's secretary, good-natured, tireless, and smart. Born and raised in Traverse City, Michigan, Fuller had joined the bureau as a "stenographer and typewriter" in 1916. Now she was not only gatekeeper to the Chief, but his spokesperson and surrogate; everyone recognized that a gentle suggestion from "Miss Fuller" was tantamount to an order from MacDonald himself, and that she had the boss's ear. She was also the only bureau employee who was permitted to step onto an elevator with the Chief. The whole building, even Herbert Fairbank, knew to take that protocol seriously.

If MacDonald found solace anywhere in the wake of Bess's death, it seemed to be on the road. He wandered for weeks at a time in the Far West, in the Sand Hills of Nebraska, in South America. And most memorably, he twice ventured to Europe, as part of a procession of American engineers drawn to Adolf Hitler's state-of-the-art *Reichsautobahnen*.

In 1936, the Chief proclaimed the finished segments "wonderful examples of the best modern road building," and a stretch headed east from Berlin "one of the most delightful drives of the world." Two years later, he had time for a closer study and again was impressed. Even by today's standards, the autobahn was a modern system. Its traffic sped along on parallel, one-way roadbeds, each two lanes wide and separated from its twin by a landscaped median sixteen feet across; it was banked and graded to enable high speeds — no official limit existed, in fact — and passed over or beneath intersecting roads, linking to some of them by ramps and cloverleafs. Road surfaces were smooth concrete. Styling was understated and modernist. The scale of bridges and viaducts was monumental.

The Chief admired the "plain design of pleasing lines" that he encountered on a drive to Hanover, and the "parking for overnight accommodation of truck drivers," and most of all the Third Reich's conscious efforts to transform highway travel into a celebration of nature and beauty. "This is the industrial area of the Ruhr river — the whole is highly industrialized — coal mining — steel," he wrote in his diary. "But the autobahn has been so well placed it runs thru miles of woods. One might very easily believe he was in a wooded agricultural district, were it not for the glimpse of smoke stacks, and other evidences of a busy, industrial life — at intervals from the road."

At some points, the roads were "carried to high grounds to give sweeping views about the whole horizon of lovely nearby and distant fields, forests, villages of purely agricultural character — streams," he wrote in his entry for July 6, 1938, when he also had dinner with the system's chief inspector, Fritz Todt. "This policy necessitates high, long viaducts even of the crossing of rather small stream valleys . . . there can be no question that the Germans are setting the highest mark in bold conception of their highway planning and design of very large scale."

But the Chief saw little about the German system that seemed applicable to American needs. Descended from highways started in the twenties, the autobahns had been appropriated by Hitler on his rise to power, and there was no mistaking that these were military roads. As *Time* pointed out in February 1939, you could drive up a ramp "at Cologne, near the Belgian border, zip past Berlin and wind up at the Polish frontier," or drive without stopping from the capital "to Falkenburg, within 95 miles of the Polish Corridor; to Hamburg, in the northwest corner of the Reich; to Saarbrucken on the French frontier."

Indeed, the roads made beelines for the country's borders, rather than serving centers of population — and by the time MacDonald made his visits, the bureau's surveys had left little doubt that such an arrangement ran counter to America's needs. The German roads were lavishly overbuilt for the volume of traffic they carried, which offended the Chief's economic sensibilities. An overbuilt road was every bit as shameful as a deficient one, in his view; unless it was justified economically, it failed, regardless of its engineering. And there was little about the autobahns that he hadn't seen back home, albeit executed on a smaller scale.*

Still, Hitler's highways made an impact on American road building. They stoked new interest among Washington lawmakers in a home-grown expressway system, and it was during this resurgence, early in February 1938, that the Chief was summoned to the White House to discuss "through national highways" with Franklin Roosevelt. Their

---

* Which made perfect sense, if you believed some American engineers, because the autobahns relied on Yankee ingenuity. Its particulars, they said, were inspired by or borrowed from Robert Moses's New York parkways, the Woodbridge cloverleaf on the Lincoln Highway, and consultations with the bureau and state highway officials. This became a popular view immediately after the war, when there weren't many German engineers around to refute it. It wasn't heard so much in 1938.

meeting included one of the watershed moments in highway history. The president showed the Chief a map of the forty-eight states on which he drew, or had already drawn, a grid of lines in blue pencil. Three crossed the country from coast to coast, and an equal number ran vertically from the Canadian line to the Gulf or the Mexican border.

Roosevelt told MacDonald that he was intrigued by the notion of building a system of transcontinental roads, and that in doodling around with the idea he'd come up with these six routes. It might be possible, the president said, to make such a system pay for itself through the collection of tolls. Or perhaps the federal government could condemn mile-wide rights of way and later sell off the property fronting the new highways at a profit — an idea exciting a lot of discussion at the time, and about which FDR made no attempt to hide his enthusiasm. He asked the Chief to look into the matter and report back.

MacDonald and Fairbank dived into the assignment, the Chief writing the summary, his assistant the briefing's actual text. Together, they made the case that the president's system was buildable, sure enough, but it would not answer the nation's real highway needs. As Fairbank put it while the work was under way, they hoped to "show that there is nothing to the transcontinental idea, that traffic is highly local in range and that congestion is a city product which exists in serious degree only in the vicinity of the larger cities and where cities are close together."

A few weeks after they delivered the paper, the Chief received orders from Congress for almost the same thing. He had until the following February to weigh the feasibility and cost of six transcontinental highways, three in each direction, and the prospects of paying for them with tolls.

But this second report, which he and Fairbank prepared with a supporting cast of dozens, was far more comprehensive, and far more important. It didn't simply answer Congress's questions; it offered the lawmakers, without having been asked, an alternative to the simple transcontinental grid, a far more ambitious system of what it termed "interregional" highways.

Titled *Toll Roads and Free Roads,* the document was divided into two parts; the first, on the feasibility of transcontinental toll roads, ran eighty-six pages, or about two-thirds of the total. It concluded "that a direct toll system on these six superhighways, in their entirety, would not be feasible as a means of recovering the entire cost of the facilities." It didn't take long to reach this judgment: it came toward the bottom of page 2.

Again, the bureau found that the six superhighways, wending for 14,336 miles and built to top standards, were "entirely feasible from a physical standpoint" and could be had for about $2.9 billion. Throw in financing, maintenance, and the costs of operating tollbooths and such, and the bill came to just over $184 million each year through 1960. But by the most optimistic reckoning, the grid would earn annual tolls of just $72.14 million, less than 40 percent of its cost.

The bureau had made a sincere effort to design the best six transcontinental toll roads. It connected major cities and used the most popular and potentially lucrative routes. Three in four miles would be only two lanes wide — not superhighways so much as faster and safer versions of what already existed, with lanes twelve feet across, wide shoulders, easy grades, broad and banked curves, no crossings of road or rail at grade. Even so, they'd lose buckets of money. The 515-mile stretch from Salt Lake City to Reno — the Wendover Road — would earn only 12.3 cents for every dollar it cost, and the long, lonely two-laner from Fargo, North Dakota, to Spokane, Washington, would earn just 9; worst of all was the road from Atlanta to Augusta, Georgia, at 7.5 cents.

Pieces of road that seemed sure-fire moneymakers were not. Indianapolis to Columbus stood to recover just 40 percent of the government's investment, and Cleveland to Buffalo, 38. St. Louis to Springfield, Missouri, a seemingly busy leg of Route 66, would make back only a third of its cost. Even the sixty-six-mile highway segment from Jersey City, New Jersey, to New Haven, Connecticut, the busiest in the U.S. system, would fail to break even. By 1960, the report said, a smattering of mileage might operate in the black, but it would be a crapshoot. If Congress insisted on experimenting with tolls, it faced the best odds of success with a highway from Washington to Boston. Nowhere else.

Then again, the numbers "definitely and conclusively" showed that no demand existed for the six toll roads, anyway. Coast-to-coast traffic amounted to only three hundred passenger cars a day; only about eight hundred traveled to the West Coast from any point east of the Mississippi. That trickle did not justify a huge public outlay.

Indeed, the data testified that not only were the vast majority of auto trips of less than twenty miles, as the bureau's surveys had shown for years, but most were less than five. Thus, only a small percentage of trips could be made on any toll road, which by definition had to limit the points at which one could enter and exit; access would be too widely spaced to suit them. So even on the legs that showed the greatest promise of breaking even, the transcontinental toll roads wouldn't suit their markets. Finally, there was some question as to how many drivers could afford to pay tolls, even if it were convenient; more than half of all cars were owned by families with annual incomes of $1,500 or less.

Toll Roads and Free Roads could have ended there, its case made. But instead came an acknowledgment that "the report should be constructive rather than negative in character" and would therefore offer an alternative to the six tollways: "the general outline of what is in effect a master highway plan for the entire Nation."

That plan comprised the fifty-five pages of Part II, which was all Fairbank. The language, like the man, was spare but elegant, clear-headed, unflinching. As he had for twenty years, Fairbank commuted to the office from Baltimore, but when burdened with a big writing task such as this he tended to tackle it at home; he wrote in longhand on unlined yellow paper, leaving blanks for the statistics that he knew would make his points; his staff, crunching numbers with hand-cranked calculators, would later fill in the blanks.

In such a manner did the bureau propose a 26,700-mile network of free highways that, in terms of its routing, bore a striking resemblance to today's interstate system — actually *was* the modern system, minus a few legs here and there. Its mileage nearly twice that of FDR's six transcontinental highways, the master plan was "believed to include substantially every major line of interregional travel in the country." It linked "the populous cities of the United States, almost without exception," and it followed "practically every one of the lines along which the population" had traveled to those places.

Most of its legs would not take the form of superhighways. The report hewed to the Chief's belief that roads answer the demand for their use, no more and no less; all that was needed in the open country was a lane in each direction, uncluttered by roadside development — a working version of MacKaye and Mumford's townless highway. Even such improvement, Fairbank believed, would revolutionize automobile travel. "Although in mileage they would represent as a system less than 1 percent of the total rural highway mileage of the country," he famously predicted, "they would unquestionably accommodate at least 12.5 percent of the total rural vehicle-mileage," and they would "effect a greater reduction in the highway accident rate than could be made by an equivalent sum spent for highways in any other way."

The truly revolutionary aspect of *Toll Roads and Free Roads,* however, was that it emphasized the need for urban freeways, something that Federal Aid legislation, with its fixation on rural improvement, had always taken pains to avoid. The report wasted no time in dismantling any lingering notion that bypasses could ease urban congestion. Not only did they become as cluttered and congested as the cities they were meant to avoid, they attempted to remedy a problem that didn't exist. Congestion wasn't caused by through traffic mixing with local; the bureau's surveys had shown that it was "caused by a multiplicity of short movements into and out of the city" — movements by locals, not out-of-towners.

By way of example, the bureau's data showed that of the 20,500 vehicles entering Washington, D.C., on any given day, no more than 2,269, or 11 percent, were "bypassable." There and in other cities, the remaining bulk of the traffic "will not only continue into, but in large part will penetrate to the very heart of the city," the report read, "because that is where most of it is destined." And on the way to the center, motorists too often found their broad path wither to streets unenlarged from their days as pikes for horse-drawn carts, and their progress confounded by cross traffic and rail lines, by curb parking and rubber-neckers on the hunt for places to park.

The answer wasn't to bend a freeway around a town's edges, but to drill it right through the middle. In bigger cities, "only a major operation will suffice," the report concluded, "— nothing less than the creation of a depressed or an elevated artery (the former usually to be preferred) that will convey the massed movement pressing into, and through, the heart of the city, under or over the local cross streets without interruption by their conflicting traffic."

This surely would be disruptive, but not necessarily in a bad way; used judiciously, freeways could help reverse the decay gripping the cores of many U.S. cities. Fairbank observed that in his hometown of Baltimore, residents with the means to do so were fleeing to the suburbs, leaving behind neighborhoods nosing into economic tailspins and, over time, stripped of hope, health, and peace; a similar exodus was gutting downtown of its business, and only a "radical revision of the city plan" would stem it. "Such a revision will have to provide the greater space now needed for the unfettered circulation of traffic," he wrote. And what better space than the depressed slums, which could be cut out like a tumor and replaced with life-infusing highways?

Time was of the essence, he pointed out, because "here and there, in the midst of the decaying slum areas, substantial new properties of various sorts are beginning to rise — some created by private initiative, some by public." These new investments could "block the logical projection of the needed new arteries." In short, it would be easier and cheaper to take advantage of the blight before the blight was cleaned up.

To read these passages today, tucked into the dense text of a little-known 1939 report, is to feel a twinge of foreboding, for the urban-renewal formula laid out in *Toll Roads and Free Roads* was exactly that adopted by cities across the nation a few years later — and because, for all of its clarity and comprehensiveness, the document overlooked an important element of the slum areas it targeted: degraded though they might be, they were home to millions of people.

• • •

Among those praising *Toll Roads and Free Roads* was Miller Mc-Clintock, the originator of the friction theory, who'd long corresponded with MacDonald; he called the report "an excellent example of economic common sense and practical administrative statesmanship." What he didn't say, but both he and the Chief knew, was that he was involved in a project that was whipping the American public into a frenzy of excitement over long-distance, high-speed expressways to a degree that no government report, no matter how groundbreaking, could approach. McClintock was the technical adviser to "Futurama," the centerpiece of General Motors' "Highways and Horizons" exhibit at the 1939 New York World's Fair and far and away the event's top draw.

The man receiving McClintock's advice was a brash, supremely un-self-conscious showman, actor, author, artist, stage designer, marketer, and visionary named Norman Bel Geddes, a native of Michigan who after a successful career in the theater had refashioned himself an industrial designer, and who in more recent years had decided to become an expert on cities of the future. Bel Geddes had sold GM's brass on an exhibit built around a simulated flight over the America of 1960, with particular emphasis on its highways, and though he busted his budget more than three times over, succeeded so convincingly that fair goers sometimes waited hours in line for the fifteen-minute experience.

He performed his magic with the biggest scale model ever built, a diorama of farm, forest, suburb, and city that covered nearly an acre and featured about half a million individually designed and crafted houses, a downtown bristling with skyscrapers ten feet tall, more than a million tiny trees representing eighteen species, and about fifty thousand streamlined cars and trucks, of which ten thousand moved on roads, bridges, and highways. Just as impressive was the vantage from which you took this in: a moving conveyor system of six hundred upholstered wing chairs, each fitted with speakers at shoulder height. The conveyor snaked high and low over the model as a male voice, at a volume barely above a whisper, commented on the sights below. In terms of a modern approximation, think Disney's Haunted Mansion.

From outside, the seven-acre pavilion loomed as a modern bunker, its slab sides painted a silvery gray. Sinuous ramps guided you inside, to a giant arcing map of the United States, 110 feet by 60, on which highways and congestion and the solution — a new network of motorways — appeared as lights. You were then directed into one of the conveyor's chairs and glided through darkness as the voice welcomed: "Come tour the future with General Motors! A transcontinental flight over America in 1960. What will we see? What changes will transpire?"

Then the conveyor swung into the light, and spread below to the seeming horizon was a vista of farms and small towns and flowing streams, complete with cattle in the pastures, apple trees heavy with fruit, and, most important, vehicles. Man "has forged ahead since 1939," the narrator intoned. "New and better things have sprung from his industry and genius. Since the beginning of civilization, transportation has been the key to Man's progress — his prosperity — his happiness." With that, your attention was fastened on a mammoth expressway, churning with traffic, that sliced across meadowlands and valleys and a mountain range toward a city you could see drawing near. There, expressways split to merge with others, ran side by side and in stacks, rolled past and through pristine high-rises. You flew over a circular airport, served by its own braid of expressways. Despite the fact that this future city was based vaguely on St. Louis, there wasn't a slum in sight. "With the fast, safely designed highways of 1960, the slogan 'See America First' has taken on new meaning and importance," the narrator said. "The thrilling scenic feasts of a great and beautiful country may now be explored, even on limited vacation schedules."

As the ride drew to a close, your attention was directed to an intersection in an urban shopping district as the voice declared: "All eyes to the future." Bel Geddes described what happened next: "Suddenly the spectator, in his chair, is swung about! He can scarcely believe his eyes. He is confronted with the full-sized street intersection he was just looking down on."

Yes, before your eyes was an exact duplicate of the model, with GM's 1939 models posing as street traffic and additional exhibits waiting behind the storefronts — a running engine fitted with quartz windows, and a Plexiglas car, and a Frigidaire paean to food preservation.

"General Motors bids you welcome to this Magic City of progress!" the voice cried. "The attendant will assist you from your traveling chair."

Most visitors found the fair a pretty amazing experience. They could step into a full-scale copy of a Moscow subway station in the Soviet Pavilion, come eyeball to eyeball with the spirochete that causes syphilis in the Hall of Medical Science, get a chest x-ray and a hearing test. Japan's building boasted a Liberty Bell made of cultured pearls, and elsewhere waited the world's largest typewriter, a pair of exceedingly tall Romanian sisters, and Jang, a Malay boy with a six-inch tail. The Loose-Wiles Biscuit Co. exhibited "a galaxy of midget stars dressed in immaculate white."

Fair goers could take in another Norman Bel Geddes exhibit — a mirror show where, the program promised, "a single dancing girl appears to be a whole chorus of World's Fairettes." And there was GM's chief competition: the Ford Motor Co.'s exhibit, starring "The Road of Tomorrow," a spiraling concrete ramp three stories high that, to look at it now, evokes a parking garage; and the Perisphere, a concrete globe two hundred feet in diameter that contained "Democracity," a model of city and satellite towns "pulsing with life and rhythm and music." The display was pretty close to the RPAA's regional city ideal, but viewing it from a pair of slowly rotating balconies didn't compare with the Futurama's on-the-wing thrill.

Then again, the GM extravaganza had been gestating for far longer. It could trace its roots to 1932, when Bel Geddes had published a picture book of his design ideas — an underwater restaurant, and a floating, circular airport for New York harbor, and a theater for staging *The Divine Comedy* (and only *The Divine Comedy*) for an audience of five thousand. *Horizons* had also shown off his sketches of finned and teardrop-shaped cars and buses, along with a future city whose population lived in cookie-cutter skyscrapers ringed by open parks and athletic fields.

Skyscraper housing was a favorite notion of European modernists, most famously the Swiss-born designer and planner Le Corbusier, and Bel Geddes became one of its fervent American proponents. In 1936, he'd been commissioned by a New York advertising agency to produce sketches of possible solutions to traffic congestion for use in a Shell Oil ad campaign. Bel Geddes had hustled to gather data on city planning, auto registrations, and highway design. Enter Miller McClintock.

Not long into their collaboration, Bel Geddes had persuaded his clients to junk the sketches and instead finance a model of his future city, complete with skyscrapers and highways; in addition to McClintock's counsel, it's apparent that he found inspiration in the graceful ramps and twisting interchanges of Fritz Malcher's Steadyflow System. When the wondrously detailed models were photographed for the ads, the results had been both artful and realistic, and Bel Geddes had the wisp of an idea.

One of its key elements was his future expressway, which had seven lanes in each direction — four to handle traffic cruising at fifty miles per hour, two for those doing seventy-five, and one for hundred-mile-an-hour, long-distance travel. Grassy strips or concrete walls would separate the sections, and eighteen-inch steel dividers would keep everyone in his own lane. At night, fluorescent strips built into the dividers would light the way.

GM hadn't been sold on Bel Geddes' vision at first; the company planned an assembly-line mockup similar to its exhibit at the 1933 fair in Chicago. Bel Geddes peddled his wares to Goodyear, but the tire maker decided against exhibiting at all. Bel Geddes returned to GM with a last-ditch second pitch, asking the company's bosses whether they could afford to create the impression that they'd had no new ideas in five years. He walked out with a $2 million budget.

This was in May 1938, just eleven months before the fair opened. In that time, Bel Geddes and his people not only built the model but engineered the 1,568-foot conveyor, on which the rubber-wheeled chairs moved at 103 feet per minute and turned at orchestrated points to face highlighted features of the diorama, each chair doing so independently of the other 599. The sound system delivered 150 overlapping copies of the narration, so that the words you heard always corresponded with what you and your three nearest neighbors were seeing.

Bel Geddes and his staff devised myriad little tricks to boost the model's realism. Airplanes in flight cast shadows. Waterfalls were shrouded in spray. Clouds of real water vapor hung over the mountains. Theatrical lighting brought on dusk, drew the eye to specific targets, manipulated mood. And the highlight, the motorway, whizzed with motion.

Not everyone was charmed by Bel Geddes' highways. Among their critics was Lewis Mumford, who in the years since cowriting the second townless highway piece had risen to fame as an author and social critic. Mumford's most recent book, *The Culture of Cities,* on the evolution of human settlement from medieval town to megalopolis, had been hailed by *Newsweek* as "one of the most significant works of creative scholarship to come out of America" and had landed him on the cover of *Time.* Eight years as a columnist for *The New Yorker* had given him a reputation as the country's toughest and most clear-eyed judge of architecture. Mumford found Futurama little but window-dressing on musty ideas, a preposterous glorification of *big,* of *more,* that reminded him of "the tinny world of a Jules Verne romance."

"Mr. Geddes is a great magician, and he makes the carrot in the goldfish bowl look like a real goldfish," he allowed, but "the future, as presented here, is old enough to be somebody's grandfather." Futurama's overbuilt expressway, he wrote, with what now seems prescience, would "prevent a motorist from enjoying anything except the speed of his journey and the prospect of getting to his destination soon."

The Chief wasn't impressed, either, and thought Bel Geddes a crackpot; the last thing the country needed was fourteen-lane bands of concrete crisscrossing the hinterlands. MacDonald was deeply annoyed when the White House hosted an informal stag dinner for the designer in late March 1939, shortly before the fair opened — even though much of the discussion centered on *Toll Roads and Free Roads.*

Perhaps sensitive to such doubts, GM's high command emphasized in public comments that Futurama was not intended as a literal forecast of the roads to come, but, in the words of company president William S. Knudsen, "to give expression to our belief that such development will take place on an important scale and perhaps within a shorter period of time than many people now realize."

Without question, the exhibit made MacDonald's job easier — nothing he did could have so whetted the public's appetite for modern urban highways. And the exhibit's timing couldn't have been much better, coinciding as it did with the release of the bureau's opus. Still, the Chief avoided acknowledging Bel Geddes. When he was called on to speak at a dinner with GM officials in November 1939, he chose a narrow path for his praise: Futurama had been good publicity for the highway industry. "Those of us who are in the highway field, as public officials, have lacked a public relations department to sell that idea to the public on the scale that you are selling it here," he said. "On behalf of the Public Roads [administrators] in the Government, and my associates in the highway field, we express our profound thanks to General Motors for doing this public relations job for us, and for doing it so well."

Within months of MacDonald's faint praise, motorists hungry for Norman Bel Geddes' vision of the future could pretend they were part of it: the nation's first road to merit the label "superhighway" opened in southern Pennsylvania. Here was a homegrown equal to the autobahns, a 160-mile-long path through the Appalachians from Middlesex, just outside Harrisburg, to Irwin, a little east of Pittsburgh, built to standards that made it a model for the interstate system to come.

The Penn Turnpike was conceived as a make-work project, like so many road jobs of the thirties, but it also served a long-term need for a passage through country that had confounded westward migration for two centuries. At the time the best road over the mountains was U.S. 30 — the Lincoln — and it wasn't all that good, being icy and snow-covered in winter, and steep, narrow, and wriggling all the year long as it negotiated the hogbacked ridges that rose, one after another, across the state's middle.

The Lincoln's veterans knew too well the obstacles, could even recite them in order: Cove Mountain, Tuscarora Mountain, Scrub Ridge, Sideling Hill, Ray's Hill, Tull's Hill, Allegheny Mountain, Laurel Hill. The turnpike would flatten the bumps, straighten the hairpin curves, and ease the anxieties that punctuated the journey — so much so, the state wagered, that a lot of motorists would be willing to pay for it; they had better, anyway, because as a toll road, the turnpike was disqualified from Federal Aid.

The state surveyed the line from 1935 to 1937. Not for the first time; its people had eyed the corridor as a train route a full century before, and in the 1840s the Pennsylvania Railroad considered running its track from Harrisburg to Pittsburgh that way. It took another path, however, and the corridor landed in the hands of a smaller railroad that did nothing with it until 1883.

That year, William H. Vanderbilt lost his temper, and in doing so he unwittingly made the turnpike a viable proposition. Vanderbilt possessed a rampaging pair of muttonchop sideburns, the world's fattest wallet — he had a personal fortune of just under $200 million — and the New York Central Railroad, the fiercest rival of which was the Pennsylvania; relics of their long competition survive in their respective depots in New York, Grand Central Terminal and Penn Station. Vanderbilt learned that the Pennsylvania planned a route up the Hudson River, a corridor his line had to itself. He decided that if he was to put up with competition, then cost be damned, so would his rival. He gained control of the idle corridor through the Alleghenies.

Vanderbilt floated $40 million in stocks and bonds, won the backing of financier J. P. Morgan, and in the fall of 1883 let contracts for tunnels and bridges along the route. Three thousand workers flocked to the job. In two years, they carved long cuts through some ridges and blasted nine tunnels through others; they built stone bridge piers across the Susquehanna; they were well along building fifty-four miles of rail bed. Then, with about eight months' work to go, Morgan forced a halt to the project, alarmed that full-on war between the railroads would prove ruinous. Vanderbilt's workers scattered. Weeds consumed the line. The unfinished tunnels filled with water and over time were colonized by white, sightless trout.

Fifty-two years later, the state embarked on a new survey, and in 1937 the General Assembly created the five-member Pennsylvania Turnpike Commission, with authority to construct, operate, maintain, and finance a road along the line. The federal Public Works Administration stroked a check for $29.25 million of the bill; the federal Reconstruction Finance Corporation covered the balance by buying up nearly $41 million in revenue bonds.

There was a catch: the feds required that most of the work be wrapped up by the end of May 1940. Pennsylvania made appropriate haste. Four days after the financing came through in October 1938, the turnpike commission advertised the first ten-mile paving contract. Twelve days later it closed the bidding. It awarded the contract on the same day. The contractor's crews were on-site less than twenty-four hours after that.

Ten thousand men worked around-the-clock shifts to move twenty-six million tons of earth and stone, cutting through hills and filling clefts along the highway's two-hundred-foot right of way. They poured 4.3 million square yards of nine-inch-thick, steel-reinforced concrete, creating parallel pavements of two lanes each bulleting straight over the smoothed terrain. In a fraction of the usual time required, they built 114 bridges, among them the six-hundred-foot New Stanton Viaduct, a graceful and gleaming concrete span that carried the turnpike over two highways, a railway, and a creek. Old-hand Pennsylvania coal miners dug out six of the old railroad tunnels to fourteen feet tall and twenty-three wide, big enough for two lanes of traffic, and shored them up with steel, concrete, and structural glass. They bored a seventh, through Allegheny Mountain, from scratch; like the tunnels through Sideling Hill and Tuscarora Mountain, it was more than a mile long.

Twenty-two months after work started, a convoy of congressmen, reporters, and government bigwigs, including a contingent from the bureau, drove the turnpike from end to end. The party marveled at its easy grades, which never exceeded 3 percent, and its straightaways, which at one point stretched for a dozen miles, and its broad, banked curves. The openness of the landscaped right of way, the long sight distances made possible by a roadway seventy-eight feet wide and cleared of obstructions, was a striking new experience; so were the tunnels, which together were nearly seven miles long. And, of course, the interchanges guiding traffic on and off the highway on looping ramps were the first many in the cars had ever seen.

Other features presaged the standards that would define the interstates, nearly a generation later: broad, paved shoulders; reflectors marking the roadside; acceleration lanes 1,200 feet long at each entrance. No wonder that *Popular Mechanics* proclaimed it "America's first highway on which full performance of today's automobiles can be realized." MacDonald was duly impressed, calling the turnpike "a magnificent accomplishment that will be a monument to the foresight of its builders." He could take some personal pride in the technical assistance the bureau had lent the project's chief engineer on any number of questions.

He was bothered only by the toll, which he believed had no place on this or any public highway. Roads were a birthright akin to free public schooling, for which motorists already paid licensing fees and taxes on gasoline and tires. To slap them with a toll amounted to a double tax — and a big one, too, because a toll of a penny a mile was the equivalent of a gas tax of 12 to 16 cents a gallon.

And tolls saddled engineers with no-win choices. To attract users, a toll road had to offer better service than parallel free roads, which limited the improvements that could ever be made to those free roads, no matter how badly needed they might be; improve the free road too much, and your state turnpike would lose customers and require subsidy. The problem remained if tolls were lifted. Now you could improve the free road, but you'd end up with two parallel highways where one would probably do — and you'd likely find the turnpike wasn't properly placed to function efficiently.

The Chief stuck to that position even after cars and trucks descended on the turnpike like the Mongol hordes, and toll income blew away all forecasts; the road had been built with a massive government handout, he noted, without which it might not be such a runaway success. After all, one of the east-west toll routes studied in *Toll Roads and Free Roads* had used essentially the same footprint, and the highway surveys had left little doubt that the Pittsburgh-to-Carlisle leg couldn't pay for itself. The bureau study had shown it would meet only 34 percent of its expenses from 1945 to 1960; at the end of the period, when traffic would be heavier, it would still be earning only 40 cents.

What was not yet apparent, but would become so, was that super-highways didn't pay much mind to projections and surveys. They were akin to mountain ranges that create their own weather — they created new users, new traffic. Build more, and the process would repeat. As fast as they were laid down, they seemed to fill with cars.

At turnoffs alongside the new turnpike, motorists could stop for gas and to stretch their legs, or to experience another harbinger of the future: a sit-down meal at a restaurant serving fried clam strips, chicken potpies, "Frankforts" in pleated cardboard troughs, and, most famously, twenty-eight flavors of ice cream. Howard Johnson's already had been around for fifteen years, but it was the chain's exclusive contract on the Penn Turnpike that really established it as an icon of the American road.

The company was a prototype for many of the restaurant chains that ply their wares at highway exits today. Howard Johnson's was reputedly the first franchise business and, decades before McDonald's or Burger King came along, built its reputation on offering the customer an unvarying experience. No matter where you were, a Howard Johnson's Frankfort was sure to be grilled and wedged in a toasted roll that resembled a miniature loaf of bread; there'd be a Friday night special on fried seafood; you'd be sheltered by a low-pitch, squint-inducing orange roof topped with a cupola in equally bright turquoise, and surrounded by architecture that married a New England town hall and a ranch house in the Orlando suburbs. And, of course, you could count on finding peppermint stick ice cream — along with butter crunch, burgundy cherry, peanut brittle, and macaroon — of an almost carnal creaminess.

The chain was the brainchild of Howard Deering Johnson, who in 1925 scraped together the cash to take over a small drugstore in a beachfront neighborhood of Quincy, Massachusetts, and enticed customers to its soda fountain by offering the richest ice cream in town, which he hand-churned with gobs of extra butterfat. He expanded the ice cream business to a stand on the seashore, adding flavors along the way, and eventually opened a bona fide restaurant in downtown Quincy. His twenty-eight flavors became a signature. His fried clams became a destination.

Johnson intended to open additional locations, but the Depression intervened, so instead a friend agreed in 1935 to share ownership in a second restaurant on Cape Cod, using the Howard Johnson's name and menu. That was the first roadside HoJo's, and both the business and the franchise arrangement were hits. The following spring, four more opened, and Johnson was honing the visual cues that would instantly identify his restaurants to hungry carloads — the color scheme, the architecture, a distinctive typeface on the oversized neon signs out by the curb, and the silhouette of Simple Simon meeting the Pie Man, replicated on signs, menus, wall hangings, and the rooftop weather-vane.

By year's end there were thirty-nine of them. By the close of 1939, when a gargantuan, thousand-seat HoJo's operated just up the street from the New York World's Fair, the chain was 107 restaurants strong. The following year, when the company opened for business on the turnpike, it had about 125 locations on highway shoulders from Maine to Virginia, plus a couple more in Florida. To ensure that a Frankfort tasted the same in Richmond as it did in Bangor, Johnson supplied all the food himself, shipping it via refrigerated truck.

Other chains sprouted alongside America's roadsides in the thirties to meet the motoring public's growing appetite for speedy service and a predictably pleasant experience. You can still spot one of these on occasion: swooping blue roof; window signs pitching discount cigarettes, burgers, pecans, and souvenirs, the closers to a campaign started by billboard thirty miles back; and overhead, a word that to this day evokes vacations by station wagon, endless afternoons of endless whining on endless four-laners, and sharp smacks from the front seat.

Hundreds of Stuckey's "pecan shoppes" dotted the web of U.S. high-ways below the Mason-Dixon Line, each in the middle of nowhere but en route to somewhere, all promising "sparkling clean restrooms," good food, and huge assortments of candy, nuts, and mementos. Stride through the door and the chain's famed Pecan Log Rolls were smack in front of you, stacked into a fortress of nut and mysterious, calorie-packed nougat, and in sizes suited to a range of appetites: The dainty two-ouncer. The whole-meal four. The mighty twelve, a shaft of crunchy sweetness big enough to qualify as instant party or deadly weapon.

It was in 1934 that Williamson S. Stuckey Sr., out of work and living in Eastman, Georgia, a nut- and fruit-farming burg south of Macon, took up selling pecans in a desperate bid to feed his family. Old Man Stuckey, as he came to be called, didn't know much about nuts, but he knew they were popular with the snowbirds traveling through town to Florida, so he opened a stand on U.S. 341, advertised with signs up and down the highway.

Before long, Stuckey's wife, Ethel, supplemented the nuts with pecan candies she cooked in the family kitchen, among them the Pecan Log Roll, the center of which she fashioned from white molasses, chopped maraschino cherries, and powdered sugar by the cubic yard. Within a couple of years, the family had several stores in Georgia and Florida, each combining an ever-expanding line of sweets with souvenirs, a snack bar, and gas.

Like Johnson, Stuckey recognized the value of the familiar. People stopped there knowing what they'd get. For children, that meant rubber snakes, milk shakes, and miniature license plates. For parents, the draws were food, restrooms, and peace offerings: an approaching store, announced on billboards bearing mileage countdowns, was handy for brokering a truce in the back seat.

Unlike modern convenience stores, which are engineered to sweep customers from entrance through purchase to exit in a smooth, speedy arc, a pecan shoppe was designed to hold them captive. Restrooms were always tucked in the far left corner, the snack bar in the far right, and getting to either required multiple turns past the merchandise. All the items geared to kids were on low shelves.

For many years, Old Man Stuckey further strengthened his stores' grip with live parrots and mynah birds, a tropical touch he reprised with coconut milk and papaya juice at the snack bars. Outposts spread like the flu, and their billboards, many of them hand-painted, with a forceful, folk-art simplicity, became a ubiquitous feature of the southern landscape.

9

F OR TWO YEARS after producing *Toll Roads and Free Roads,* the government's engineers fussed with its details, refining the network's routes and extending them, in myriad small additions, to 29,300 miles. They had plenty of time to fiddle, because the report earned no action from the White House or Congress; war was almost surely coming, and Washington's attention was fixed on girding the country for a fight.

But in April 1941, with Pearl Harbor still eight months off, Franklin Roosevelt was already thinking beyond the struggle against Germany and Japan. He recognized that the feds needed a plan for absorbing millions of fighting men into the economy and retooling the country's high-revving war industries once the shooting stopped — and they needed to start work on the plan soon, rather than wait until victory approached. His interest returned to highways.

That month, the president appointed a committee to revisit the bureau's 1939 recommendations and, if they held up, work out the details of a "limited system of national highways." The new panel was an interdisciplinary bunch, its members the Chief, a former governor, a couple of state highway officials, and three big-name planners. At its first meeting that June, the group elected MacDonald its chairman and appointed Herbert Fairbank its secretary. The pair who'd envisioned America's highway future in *Toll Roads and Free Roads* thus oversaw its refinement into a virtual blueprint of the interstates to come.

The committee first reconsidered the size of what it called "inter-regional" highways. It mulled a bare-bones system, just 14,300 miles long, that resembled what the president had sketched for the Chief in 1938, and a 78,800-mile option that approximated the War Department's Pershing Map of years before. It weighed other varia-tions that split the difference between these two extremes and, using hard data from the highway planning surveys, eventually decided that a 39,000-mile model made the most sense; its average daily traffic was about as high as could be achieved, it passed through counties that were home to 45 percent of the rural population, and it connected all of the country's principal cities — the biggest not actually touched by the roads were Akron, Canton, and Youngstown in eastern Ohio, and they weren't far off the grid. It would span "as much as possible of the productive agriculture area of the Nation," as a committee draft said, and "include the more important routes of the strategic network of principal traffic routes of military importance." Plus, it would "give convenient access to principal recreational areas."

Motorists on the interregional system would be able to punch their speed to seventy-five miles per hour with confidence. Curves wouldn't exceed three degrees and climbs wouldn't top a gentle 3 percent, or a gain of just 158 feet over the course of a mile. Lanes would be wide enough to "relieve the strain of holding the vehicle to a narrow path," as the draft said, "especially when passing large vehicles." The right of way would be 300 feet wide whenever possible, and overpasses (always made of steel or reinforced concrete) would give drivers at least 14 feet of headroom.

This was an amazingly big vision. No highway system in the world had such specifications. And consider when it was born: the coun-try was at war on two fronts and just emerging from a decade-long depression; money was nonexistent. The scheme was so vast, and so expensive, that it must have struck many as an impossible abstraction, nothing more than an academic exercise in wishful thinking. That may well have been a blessing; with the prospect of actual financing, the committee might have aimed for a feasible, best-we-can-do system, rather than the ideal indicated by the data. Hard times, in this odd sense, might have freed it to conjure up the costliest public works project in history.

Like *Toll Roads and Free Roads,* the committee didn't argue for a uniform system of superhighways. It insisted that all of the dream network be limited-access but suggested that twenty-one thousand lightly traveled, rural miles could remain two-lane, undivided roads. What's more, those sections attracting fewer than three thousand vehicles on an average day wouldn't have to pass over or under crossroads; they could meet at grade.

On a panel led by Thomas MacDonald, this was hardly a surprise. He was as staunchly opposed as ever to big freeways in the boonies and would stay that way. He'd call them "an extravagance" in one 1946 interview, adding: "We can't afford them. We don't need them. And we probably won't ever need them." Two-lane rural highways were "much more useful," in MacDonald's view, though that rule of thumb certainly had exceptions. In places where the terrain made passing unsafe on a two-laner, where a driver couldn't see far enough ahead to safely swing into the oncoming lane at high speed, the committee decreed that an interregional highway would widen and split into two lanes each way, separated by a median at least fifteen feet wide. That would be the standard along parts of the system that saw heavier traffic, too — side-by-side, two-lane, one-way roads, built as independent units so that each followed the topography and the width of the median varied. Along these stretches, all cross traffic would be carried over or under the interregional highway and reached via ramps. The same went for stretches that carried more than fifteen thousand vehicles on the average day and thus warranted three lanes each way.

As envisioned in 1943, many of the new highways would be laid smack on top of existing roads; all that was needed was to improve what was already in place. The committee didn't have a beef, in other words, with *where* U.S. 1 or 11 or 60 was; it was *how* those roads were that needed a fix. Granted, in some places it might prove necessary to build a completely new road, separate and distinct from anything already on the ground, but the committee left unaddressed where either option might be used.

So the proposed system's mileage — about 29,450 miles in the open country and 4,470 in towns, plus 5,000 or so miles of metropolitan beltways and loops that would be added later — was ballpark, at best. The exact location of its path, the report read, "will be a problem for local reconnaissance study." That was especially true for the urban mileage. *Interregional Highways* included no maps of routes through cities, and no description of them beyond a catalog of possibilities, because the problems of extending four- and six-lane highways through dense settlement were simply too complicated and too local to generalize — besides which, it was a decision best made by the states and municipal authorities. "How near they should come to the center of the area, how they should pass it or pass through it, and by what courses they should approach it, are matters for particular planning consideration in each city," the committee decided, though it observed that surface streets carrying the heaviest traffic loads generally "pass through or very close to the existing central business areas."

Fairbank again did most, if not all, of the writing, and this time his passages on urban expressways included a cautionary note. However they were located, the new urban highways would do more than simply carry traffic; they would be "a powerful influence in shaping the city," the report predicted, and "should be located so as to promote a desirable development or at least to support a natural development rather than to retard or to distort the evolution of the city.

"In favorable locations, the new facilities, which as a matter of course should be designed for long life, will become more and more useful as time passes; improperly located, they will become more and more of an encumbrance to the city's functions and an all too durable reminder of planning that was bad."

That warning was resounded by the Chief's boss, retired army major general Philip B. Fleming, who pointed out that highways had "built cross-roads communities into thriving cities" but had "just about wiped out other towns.

"So it seems to me that the highway planner needs to approach his task in a prayerful attitude," Fleming said. "He is building not only for the present but for the long future, and thereby helping to shape the coming pattern of our civilization."

• • •

The committee didn't finish its 184-page report, *Interregional Highways,* until January 1943. FDR submitted the document to Congress a year later, urging prompt action to "facilitate the acquisition of land, the drawing of detailed project plans, and other preliminary work which must precede actual road construction."

It received a warm reception on Capitol Hill. By then, it didn't take an engineer to see that America's streets and highways desperately needed a boost. The war effort had diverted materials and manpower from construction and maintenance, and all about, concrete and asphalt crumbled. New highways won approval only in short stretches, and only if they directly served military installations or suppliers — in places such as Charlestown, Indiana, where in the space of weeks a cornfield sprouted a mammoth DuPont gunpowder works; and San Diego, where the population had leaped by fifty thousand in a single year; and Norfolk, a great knot of harbor, shipyard, and military base that became a factory of war.

Otherwise, road building had simply stopped. In the two years before Pearl Harbor, Federal Aid put more than 20,000 miles of highway under construction. In 1942, it produced just 1,869 miles, and in the first ten months of 1943, a paltry 722. The traffic on this disintegrating network got heavier every year. There now was a registered vehicle for every 4.5 people; if it so chose, the entire population could go for a drive at once. Congealed streets turned the simplest midday errands into ordeals in Boston and Philadelphia, in Chicago and Denver, even in Honolulu.

Over several months in 1944, lawmakers incorporated the committee's recommendations into the annual highway bill. They did so with little drama, making only one significant change: Republicans chucked the system's "interregional" name for "interstate," after inferring that the original had been coined by planners whom they regarded as leftist pains in the neck, and after the Chief assured them that "interregional" had "absolutely no significance."

And so, deep in the Federal-Aid Highway Act of 1944, there appeared a section that opened: "There shall be designated within the continental United States a National System of Interstate Highways," and which specified that such a system should not top forty thousand miles in length, and should be "so located as to connect by routes, as direct as practicable, the principal metropolitan areas, cities, and industrial centers, to serve the national defense, and to connect at suitable border points with routes of continental importance in the Dominion of Canada and the Republic of Mexico."

The bill also cleared the way for Federal Aid money to be used in the cities, as the report had urged — to the tune of a quarter of each year's appropriation. It provided no special financing for the interstate system, and no word on when or where construction would begin. Even so, it committed the interstates to paper. It made them the continent's principal roads. It now remained only to find the money to build them.

At congressional hearings on the bill, 110 witnesses testified, the great majority backing the plan. Just before Christmas, it became law.

Interregional Highways not only called for expressways in the nation's cities, it suggested that they were a logical place to start construction. City fathers throughout America agreed; they were thrilled by the prospect of big roads cleaving the fast-spreading suburbs to bring new life, new business, to downtowns strangled by car and truck traffic — a congestion that grew exponentially worse with the war's end.

Peace brought an abrupt halt to rationing and an explosion on Detroit's assembly lines. From thirty-one million at the Japanese surrender, vehicle registrations leaped to nearly thirty-eight million in 1947, on the way to an incredible forty-nine million in 1950 — an increase of almost 60 percent in five years. The boom showed no sign of slowing. Americans were flush with cash, emboldened by easy credit, and thirsty for speed and wide-open spaces. As one Public Roads official put it, car ownership was headed "upward as rapidly as vehicles can be manufactured."

Arranged bumper to bumper, the cars produced in 1949 would have stretched more than twenty thousand miles, which vied with the year's output of improved road. America spent more on transportation, $40 billion, than on anything except food, and that exception was a matter of doubt. Its transportation spending trumped that of all the rest of the world lumped together, even topped the total income of Great Britain. Three out of four cars on the planet were in the United States.

And the great majority of the new cars squeezed into overcrowded cities that had outgrown their streets during the conflict. Baltimore's population grew by 73 percent during the forties; New Orleans's head count doubled; San Francisco swelled to two and a half times its pre-war size. With all those new people came traffic that surpassed the wildest imaginings of highway officials and city planners. In 1949, it topped the forecasts for 1960.

You find your morning commute trying now? In most places, it can't compare to the glacial pace of negotiating the logjammed streets and overstuffed parking lots of the pre-interstate years. The new program shimmered on the horizon, promising relief from the building crisis. "If we are successful in executing the plans now being formulated in practically every large city in the country," the Chief wrote in a maga-zine essay, "access to the main business districts will be enormously improved. People from the outer portion of the city and the surround-ing area will travel safely and without stops or delay of any kind to the downtown area. More traffic than ever will pour into the business district."

Now came the difficult task of choosing where to put these urban routes. Public Roads wasn't looking to pinpoint them exactly — that could wait until it came time for the states to acquire rights of way — but it did need to decide on approximate corridors in the inter-est of refining its mileage calculations. Problem was, the tried-and-true techniques used in the highway planning surveys wouldn't work; traffic couldn't be stopped for interviews in the midst of an evening rush hour. The agency tried a number of approaches before it hit on population sampling, then being pioneered by pollster George Gallup. With help from the Census Bureau, MacDonald's people divided a city into squares and targeted a certain percentage of homes in each. "Each interviewer is given a list of the dwelling units in his territory selected for inclusion in the sample, and he is instructed to obtain interviews in these dwelling units and no others," explained John T. Lynch, who led the effort. "He obtains information concerning all trips made by automobile or by public conveyance on the preceding day, including the means of travel, the origin and destination, the purpose of the trip, the times of starting and arrival, and other information which varies somewhat from city to city."

The travel patterns that emerged in each square were linked with those in others to form "desire lines" through a city. When Public Roads found that such desire outran the capacity of existing streets, it launched studies of the costs and benefits of bigger, limited-access alternatives.

Some of the coming construction might be tough medicine. "Admittedly, an expressway through a densely populated area does involve razing numerous buildings, including many dwellings," MacDonald wrote. But "in most instances" the selected routes aimed for "sections where property values are low, and most of the buildings are of the type that should be torn down in any case, to rid the city of its slums."

MacDonald's boss, General Fleming, went so far as to propose that Truman assign him the nation's entire urban renewal effort, arguing that highway and housing officials would be able to better choreograph their efforts. The president wasn't interested; he instead backed what became the Housing Act of 1949, which replaced decrepit slums with often-bleak public housing projects.

Still, the Chief threw Public Roads into its part of changing the cityscape. Surveys were under way in Little Rock and Tulsa even before the 1944 act was put to a vote. In six years, they spread to eighty-five major cities. By August 1947, the agency could announce that it had nailed down rough locations for 37,681 miles of the system, including 2,882 miles that ran through urban areas. That left 2,319 miles unassigned, under the system's 40,000-mile cap. The Chief reserved that mileage for future beltways, spurs, and loops off the main routes.

In retrospect, the surveys were self-fulfilling — their yardsticks were motorist safety, travel time, gasoline use, and incidence of repair, all facets of the driving experience. The effects on those not using the roads were neither as easily tallied nor as eagerly sought. And they rested on a fundamental assumption that would soon prove flawed:

that in the years to come, white-collar jobs would remain clustered in downtown office buildings, along with most retail shopping and nighttime entertainment, and blue-collar work would stay concentrated in well-established industrial zones. Most urban traffic, then, would continue to move back and forth between these few defined destinations and a city's residential neighborhoods.

The Chief failed to grasp that his roads would change the old patterns, that in addition to addressing traffic that already existed, they would spawn new centers for business and entertainment, and fartherflung subdivisions — that they would explode the traditional city built around a nucleus, something resembling a cell, into a blob sprinkled with smaller nodes of activity. But in the first years after the war, that wasn't yet apparent. On paper, the highways came off as almost unassailable.

That didn't, however, get them bankrolled in a hurry. The highway community had met Harry Truman's ascension with excitement, for the new president was a roads man of long standing. He'd sought his first office, a county judgeship, on a better-roads platform, had led the Kansas City–based National Old Trails Road Association, was a card-carrying member of the American Road Builders Association, and had logged thousands of miles behind the wheel while campaigning for the Senate. Truman loved cars, loved roads, and loved to drive.

But he did not usher in the expected windfall for highways. No money was earmarked specifically for the interstate program; the states were expected to build it from their regular Federal Aid handouts, matching the federal contribution dollar for dollar. Few could afford the arrangement.

Framing the interstates as key to the national defense didn't shake loose any cash — not even when, in an appendix to a March 1949 Public Roads report, defense secretary James V. Forrestal made an Atomic Age pitch for urban superhighways, noting that "methods of modern warfare . . . may require movement of much of [a city's] civilian population and industry." Those "methods," of course, meant nuclear attack; interstates radiating from America's downtowns would be an important tool for herding populations away from ground zero — assuming they were built wide, which "in event of bombing would reduce to a minimum the rubble that would fall on at least a portion of the traveled way." Forrestal's comments, among the few on the subject in any Public Roads document of the period, evidently didn't resonate with the president; Truman gave the report only a distracted nod.

By the time they met in December 1950, state highway officials worried that the nation's "vast transportation systems" were "now in a seriously weakened condition." Because the interstate system would "greatly contribute to the execution of the defense program," the officials urged Congress and the states "to do everything possible to expedite the construction" of the network.

Nothing happened. The existing highway system, already pounded by overloaded trucks and curtailed maintenance during the war, slipped into further disrepair, even as auto plants disgorged new models by the millions. New York State figured it would take nearly a billion dollars to restore its highways to the efficiency they'd enjoyed in 1930. On the Federal Aid system, fifty-two thousand bridges were rated as "below standard." Half the nation's busiest rural roads remained less than twenty feet wide. "On each such mile of highway," the Chief complained, "over sixty times per hour, or once each minute, a vehicle is encroaching upon the left lane when meeting an oncoming vehicle."

With no federal help on the horizon, several states turned to building their own expressways, all of them — the bureau's warnings be damned — financed through tolls. Maine opened a turnpike from Portland to the New Hampshire line in 1947. New York created an authority in 1949 to build and manage a "thruway" linking New York City, Albany, and Buffalo. The same year, West Virginia created an authority and Ohio a commission to build toll roads.

Oklahoma legislators broke ground on a turnpike linking Tulsa and Oklahoma City, and in New Jersey, construction crews got busy on a 118-mile toll highway running the length of the state, with seventeen interchanges and construction standards largely borrowed from the interstate system. Its backers defended toll financing by pointing out that they really had no choice; if they spent all their regular highway money on the turnpike alone, they wouldn't be able to finish it as a free road until at least 1961.

Metropolitan areas around the country conceived of their own expressways, too, many of them bankrolling the projects with big bond issues. Booming Houston built a six-lane freeway that ended in a spray of ramps into its downtown. Kansas City started work on a belt around its middle, fed by arterial highways, and Washington and Baltimore planned to do the same. Los Angeles began to lay down its great tangle of concrete. And in Boston, which had made few accommodations to the automobile and seemed to take odd pride in the foulmouthed logjam that each rush hour brought to its crooked, narrow streets, state highway men started work on an elevated expressway that would chew a curving path straight through the city's heart.

Frustrations over worsening congestion aside, Thomas MacDonald was a contented man. He was serving his sixth president; only the FBI's J. Edgar Hoover would outlast him as the head of a federal bureau. Truman had awarded him the government's Medal of Merit for his "energetic leadership" and "exceptionally meritorious service" during the war — not least, for overseeing the breakneck construction of the Alaska Highway across more than a thousand miles of Canadian wilderness. He'd achieved an almost unrivaled respect in the capital, his integrity and expertise held in such esteem that his testimony was unquestioned; lawmakers of both parties assumed that if the Chief told them a highway was needed in such and such a place, he had the research, the figures, to back up the statement.

Of even greater note, in the years since Bess's death his relationship with his secretary, Caroline Fuller, had deepened into a formal, pragmatic brand of love. She had much in common with the late Mrs. MacDonald. Like Bess, Fuller had been a schoolteacher before going into secretarial work, and like Bess, she brought a prim efficiency and a sharp intelligence to her work; not only was she authorized to exercise "her own judgment in disposing of" visitors, she contributed to bureau policy and procedure to a degree matched by few others in the organization, deputy commissioners included.

Her duties, according to the Chief, called for "maintaining a current and comprehensive knowledge of the thinking and operating methods of the Commissioner," and evidently, she succeeded. When, exactly, their relationship morphed is suggested circumstantially. Through March 1942, she invariably earned an "Excellent" on her annual performance appraisals. After that date, her ratings dropped to "Very Good." It would be just like the proper MacDonald to feel he could no longer give her top marks, lest he be suspected of bias.

The two betrayed nothing of their affair in public. She continued to address him as "Chief" and signed her notes and telegrams to him with "Fuller" or "CLF." She continued to share an apartment with her spitting-image sister; the Fullers and MacDonald often went about as a trio.

In July 1951, MacDonald turned seventy, the federal government's mandatory retirement age. The Truman White House asked that he extend his career for at least another year, to which he happily agreed. The *Fort Worth Star-Telegram* approved: "We think it would have been a costly mistake to dispense with the services of a man of Mr. MacDonald's ability and to lose his valuable experience," the paper surmised, "especially when his physical condition is such as to permit him to remain in the harness."

A year later, with his attention devoted to the war in Korea, Truman again asked the Chief to stay on. Again, he agreed. So it was that MacDonald was still on the job when, at long last, the interstate system finally received its first dedicated federal check. In the spring of 1952, Congress earmarked $25 million a year for the network in its highways budgets for fiscal 1954 and 1955.

It was a token amount, too little to get much of anything started, at a time when suburbs were blooming and traffic was worse than ever. The Chief said as much in his annual speech to AASHO, noting "ample evidence that highways today are only fractionally as adequate for today's traffic demands as they were two decades ago."

But it was a start. The National System of Interstate Highways was moving from blueprint to concrete.

It bears noting that the man most often celebrated for creating the interstates played no role in any of this. The conception of the system, its routing, its design — all that took place while Dwight Eisenhower was busy elsewhere.

On the day Franklin Roosevelt called the Chief to his office to draw his six blue lines on the map, the future president was half a world away in the Philippines, serving none too happily as chief of staff to Douglas MacArthur and helping the boss whip the island territory into shape for the coming war. The following year, when *Toll Roads and Free Roads* made its way to Congress and Futurama wowed crowds in New York, Eisenhower was at Fort Lewis, Washington. In April 1941, when Roosevelt appointed the committee to study interregional highways, Ike was a newly minted colonel stationed in San Antonio. When the committee finished the bulk of its assignment late that year, he was helping to draft the nation's war plans in Washington, D.C.

As the Chief and Fairbank tweaked their recommendations on urban highways, Eisenhower was leading the Allied invasion of North Africa. The same month FDR submitted the committee's report to Congress, he assumed command of Allied forces in Europe. The very day that the landmark 1944 highway act became law, and the interstate system moved from proposal to legal reality, Ike earned his fifth star while overseeing the Allies' eastward sweep across France. The year after the rural sections were designated, he was telling a reporter that he couldn't "conceive of any circumstance that could drag out of me permission to consider me for any political post from dogcatcher to Grand High Supreme King of the Universe." And at the point that the system received its first paltry handout, the general was the head of the West's cold war alliance in Europe and not yet a candidate for president.

Eisenhower was a lot of things: an officer who never saw time at the front, but who would be remembered as one of history's great commanders; a middling student at West Point who proved himself a genius for organization and planning; a guy who spent most of his career in frustrated, go-nowhere obscurity, only to rise from major to general of the army in eight years.

But he was not, by any means, the father of the interstates. Over the years a fable has gained currency that the system was inspired by two events in Eisenhower's life: the 1919 motor convoy expedition, on which the young Ike first grasped the nation's highway shortcomings; and the Allied advance on Berlin in World War II, when he experienced Hitler's autobahns and came to appreciate the promise of modern expressways. He returned from the war with a vision of how America's security, fraternity, and commerce would be bolstered through a vast superhighway grid, it's claimed, and so made it happen as president. It's a satisfying story, one that Eisenhower told himself, and indeed, there's no doubt that Ike was affected by both experiences. But they did not beget the interstates. The system was a done deal in every important respect but financing by the time Ike entered politics.

He would certainly have a role to play, and an important one, but it would be far more limited than that with which he's commonly credited. As for the system's true paternity — well, by now it should be obvious that it belonged to more than one man, and who they were.

PART III

The Crooked Straight, the Rough Places Plain

10

- - - - - - - - - - -

WHEN DWIGHT EISENHOWER took office in January 1953, the Interstate Highway System had officially existed for more than eight years, and the Bureau of Public Roads had taken to speaking of it as if the concrete were already poured; bureau reports and press releases often mentioned the "forty thousand-mile" network alongside descriptions of the very solid primary and secondary Federal Aid highways.

In reality, of course, the system was made of paper. Ike knew little, if anything, of this abstraction. He entered the Oval Office professing an interest in building "a network of modern roads," rating it "as necessary to defense as it is to our national economy and personal safety" but having conducted little, if any, research on the subject. He didn't know that the executive and legislative branches had already worked out the details of the network he sought. He had no idea that the Bureau of Public Roads had produced two reports, more than a decade before, that spelled out its design and approximate footprints. His own views about highways were at odds with those of the government's experts: unaware that the greatest need for expressways was in cities, he favored a strictly rural network; and not knowing that the bureau had concluded that a national program could not be financed with tolls, he favored "self-liquidating" highway projects, or those that generated the revenue to repay their costs.

How to explain this? Well, the thirty-fourth president wasn't much of a reader and couldn't sit still for long briefings; he preferred information delivered via terse reports from subordinates to whom he delegated the complicated business of actually running the government. Oddly, incredibly, it seems none of them mentioned to the boss that such a system was on the books — or so he later claimed.

This is what he did know, and perhaps it's all he needed to know: That building new highways would supply jobs to homecoming soldiers when the Korean conflict ended, and a ready source of employment and spending whenever the economy required it. That modern expressways could provide a long-lasting boost to interstate commerce, promote tourism, reduce the cost of goods and shipping. That they might put a dent in the automotive death toll. And that they would ease congestion, at a time when vehicles continued to multiply and the daily commute was lengthening for millions of Americans decamping from city to suburb.

So Ike got started on a program even before he moved to Washington, asking a golfing buddy and New York securities broker named Walker G. Buckner for his thoughts on how a highways program might be approached. Buckner's thirteen-page response, delivered just days after Ike took up residence in the White House, roughly outlined a new grid of self-liquidating turnpikes that would augment those already open or contemplated in the various states: one from Washington, D.C., to Jacksonville; another from Chicago to New Orleans; a third from Chicago "to the neighborhood of San Francisco by Springfield, Kansas City, Salt Lake City." Buckner appended a gas station map marked with those and other routes he favored: San Diego to Seattle, Kansas City to Houston, and an extension of the West Virginia Turnpike north to Cleveland and south to a junction with the Washington-Jacksonville route near Charleston, South Carolina.

Most bore little resemblance to the interstate routes already mapped out by the Bureau of Public Roads. In fact, though the report opened by noting that Buckner had consulted "men who have participated in at least seventy percent of all existing toll bridges, roads, parking facilities and arterial highways," it offered no evidence that its author was any more aware of the existing interstate program than the new president.

But Eisenhower didn't know what he didn't know. Buckner's report prompted the president to ask Gabriel Hauge, his administrative assistant, to launch, "with interested departments of government," a more formal study of the highway situation; he was convinced, he wrote, that any initiative should be part of a "constructive program that will be designed to meet, in a well-rounded and imaginative way, the constantly increasing needs of a growing population.

"Our cities still conform too rigidly to the patterns, customs, and practices of fifty years ago," Eisenhower observed. "Each year we add hundreds of thousands of new automobiles to our vehicular population, but our road systems do not keep pace with the need. In the average city today, many of our streets become almost useless to traffic because of the necessity of home owners for using them for parking.

"While this entire subject of vehicular traffic is but a small segment of the great program that must attract our attention, there is nevertheless no reason why we should not proceed to its thorough study so as to have it ready for inclusion into a broad plan to be developed later."

He further told Hauge that he would "like to have plans crystallized and developed so that significant parts of it could be initiated without completion of the entire plan, but with the certainty that the part started will fit logically and efficiently into the whole." His sign-off was very much in character: "From time to time, please give me an informal report of progress."

That February 4, 1953, memo signaled the Eisenhower administration's official entry into the interstate highway saga. Hauge passed Buckner's paper on to the Commerce Department, where it apparently was filed away; nothing came of it.

The administration's second highway-related undertaking came a little more than a month later, when Eisenhower's commerce secretary, Sinclair Weeks, summoned the Chief to a meeting. The bureau had been shifted into the Commerce Department during Truman's presidency; MacDonald knew his new boss, with whose father he'd worked thirty years before, in his first days at the bureau — John W. Weeks had been secretary of war during the development of the Pershing Map.

But trouble had been in the air. Just after taking office, the new secretary had created the post of undersecretary of commerce for transportation, with the power to change or assume the bureau's responsibilities as he saw fit. It was difficult to take the development as anything but a vote of no confidence; the Chief had been knocked down a rung in the federal hierarchy and replaced as the secretary's principal adviser on highways. He wouldn't be representing the administration before Congress, either, unless it was with the blessing of this new undersecretary.

Exactly what was said in Weeks's office has been lost, but not so the gist. The time had come, Weeks announced, for MacDonald to pack his bags. His service would not be extended. After thirty-four years as the country's top highway man, as the longest-serving head of any major government agency to that time, as trustee of more public spending than any federal official in peacetime history, he was done.

Several theories emerged as to why he wasn't allowed to simply serve until his birthday rolled around again that summer. They generally fell under two headings: Weeks wanted firmer control of the biggest budget in his department; and Eisenhower wanted to jump-start the country's response to burgeoning congestion and highway disrepair, and figured new leadership, loyal to his administration, was key to making it happen.

On paper, MacDonald's departure was his own doing. On March 9, 1953, he wrote to Weeks that he had continued so long as commissioner "at the request of, and wholly at the pleasure of" the Truman administration. "If it meets your convenience," his letter concluded, "I now request your concurrence in my release from my present position at the end of the current month, March 31st."

In truth, there was nothing voluntary about it. At the meeting's close MacDonald chugged back to the bureau's offices and straight to Miss Fuller's desk. "I've just been fired," he reputedly told her, "so we might as well get married."

Reactions, most of them shocked and saddened, poured in. "Personally, I am awfully sorry that you will not continue at the head of the Bureau," Georgia congressman Carl Vinson wrote the Chief.

John A. Anderson, Virginia's highway commissioner, ended a note praising MacDonald's "work well done" with "Honor to you for ever." *Engineering News-Record* saluted his "unquestioned integrity and unyielding adherence to principle," concluding: "Tom MacDonald brought great honor to the civil engineering profession."

On March 18, Weeks's office went public with the Chief's replacement: Francis V. du Pont, a fifty-eight-year-old businessman and heir to a chemicals fortune who'd devoted much of his adult life to an inherited passion—building and promoting highways in his adopted state of Delaware.

His father, T. Coleman du Pont, an early leader of the Good Roads Movement, had built his own hundred-mile highway from Wilmington to the Maryland line and eventually donated it to the state. Francis had followed his father to MIT, where he obtained a degree in mechanical engineering in 1917, then served in the war, spent time in the family business, and worked as a Cadillac research engineer. In 1922, he'd landed a seat on the Delaware State Highway Commission; he spent twenty-seven years on the panel, all but four of them as chairman, and was a central figure in the planning, design, and construction of the Delaware Memorial Bridge linking his state with New Jersey, among the biggest bridges of any kind when it opened in 1951.

A government job paying $16,000 a year was the last thing Francis du Pont needed; not only did he enjoy a fat inheritance, he was treasurer of several landmark hotels, president of New York City's Equitable Building, and president of the Delaware-based Equitable Trust Company. But the gracious, lantern-jawed millionaire was excited by Ike's presidency and the prospect of building highways on a national scale.

Du Pont sent a two-page telegram to the Chief, stressing that he was honored to succeed him and planned to continue his policies. MacDonald returned du Pont's cordiality. In the last week of March, he showed the new man around the office, making introductions, explaining bureau procedure. After finishing his last day of government service, MacDonald agreed to preside over a farewell dinner thrown by his closest friends and colleagues at Washington's Metropolitan

Club. The next day, he left town for Texas. An old friend there, former state highways boss Gibb Gilchrist, headed Texas A&M University. He'd been after the Chief to retire to College Station for years, offering him a leadership post in a program for the study of transportation. Now he had a taker.

MacDonald's close lieutenants assumed that they were finished themselves. Many were indistinguishable in outlook and philosophy from their departed boss; they shared the old man's unwavering faith in the certitude of technical expertise over political influence, in the federal-state partnership, in the sacredness of empirical data.

The new commissioner surprised everyone. He moved into his office without fanfare. He brought a lawyer with him, but no other staff, not even a secretary; he made it clear from his first day that he admired the bureau's past performance and could only hope to do as well, and that he knew he would need the agency's veterans to succeed.

Du Pont instituted weekly staff meetings, something the Chief had always avoided, and solicited his deputies for their anonymous suggestions on how they would change the place. Then he convened a series of meetings to find, as he put it, "the common denominator of changes that were desirable." He kept the Chief posted on what he was doing. "I want to assure you," he wrote after six weeks on the job, "that all of your assistants have been most courteous and helpful in our effort to carry on the good name and good will which you created during your administration."

In short, it was hard not to like the guy. It didn't hurt that du Pont was a solid engineer, that he knew highways as well as anyone in the building, and that he enjoyed friendships and influence in Congress, the executive branch, and industry. Even Herbert Fairbank was won over. "Don't worry about your Bureau or your friends in it," he wrote MacDonald. "Both it and they, I think, are coming through all right."

The Buckner report having vanished into bureaucratic limbo, highways languished for the rest of Eisenhower's first year in office. Then, on April 12, 1954, Ike again spurred his staff to take up the issue, instructing Francis du Pont, a former West Point classmate named

John S. Bragdon, and Sherman Adams, the White House chief of staff—a gruff, dour, and forcefully efficient former governor of New Hampshire—to come up with a $50 billion highway scheme.

He stayed on them as much as he stayed on anything, given his rigorous golf and vacation schedule. In a May 11 memo he asked Adams: "Where do we stand on our 'dramatic' plan to get 50 billion dollars worth of self-liquidating highways under construction?" Where they stood was toe to toe. Bragdon, a retired army major general and member of the president's Council of Economic Advisers, was an unabashed fan of toll financing who firmly believed that by using the excess income from busy toll roads to subsidize weaker links, America could build a thirty-thousand-mile superhighway system that wouldn't cost a penny in taxes or debt. If he had his way, it would be built and managed by a National Highway Authority, led by cabinet members, that would replace all existing state and federal highway agencies to wield supreme road-building authority. Adams differed with all that, preferring to stick with the tried-and-true federal-state partnership.

In the resulting tussle, not a lot was accomplished. Exasperated, the president decided to delegate the task yet again, this time to the governors of the forty-eight states, who were meeting in July 1954 at a lakeside resort in New York's Adirondacks. This was a politically daring move, seeing as how governors had been agitating for years for Washington to get out of the highway business, or at least to drop its tax on gasoline, which in 1954 stood at 2 cents; they preferred that the taxes be collected instead by officials of the individual states, who didn't need the bureau or anyone else telling them how to use the money.

Ike didn't reveal the subject of his address ahead of time, explaining that it would be "informal." As it happened, his sister-in-law died shortly before he was to head to Lake George, prompting him to send Vice President Richard Nixon in his place—so that for one of the highway-related events for which he is best remembered, and can be granted credit for truly making a difference, Eisenhower wasn't even present.

Nixon had more than mere notes on which to rely. The president gave him a well-crafted speech observing that the country had "a transportation system which in many respects, it is true, is the best in the world, but far from the best that America can do for itself," and that highways were "inadequate locally, and obsolete as a national system." By way of explanation, he offered a neat summary of the network's history:

> It is obsolete because in large part it just happened. It was governed in the beginning by terrain, existing Indian trails, cattle trails, arbitrary section lines. It was designed largely for local movement at low speed of one or two horsepower. It has been adjusted, it is true, at intervals to meet metropolitan traffic gluts, transcontinental movement, and increased horsepower. But it has never been completely overhauled or planned to satisfy the needs ten years ahead.
>
> Now, what are the penalties of this obsolete net which we have today? The first, most apparent: an annual death toll comparable to the casualties of a bloody war, beyond calculation in dollar terms. It approaches forty thousand killed and exceeds 1.3 million injured annually.
>
> And second, the annual wastage of billions of hours lost in detours, traffic jams, and so on . . . amounting to billions of dollars in productive time . . . Third, of the civil suits that clog up our courts, it has been estimated that more than half have their origins on highways, roads and streets.

Inadequate highways also retarded industry and, of great and growing concern in 1954, failed "to meet the demands of catastrophe or defense, should an atomic war come." But a solution was at hand, the vice president declared: "A $50 billion highway program in ten years is a goal toward which we can — and we should — work."

No one in the room had seen this coming, besides the guy at the dais. The president believed, Nixon rolled on, that America needed a "grand plan" for highways that enabled fast and safe long-distance travel, connected farms to their markets, and loosened urban bottlenecks — and which, to the extent possible, paid for itself. He asked the governors to study the matter and recommend action to get such a system started.

The governors' initial reaction was a blend of anger and confusion. They'd been blind-sided, challenged on a matter they were on record as opposing. It was only after a flurry of White House clarification (that, for instance, the $50 billion of which Nixon spoke was new money, piled on top of the billions already spent on Federal Aid) and back-room reassurance (that the states would have a leading role in developing this highway system) that two days later the conference adopted a resolution of support and backed it up by appointing a seven-man committee to do as the president had asked.

Eisenhower hedged his bet. Over the following month, he created two committees on the same topic within his administration. He asked Sinclair Weeks to pool representatives from various departments into what became known as the Interagency Committee; among its members was John Bragdon, who was still espousing the glories of tolls and a national highway authority. That group would offer ideas and support to the second panel, this one comprising citizen-businessmen and led by an old friend, retired army general Lucius D. Clay, the president's deputy during the postwar occupation of Europe and overseer of the heroic, 324-day Berlin Airlift of 1948–49. Its official name was the President's Advisory Committee on a National Highway Program, though Washington preferred the shorthand "Clay Committee."

Lucius Clay, hawk-nosed and towering, was both supremely self-confident and, thanks to a long career in the officer corps, accustomed to getting his way. Colleagues mockingly compared him to a distant forebear, the nineteenth-century senator and diplomat Henry Clay, who'd won renown as "the Great Compromiser." General Clay was "the Great Uncompromiser" or, alternatively, "the Kaiser." Even Eisenhower found him overbearing at times, writing in his diary that Clay's "usual tactics" were "aimed at overpowering all opposition and at settling the matter without further question."

Clay had a lot on the ball, however. He had a photographic memory, for one thing, and the ability to retain and later retrieve numbers, dates, and facts at will. He also had a strong engineering background — his prewar commands had included big construction jobs — and a gift for organization on a grand scale, which he had demonstrated so convincingly during the airlift. At its height, his answer to the Soviet blockade of West Berlin supplied food and supplies to the population at the rate of four planes a minute. That triumph overshadowed his insistent push for the postwar reconstruction of Germany, which helped spawn the Marshall Plan.

Clay had retired from the army just after the airlift, had come home to a ticker-tape parade in New York City, and had since taken over the chairmanship of the Continental Can Corporation. He'd also helped Ike corner the GOP's presidential nomination and had wielded great influence in selecting the president's cabinet. No surprise, given the styles of both men, that Eisenhower left the membership of the Clay Committee up to the general. Clay selected a builder, a banker, a manufacturer, and a union boss.

Not a highway man among them. For that expertise, the committee would come to rely heavily on a bureau up-and-comer, a Thomas MacDonald protégé named Francis Cutler Turner.

Even at gatherings of men in the highway field, short, bespectacled Frank Turner could be easy to overlook. A teetotaler and homebody, quiet to the point of reticence, he found social events more wearying than the thick satchel of paperwork he carried home most nights, and he tended to blend into the wallpaper of any room he entered. But he had an almost superhuman capacity for work, and in 1954, Turner was midway in a career without equal in the history of American roads. Starting with his appointment to the Clay Committee's staff, it would be he, more than anyone else, who would midwife a conceptual network of superhighways into the concrete and steel octopus that now spans the continent.

Born in December 1908 to an engine man for the Missouri-Kansas-Texas Railroad, Turner had spent most of his childhood in Fort Worth, in a hipped-roof shotgun shack in a working-class neighborhood sandwiched between the Meridian Highway, two blocks to the east, and the rail yards just to the west. It was an unadorned upbringing, one of hand-me-down clothes and barefoot afternoons and sweating out the Texas heat in the shade of a tiny front porch.

As a boy he spent a few weeks each summer in Oklahoma, visiting his paternal grandfather on his farm east of Lawton. The surrounding roads were unimproved dirt; after a rain, Frank would help run a split-log drag over the ruts, sometimes driving the mules, otherwise standing on the drag to give it more bite. Once a year, the Turners would hitch a county-owned blade to the family tractor, to grade the roads and pull the ditches. Which is to say that even before he was out of grade school, Frank Turner had worked on roads and had experienced their limitations firsthand.

His grandfather, an educated man who recognized the change then sweeping the country, often remarked that roads were "the coming thing," and that if he were a young man starting out, he might look into the highway business. That reinforced what Frank was hearing back home, where he sometimes joined his father aboard a steam locomotive in the yards. Linnaeus Turner steered his boy away from his own life's work, saying: Careers in the railways, Francis, they're not looking good. The lines have all been built. But, roads — that's where the future lies.

Soon enough, Turner could see that for himself. Fort Worth's dirt streets were crowded with automobiles when he started classes at North Texas Agricultural College, a local satellite of what's now Texas A&M University, and even more so when he transferred after two years to the main campus in College Station. The highway engineering curriculum did not inspire confidence: "The books that I studied in college," he would remember, "they talked about gravel roads and how to build a gravel road and how to build a macadam base" and were busy with "pictures of horse-drawn equipment." But in the spring of 1928, Public Roads sent a man around, as it did every year, on a hunt for talent. The bureau's man impressed Turner, and he the bureau's man; the following year, his last at A&M, he received word from Thomas MacDonald that he qualified for appointment as a junior engineer, making $2,000 per year.

Turner accepted. When he left the college in June 1929, the east end of campus was a construction zone. An administration building was to go up at the head of a grand new avenue onto the grounds. A college laid out on an axis defined by its railroad station, in a town that took its name from the depot, was reorienting itself to the automobile.

A quarter century later, Turner had worked virtually every sort of engineering job the bureau had to offer. Days out of college, he'd reported for duty with the bureau's Division of Management, and an assignment as an observer and analyst. Issued a 1927 Ford Model T touring car, he'd studied road-building jobs all through the West. "We would sit on the side of the bank there with a clipboard and a pencil and a stopwatch," he recalled late in life, "and time the movement of [a] shovel, digging, swinging, loading it in the truck and then back. What did he do there? How far did he swing around? What effect were these movements on productivity? How many cubic yards did he move? How many truckloads did he move in an eight-hour period?"

On a job in Victoria County, Texas, he reported that a poor hauling road so slowed the trucks supplying a concrete mixer that the machine was idled about two and a half hours a day — wasting $112.50 of the government's money, which Turner figured would have covered the cost of fixing the road, with plenty left over. The spring of 1930 found him testing the strength of concrete mixed in larger batches. He moved on to jobs in Santa Cruz, California, and Sheboygan, Wisconsin, others in Wyoming. It was an exciting time to be building roads. New machines were coming online that could carve great notches in previously impenetrable mountains, fill hundred-foot-deep ravines — accomplish in weeks what would have taken years in the days of horse wagons.

And it was an exciting time off the clock, as well. In December 1930, Turner married his longtime sweetheart, Mable Marie Nanney, a fellow Baptist and the daughter of a railroad man. The two made a good couple; Frank was content to listen as others did most of the talking, and Mable, while shy in groups, enjoyed talking to Frank. He was prone to smile with his eyes; Mable laughed for both of them. Neither touched alcohol. And both were optimists; the motto under Frank's senior picture in the Fort Worth Central High yearbook had read, "Everything is for some good." She was pregnant in a matter of weeks; their daughter Beverly was born while Turner was conducting a study in California.

In the summer of 1933, he was transferred to the bureau's outpost in Little Rock,* where he had responsibility for about a third of Arkansas and found that the partnership envisioned in Federal Aid legislation was flesh-and-blood reality. When a highway project existed only on paper, Turner would venture into the boonies with a state survey engineer to eyeball route alternatives. They would whack through thicket and swamp side by side, gauging the lay of the land, discussing what they saw, how a road might work better here than there, and together arrive at a recommendation.

He would team up with the Arkansas specialists in design and construction the same way, the pairing usually so harmonious that a bystander would be hard-pressed to tell the federal man from the state. Sometimes Turner and an Arkansas engineer would be on the road for two, three days at a time, visiting multiple job sites, and more often than not they would share a car, take all their meals together, stay at the same hotels. Patient, judicious, Turner became a great ambassador for Federal Aid. He avoided pulling rank, never assumed the final word on any decision. As far as he was concerned, it was the state's road, and it would be Arkansas' lot to live with the finished product; he was there merely to help get it built. He and the state man might disagree about a detail now and then, might even "argue loud and vociferously," as he put it, but they would eventually reach some solution that worked for both. This was, after all, engineering. It relied on a logical framework, on mathematics and measurement. On numbers.

The bosses took notice. Turner was praised for his "unusual capacity for work," for handling "a large volume of work in a most commendable manner," for his energy and thoroughness. In 1935 he won promotion to assistant highway engineer, and later to a post as top maintenance inspector on Federal Aid jobs in and around Washington.

---

* Not willingly. Told he would be transferred, Turner listed Denver as his first choice and Fort Worth as his second — but only if he worked in the main office, and not one of the four state branches; life in Austin, Baton Rouge, Oklahoma City, or Little Rock, he wrote, "would not be very satisfactory from my viewpoint." Alas, Public Roads was no democracy.

Then, in March 1943, Turner was summoned north, to the wilds of British Columbia and the Yukon Territory, and to a leading role in the biggest Public Roads undertaking to date. An army of soldiers and civilians had been up there for nearly a year, hacking a two-lane, all-weather road out of the wilderness, extending the North American highway system from Dawson Creek, British Columbia, a tiny farming town five hundred miles northwest of Edmonton, to Alaska, until then reached only by air or sea. Mindful that the sprawling territory was open to Japanese attack, the U.S. and Canadian governments had hatched a plan for the Army Corps of Engineers to build a pioneer trail, more or less the first draft of a more substantial highway that Public Roads would lay down with the help of fourteen thousand civilian contractors.

It wasn't long before each side wore on the other's nerves, and it was in the name of patching things up — or, as he put it, "effecting a closer liaison with the [army] to expedite completion of the highway" — that Turner was dispatched on a field inspection in mid-August 1943. His first morning in the Yukon, he stopped in at Public Roads' Whitehorse office to find the resident engineer, Frank E. Andrews, deeply unhappy that an outsider had been sent to do what he reckoned he was already doing pretty well. Andrews was even unhappier that the assignment had been given to some backwoods Arkansas greenhorn who knew nothing about anything, and he told Turner flat-out that he didn't want him around. Turner's reply testified to his soft-spoken tenacity, not to mention restraint. "I said that I appreciated his frankness in telling me where I stood," he reported to his boss, "and that I was confident I would operate in a manner which would force him to revise his opinion of my ability to handle this assignment — that I considered his statement a challenge — and that I accepted it with enthusiasm and much interest, knowing the disadvantage under which I was operating with him."

That got the attention of the higher-ups. Three weeks later, at the War Department's request, he was loaned to the army to help organize its efforts and, after a breakneck second building season and with the "finished" highway 96 percent complete, was kept on as a consultant.

By that time, Mable had joined him; after a few months she returned for the couple's children — daughter Beverly now had brothers Marvin and Millard, or "Jim" — and the reunited family settled in Blueberry, a maintenance camp of tarpaper shacks and Quonset huts fifty-two miles up the highway from Fort St. John, itself no thriving metropolis.

Few people called the camp by its name; it was "One-oh-one," a reference to its distance from Dawson Creek. Mileposts were Turner's doing, a tribute to his father's stories about his runs on the rails: "Down at 820," Linn Turner might have said, or, "When we were coming up on 671," and his fellow engineers had nodded, understanding the exact spot he meant. Railroads had long used mileposts to mark their routes, as well as every bridge and tunnel, every siding, every town, and their crews mentally logged the mileposts of dangerous crossings and notorious curves; the numbers were far more precise and far less wordy than trying to pinpoint a place by nearby town or landmark, especially when reporting a wreck or damage to the track. Adapting the system to the highway had seemed natural — as it would, years later, on the interstates. So the maintenance camp at Fort St. John became 49, and the base camp at Whitehorse, 911. Everyone on the highway soon knew Milepost 1221.4 was the boundary between Alaska and the Yukon. And for better than a year, 101 became home.

The family's hut was insulated with sawdust. The cookstove was wood-fired, and the fridge was a wire cage nailed to a tree outside. Another shack served as one-room schoolhouse, church, and community center. Groceries took a week to arrive by truck. And camp life was not without its dangers: though Turner might deadpan in a report that recent days had been "quite cool" before revealing that he meant "from minus 15 to minus 38," the weather could kill.

In December 1944, all of the children at 101 piled into a carryall and took off for a Christmas program in Fort St. John, chaperoned by a driver and a schoolteacher. While the children watched the show, the driver slugged from a bottle outside. Headed back to camp, he missed a curve, ran off the road, and plowed the truck into a snowbank.

The party had no radio. It was dark. It was snowing. It was well below freezing and getting colder. The children huddled in the back, their toes and fingers growing numb, for "probably close to a couple hours," Marvin Turner, who was ten at the time, later recalled. Finally, headlights appeared, moving up the highway from the south.

It was Turner in his government car. Once he'd checked on the children, he walked around to the truck's cab, where the driver sat reeking of alcohol. Turner stood five foot six and weighed all of 138 pounds; just the same, he pulled the man from the truck with one hand and threw him against the vehicle's side, then yelled for someone to get him a rope, that he was going to tie the guy to a tree and leave him.

The Turner children had never seen their father lose his temper, let alone contemplate homicide. The teacher gently suggested that perhaps it wasn't a good idea. Turner, regaining his cool, fired the man instead.

Frank Turner proved so indispensable to the Corps of Engineers that in 1944 it requested his services indefinitely. By the end of the year he could boast that the highway bordered on the civilized. "There will be no difficulty at any season of the year," Turner wrote, "for a tourist to drive from any point in the United States directly to Fairbanks or Anchorage, Alaska, in an ordinary passenger car, with no special equipment." That winter, despite heavy snow and bone-cracking cold, the highway was never closed for more than four hours.

The job finished, the Turners drove home to the D.C. suburb of Arlington, where they discovered that the widening of the Lee Highway, U.S. 29, was slated to carve so deeply into their corner lot that they would lose a porch; a door opening onto the structure would be just a handful of feet from the curb. Frank was philosophical about it; they simply wouldn't use the door.

They were not inconvenienced for long. On his return to the office, Turner was told that he wouldn't be getting a job in one of the bureau's district offices, as expected. Impressed by his obvious skills as a logician and diplomat, the Chief had chosen him to oversee the reconstruction of war-ravaged roads in the Philippines.

Freshly vaccinated against tropical diseases, he arrived by military cargo plane in November 1946 to a country in ruins. He had to "rebuild 3,500 kilometers of road and about nine hundred bridges each year," he figured, in a program that crowded "into four years what normally would be about a twenty-year schedule of operations." Turner recruited a force of American engineers and put them up in a village of Quonset huts and apartments abandoned by the navy, which he transformed into a comfortable, fully self-contained American suburb. He claimed one of the biggest Quonsets, a three-bedroom model near the front gate, and sent for reinforcements. Mable and the kids pulled into Manila Bay on a freighter out of San Francisco.

It was not an especially easy place to live. Crime and political violence were chronic worries; the compound was twice ringed by barbed-wire fence and guarded around the clock by armed soldiers. On or off duty, travel beyond the city limits was "rough," Turner told the Chief. "When overnight stops are involved the traveler will find that it is not safe to travel after dark, that it is hard to find a 'suitable' place to sleep, and that it is almost impossible to find a clean place to eat," he wrote. "Amoebic dysentery is very prevalent."

On the job, corruption was a persistent enemy. In October 1948, he caught wind that contractors were being strong-armed into hiring "certain favored individuals," as he put it, and "additional persons not considered to have been required for the efficient prosecution of the work" — behavior that deeply offended Turner, whose years of efficiency studies and fieldwork had ingrained in him the expectation that the public should get an honest dollar's work for every dollar spent.

In one of his son Jim's most vivid memories of the Philippines, the Turners were driving from Manila to Camp John Hays, an army weekend getaway in the mountains, when they came upon a crew rebuilding a bomb-cratered road. Turner got out to speak with the foreman, and when he returned, Jim could see that he was upset. All of the contractor's vehicles displayed tags reading "On Test," Turner fumed. They were being passed off as experimental, which enabled the contractor to duck paying for license plates. The government paid him good money to do a job, and he was cheating it. And if he cheats on that, Turner said, he might cheat on the big stuff.

In April 1949, the State Department asked to borrow him from Public Roads to oversee all nine agencies involved in the Philippines re-habilitation program. Again, he excelled. Ambassador Myron Cowen nominated him for a government medal, testifying that he'd "done a superb job in all respects." The heads of all the American agencies in Manila lauded the "mild-mannered son of the Lone Star State" in a resolution: "You have carried out your trust and have never let us down," it read. "The words 'above and beyond the call of duty' come to mind." And as Turner's assignment neared its end, the Philippine government's public works director wrote that his advice had been "of incalculable value," and that his "sympathetic understanding has contributed largely to the speedy rehabilitation of the highways and bridges of my country."

His stints in Alaska and the Pacific imbued Turner with skills that would prove vital in the years ahead. He learned statecraft, how to bridge divides between cultures, both regional and organizational; he learned how, with careful organization and planning, even Herculean tasks could be broken into their component parts and accomplished; he was called on to apply his training in imaginative ways, to sur-mount engineering challenges unknown to Public Roads at large; and not least, he became expert at stretching a dollar.

But the assignments were to prove more important to highway history for what they taught the Chief, for in his eyes, they boosted Turner high above his contemporaries. They made a star of the very sort of worker who's all too often overlooked for promotion: the infi-nitely capable and universally respected guy who's too shy, too frumpy, too beige to excite the boss.

Beneath his diffident exterior, Frank Turner nursed an adventurous streak and revealed it on the trip back to the States. Weeks before his stint in Manila ended, he asked his daughter, Beverly, to plot a grand, six-week course home, a westbound route through Asia and Europe, most of it by air, with stops at major sights and cities. At 8:06 A.M. on July 2, 1950 (the time recorded by the detail-oriented Frank in a travel diary almost wholly devoted to weather, exchange rates, and roads), the Turners lifted off in an Indonesian DC-3 for Borneo, then Surabaya ("clean neat town, fair size, large busy port, good harbor — concrete buildings and red tile roofs — good airport with asphalt runways"), then Jakarta and Singapore.

Turner's entry for Bangkok: "Settled hotel bill — double room 50 ticals per person per night — three at 45 each — meals 15 ticals for breakfast, 12.5 to 18 for lunch and 16 to 20 for dinner — all plus 20% government tax. Hotel bill=1861 ticals plus laundry 99 ticals. Sightseeing trip Saturday 420 ticals, car hire about 40 ticals per hour for 5-passenger car. Rate of exchange 21.77 at Bank of America today."

In New Delhi, Turner hired a car for the 122-mile excursion to the Taj Mahal. "Road fairly well aligned," he reported. "12 ft width of asphalt surface treatment with bricks showing on edges looks like original road may have been of brick. Lined completely for entire length with large trees both sides of road. Follows river valley — fairly flat, no grades." In Calcutta, son Jim wrote in his own diary, "We took pictures mostly of the traffic."

They visited the Holy Land and rode camels in Egypt, explored Athens, and drove out of Rome to the Appian Way — precipitating a two-hour monologue from Turner on how ingenious the Romans had been, and a frequently aired complaint from Mable that they could go nowhere without a lecture on highways.

Once back in D.C., Turner wasted little time getting the family settled in a rented house and returning to the bureau, where Thomas MacDonald, impressed by Turner's knack for problem solving with little guidance or money, named him his assistant. An unknown engineer in Arkansas ten years before, Turner was transformed, at age forty-one, into one of the bureau's most influential leaders. It must have been apparent to others in the organization that the Chief was grooming him, an impression bolstered with the news that Turner would, as part of his duties, oversee the bureau's foreign programs — highway building in Turkey, Ethiopia, Liberia, and the Chief's pet project, the Inter-American Highway linking the United States and South America.

At about this point, Turner went home to Fort Worth to visit his parents and found a surveyor's stake in their front yard. The couple had moved out of Frank's boyhood home years before but had not strayed far; their bungalow on Colvin Avenue was just a few blocks to the south. Now Texas was turning the old Meridian Highway, U.S. 81, into a limited-access expressway; at Colvin it would be depressed so that Morningside Drive, a short block farther south, could pass overhead, and on either side of this ditched highway would run an access road, to which the expressway's ramps would link.

The Turners' corner lot sat smack in the right of way that Texas highway officials had drawn up a year before, and right where northbound traffic would soon be whizzing. The parents of a high-ranking federal highway official were about to have a superhighway blast through their front door.

We have to move, Turner's mother told him.

Yes, he replied. It appears so.

11

- - - - - - - - - - -

YEARS LATER, FRANK TURNER described his role on the Clay Committee as "developing the papers, the numbers and all of the mechanics — what do we want to do, how do we do it, how do we find it — and converting all of those into proposals which the president would then transmit to the Congress." As encompassing as that sounds, it understates his actual duties. He was the chief source of statistics and technical background for the committee, the explainer of why things were as they were and what had been tried, successfully and otherwise, in years past — the font to which the members turned again and again to check their assumptions and ideas. He was the recorder of meetings, the writer of letters, and the author of every draft of every paper the group produced. He was the chief of the committee's staff, which was drawn from the bureau's ranks. He also served as liaison with an advisory panel of industry experts, who brainstormed ideas the main committee might consider. Turner also described himself as "kind of a glorified gofer" but admitted that in this "very 'hey you' type of organization, very informal," it was the "gofers doing the actual work."

General Clay had three main assignments: determine what kind of highway system the country needed, find out how much it would cost, and decide how to pay for it. In addition, he was to work with the governors' committee to ensure that whatever he came up with was OK by them. The first question, as far as Turner and du Pont were concerned, was decided — improving primary and secondary roads and building the long-planned interstate system would do the trick.

The money question would be answered by a study already under way at the bureau. Though incomplete — the inquiry wouldn't be released until months after the Clay Committee's work was finished — it showed that the nation's road and highway needs over the coming ten years carried a bill of about $101 billion. That was for *all* roads and highways. Of that total, the bureau reckoned it would cost $23.2 billion to build the interstate system laid out in 1947, not including the segments yet to be designated in and around cities. Clay accepted the bureau figure and chipped in another $4 billion for the city segments — a token amount, as the committee knew; it was careful to say the $4 billion would cover "only the most important connecting roads and is not intended to meet the total needs in this category." That qualification was soon forgotten; the estimated cost of the interstate program soon became lodged in the public consciousness as $27.2 billion.

The remaining three-quarters of the $101 billion would bring America's other three million miles of road up to a condition "adequate for traffic demands in the year 1974," as Clay put it, when the load carried by highways was expected to be about half again as great as that of the mid-fifties. Left unchanged, state and federal taxes and fees over the construction period would bring in about $47 billion, so the committee had to find new sources for some $54 billion.

The general was undaunted. His committee "accepts as a starting premise the fact that the penalties of our obsolete roads system are large and that the price of inefficiency is paid in dollars, lives and national insecurity," he said. He had to succeed, and damn it, he would.

For two days in early October, a procession of auto industry, trucking, and road-building spokesmen testified before the panel. The Automobile Manufacturers Association urged "special emphasis" on the interstate system. AASHO suggested that the feds pay the whole interstate bill to assure a quick finish. The committee heard from John Bragdon, too, via a barrage of memos on the virtues of — once again — toll financing, as well as his own scheme for an interstate system of 26,000 miles that would bypass urban centers. Clay paid him little mind; though turnpikes were the rage at the time — some 5,242 miles of toll superhighways were open, being built, financed, or authorized in twenty-three states — he'd come to share the bureau's view that few could pay their own freight.

Instead, Clay favored bond financing for the new highways. Advisers warned that the idea would face a rough reception in the Senate, where Virginia's Harry F. Byrd, chairman of the powerful Finance Committee, was known to be pathologically opposed to bonded debt. The Great Uncompromiser paid the counsel little heed.

So it happened that the committee recommended the creation of a Federal Highway Corporation, its board appointed by the president. This corporation would exist only to issue bonds and, over a ten-year period, use the proceeds to pay the states for the cost of building the already-designated interstate system. The bonds would be paid off with outlays from the treasury equal to receipts from the federal taxes on gasoline and lubricating oils.

"It will," Clay promised, "achieve our objective while entailing no increase in either the Federal tax rates on these items or the national debt limit." At the insistence of the governors, the committee would place only minimal burden on the states; Washington would cover 90 cents of every dollar spent on the interstates.

By late December, Turner had taken the report through at least three drafts, each written in longhand, augmented by scribbles on White House scratch pads, and typed late at night at home in Arlington. Successive drafts were mimeographed, distributed to the membership, edited, and returned to Turner, who would consult with Clay on any changes. Turner's final draft declared a "safe and efficient highway network" to be "essential to America's military and civil defense" and played up the latter. "Large-scale evacuation of cities would be needed in the event of A-bomb or H-bomb attack," he wrote. "The Federal Civil Defense Administrator has said the withdrawal task is the biggest problem ever faced in the world. It has been determined as a matter of Federal policy that at least seventy million people would have to be evacuated from target areas in case of threatened or actual enemy attack. No urban area in the country today has highway facilities equal to this task."

A federal role was essential. "State highway departments cannot meet the need for this type of facility," Turner wrote. "At the current rate of improvement, the interstate network would not reach even a tolerable level of efficiency in half a century. It is clearly necessary in the national interest to accelerate the program."

Had Turner's contributions to the interstates ended there, with authoring the Eisenhower administration's grand plan, he would still be remembered by the program's students. Francis du Pont, vacationing in Europe, dropped Turner a line from Rome to thank him for "the outstanding job you have done for Lucius Clay and I hope posterity." The committee's report went to the president on January 11, 1955; three days later, du Pont, having returned to the States, quit his bureau post to campaign full-time for it.

But as predicted, the committee's work was in for a rough ride. Congressmen balked at a provision that would reimburse states for the cost of turnpikes they'd already built. Others scoffed at the administration's insistence that the bond financing didn't really count as debt. Still others objected to the $11.5 billion in interest payments due over the thirty-year life of the bonds; that was money, they felt, better spent on actual roads. The new chairman of the Senate's Subcommittee on Roads, Albert Gore of Tennessee, called it "a screwy plan which could lead the country into inflationary ruin." Criticism bubbled up even within the cabinet. Sinclair Weeks passed du Pont a note questioning the need for the Federal Highway Corporation. "A new agency as proposed seems to me unnecessary and undesirable," he wrote. "There are too many independent agencies in the Government already."

Eisenhower crafted an elegant cover letter to the report, observing that "together, the uniting forces of our communication and transportation are dynamic elements in the very name we bear — United States," and did his best to soften congressional resistance in meetings with leaders of both parties. He made little progress before presenting the report to Congress on February 22, 1955 — where, in hearings before Gore's subcommittee, Harry Byrd lived up to expectations. A native of Virginia's Shenandoah Valley, Byrd had rescued his family's small-town newspaper from failure and served four years as the commonwealth's governor, guided in both ventures by one hard-and-fast principle: debt was trouble. Public debt was even more so, amounting, in his view, to a mortgage on every house, property, and transaction. Virginia had not borrowed a dime on his watch. In fact, he boasted, it hadn't issued highway bonds since 1835.

Byrd's testimony, typed single-space, occupied seven legal-size pages. The Clay plan would "destroy sound budgetary procedure," he said. It used "legerdemain" to disguise debt. It removed the government's highway appropriation from annual congressional review. "Nothing has been proposed during my twenty-two years in the United States Senate that would do more to wreck our fiscal budget system," Byrd warned. "As we spend and spend and borrow and borrow, the least we can do for future generations — our children and grandchildren, on whom we would place astronomical burdens — is to keep an honest set of books so they will know what debts we of this generation have incurred for them to pay."

Among Clay's defenders was treasury secretary George M. Humphrey, who argued that critics were reading the proposal all wrong. The gas tax was a form of toll, every bit as much as one collected in a booth; it was just based on fuel consumption instead of distance traveled. And the $11.5 billion in interest wasn't wasted. "By paying the interest you will have roads for several years when you wouldn't otherwise have them," he pointed out. "Don't say you don't get anything for the interest money. You do get years of use."

Still, Clay's proposal was doomed. The Senate killed it by a two-to-one margin on May 25, 1955, opting instead for a bill written by Gore that provided a third as much money for interstates, spread out over five years. Over in the House, it seemed plain to Rep. George H. Fallon, chairman of the Subcommittee on Roads, that both the Gore and Clay bills were headed nowhere. He decided to draft a compromise and turned to Frank Turner for help.

Tall, bespectacled, baldheaded, Fallon shared Turner's mild manner and devotion to roads. No other subject so captured the energies of the congressman: his rare floor speeches were invariably about highways, which was what, his colleagues joked, his middle initial stood for. The fifty-two-year-old Fallon's only newsworthy moment had come in 1954, when four Puerto Rican nationalists opened fire on the House from the visitors' gallery, spraying the chamber with about thirty rounds. The Big Man from Baltimore, as he was sometimes known, had been a big target; he'd caught two slugs in the hip.

Now he and Turner crafted a bill doling out $24 billion for what Fallon renamed the National System of Interstate and Defense Highways, and relying on tax hikes on fuel, heavy trucks, and tires to cover Washington's 90 percent share — a "pay-as-you-go" feature to satisfy Byrd and other fiscal conservatives. The bill seemed a winner. Lawmakers were predisposed to like the interstate system — after all, it promised federal money, and lots of it, to every state — and Fallon offered a practical plan to pay for it. Except that the U.S. trucking fraternity cared for neither a doubled tax on diesel fuel nor jacked-up levies on tires; both, it complained, would saddle truckers with a disproportionate share of the system's costs. The industry buried the Capitol in a hundred thousand telegrams, ten thousand of them to Fallon alone. The oil and rubber lobbies were vocal in their opposition to the bill, too. Stout hearts quavered on the Hill, and more trouble, of a parliamentary nature, erupted behind closed doors. On July 27, a short while after they killed the Clay bill, congressmen clubbed the Fallon measure to death by a huge margin, 292 votes to 123. His Democratic brethren abandoned Fallon in droves.

The defeat came as a shock to the bureau, the press, even congressional leaders. It was crushing to Turner, who between the Clay and Fallon bills had been slaving around the clock on highway legislation for close to a year. Francis du Pont passed his office and saw him sitting, stricken, at his desk. Du Pont hurried to his own office and returned with a high-end watch that he'd bought for Turner on his trip to Europe, and that he'd planned to award him on the bill's passage.

As he presented it, he explained that time was their ally; Turner's patience and hard work would eventually, inevitably, pay off.

• • •

Dwight Eisenhower assuaged his disappointment over the events in Congress by fleeing Washington for most of August and September, splitting time between his farm in Gettysburg and his wife's home place in Denver, where on most days he squeezed in a little government business among long stretches of golf at the Cherry Hills Country Club. It was while playing a round with the club pro on September 23 that Ike first complained of what he mistook for indigestion, blaming his lunch — a burger with Bermuda onion — and pesky telephone interruptions from the State Department. In the wee hours of the following morning, Mamie and the president's doctor drove him to Fitzsimons Army Hospital, where all learned that he was having a major heart attack.

He was still recovering on January 5, 1956, during his State of the Union message. Ike was relaxing in Key West at the time; a clerk read the address to Congress, meaning that a second of the president's important speeches in which he beat the drum for highways was delivered *in absentia*. "Legislation to provide a modern, interstate highway system is even more urgent this year than last," the speech read, "for twelve months have now passed in which we have fallen further behind in road construction needed for the personal safety, the general prosperity, the national security of the American people."

Indeed, travel had jumped by a third since 1950. America was home to 62.8 million vehicles, a fast-growing percentage of them trucks that shared, or failed to share, the nation's skinny numbered highways. The average weighed more than twelve tons.

"If we are ever to solve our mounting traffic problem," the president's message continued, "the whole interstate system must be authorized as one project, to be completed approximately within the specified time. Only in this way can the required planning and engineering be accomplished without the confusion and waste unavoidable in a piecemeal approach." He repeated the pitch eleven days later in his annual budget message. Authorize the system as a single unit, he urged, "in order that it may be accomplished over a period of approximately ten years with the greatest economy."

The president's highway fever aside, there was little to give a wagering taxpayer much reason to bet on an interstate bill in the coming session of Congress. But much was happening behind the scenes. Back in the late summer, immediately after the Fallon bill's defeat, the trucking lobby had been exultant — its successful campaign against higher taxes had been a glorious success. It was only after the heady rush of victory dissipated that the truckers came to realize: Hey, wait a minute — we're not going to get highways. And with that came the sober judgment that they would benefit far more from the proposed interstates than they would give up in taxes and fees.

By January 26, 1956, when George Fallon introduced a new highway bill, the truckers had softened their position, and the naysayers in Congress, having had months to mull over their failure to deliver a boon to their constituents, had done likewise. What seemed a lost cause when Ike had his myocardial infarction was beginning to attract something a lot like optimism.

Fallon's new bill, again crafted with the help of Frank Turner, was much like the old one. It called for 90 percent federal financing of a forty-thousand-mile interstate system, to be built over thirteen years. Fallon called for pay-as-you-go financing but left the details to a separate bill being stitched together by Rep. T. Hale Boggs, a Louisiana Democrat on the Ways and Means Committee.

On February 6, Boggs introduced the resulting Highway Revenue Act of 1956, which dictated that road-related taxes be set aside for highway purposes. The following week, treasury secretary George Humphrey testified that to really restrict car-related tax money to roads, the government would do well to "follow a practice similar to the practice that is followed for Social Security." The practice in question was a trust fund.

Congressmen seized on the idea. For the first time in the automobile age, as Boggs told his colleagues, the American motorist would "pay these taxes with the assurance that he will be the direct beneficiary of every penny which he pays and he will pay with the knowledge that every cent derived from these taxes will be devoted exclusively to his personal convenience and safety." In April, Fallon introduced the Federal-Aid Highway Act of 1956, combining his own bill and Boggs's.

Carl Graham Fisher — cyclist, autoist, and speed demon, and the father of America's first web of long-distance motor roads.

Library of Congress

The fearless Fisher poses at the wheel of a race car in 1904. Five years later in Indianapolis, he learned the hard way that horse-drawn road technology wasn't up to the demands of high-speed auto traffic. *Chicago History Museum: Chicago Daily News/SDN-002710*

All photos courtesy of the Federal Highway Administration unless otherwise noted.

Thomas Harris MacDonald at the turn of the century, when he left home for Iowa State and began his career as America's greatest road builder.

Courtesy of Lynda Weidinger

A common scene in the early years of automobility: horses running side by side (and nervously) with motor cars.

Herbert Fairbank, MacDonald's ideological right hand. His vision of how superhighways might ease congestion in the cities — and wipe out slums at the same time — helped launch the interstate program before World War II.

MacDonald takes a break to shoot pictures on a trip out West. Almost painfully formal, "the Chief" was rarely without a jacket and tie, even while camping and hiking. *Courtesy of Lynda Weidinger*

Short, shy, and the very antithesis of flash, Frank Turner spent years laboring as a public roads engineer before his work on the Alaska Highway brought him to the Chief's attention — and launched his rise to the bureau's top.

Caroline Fuller MacDonald (right) poses with her lookalike sister, Jane, outside the MacDonald home in College Station, Texas. An unheralded influence on U.S. highways for three decades, she married the Chief after his dismissal.

Courtesy of Lynda Weidinger

Dwight Eisenhower receives the Clay Committee's report, which was fated to suffer an icy reception in Congress. Lucius Clay stands at far left; beside him is the committee's secretary, Frank Turner.

Army trucks roll over one of the loops of the AASHO Road Test near Ottawa, Illinois. The experiment, the grandest of its kind ever attempted, yielded valuable data on the relative merits of various pavements.

San Francisco's Embarcadero Freeway, a double-decker eyesore that separated the city from its famed waterfront and passed just feet from the beloved Ferry Building. The highway's sins provoked the first shot in the Freeway Revolt of the 1960s.

Though intended to handle the traffic of the mid-seventies, early urban interstates seemed to breed new users and filled with cars far ahead of schedule. Here, Chicago's Northwest Expressway in 1961.

Joe Wiles of Baltimore: Quiet and capable, this scientist and family man helped lead opposition to highways that promised to uproot thousands of citizens.

Courtesy of Carmen Wiles-Artis

The shape of things to come: A classic cloverleaf marks the intersections of Interstate 280 and Stevens Creek Road in San José, California.

The land-gobbling nature of superhighways was particularly apparent in cities, where the fat ribbons of concrete claimed thousands of homes and businesses. Here, Interstate 70 swoops into downtown Kansas City, slicing through a neighborhood along the way.

The juggernaut: A construction crew lays down the bed of the future Interstate 94 in North Dakota, 1967.

In an exercise repeated some 55,000 times throughout the system, workers bridge the Alamosa River near Truth or Consequences, New Mexico, for Interstate 25.

From the air, the interstate system's curves and overlaps achieve a beauty often lost at ground level; witness the interchange of interstates 5 and 10 in Los Angeles.

The debate that commenced on the House floor a few days later offered more friendly banter than rhetorical combat. Freshman Democrat Kenneth J. Gray of Illinois walked to the well with a bouquet of artificial flowers representing Fallon's 1955 bill. "Everything looked rosy last year, until the powerful trucking lobby removed one rose from our bouquet," Gray said. He snapped a rose from the bunch, then did the same for the other interests he blamed for killing the measure. "When we were finished, nothing remained but stems that were completely barren."

Now, he said, it was up to the House to make amends. He urged his colleagues to pass the new bill, to "transform the barren stems into a beautiful and growing bouquet of roses." With that, he pressed a spring-loaded trigger in the bottom of the bouquet, causing a spray of white roses to burst into view. His fellow congressmen roared.

Gray was pranking to the choir. When it came to a vote, the bill passed, 388 to 19.

Over in the Senate, the Fallon-Boggs bill was split in two and the halves referred to different committees. Public Works got Fallon's part, chopped out most of its text, and substituted language from Albert Gore.

The senator was, of course, father to the future vice president and Nobel laureate. The senior Gore had grown up in the Cumberland River valley of north-central Tennessee, had paid his way through the State Teachers' College by fiddling at barn dances and teaching in the rural schools thereabout, and had attended night law school at the Nashville YMCA. He'd eventually won a seat in Congress but had quit to join the army, and while fighting in Europe had a formative experience not unlike that which Ike would later claim: Gore led an attack on a German outpost only to find, once he'd captured it, that the enemy troops had sped off on the autobahn. "They had left that town very quickly," he later said. "It occurred to me then that our country needed something like that for defense, as well as economic development purposes."

As Tennessee's junior senator he had a second epiphany, this one in the company of Frank Turner. "He invited me to see a new federal highway about a hundred miles from Washington," Gore said, recalling that the journey posed "no big trouble as we went down.

"But we came back at night and every little piece on each side of the new road there was a honky-tonk or a service station," he said. "In three years there had been so many wrecks that it had been nicknamed 'Suicide Alley.' This drove home to me the absolute necessity of the cloverleaf."

Now he offered a bill that differed only in minor respects from Fallon's. The Boggs half of the House bill, meanwhile, was sent to the Senate Finance Committee, which held two days of hearings on the measure. Again, Treasury Secretary Humphrey testified, and again he made a major contribution. He endorsed the bill with enthusiasm, he told the committee, but according to his projections, Washington's obligations to the states could exceed the trust fund's balance about six years into the program. The feds' regular payments into the kitty would generate a surplus early on, and again at the program's end, but might fall short in the middle, as construction kicked into high gear. He offered a simple solution. And so the bill acquired what became known as the Byrd Amendment, which limited spending each year to the cash expected in the fund. If the treasury secretary projected a shortfall, the payouts to each state would be reduced proportionally to balance the books.

The amended bill passed both houses on June 26. "It is hereby declared to be essential to the national interest to provide for the early completion of the 'National System of Interstate Highways,'" Section 108(a) of the Federal-Aid Highway Act of 1956 opened. "It is the intent of the Congress that the Interstate System be completed as nearly as practicable over a thirteen-year period and that the entire System in all the States be brought to simultaneous completion. Because of its primary importance to the national defense, the name of such system is hereby changed to the 'National System of Interstate and Defense Highways.'"

The finished document extended the interstate system to forty-one thousand miles, all of it designed and built to uniform standards and to accommodate the traffic projected for 1975. It authorized spending $25 billion on the roads over thirteen years, with the biggest outlays in the program's middle, from 1960 to 1967. It further boosted the taxes on gas, diesel, and tires, as expected, as well as the sales tax on trucks and buses; applied a new tax on the camelback rubber used in tire retreading; and imposed an annual registration fee on heavy trucks.

In other words, it bore little resemblance to the bill Ike had sponsored; the chief contributor to the system's financing in the executive branch wasn't the president, but Frank Turner. Eisenhower was back in the hospital, this time recovering from surgery for ileitis. He signed the bill into law in his room at Walter Reed, without witnesses or fuss, on June 29, 1956. Eighteen years after Thomas MacDonald and Herbert Fairbank first committed them to paper, a dozen after Congress formally created them, the interstates were at long last on the way.

Frank Turner's hand in the success was plain to everyone in the bureau. "Mr. Turner completed his many arduous assignments of a widely varying nature through application of great administrative wisdom, tact, and diplomacy," Cap Curtiss, now the bureau's chief, wrote in a May 1956 performance evaluation. "In addition, he contributed unselfishly of his own personal time to the interests of Public Roads, working long days and weeks continuously.

"Specifically, his assistance to the committees of Congress considering highway legislation was superb inasmuch as his technical guidance was unusually sound and his personal associations with members of Congress were so well conducted that he added materially to the prestige and confidence of Congress in the Bureau of Public Roads."

Even before the final votes, Curtiss presented Turner with a $750 check, the largest that the Department of Commerce had granted one of its own as part of a civil service incentive program. The quiet force of Turner's opinions had helped frame committee discussions. His humility, along with his ability to provide the members with virtually any useful statistic, cemented their trust. His obvious devotion to public service earned their respect.

And he'd had another weapon in his arsenal. All through the previous year, while the Clay Committee had finished its report and the White House had greased the skids for its release, while Congress had debated and killed the highway bills placed before it, planners in the bureau had remained focused on refining the network's routing. In January 1955, the bureau had requested that the states submit requests for interstate mileage in their cities, to be parceled out from the 2,300 leftover miles authorized back in the forties but still unassigned.

Most highway departments were ready to do so; they'd been planning those urban routes for the better part of a decade. In September, the bureau had released the results — a slim book titled *General Location of National System of Interstate Highways Including All Additional Routes at Urban Areas*. That title was nearly as long as the text, which consisted of three sentences; the pages were otherwise devoted to simple maps of every major city directly served by the network, with the approximate routes of interstates through and around them rendered as thick black lines. Its title being too much of a mouthful even for engineers, it became known by the color of its jacket: the *Yellow Book*.

It was not intended to be a landmark document. Turner later dismissed it as "a kind of routine scratch pad memorandum to ourselves," an exercise "to diagram these routes that we had reserved for the urban areas, even before we got around to actually locating them on the ground.

"They were never intended, never thought of as being designated routes," he said. "You couldn't tell within a mile of where a route was going to be on the ground."

Indeed, the renderings were ballpark. Fort Worth, for example, was partially circled by a beltway that doesn't much resemble the full loop of today, and the crisscrossing highways coming into town from north, east, and west didn't correspond closely with reality, either; only the freeway over Turner's parents' house was depicted close to its actual line.

Still, you can figure out which interstates the 1955 lines represent, and in similar fashion most other maps — those for St. Louis, San Antonio, and Richmond, for Tulsa and Des Moines, Norfolk and Portland, Rapid City and Roanoke — were simplified, stylized versions of what we got.

Big deal or no within the bureau, outside the agency the *Yellow Book* packed a wallop, especially among elected officials who for the first time saw how the talk of urban interstates would translate into steel and concrete. To them, the imprecise maps read like wonderful promises.

No doubt Turner had understood as much. Late in 1955, after the defeat of that year's highway bills, the bureau had sent the *Yellow Book* to every member of Congress.

12

- - - - - - - - - - - -

THE AMERICA OF 1956 was a baby factory. American women of the period bore an average of 3.7 children, and families were outgrowing their cramped urban quarters. The American dream had morphed in the postwar years to include a rectangle of lawn and a split-level rambler, a patio and a grill, and to slake the nascent demand for this ideal, builders were buying up cropland at every city's fringe and putting up cookie-cutter houses on quarter-acre lots, one beside the next, by the thousands. The tools with which Americans commuted between work and these far-flung new subdivisions were not up to the job. Aside from a few short, overloaded expressways in a handful of cities, the main drags to the edge of town were narrow and glutted with machines that bore little resemblance, beyond the basics, to those we drive today.

Consider that today's new cars routinely cover a hundred thousand miles without a spark-plug change and are expected to achieve double that mileage over their useful lives; engines are computer-timed to the thousandth of a second, the better to ensure clean ignition, maximum compression, optimal power; bodies are crash-worthy, aerodynamically clean, rustproof. Contrast all of that with the spindly, underpowered, brittle confusion of moving parts that Carl Fisher drove home from the New York auto show in 1900 — its horsepower measured in single digits, its steering by tiller — or the stripped-bare Winton in which Dr. Horatio Nelson Jackson lurched across the country three years later.

The halfway point between those pioneer horseless carriages and today's cars can be found in the models for sale the autumn after Eisenhower signed the 1956 act: the '57 Ford, the '57 Plymouth, the year's DeSoto and Caddy and Chrysler, and in particular the iconic '57 Chevy. They're now as far in the past as the first wheezy buggies to ply American roads were when work began on the interstates, and as different from modern cars as they were from Carl Fisher's first ride.

Behold the Chevy. It didn't come in different models of compacts, mid-sized cars, or land yachts in 1957. Besides the Corvette, the company's only model was simply the Chevy; distinctive nameplates such as Impala, Chevelle, and Nova didn't come along until later. A buyer was instead bombarded with variations on a single theme. That one Chevy came as a two-door or four-door sedan, a two-door hardtop, a four-door hardtop, a two-door or four-door six-passenger wagon, a four-door nine-passenger wagon, a two-door Nomad "sports" wagon, and a convertible. Within most of those styles were three trim levels: the economical 150, with a bare-bones interior and little chrome decoration on the skin; the midline 210, with nicer seats and more bling; and the Bel Air, the top-of-the-line, all-luxe version, with shiny aluminum inlays along its flanks and golden accents.

Just among wagons, one had more than a dozen options, what with the available six-cylinder engine, the 265-cubic-inch V8, and the Turbo-Fire 283 introduced with that year's model — which came with a two-barrel carburetor, a high-performance four-barrel, or the first fuel-injection system ever offered on a production car.

Every variation was a stylish machine. Most memorably, the Chevy had fins — gargantuan, chrome-edged things that jutted a foot aft of the trunk or hatch, so Jet Age and out of scale that they'd have been dismissed as ridiculous, as whimsy run amok, had they not looked so damn *great*. They weren't the car's only Buck Rogers touches. The taillights resembled fighter plane exhausts. Chrome gun sights were fitted into the curving hood. The bumper guards bore crosshairs, unless covered with optional rubber warheads.

The Chevy line shared weaknesses, as well. By today's standards, the cars were primitive — unreliable, quick to wear, blundering, dangerous. Chevrolet boasted that its small-block V8, married to a new Turboglide automatic transmission with "triple-turbine-takeoff," was "as quiet as a contented cat and as smooth as cream," and "cat-quick in response when you ask for action!" But it wasn't uncommon to see a '57 pulled to the roadside on a hot summer day, hood up and radiator steaming; thermostats of the period were notoriously untrustworthy, radiators too, and even new cars boiled over. It was no rare event to find the car stranded in an icy driveway, either, immobilized by a frozen fuel line or balky mechanical fuel pump. Tires had tubes prone to catastrophic blowouts. Nylon-ply models were leaky, quick to bald, weak at the sidewalls.

Carburetion, the blending of gasoline and air on which combustion depends, called on a choreography of twitchy parts. Generating the spark necessary to begin the process relied on points, gaps, and a battery that had to be watered like a fern. The Chevy jounced along on heavy springs and relied on Stone Age brakes that quit working when wet. Rust set in at the faintest hint of sea air or road salt. The car was middle-aged at thirty thousand miles; flipping the odometer into six figures was a rarity.

The Chevy was unforgiving, too. In a collision, the '57 didn't absorb energy; it was a battering ram a foot longer than a Hummer H3, nearly two tons of dumb metal strapped to a big-assed engine, its steering column a spear aimed at the driver's breastbone, its beltless passengers free to carom about an all-metal cabin softened only by a thin layer of paint.

Imagine this car by the millions crowded onto the narrow U.S. highways linking city and country, too heavy and big and loose to handle unexpected curves or come to a fast, safe stop, flanked by driveways and intersecting streets that at any moment might spit cross traffic the Chevy was ill equipped to evade. Imagine a long, wearying vacation trip in such a car, stoplights confounding your attempts to maintain a reasonable pace, tractors and slow trucks hogging and clogging even the biggest and best roads: four punishing days from New York to Miami; close to two weeks to go coast to coast. And imagine how strange and wonderfully liberating it must have been to steer that lumbering beast up a new interstate entrance ramp.

It didn't take long for the states to jump on the program. Barely a month after the president signed the Federal-Aid Highway Act of 1956, they had more than $800 million worth of projects in the planning pipeline and a slew ready to advertise for bids. Eisenhower declared himself "gratified."

Cap Curtiss, the bureau's top man, tried to cool expectations that work would start so swiftly everywhere. "A few drivers will see actual construction beginning in their particular areas within the next few months," he told an interviewer, but though the interstates would "spread rapidly in terms of a national total . . . the sheer magnitude of the job and the thousands of individual projects mean that there will be no magical overnight relief."

Ike was among the impatient, however. He decided it might goose things along to put a new boss in charge of the project — a presidential appointee who'd be confirmed by the Senate, and who'd be able to use his higher national profile to better herd the states. At the president's behest, Congress created the post of federal highway administrator, who'd be top adviser to the White House on roads policy and oversee the interstate program while Cap Curtiss ran the bureau's day-to-day operation.

That October, word came that the job would go to "one of the world's greatest builders of roads," as the newspapers knighted him — Bertram D. Tallamy of New York, architect of the 562-mile New York Thruway, the longest toll superhighway in America. The tall, mustachioed Tallamy had spent several successful years in contracting before chucking his private-side career for public service, helping devise New York's highway design standards, working with cities to develop regional plans and arterial routes, and eventually overseeing all of the state's public works. Tallamy was an avid driver, averaging 40,000 miles a year behind the wheel. He'd planned and built the limited-access Thruway in six years, during which he'd demonstrated a passion for walking, too; he'd covered all of the expressway's 427 miles between New York City and Buffalo on foot.

Tallamy wanted the job but had obligations in New York that would keep him there for several months. For the interim, Eisenhower appointed another well-known engineer, John A. Volpe of Massachusetts, who'd built an international construction company from scratch before serving three years as his state's public works chief. Volpe was sworn in with Ike holding the Bible and thus became the first person in what remains today the nation's highest highway post, the equivalent to an assistant secretary. Consulting all the while with Tallamy, Volpe rejiggered the bureau to better shoulder its new, unwieldy responsibilities. More decisions would fall to the field offices, ensuring limber response to state needs. Departments were split up, functions shifted. And on January 1, 1957, Frank Turner got a promotion.

He was now deputy commissioner and chief engineer, second only to Curtiss among the bureau's career employees and in essence the agency's chief operating officer. Officially speaking, responsibility for the interstates might fall to the federal highway administrator, but as a practical matter, it was Turner's hide on the line. As an official description of his duties reported, he had "specific responsibility for evaluation and progress" of the largest highway program in history—an undertaking that "involved new concepts of design and construction, right-of-way procedures, financing, recruitment and utilization of engineering manpower, and the coordination of and cooperation with the nation's entire highway plant."

Turner's new title and responsibilities had no discernible effect on the man. He rode the bus to and from work most days, for all appearances a midlevel functionary—a quiet, short guy in a dark off-the-rack suit lugging an overstuffed briefcase, one among faceless thousands in the capital.

As the first concrete was poured on widely scattered bits of the system, AASHO adopted, in July 1956, the major design features that would govern its form. They were lifted straight from the bureau's work in the thirties and forties: divided highways of at least four lanes and with access limited to grade-separated interchanges, except in lonesome western stretches; lanes twelve feet wide; grades, banking, and sight distances to permit speeds of seventy miles per hour on the flat.

The bureau and AASHO also mulled how they might label the new highways to distinguish them from the existing numbered grid. They received a lot of advice. One New Mexico official, convinced that a new arrangement of numbers laid over the old would ask too much of drivers, pitched the idea of using letters. "This would allow as many as twenty-six route designations by single digits," he pointed out, "and at the same time, avoid confusion." Once the twenty-six were exhausted, the system could move to two-letter combinations.

But Edwin W. James's 1925 system had worn well for more than thirty years. Following numbered highways was simple, logical. The public understood them and appreciated that a driver could discern much about his location simply by the number of the highway he drove. The nation's highway engineers weren't much for replacing something that worked.

So AASHO's Route Numbering Subcommittee proposed recycling the old arrangement. As in James's system, east-west interstates would be even-numbered, with the longest and most important ending in zero, and north-south freeways would carry odd numbers, the principal routes ending in 1 and 5. Only this time the order would be reversed — the lowest interstate numbers would be in the far Southwest, where the U.S. highway system had its highest. Interstate 5, running from San Diego to Blaine, Washington, would be the westernmost major north-south interstate, occupying roughly the same corridor as old U.S. 101. I-95 would be the easternmost, alongside U.S. 1.

The only places where you might encounter numbers that overlapped with those of the older highways were a broad strip across the country's waist, and another running a couple of hundred miles either side of the Mississippi. To stave off having both areas crowded with too-similar numbers in the fifties and sixties, AASHO ditched the use of I-50 or I-60 and proposed that there be no interstate and U.S. highway with the same number in any state.

All of the numbers would be one- or two-digit. It wasn't until more than a year later that three-digit numbers came along, identifying auxiliary interstates — beltways and loops, which have an even-numbered prefix tacked onto the number of the interstate to which they connect at both ends, and spurs, which are connected to the main line at just one end and bear an odd-numbered prefix.

Not only did the numbering run from west to east and from south to north, but the roads themselves did, too. Mileposts, borrowed from Frank Turner's boyhood, would begin at zero on a state's southern or western borders and climb as the road headed north or east.* Thus, the mapped system runs left to right and bottom to top; Bostonians might think of I-90, at 3,099 miles the longest interstate, as starting near their city's airport, but you could argue it actually ends there and starts in Seattle.

Under the new system, I-90 and two other principal east-west routes ran all the way from the Pacific to the Atlantic. I-10 would stretch from Los Angeles to Jacksonville, Florida; and I-80, from San Francisco to New York, for the most part shadowing the Lincoln Highway. A fourth, I-40, would come close to going the distance, beginning a couple of hours northeast of L.A. in the desert outpost of Barstow and ending in Wilmington, North Carolina.

Interstate 20 (Kent, Texas, to Florence, South Carolina) and I-70 (Denver to Baltimore) would cross a fair piece, but not all, of the continent. As for I-30, well, it didn't fit the mold of principal highway at all, covering only the 367 miles from Fort Worth to Little Rock. Like the numbered U.S. highways, the interstate system was peppered with exceptions to its rules.

On the same day they unveiled the numbers, highway officials also introduced Americans to the system's jazzy new logo. The AASHO subcommittee had received scores of ideas for a new interstate sign, in a slew of shapes and colors; one, for instance, displayed the route num-

---

* Turner argued for years that exits should be numbered according to their mileposts, too. A good many states disagreed, preferring sequential numbering. Not until 2009 did the feds mandate that Turner's approach would be a system standard; the seven states still numbering their exits in sequence were given until 2020 to make the switch.

ber within an outline of the contiguous states; another, inside a rather Teutonic eagle; a third surrounded the number with a fat letter *I*.

The subcommittee whittled the pile down to four and had them erected on the side of an Illinois back road, so that they could be judged in all weather, at all times of day. The winner was mostly the brainchild of Richard Oliver, a senior traffic engineer in the Texas Highway Department. It was, of course, the universally recognized red, white, and blue shield still used with only slight alteration today: a sleeker, simpler shape than that used on the U.S. highways, bordered and lettered in white, a thin strip of red across the top bearing the word *Interstate*, the balance a field of blue on which the state's name and the route number were printed.

AASHO was picky about the colors, dictating that the white be "relatively free of yellow or silver hues," and that the red have "a slight orange tint that is better for color-blind people." The dominant color would be "a true blue without excessive purple or gray hues" and "essentially the same color at night under incandescent headlight illumination as during the day." AASHO eventually had the design trademarked.

Turner and his colleagues devoted considerable discussion to the network's other signs, such as those announcing exits and the mileage to upcoming cities. The bureau had been experimenting with sign technology for a couple of years. In March and April of 1955, it had hired a corps of volunteers to drive 1951 Pontiacs across a darkened parking lot, peering at signs containing six words — BALK, FARM, NAVY, STOP, ZONE, and DUCK — in different combinations of typeface and spacing; the experiment showed that some fonts were easier to read than others, and that as distance increased between letters, so did the distance at which a driver could make out the words.

Now it had to decide what color the signs should be. Tallamy favored blue, the color used on his New York Thruway. Others in the bureau liked green. The question was settled with another experiment, a two-week trial in which signs in blue, green, and black were posted along an unfinished leg of Washington's Capital Beltway and eyeballed by hundreds of volunteer drivers. Nearly six in ten voted for green, and most were partial to up-and-down lettering versus all caps. Tallamy approved the white-on-green design in January 1958.

It remained to standardize the surfaces of the roads themselves. In 1950–51, the bureau had collaborated on a series of wear tests in Maryland and in 1952–54 had undertaken a $3 million test of asphalt surfaces in Idaho, but a program as big as the interstates demanded a more comprehensive effort. It behooved the bureau to nail down what mixes and thicknesses of pavement lasted longest, and at the same time to establish the maximum loads that pavement should bear, a number on which the states had never achieved consensus.* Turner turned to the Highway Research Board for help and, with backing from an old Arkansas colleague, Alf Johnson, who was now executive director of AASHO, devised what still ranks among the biggest civil engineering experiments in history. On the plains west of Chicago, the bureau and its partners built a chain of six looping test tracks, each a quiltwork of paving types, thicknesses, and base layers, 836 test sections in all.

Then they moved a company of army Transportation Corps soldiers into a barracks at the complex, put them behind the wheels of 126 trucks — everything from pickups to big semi rigs, all loaded with concrete blocks — and sent them around the loops. Nineteen hours a day they drove, every day for two years, maintaining a steady thirty-five miles per hour on the straightaways, thirty in the curves. They racked up more than seventeen million miles.

Along the way, the strain the trucks caused was measured by electric gauges, until three hundred million pieces of data had been recorded on punched paper tape. While a big Bendix computer deciphered the readings, the staff of what would be known as the AASHO Road Test

---

* This is how senseless and arbitrary some load limits were: A half-dozen states had limits dating to the early twenties, when trucks ran on solid rubber tires. Those tires were thought capable of handling 800 pounds of load per inch of tread width, and the widest tires on the market measured fourteen inches across. That meant the maximum load per tire would be 11,200 pounds, and because an axle had a tire at each end, *voilà* — the laws capped loads at 22,400 pounds per axle. Unfortunately, while this might have preserved some truck tires, it did nothing to preserve roads. And by the 1950s, no truck had run on solid rubber in decades.

were measuring the pavement's roughness and grading it on a five-point scale, zero being impassable, five being glass-smooth.

What they learned filled six volumes and came down to this: The thicker the pavement and subgrade, the better. And: Trucks wear out roads in a predictable fashion. As Turner later explained, "We got a fairly simplified equation out of the thing, that X number of trips generated Y amount of damage in Z . . . period of time."

The test had limits. It was conducted in a single location and climate, over a fairly short period of time, and its science was only as good as the art to which it was married — predicting traffic volumes and the mix of vehicles for a particular stretch of pavement. As Richard Weingroff, the Federal Highway Administration's unofficial historian, points out: "Life has a bad habit of ignoring predictive formulas."

Just the same, the experiment contributed immensely to the interstate surfaces we drive today. And it continues, after a fashion. The four biggest test loops were incorporated into the lanes of Interstate 80, which had been under construction to the east and west while the soldiers drove. But one of the others, Loop 1, survives a mile or so west of Ottawa, Illinois.

This was the only loop on which trucks didn't roll; Loop 1 was intended merely as a venue to study the effects of weather. More than fifty years later, some of its test sections have devolved to loose gravel, and waist-high weeds sprout from the joints in its concrete.

But when I visited the loop in the summer of 2008, I found that here and there, the pavement looked almost new.

Thomas MacDonald didn't get to see his penchant for research so rewarded. Since leaving the capital, he'd embarked on a new career at Texas A&M, building what is today known as the Texas Transportation Institute, among the nation's leading transport think tanks. His official title was "distinguished research engineer," his duties "to think, suggest, advise and guide." He'd hired a staff of research engineers and built a library. He'd become well known on campus for the big $5,000 car he pulled into the lot every day.

He and Caroline Fuller had married in November 1953 and set up house in College Station with Caroline's sister, Jane. They'd traveled a lot together on the highways that both had worked for so long to build; one year the couple drove more than six thousand miles through fifteen states. The Chief had grown comfortable.

But he'd also grown old. Suffering from an undisclosed ailment, he spent time at the Mayo Clinic in Rochester, Minnesota; afterward, he wrote to a friend that the trip "was very much worth while," as the "people at the Clinic inspire confidence and I feel sure we will be successful in overcoming some difficulties with faithful effort."

He'd been similarly upbeat about another illness in an April 5, 1957, letter to an Illinois colleague: "Some weeks ago," he wrote, "some virus bugs moved in and apparently became quite bad tempered over my failure to show them proper respect by calling in any medical treatment, so they established a play ground of infection which has brought the Doctor in and he has taken over decision as to what I can and cannot do."

The condition evidently had cleared enough that two evenings later, the Chief felt up to going out with Caroline, her sister, and another couple. They had a fine dinner, after which MacDonald bought a cigar; while waiting to attend a play in the university's Memorial Student Center, he settled into a sofa to smoke it. And there he died.

The distraught Caroline could not bring herself to accompany his body back to Washington, where he was to be interred beside his first wife. Texas A&M's Gibb Gilchrist went in her place. He and the casket found a large delegation waiting in Washington's Union Station — Frank Turner, Herbert Fairbank, and other bureau employees, state highway officials, industry bigwigs.

They went to breakfast, then stopped by the funeral home to collect MacDonald's children for the ride to Cedar Hill Cemetery, across the Anacostia River in Suitland, Maryland. The Chief had requested little ceremony and no flowers; on this occasion, his men defied him. Two hundred people, give or take, gathered around the grave. Flowers were everywhere.

Turner and Fairbank were among the honorary pallbearers. The

Presbyterian minister kept his remarks brief. "This is not the time or place to laud the man," he said. "Rather, it is the place to call on those who follow him to carry on the great work which he has done for the people of his country and the world."

More expansive eulogies came later. The *Washington Post* wrote that the Chief "left an inheritance to his fellow Americans which will stand enduringly as a monument to his memory," that everyone "who drives a car or truck, for business or for pleasure, across the face of America stands indebted to this quiet, forceful public servant who earned the title, 'the father of all good roads in the United States.'" AASHO's Alf Johnson figured him "more responsible for the United States leading the world in highways and the use of motor transportation than any other one man."

Fairbank delivered his tribute later in the year, when he was named the first recipient of AASHO's Thomas H. MacDonald Award, the organization's highest honor. The Chief's old deputy was ailing himself; while vacationing in Italy with his sister in the summer of 1954, Fairbank had contracted an illness that the doctors could not identify and that he could not shake. It had forced his retirement in 1955 and continued to limit him.

"Any award made in the name of Mr. MacDonald would have for me now a heightened significance," he said, "because I have been devoting a substantial part of my time during the last six or seven months to a study of Mr. MacDonald's life and work." Fairbank had been examining the Chief's accumulated papers, he said, "from the beginning of his career in 1904, at the very dawn of the modern era of highway building, in the early infancy of automotive transportation, until the moment of his passing from us seven months ago, at the very moment when all he had worked for and hoped for through more than half a century of his life was coming to fruition, a great fruition, that he so clearly and so long foresaw.

"From this review," Fairbank declared, "I have gained, as never before, the conviction that if ever a man deserved the name of prophet it was he. If ever a public servant could truly boast of an administration of the people's business virtually without flaw, it was he. If ever in any man there can be combined just that conjunction of the qualities of the able engineer, the perceptive political economist, the skilled diplomat and the sure and faithful administrator, that it takes to make a great highway engineer, it was in Thomas H. MacDonald that these qualities found their rarest blending."

13

BY THE 1956 ACT'S first anniversary, the bureau had reviewed and OK'ed about thirty-two thousand miles of the system's routing. Construction was under way or about to begin on nearly two thousand miles of highway, and contracts had been awarded on more than a thousand bridges. Nearly $2.6 billion had been committed to the work. "We have progressed at a gratifying rate," wrote Bert Tallamy, who by now had assumed command of the Federal Highway Administration, "and we are on schedule."

On paper, the program seemed to be moving briskly. But it didn't always look that way to a public salivating over the prospect of driving faster, farther, *more*. For most Americans, getting by without wheels had become not only unthinkable, but repugnant. Indeed, with gas cheap and wallets fat, the country's demand for everything automotive seemed unquenchable. Drive-in movie theaters sprang up by the thousands. So did drive-in banks, drive-in laundries, and drive-in restaurants, which often served beer along with burgers, even to patrons behind the wheel.

Detroit could barely keep up. For years, the most optimistic industry forecasts had shortchanged the demand for new iron: 5.8 million cars sold in 1953, 5.5 million during the recession of 1954, a record-breaking 7.4 million in 1955. By the time the Clay Committee convened, there was a car registered for every 3.5 citizens, a truck for every 18 — enough rolling stock, *Science Digest* claimed, to form a nose-to-tail string of autos two hundred thousand miles long.

Those purchases, and the subsequent cost of keeping cars on the road, devoured an ever-greater share of the family budget: 7.3 percent of the average worker's after-tax income by 1956, and the percentage was rising. Cars gobbled vast stores of steel, lead, zinc, rubber, corn, and beeswax; each year the auto industry further consumed the wool of seventeen million sheep, the hides of a half-million cattle, and a mountain of ground walnut shells, which were put to use in automatic transmissions.

With the interstates still on the drawing board in most places, the flood of new cars pouring onto the already choked U.S. highways brought spectacular jams. The Hollywood Freeway, designed for one hundred thousand cars a day, carried half again as many a year after it opened. Eight-mile backups were not uncommon on the San Francisco–Oakland Bay Bridge. Snarls at New York's George Washington Bridge were traced back eighty-four miles — seriously, eighty-four miles — to Monticello, New York.

By one estimate, tie-ups cost New Yorkers more than $1 billion a year in fuel, engine wear, lost productivity, missed sales; a quarter of all the gasoline consumed in American cities was burned, it was said, while motorists sat in traffic. Another forecast held that by 1970, New Yorkers would have to make an overnight trip to reach open country. Travel by horse and buggy had been faster.

No surprise, then, that the new highways couldn't come fast enough. Americans loved everything about their cars, loved driving, loved that they could follow an impulse to go wherever they chose, without a thought to routes or timetables. They loved that they lorded over their surroundings while they did it. They were cocooned, protected from the world, even as they were free to explore it. They could ride in silence or with the radio blaring, need never surrender personal space to a sweaty, foul-smelling stranger, need not suffer inane chatter.

They thrilled to the sensation and sound of movement, the buffet of air through an open window, a big engine's growl and punch. They embraced the status reflected in chrome trim, the subtext each model offered as to income and station and sex appeal.

What wasn't to love about the car? Americans took to it not only willingly, but with gusto. They did not have an automotive life foisted on them; they did not buy homes far from work, or forsake mass transit, or pave over their cities because they were manipulated into doing so by Detroit fat cats, or a government-industry conspiracy, or anyone else. No such subterfuge was necessary. The people chose their path. They wanted what they were getting.

Now they wanted the barriers to their automotive pleasure lowered. They wanted interstates, and damn it, they wanted them pronto.

Among the few voices raised against this almost universal enthusiasm was that of Lewis Mumford, who a quarter century before had teamed with Benton MacKaye to call for townless highways and who, in the intervening years, had grown into a celebrated critic of art and architecture, a force for deliberate city planning, and a thinker and writer of national renown.

His rise had been unlikely, at best. Born out of wedlock, raised by a drifty and self-obsessed mother, plagued by rotten teeth and bouts with both malaria and tuberculosis, Mumford had abandoned his formal education after a brief flirtation with college, choosing instead a course rare even a century ago: he fashioned himself into a self-taught man of letters, an intellectual without academic credentials, taking his schooling from books, mentors, a circle of brilliant friends, and from firsthand observation on his travels both near and far from home.

Beginning with walks. They were a habit formed in his early childhood, when his retired step-grandfather had taken him from his Upper West Side apartment on daily explorations — to Central Park, the Metropolitan Museum of Art, and the American Museum of Natural History; to the west along Riverside Drive, a promenade lined with shade trees and big, fine houses overlooking the Hudson; through an Upper West Side still sprinkled with loose chickens and vegetable gardens. By the time he started school, Mumford had encountered a few backfiring, clattering horseless carriages. He responded the way pretty much every city kid did at the turn of the last century; he yelled, "Get a horse!"

As the years passed, he'd ranged farther from home, almost always on foot, past workers erecting early skyscrapers, among block on block of Irish tenement, down streets echoing with the clop-clop-clop of hooves on cobblestone. New York had been an intimate city, by today's standards. Smells filled the air — of cooking, and manure, and slaughterhouses — and shouts, too, of merchants and teamsters, arguing couples, children playing in the street.

Before his eyes, it all had changed. Electric streetcars pushed the city's edges outward. On his forays beyond the East River, into Queens, Mumford had found truck farms, bogs and untidy forest studded with surveyor's stakes, and trolley tracks dissecting open ground that soon would sprout houses by the hundreds, by the thousands.

Digging the subways had started in 1900; within a few years, trains ran underground from the Battery to beyond Harlem and into the Bronx. Manhattan underwent spectacular change, ever-taller buildings colonizing the island's middle, chicken pens giving way to new housing. And everywhere came cars and trucks, and the din of horns, engines, and brakes, the burps of choking exhaust.

Mumford had gained a framework for his observations in the fall of 1914, when while browsing in a library he encountered a slim book titled *Evolution,* its coauthor a lanky, bearded Scot named Patrick Geddes — no relation to Norman Bel — most often remembered today as the father of modern city planning. Actually, Geddes was a biologist who defined his science broadly. He believed that one could not study an organism, man included, without exploring the context in which it lived and whatever mechanisms for living such a creature devised. In the case of humans, the greatest of mechanisms was the city, which in Geddes' view was as much a part of the natural world as a bear's den, a rabbit warren, or a beehive, and which was best judged by whether it enriched the lives of its occupants. Cities "worked" not just when they balanced their books, or kept crime off the streets, or picked up the garbage in a timely fashion, but when they fulfilled their more important function of facilitating human interaction — which was, after all, the reason people gathered in cities in the first place.

By extension, good architecture incorporated as much sociology as it did engineering or design. A building's scale and orientation, its relationship to its neighbors, the mood it created in those who beheld it, could fuel a neighborhood's vitality or hamper it. The width of streets, the presence of trees, the press of high-rises — all were part of the agar in the municipal Petri dish.

Mumford had become an enthusiastic disciple. After a brief stint in the navy at the close of World War I, he'd offered a short essay on housing ideas to the *Journal of the American Institute of Architects*. It owed much to Geddes but boasted Mumford's own sure and elegant writing voice; articles followed for the *American Mercury*, the *Freeman*, and the *New Republic*, and he'd landed a short-lived position on the staff of a small socialist magazine called the *Dial*.

He'd also fallen hard for its editor's dark-eyed secretary, Sophia Wittenberg, whom he married after a long and uncertain courtship. The same year, 1922, he'd hit on the idea for his first book, a history of utopias. He'd researched it by the end of March and turned in the finished manuscript in June; it was in stores by the year's end.

The turning point of Mumford's career had come in 1931, when the college dropout was a visiting professor of art at Dartmouth College and published a well-received book, *The Brown Decades*, that chronicled the flourishing American arts in the wake of the Civil war; among the architects, visual artists, and writers it celebrated was landscape genius Frederick Law Olmsted, who, seventy years before Radburn or the townless highway, had used underpasses to separate pedestrian and carriage traffic in New York's Central Park.

The same year, Mumford had embarked on a project that would consume him for the next two decades: a series of four books in which, he would later say, he hoped "to bring together, within a common frame, the ideas I had so far formulated on machines, cities, buildings, social life and people." The first volume, *Technics and Civilization*, recounted man's early flirtations with machines and his evolving relationship with them since; Mumford came across as an optimist about technology's potential for bettering everyday life.

He'd also ballooned his audience and solidified his reputation as a critic by taking over "The Sky Line," an architecture column in *The New*

Yorker. Mumford's columns minced no words in meting out praise or damnation. An architectural detail he didn't like was "the new cliché" and would "soon belong in the done-to-death department." A proposed bridge was "one of those plans that should be firmly discarded and never mentioned in anyone's presence again." A Manhattan milk bar was such "a monstrosity" that "it would take a lot of ingenuity to create anything more massively vulgar."

His "Sky Lines" had earned immediate and lasting notice. *Time* praised them as the "most perceptive, severe and expert column of architectural criticism in the U.S.," noting that "Manhattan architects, conscious of having blundered or faked, have learned that if nobody else will discover it, Critic Mumford probably will." In short order he was invited to tackle the magazine's art criticism, as well, giving him a regular footprint in its pages and a rare prominence, bordering on celebrity, among American critics.

As he'd settled into his new role, New York had continued to change around him with alarming swiftness. The Chrysler Building, the Empire State Building, and Rockefeller Center rose in midtown, Depression be damned. Suburbs crept eastward across Long Island, slowed but not stopped by the nation's economic woes. And Robert Moses, Carl Fisher's old adversary at Montauk, built a corona of parkways radiating through the growing sprawl to countryside and beach.

Early on, Mumford had admired Moses's landscaped roads, which were the closest thing the country had, at the time, to townless highways. They were smooth, concrete four-laners with no at-grade intersections, no commercial traffic (thanks to low underpasses that kept buses away, as well as trucks), and visual insulation from the rude metropolis beyond their wide rights of way; no billboards intruded on the pleasure of the drive, no slapped-together snack stands. He'd been taken, too, with Moses's prewar transformation of the Hudson's muddy and trash-strewn waterfront into a park-lined expressway; Mumford had found it "thoroughly modern" and the "finest single piece of large-scale planning the city can point to since the original development of Central Park." His description of the West Side Highway's interchanges had bordered on rapture: "The visual key to the design is the great traffic intersections, with their clover-leaf form, their changes of level, their vigorous curves postulated by the necessity for swift, uninterrupted motion."

But even as he'd written those words, Mumford's views on the automobile, and on Moses, were starting to shift. Traffic congestion was all but paralyzing, and schemes to ease it were even more vexing. Soon Moses wanted to punch three huge expressways 160 feet wide through Manhattan, one clear-cutting the skyscrapers lining 30th Street, another burying Washington Square. He started demolition for the Cross-Bronx Expressway, a ditch bulldozed through the borough's heart that felled apartments by the tens of thousands, crushed small businesses, split neighborhoods; and he envisioned a tangle of similar highways across Brooklyn, Queens, and beyond, out through the far satellite towns of Long Island. Cities all around the country were embarking on their own crosstown highways — Boston, Kansas City, Chicago, Fort Worth — but Moses's New York expressways and bridges dwarfed them all in scope and collateral damage.

By 1947, Mumford was writing a friend that it was "hard for an honest man to tell" whether Moses had "done the city more harm or more good, on a balance of considerations." His magazine pieces soon made it clear that he'd arrived at an answer. The United Nations headquarters complex overlooking the East River, in which Moses was deeply involved, was an architectural mishmash on a too-puny site (a "fleabite," to use Mumford's term). Moses's Stuyvesant Town, a knot of Corbusian high-rise apartments on a fenced and guarded superblock, was the "greatest and grimmest" of the city's new housing, "a caricature of urban rebuilding," an exponent of "the architecture of the Police State, embodying all the vices of regimentation one associates with state control at its unimaginative worst."

Moses had responded with a letter calling Mumford's views "bunk," and "grotesque misstatement," and "mumbo-jumbo," and "just plain tripe," and charged that Mumford was "poisoned by jaundice and envy" and must hate New York. "It is a sad bird," he wrote, "who fouls his own nest." The magazine published the letter with footnotes, supplied by Mumford, refuting its arguments point by point.

From that exchange on, the two had disagreed on practically every-thing and didn't do so quietly. Moses devoted himself to highways and bridges without pause, and Mumford, the early champion of the ex-pressway, the one-time admirer of the cloverleaf, came to see no other aspect of city planning — or lack thereof — as so potentially wasteful, disruptive, or stupid; Moses's calls for more high-speed auto roads were "temporary and futile palliatives," Mumford wrote, that "absorb funds badly needed for schools, hospitals, homes for the aged, libraries and other facilities already in stringently short supply."

He'd lost every one of their fights. Moses leveled great swaths of the city for his expressways. As a consultant, he recommended the same treatment across the country — in Portland, Oregon; in Hartford, Connecticut; in New Orleans. Motorists, which to an increasing de-gree meant just about everybody, seemed to side with the builder; in New York, especially, they greeted his new highway proposals with enthusiasm. Mumford's status as lone prophet was even reinforced in the pages of his own magazine. One of his columns detoured around a big Chevy ad that depicted a guy happily tooling up Moses's Saw Mill River Parkway, north of the city.

But when few others were objecting that building new high-ways into New York didn't alleviate the crush of traffic but spurred it on — seemed, in fact, to actually breed it — Mumford was making the point. And when few suggested that the automobile no longer simplified American life but in fact complicated and tainted it, Mumford — who, like Moses, never learned to drive — was practically shouting it.

In 1955, Mumford stepped up his criticism of the automobile's noxious effects with a four-part essay in *The New Yorker* titled "The Roaring Traffic's Boom." It was largely an attack on Moses, who was about to begin building the Long Island Expressway and planned a host of new bridges in the region — which, Mumford observed in his first piece, would pump more cars onto city streets already so packed that "af-ter ten in the morning, a reasonably healthy pedestrian can get across town faster than the most skillful taxi driver." You could say that Moses and his colleagues were leaving a baby on the doorstep, he wrote, but it was more like "dumping a whole orphanage on an overcrowded and bankrupt home."

Mumford's anger was not confined to the situation in New York. Readers all over the country could find application to their cities and local highways in the essay — such as when, in that same opening piece, he decried a planned bridge approach as "one of those vast spaghetti messes of roads and clover crossings and viaducts that provide excellent material for aerial photography but obliterate the towns they pass through as mercilessly as a new Catskill reservoir."

Or in the second installment, when he castigated highway engineers for behaving "as if motor transportation existed in a social vacuum" and "building more roads, bridges, and tunnels so that more motorcars may travel more quickly to more remote destinations in more chaotic communities, from which more roads will be built so that more motorists may escape from these newly soiled and clotted environments."

"Our transportation experts are only expert whittlers," he wrote, "and the proof of it is that their end product is not a new urban form but a scattered mass of human shavings. Instead of curing congestion, they widen chaos."

Or in the series' third part, where he pointed out that the "fancy cures that the experts have offered for New York's congestion are based on the innocent notion that the problem can be solved by increasing the capacity of the existing traffic routes, multiplying the number of ways of getting in and out of town, or providing more parking space for cars," when the reality was that the city screamed for redesign and the dispersal of its crowd-generating employers, stores, and public amenities.

"We have consistently acted," he wrote, "as if there were no relation between the number of people we dump on the land and the amount of congestion in the streets and arterial traffic routes."

Finally, in the fourth installment, he likened city congestion to an arterial thrombosis "aggravated by the reckless subsidized building of superhighways" and offered this flourish: "Highway engineers currently act on the principle of the hostess who, spying at opposite ends of a crowded drawing room two people who have not yet met, thinks only of how to bring them together, though in doing so she may jostle and squeeze against her other guests, interrupt conversations, knock the cocktail tray out of the butler's hands, and embarrass the two recipients of her intentions, who would have been far happier had they been left alone."

"The Roaring Traffic's Boom" was a call to arms. Here was a smart, sustained, and high-profile critique of the Futurama freeways that, just a dozen years before, Americans had welcomed as the cure for their urban transportation woes. Even before the interstate system was a fact, Mumford was raising the possibility that these wonderful roads might forever change, in less than wonderful ways, the very towns they were engineered to preserve.

And here was an attack on highway engineers as a class — men who, since the dawn of the motor age, had been treated as saviors by the press and the motoring public. To Frank Turner and his colleagues, Mumford must have come off as a raving maniac. Couldn't the writer see that highway engineers were first and foremost public servants, dedicated to improving life for all Americans? Couldn't he see that for decades, they'd done just that — that without highway engineers, farmers would still be marooned, the city-bound would go without fresh meat and greens, the price of clothing, furniture, appliances, books, just about everything, would be higher? And equally important, couldn't he see that the highway engineer's work was divorced from politics — that his decisions were fact-based, numerically supported, scientifically derived? That the numbers didn't lie?

Apparently, no. Such arguments would have had little traction with Mumford, who so passionately believed in the organic aspect of cities, and in their atmosphere, their personality, their feel. Besides, he could offer some numbers of his own. New superhighways pumped an ever-heavier flow of cars onto streets and avenues designed for a New York of four-story buildings. Now "we have in effect piled from three to ten early Manhattans on top of each other," he wrote. "If the average height of these buildings was only twelve stories, the roadway and sidewalks flanking them should, according to the original ratio, be two hundred feet wide, which is the entire width of the standard New York block."

Mumford's words especially resonated in the handful of cities that had started to build their own urban expressways while the interstate system lay dormant, awaiting federal money — cities whose people had been uprooted from their homes by advancing concrete, had already seen their downtowns cleaved, had already realized that expressways were inventions best beheld from the air, from such heights that concrete and steel acquired an airiness, ramps slimmed to filaments, loops formed delicate lacework — that only with altitude were highways and interchanges things of beauty, of pleasing symmetry, of order imposed on otherwise wild and untidy terrain.

They were a small minority, at that point. Most folks were impatient for the new roads. By the late summer of 1957, the press was grumbling that the vaunted interstates had started to appear in a few dislocated bits and pieces but looked nothing like a system, and surmising that the program must have stalled. *U.S. News & World Report* decided it was "apparent that the construction period will be a good deal longer than the thirteen years originally estimated." *Look* magazine, while allowing that "any program of this magnitude takes a good many months to get rolling," incited its readers: "Meanwhile, however, the states and federal government have been collecting more and more tax money from highway users, and motorists may soon be justified in asking: 'Where are all those new roads we were promised?'"

Frank Turner countered that a project bigger than the Panama Canal, the Pyramids, and the Great Wall, combined, couldn't be built overnight. "Each step," he explained, "takes time — planning the roads, holding public hearings on the routings, designing the highways and the structures involved, getting the necessary approvals, relocating factories, homes and utilities that may be in the path of the new highway, advertising for bids, awarding contracts, waiting for materials and, finally, the actual construction.

"We hope the public, which is already paying for the interstate system, will be patient," he said. "By 1960 there will be something substantial to show for all the effort and money going into this project."

14

I N YEARS TO COME the feds published a map every three months that was shaded to demarcate the sections of interstate completed, under construction, left to be built. You could make a flipbook of those maps, see in the whir of pages the steady fusion of the web's strands — could watch Interstate 10 crawl across the deserts of California, Arizona, and New Mexico, and the swamps and thickets down South; could watch I-90 arc through the Badlands, I-25 push north along the Rockies' eastern face in Colorado, and I-30 span the dirty-footed villages and rice paddies of rural Arkansas that Frank Turner had explored in his early career.

But most Americans first experienced the new highways close to home, in the suburbs, where an ever-growing share of them already lived. The burbs were generations old by the mid-fifties and had exploded in the decade since the war's end. The desire for fresh air, cool breezes, and room to stretch their legs, for an opportunity to buy more house for the money, for relief from overcrowded apartment blocks that too closely evoked the barracks and berthings in which they'd spent the fight, had spurred millions out of the cities long before the interstates came along. Houses sprang from the soil after the Japanese surrender at double the rate of the previous fifteen years, the overwhelming majority of them in subdivisions carved from forest and field on the urban fringe; between 1950 and 1955, the suburban populations of the country's 168 metropolitan areas grew by almost 28 percent, while those of the central cities grew by less than 4 percent. By 1963, when the interstates were just making tentative inroads into most urban areas, the population of America's suburbs surpassed that of the cities they ringed.

The new houses came fast and cheap, thanks to mass-production techniques that had stamped out hundreds of Liberty ships and thousands of bombers during the war. Their downside was that this factory approach to construction demanded limited variation in the product. A Virginia newspaper labeled tract homes "mass individualism," noting that it was up to homeowners to personalize their look-alike ranchers; in the meantime, they offered the young buyers of 1955 "the home that would have been merely wishful thinking ten years ago."

The subdivisions in which these homes rose didn't vary much, either. They borrowed, here and there, from the Radburn design manual. Their concrete lanes curved sinuously, whether or not the terrain dictated they should; cul-de-sacs, virtually unknown in the horse-and-carriage days, often branched off the principal streets. But they bore a very different relationship to the mode of transportation that made them possible: Radburn had been billed as the first town designed for the motor age but had segregated the automobile from home life, hidden it away out back; the new suburbs passed themselves off as escapes from the noise and congestion and evil air of the too-crowded city but treated the family car as a vital element of home — in the form of a concrete driveway in every front yard, and a garage door that faced the street and dominated a rambler's façade.

James W. Rouse, a Baltimore developer, succinctly described the exodus from town: "A farm is sold and begins raising houses instead of potatoes, then another farm; forests are cut; valleys are filled; streams are buried in storm sewers; kids overflow the schools; here a new school is built, there a church. Traffic grows; roads are widened; service stations and hamburger stands pockmark the highway. Relentlessly, the bits and pieces of a city are splattered across the landscape."

All of which is to say that the suburbs were cooking along years before the 1956 act became law, were seeping farther and farther from every downtown, were fostering "a new kind of urban tissue," as Lewis

Mumford put it in the spring of 1956, "a little looser than that of the central core but equally disadvantageous to a self-directed life, and often even more lacking in collective alleviations."

It wasn't just households moving out. The Urban Land Institute observed that during the postwar boom, from 1948 to 1954, retail sales grew by 23 percent in central cities, and by a whopping 59 percent outside of them. In October 1956, Southdale, the world's first fully enclosed, climate-controlled shopping mall, opened in Edina, Minnesota, outside the Twin Cities.* Its architect, Austrian-born Victor Gruen, also opened three big suburban shopping centers that helped remake metropolitan Detroit. A month after Southdale's debut, *Business Week* worried there might be too many shopping centers in the suburbs. The ink on Ike's signature had barely dried.

A city's circumferential interstate, the big ring road on which traffic orbited fifteen or twenty miles out of downtown, was usually among the first urban legs on which construction started. Way out on a settlement's edge, beyond all but the most ambitious commutes, it proved relatively easy for state highway departments. Existing development out there was of such low density that few homes and businesses stood in the way; in some places, the beltways had been planned for so long that much of the right of way had already been acquired.

So in Washington, D.C., and Baltimore, in St. Louis and Houston and Atlanta, stretches of the loops materialized — and instantly changed public perception of each city's size and shape. Houston was no longer a messy, fast-spreading stain, its edges as ragged as a cancer's; on maps, it became the neat circle of Interstate 610. In St. Louis, the city's crescent shape was mirrored by an arcing interstate a half hour's drive from the city limits, beyond the dozens of suburban satellites that had sprung up in St. Louis County. Cincinnatians saw the beginnings of a belt eighty-four miles long that would eventually pass through three states.

---

* Note that this was the first modern, indoor mall, though the concept of a shopping center ringed by parking lots, its storefronts turned away from the surrounding streets, dates to 1931, when Highland Park Village opened in suburban Dallas.

Even while they were still under construction, the loops formed a psychological barrier to further development, a seam between metropolis and countryside — a role captured most literally by Atlanta's name for I-285, the Perimeter. But before long the circumferentials, and the radial interstates shoving their way into the central cities, enabled the burbs to push farther from the center, much farther, and the development they fostered was of an odd, new type. Subdivisions and shopping centers didn't simply appear on the roadside; the old motor slum that Benton MacKaye had so chastised wasn't suited to an expressway that you couldn't enter and exit wherever you wished. Instead, they popped up around interstate exits, in nodes that planners called "nucleated" development.

To fly over an outer suburb of the early sixties was to look down on islands of houses, stores, and industry, sometimes separated from their neighbors by miles; builders looking for cheap land leapfrogged those exits already claimed to put down stakes farther out. In time, the open space between islands filled with newer subdivisions, newer schools, newer shops and offices, until most of the American metropolis became a rambling patchwork of lawns, streets, and parking lots.

Once development leaped the outer rings, it wasn't long before the farm burgs beyond morphed into bedroom communities. Harry Truman's once-rural hometown of Independence, Missouri, saw 1,500 homes and eleven apartment complexes sprout alongside I-70 in eighteen months. Cropland outside Atlanta yielded galloping subdivisions. And on the strength of three-bedroom "Caribbean cottages" for just over twelve grand apiece, little Irving, Texas, population 2,621 in 1950 — a place where, as *Architectural Forum* put it, "cows were lonely" — had by 1961 ballooned to 45,489 souls scattered chaotically over twenty square miles. "There are just houses, roads, cars, children, and signboards promising more houses," the magazine reported.

Land values at the exits leaped crazily. Outside Louisville, a run on interchange property three or four years ahead of highway construction boosted the price of tobacco farms by 250 percent or more — and in one instance, fifteen times over. In Robeson County, North Carolina, an average acre near I-95 leaped from $1,684 to more than $26,000.

Farther out in the country, beyond the cities' gravitational pull, the new roads touched off an economic revolution no less profound than that ushered in by the railroads a century before. Manufacturing jobs left the cities for rural property that was abundant, cheap, and alongside the new or planned interstates, which promised companies a ready distribution network. Factories mushroomed beside I-80 in Pennsylvania — a mobile home company in Pottsville, a U.S. Rubber building in Wilkes-Barre, a Japanese plastics firm in Hazleton. Chrysler cited the proximity of I-90 for its decision to build a $50 million factory in tiny Belvidere, Illinois, and of I-44 for its construction of another assembly plant in the Ozark foothills southwest of St. Louis. Interstate 35 spurred E. I. du Pont de Nemours & Co. to locate a cellophane plant, and the Hallmark Co. a ribbon and gift wrap factory, in eastern Kansas.

Spartanburg, South Carolina, saw thirty-one new plants or expansions in a single year, part of an industrial boom on and near I-85 that stretched from Danville, Virginia, to Atlanta. The surge spawned severe labor shortages — companies couldn't recruit outside workers for lack of housing, and new housing couldn't be built for lack of workers — and unforeseen social change; hungry for labor, firms offered better working conditions, higher wages, and new opportunities for blacks.

Mount Vernon, Illinois, at the junction of Interstates 64 and 57, found itself new home to a slew of interchange restaurants and motels, a General Tire plant boasting 1,800 jobs, and a five-hundred-bed regional hospital. The population was swelling, household income on the way to doubling, and soon townsfolk could take in live music any night of the week at the Ramada Inn lounge. "The day we cut the ribbon on I-57," the mayor later said, "it was like turning on a spigot."

As Frank Turner had promised, soon pieces of the system were under construction all over the country. For all this encouraging progress, he and his lieutenants were wrestling with an unforeseen difficulty on both suburban and rural legs. As the bureau and states had planned to run a good many of the new routes right on top of the old U.S. highways they would supersede, they expected that they would have to buy only so much land for the system; the existing resources, they figured, merely needed an upgrade. But as plans moved toward construction, it became obvious that in most of the country, that approach wouldn't work.

Virginia's experience with Interstate 81 illustrates why. The commonwealth had initially resisted plans to upgrade U.S. 11, a critical but narrow link between the Deep South and the Northeast that within the state ran 343 miles up the Shenandoah Valley from Bristol, on the Tennessee line, through Roanoke and Staunton to West Virginia. It was among the country's most historic corridors, the descendant of the Valley Road on which early European settlers had ventured beyond the Blue Ridge, and of the Wilderness Road on which Daniel Boone had struck farther west. In the eyes of the state's highway bosses, it was just fine as it was — a two-laner that here and there widened to three or four.

The feds convinced them that the corridor needed Interstate 81, and that the new road would have to hew to a four-lane standard. But building a much bigger highway on the old road was no simple matter, because over the centuries, a lot of people had settled alongside U.S. 11. Farmers depended on the highway to get their crops and cattle to market; restaurants and stores catered to the travelers who streamed past at all times of day, as well as residents of nearby towns and colleges; churches and filling stations abounded. All of these properties had driveways opening onto the road.

If built on top of the existing road, the limited-access interstate would run right past their front doors but deny them entrance. Many, if not most, had no other way on and off their parcels. And that, as Turner would recall years later, spelled trouble. "The right of access to a public highway was considered a property right by law," he said. "And therefore, it had a dollar value." So did the property itself. If you run a restaurant and the state barricades you from your customers, that's denying you a right beyond simple access; you're being deprived of livelihood. The state likely would have to buy your whole property, and chances are, you wouldn't settle for a lowball offer; commercial real estate, because appraisers consider it a "highest and best use" of a tract, always costs more than, say, pastureland.

Which is not to say that farmland would come cheap. "Every drive-way to a rural farmstead," Turner said, "had the potential of costing us virtually the price of the farm itself, at least." Had Virginia tried to buy access rights and properties along the highway's length, it would still be paying for them today.

Instead, after a great deal of haggling with Turner and company over the details, Virginia moved the interstate away from the existing highway, surveying a line that ran parallel to U.S. 11 but passed a few hundred yards behind the farmhouses and businesses. Because their owners had no right of access to a road that had not previously existed, prices were kept to a minimum.

That scenario played out all over the country. It turned out that three miles of every four had to be built on new alignments. One happy by-product of these new paths was that they tended to be straighter, and thus shorter, than the U.S. highways on which estimates of their lengths had been based—1,102 miles shorter, system-wide, meaning the bu-reau had that much in extra interstate to parcel out. It was enough, when added to the 1,000 miles that Congress had tacked onto the orig-inal 40,000-mile cap, for nine intercity additions to the network—in-cluding one from Pittsburgh to Erie, Pennsylvania, a 102-mile highway that became I-79; another from Charlotte, North Carolina, to Canton, Ohio, to be known as I-77; and most dramatically, a 547-mile exten-sion of Interstate 70 through the Rockies, from Denver to Cove Fort, Utah. It also added mileage in the cities, in part to satisfy the military's desire for "traffic to pass around potential target areas."

Still, satisfying the property-rights question added time and ex-pense to planning and construction. Clearing a path for the interstates required the taking of more than 750,000 properties. In just the first ten months after Ike signed the 1956 act, the bureau allocated $321 mil-lion to the states for real estate.

With such money on the line, it was a given that some might try to take advantage of the right-of-way process. The first scandal broke in Indiana, where the chairman of the state highway commission was sneaking inside dope about upcoming land acquisitions to his friends, so that they could beat the state to the properties, then sell them to the taxpayer at jacked-up prices. The bureau increased its scrutiny of land deals, which further delayed construction. And the challenges didn't ease. Before long, New Mexico suspended all interstate construction because land in the rights of way was selling for thirty times its appraised value.

More trouble loomed. One provision of the 1956 act had required the Department of Commerce to update Congress every couple of years on adjustments to the system's costs, and the first such report came in January 1958. What with soaring construction costs and right-of-way prices, not to mention the lowball amount originally earmarked for urban routes, the projected outlay had jumped from $27 billion to $37.6 billion; the interstates were now expected to average close to a million bucks a mile.

Rudely shocked by the new figures, some members of Congress concluded that states fat with Washington's money were tossing cash around—or worse, had succumbed to corruption. "Congressman after congressman got up on the floor of the House and made wild speeches, frightening speeches," one Democratic member, John A. Blatnik of Minnesota, later recalled, "saying we had a shortage of funds because the States were playing fancy-free and foot-loose with the taxpayers' dollars." So strident was the talk that in September 1959, the House mustered a Special Subcommittee on the Federal-Aid Highway Program to look into the matter, led by the same John Blatnik, a former high school chemistry teacher and World War II veteran of the Office of Strategic Services, the forerunner of the CIA.

Blatnik and his eleven fellow committeemen were "real gung-ho" about the assignment, Frank Turner later recalled, and "took an antagonist confrontational approach" to their dealings with the bureau. The press piled on with gusto. In July 1960, *Reader's Digest,* then among the biggest magazines in America, published a blockbuster story titled "Our Great Big Highway Bungle," which labeled the highway program "a multibillion-dollar rathole" of graft and incompetence, overseen by an "inept" bureau and carried out by states with "an easy-come, easy-go attitude."

"Judging by the record to date, it is time to stop and evaluate," the story suggested, "to make every possible effort to cut out the waste, graft and stupidity, if that beautiful dream we all once had is to come true."

Parade followed suit in February 1962, with "The Great Highway Robbery," by veteran muckraker Jack Anderson, who quoted Blatnik as saying that corruption "permeates the highway program." NBC's David Brinkley brought up the rear, with a special that repeated the accusations.

In fact, the committee did turn up some rotten business. In New Mexico, investigators found that contractors ran roughshod over roads officials, exhibiting "open contempt" for construction specs and quality controls as "a continuing course of conduct over a period of almost ten years." They got away with it, Blatnik's people found, because the state didn't know enough to object; its highway department was managed by unskilled laborers who had been advanced up the ranks without a lick of training. Some state men testified that they didn't know how to test roadbed materials, so they OK'ed all that came before them. Their boss admitted he wasn't schooled on how to do his work until after it was finished. The committee discovered one stretch of highway that was in the act of collapsing even as New Mexico officials signed off on it.

The bureau stopped payments to New Mexico until it got itself together, and did the same to Massachusetts and Oklahoma. Its position was that the problems uncovered by Blatnik's sniffing were probably inevitable — officials were human, after all, and big money was involved — but that they were nonetheless rare. And indeed, they were; the vast majority of states stood up well to the committee's scrutiny.

Still, the bureau put some new safeguards in place, instituting drop-in inspections and materials testing, and creating, in July 1962, two new offices: Audit and Investigations, led by a former FBI agent, would dig into any charges of fraud, sweetheart dealmaking, and the like; the Office of Right-of-Way and Location would verify that property for the system was obtained on the up-and-up and at a price that made sense.

• • •

Much to Turner's chagrin, the Blatnik committee didn't restrict its inquiry to corruption and waste. It attracted almost as much attention investigating whether the "national and defense" highway system could accommodate the military — in particular, whether its overpasses left enough clearance for the army's tanks and heavy trucks. Those clearances, which the bureau initially set at fourteen feet, were revised up to sixteen shortly after the committee convened, but some army vehicles needed much higher clearance than that, and Blatnik's people smelled negligence. How else to explain defense highways that were too puny for the job? One trucking company president testified that low overpasses so slowed down his crews that it took nine days to deliver an Atlas missile from its California factory to its Florida launch site. The trucks were equipped with hydraulic shocks that enabled them to duck under some bridges, but even so, drivers often had to let air out of the tires to make it.

Here was evidence, the committee charged, that the bureau had ignored the needs of the Defense Department. Turner knew better; he and "all of us at the staff working level had been working for years on these kinds of things," he later explained with some bitterness. Both the bureau and the military were well aware, and had been all along, that some gear wouldn't fit under the bridges, but they'd agreed that only a tiny number of vehicles would be blocked, and that the army probably wouldn't want them rolling down the interstates, anyhow. So, rather than spend extra billions for soaring overpasses, the parties simply came up with alternate routes. A too-high truck might go around an overpass on a diamond interchange or parallel the interstate for a short way on a feeder road. All these Plan Bs were mapped and well known to Defense officials.

To Turner, the whole inquiry smacked of a misunderstanding about the nature of the system's "defense" role. A myth persists today, as it did in Blatnik's hearings, that the interstates were designed for the rapid movement of troops — "boys in brown uniforms riding in trucks, an infantry battalion or something," as Turner put it, when they were really "a 'goods movement' facility, rather than a 'human-persons movement' kind of thing."

Another piece of conventional wisdom, still alive on the Internet, was that every fifth mile of interstate was designed as a straightaway so that warplanes could use it as a runway in national emergencies. This may have had its origins in talks between the bureau and air force that did, in fact, occur early in the acquisition of the system's right of way. Turner later said that he was "pressured pretty hard" by the service to build a runway capability into the highways, and that he did his best to accommodate it. The bureau strove to "twist the alignment here to get in the wind directional considerations, and the low gradients and lack of obstructions" necessary for such double duty, hoping that "every forty or fifty miles, we'd have about a three-mile section there that would meet those requirements." He even sent a team over to Germany to reexamine the autobahns. Ultimately, however, he decided it couldn't work. Just from a traffic standpoint, the interstates could not serve two masters. They're strictly for ground traffic.

PART IV

-- -- -- -- -- --

The Human Obstacle

15

- - - - - - - - - - -

WHATEVER THE CHALLENGES the states and the bureaus faced in buying and building in the countryside and low-density suburbs, they confronted a much tougher task in America's central cities, particularly those that had been around for a century or more: Providence and Philadelphia, Boston and Chicago, San Francisco, Cleveland, Detroit — settlements of closely packed neighborhoods, narrow streets, shoulder-to-shoulder industry. In a nineteenth-century cityscape, the destruction that attended bulldozing space for the new roads was extreme. In Washington State, engineers gutted a long belt of old neighborhoods and businesses to force Interstate 5 through Seattle's clotted heart; in Wilmington, Delaware, I-95 split the downtown, mowing down hundreds of homes and businesses and four historic churches; black neighborhoods in St. Louis fell to one interstate, a famed Italian enclave was nicked by another, and the downtown was separated from its Mississippi riverfront by a wide and deep ditch, a second river filled with speeding traffic.

As the Chief had warned, urban interstates would bring pain. And one city that stood to feel as much as any was Herbert Fairbank's hometown, the bureau's very model for how such highways might transform cities for the better: Baltimore.

In the fifties Baltimore was, as it remains, a gritty industrial port town with as much in common with cities in the Northeast as with its sisters in the South. Settled in the late seventeenth century, it is situated on a great natural harbor convenient to the agricultural fields of Pennsylvania and Ohio. First as a shipping center for tobacco, later for corn and other food crops, and eventually as a major exporter of flour, Baltimore expanded until, by the early 1800s, it was the second-largest city in the country.

As was the case with other colonial settlements, its streets were narrow and crooked and met at odd angles, making traffic a nightmare even before the Civil War. In the century since, the population had erupted to nearly a million, much of it packed into Baltimore's famed brick row houses. Two of the country's most important highways crossed the city — U.S. 40 from west to east, and U.S. 1 on a diagonal, carrying traffic to and from Washington, to the southwest, and Philadelphia, to the northeast. In Baltimore's heart these big roads dwindled to doglegging lanes and became, as Fairbank had put it in *Toll Roads and Free Roads*, "the despair of the stranger and the daily inconvenience of [Baltimore's] own citizens." The halting flood of autos, trucks, and streetcars, whether bound for the next block or two states away, created a fatal sludge. Congestion was epic.

In 1944, Baltimore had been among the cities to tap Robert Moses for a solution. He found the lay of the place vexing. The southeastern quarter is dominated by the Patapsco River, a tidal estuary of the Chesapeake Bay, which enters the city two miles wide, then splits three ways, throwing up myriad obstacles to crosstown travel. The Patapsco's southern two forks dead-end among piers and factories. The third, North Branch, splits off at Fort McHenry, where in 1814 Francis Scott Key witnessed the Star-Spangled Banner survive a British siege, and bends northwest toward Baltimore's center. It is the narrowest of the forks, lined with shipyards, foundries, and old brick homes and warehouses, and swings first left, then right, before ending at a squarish basin. Today, this Inner Harbor is Baltimore's showplace, encircled by high-rise apartments and offices, shops, restaurants, and the National Aquarium, the nighttime lights of all reflecting almost magically on the water. Hotels rise from docks where excursion boats tie up, and a few blocks away looms the celebrated Oriole Park. But in 1944, few tourists ventured anywhere near the Inner Harbor, which was oil-fouled and trash-strewn and home to a transient population almost as unsavory as the stinking water itself. The central business district kept its distance, clustering several blocks to the north.

One question confronting Moses was whether to locate his expressway along the Inner Harbor, thereby serving the downtown area from its southern fringe, or to route it through densely packed residential and commercial blocks to the north. Moses chose the latter; he called for a six-lane, mostly depressed expressway that entered Baltimore from the southwest, then made a hard turn east to run between two parallel streets, Franklin and Mulberry, past downtown. It continued on that eastward line, varying no more than a block or two, clear across the city. He called it the Franklin Expressway.

The alignment not only made for an arrow-straight highway, it wiped out the city's worst slums, which were concentrated to the west of downtown. Some of the back alleys there were truly wretched, reeking of garbage and overfilled privies. "Flies swarm by the thousands," the *Baltimore Sun* reported. "Rats scurry from piles of garbage into pock-marked, cementless yards where they make their homes. Dogs paw through discarded foodstuffs dumped indiscriminately in yards and alleys. Wooden fences around back yards are falling down, some due to the tenants tearing out boards to use for heating purposes." Because slum land could be snapped up for a song, the Franklin Expressway was also affordable, as Fairbank had foreseen.

But the slums, grotesque though they were, housed a large chunk of Baltimore's population, and the Moses proposal was sparking dissent months before it was finished. A protest group sprang up to argue that the Franklin Expressway would be unnecessarily destructive and wouldn't really fix the city's congestion woes; traffic surveys showed the busiest streets ran north-south, not east-west. Others protested that the highway would create a "Chinese Wall" dividing Baltimore in half.

Moses had little patience for such trifling worries. Sure, the road would put nineteen thousand people out of their homes, but "the slum areas through which the Franklin Expressway passes are a disgrace to the community," he wrote, "and the more of them that are wiped out the healthier Baltimore will be in the long run." As for the talk of a Chinese Wall, well, that was "an old chestnut" that had been hung on "every parkway and express artery since the internal combustion engine was perfected." Progressive communities mounting such objections had "lived to retract their epithets," he wrote, then sneered: "Some are beyond conversion, but these are the same people who don't believe in automobiles, live in the past, and honestly believe they have no debt to the future." The Franklin Expressway, he assured Baltimore, would be "a genuine municipal improvement."

The city's business community got behind the plan, producing a brochure that called it a key to postwar prosperity. The citizenry was unconvinced. When the City Council considered the plan in March 1945, a crowd of 1,500 taxpayers showed up, and a long parade of speakers denounced it to a chorus of cheers and shouts. The last to speak, one Mrs. Rufus Gibbs, read a letter from acerbic *Sun* staffer and syndicated columnist H. L. Mencken, saying he figured the expressway would win approval. It had "everything in its favor," he explained, "including the fact that it is a completely idiotic undertaking."

To Mencken's happy surprise, he was wrong. The proposal died. Not so the thinking behind it, however. In its place, City Hall mulled a more complicated highway scheme of radials and loops. This new plan prompted an appearance by Herbert Fairbank, who told his hometown's advertising club that Baltimore, like every other old city in America, faced a choice: shake off its resistance to change or witness its downtown suffer a lingering death. Employment there had seen no growth in more than a decade. Property values were in free fall. Empty loft and warehouse space abounded; vacancies were so high in some buildings that their cash-desperate owners tore them down for parking lots. Sales were dwindling at the big flagship department stores. Not a single new office building had been erected since the twenties.

"The arteries are clogged, and when the arteries clog, the body dies!" Fairbank warned. "You are going to have to do something about it. And the answer is: expressways." The city needed a system of fast, free-flowing radials sprouting from a beltway around the central business district, a setup "very much like the hub and the spokes of a wheel" and linked to a rim out in the far suburbs. "The whole system is needed," he insisted, and to the city's good fortune, the first step to getting it was already figured out: the proposed highway running across town between Franklin and Mulberry. "We are satisfied that this proposal is thoroughly sound," he said, "and will approve it."

Baltimoreans weren't nearly so satisfied. A few weeks later, the city's chief engineer was booed loudly by residents at another packed City Council session. He told them he sympathized with their position but didn't "feel like laughing off" the millions of dollars the feds would contribute to the project. That would become an oft-heard refrain of city leaders and state highway officials across America in decades to come: they couldn't afford to refuse Washington's money.

While all this excitement was unfolding, a quiet, studious young black scientist named Joe Wiles moved to town. He was a New Yorker, a native of Brooklyn, raised in working-class Prospect Heights by parents who'd immigrated from Barbados. Neither his father, a printer, nor his mother, a homemaker, had much education. Still, they'd infused Wiles and his four younger brothers with a hunger for learning and service, and with an understanding that "community" meant more than lines on a map. So young Joe Wiles had earned admission to Brooklyn College, where he'd studied biology for five semesters, then had transferred to Morris Brown College in Atlanta on a basketball scholarship. He'd started graduate work at Atlanta University, intending to eventually enter medical school, and had performed brilliantly.

On visits back to Brooklyn he'd passed time shooting hoops outside of P.S. 35 and had caught the eye of Esther Ogburn, the pretty daughter of a local Episcopal priest. One day Wiles left his bike lying around, and Esther's father, Rev. John T. Ogburn, drove his car over it; the accident gave Esther and Joe a few minutes to talk. They reconnected in more relaxed fashion at church socials, where Wiles wowed the girls with his dancing. He soon had a steady partner, and before long, the two were seeing each other all the time. That ended when his draft notice arrived.

The army had sent him first to Fort Benning, where he was given an intelligence test. The cadre quickly accused him of cheating; Wiles's score blew away those of his fellow conscripts, which wasn't expected of a black man with a New York accent, and they had him take it again while they sat in the room. He topped his previous score. Ah, one of the officers said, we have ourselves a smart one. They made him a medic.

Wiles and Esther had written each other throughout his training, kept up their correspondence when the army shipped him overseas, and in one of his letters he proposed. When Germany collapsed, the army transferred Wiles to the Pacific, with a stateside furlough on the way. He used it to marry Esther in her father's church.

Freshly discharged in July 1946, Wiles had landed a job at the Edgewood Arsenal, an army chemical and biomedical research lab northeast of Baltimore. Housing for blacks was not to be had nearby, so he and Esther moved into a one-room apartment on Baltimore's west side. It was so tiny they couldn't get dressed at the same time, and almost an hour's commute from the lab on busy U.S. 40, but it wasn't far off Pennsylvania Avenue, Baltimore's black shopping and entertainment district of the day, and convenient to Druid Hill Park, a massive preserve just to the north, and they made a home of it. Little more than a year after they married, Esther was pregnant with their first daughter, Carmen.

With her arrival, the Wileses found a bigger place in Mount Washington, north of the city in rural Baltimore County, where not long after, Esther gave birth to another daughter, Carole. And not long after that, with the cold war threatening to go hot in Korea, Wiles was called up by the army. Stuck in a succession of stateside posts, the only black sergeant in his unit, he wrote Esther of conversations with white noncoms that made him feel "very envious and jealous" of the homes they owned, when he was "older than them and had two children and didn't have a home to offer you or them either."

The conversations left him with a hardening resolve. He wrote Esther that it was now his "prime aim to direct all of our resources, energy and ambition towards getting a place that we can call ours and fixing it up so that we can live comfortably." He begged her not to "run up any more bills," to sock away all available cash. And he shared with her a detailed picture of what he had in mind: "one of those fine red brick two story affairs with a nice large cemented cellar," three bedrooms, a big front porch, "paneled painted walls with indirect lighting in the living and dining rooms," and a "modernistic" kitchen with "inlaid linoleum and tile walls, fluorescent lighting, built-in wall cabinets."

"That's a beautiful picture, isn't it, honey?" he wrote. "I can dream, can't I?"

He could. He did. Once out of uniform and back at Edgewood, Wiles bought a house that fit this description in virtually every respect, in a solidly middle-class corner of west Baltimore called Rosemont.

The Wiles family was at the vanguard of a westward migration of Baltimore's middle-class blacks. Long penned in overcrowded streets and alleys that hugged the city's downtown (the very neighborhoods that Robert Moses had targeted), they shared a postwar hunger for safety and shade trees, decent schools and a little privacy, and found them in traditionally white neighborhoods along U.S. 40. Some parts of town saw their racial makeup flip practically overnight.

So as the Wileses moved into their new place and other black families did the same, Rosemont's remaining whites prepared to flee to the county's fast-rising suburbs. Just as Wiles had imagined, the family's new row house was two stories tall and brick, with a big azalea in the yard and a façade dominated by a deep wooden porch. It had airy living and dining rooms, a dry basement, and a nice kitchen with plenty of room for a table. A detached one-car garage opened onto the paved alley out back. Its surroundings were tranquil; traffic was light, the sidewalks were safe, and everywhere they turned was green. The front porch looked onto a dense thicket of hardwoods — houses ran up only one side of Ellamont Street — and just across the back alley, and forming the central two-thirds of the block, was a low wetland tangled with vines and scrub and reputedly full of snakes.

Wiles draped a canvas awning from the front porch, put a metal glider out there for warm summer nights, and started transforming the basement into a game room. He bought concrete flower boxes in which Esther planted geraniums. The girls instantly made a passel of friends and spent afternoons playing jacks, jumping rope, and riding bikes in the alley. Rosemont became home.

Yet Wiles saw that nice as the neighborhood was, it had lost an important piece of itself when the population turned over. Its new residents had no shared memories, no common traditions, no consensus as to what or how the community should be. Mature trees or no, it felt a little like a new subdivision. So in 1952, he and a few of his neighbors organized the Rosemont Neighborhood Improvement Association, and at its first meeting, despite his soft-spoken, almost shy manner, Wiles was elected president.

The association met monthly in members' homes and on weekends embarked on cleanups of the vacant lots scattered among the houses and the weedy open land straddling the railroad tracks that curved by a few blocks to the south. Its members helped older residents with big maintenance chores and kept an eye on each other's kids. The culture of involvement fed on itself; Rosemont came to seem a village in the city.

Always, Wiles had an eye for further improvements. Some of Rosemont's men decided the neighborhood's boys could use a little structure, and they organized a troop of the Kadets of America, a patriotic youth organization big on military-style marching drills. A couple of years later, Wiles started a girls' troop that Carmen and Carole joined, and he drilled the unit a couple of times a week. He was serious about it, as he was about anything he took on, and the girls held their own in weekend competitions with Kadet troops from out of town.

He and the neighbors decided the jungle in the middle of the block was wasted opportunity and resolved to clean it up. They whacked down its brush and high grass to expose a sloping, two-acre clearing and eventually convinced the city to fill and level it. The association put flower boxes around the trees and built picnic tables, and it became a neighborhood jewel.

He preached to the girls the value of having a plan and working toward it, and the house around them bore witness to his methodical nature. The yard matured into a crisp arrangement of lawn and flower beds. The basement acquired paneling, a full bath, and a bar. The same went for Wiles's performance at Edgewood; he steadily rose through the ranks at the biomedical lab and on the side authored a growing body of scientific papers, even patented an inoculation gun.

His calm determination was especially useful when Rosemont confronted crisis. The first came five years after the family arrived, when the association learned that a box factory was to be built down by the railroad tracks. Wiles and his neighbors organized a protest that drew five hundred people to a local Baptist church. They met with members of the City Council, too, and won a promise of help. It turned out the property had been zoned for just such a purpose for twenty-five years or better, and the councilmen couldn't block it, but the experience spurred the association to pursue zoning changes that would discourage industry and apartments, and to develop an expertise in navigating City Hall.

At almost the same time, the Wileses and twenty-five other families whose homes backed onto the open field learned that the school board planned to condemn their properties for a new elementary school there. Wiles convinced the city to instead condemn the woods across Ellamont.

It was a close call. And, it turned out, a warm-up for battles to come.

The *Yellow Book*'s map of Baltimore resurrected talk of an east-west expressway. It depicted the highway making a straight shot across the city's waist on top of U.S. 40, which formed Rosemont's southern boundary. But by the autumn of 1956, city planners mapping out the specific right of way for what was to be Interstate 70 had come up with a decidedly different path. Looking to avoid the expense and hassle of buying commercial property along U.S. 40, they chose a route through two big city parks west of Rosemont, then swooped it south to join 40 in the Franklin-Mulberry corridor. In the process, they penciled in a route that drilled straight through Rosemont's heart.

If built as proposed, I-70 would pass within a yell of the Wileses' house, in two directions. It would cross Ellamont to the south and come up behind the school now planned for the woods across the street. It would dominate the view from the front yard. It would obliterate the quiet. It would cut the neighborhood in half. And the Wileses would have to count themselves lucky, because the expressway also would flatten 880 of their neighbors' homes.

Wiles and those neighbors knew that a parade of expressway proposals had come and gone over the previous decade, and that this one might well meet the sort of shout-down that had killed its predecessors. Still, it was galling. Rosemont was a genuine success story. Its household income exceeded the city's average. Its people were better educated than most of their fellow Baltimoreans. It had a higher-than-average rate of home ownership. Why target such a place?

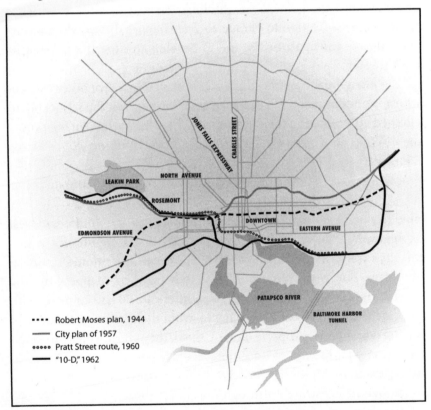

By 1962, city and state officials had considered four main paths for Baltimore's east-west expressway, along with a slew of quickly forgotten variants. Three of the four had in common an alignment through Leakin Park and Joe Wiles's well-educated, middle-class neighborhood of Rosemont.

The question went unasked — and certainly, unanswered — outside Rosemont. The press and most of the population concentrated their outrage on what the road planners had in mind for the white neighborhoods to the east. Nearing downtown, I-70 would encircle history-rich Mount Vernon Place (and the nation's first monument to George Washington) to meet a partially built north-south radial, the future I-83, in a lavish interchange. From there, it would bull eastward through a half-dozen communities, displacing thousands. Most outrageously, in the view of many Baltimoreans, the six-lane freeway would blast through Tyson Street, where a band of artists and professionals had won national acclaim by transforming an enclave of derelict houses into a bright, funky arts district.

At first, the planners said they might be able to adjust the route to spare the "Pastel Block," as Tyson was nicknamed, but that was before they muscled up the proposed interstate to eight lanes; by the summer of 1957, the city was saying that the street's future was "bleak — almost nil." And to add insult to injury, I-70 would be double-decked and elevated for most of its swing through town, so that its upper level stood nearly sixty feet off the ground.

To this point, Baltimore's citizens had been neither asked whether they wanted an expressway nor consulted about its route and design. It was handed to them as a done deal; by the time they were briefed on its specifics, the decisions about where and how and whether it went seemed unalterable. Baltimoreans didn't care for being treated this way, and they didn't keep it to themselves. Letters poured into the newspapers condemning the coming Chinese Wall. Property owners in Mount Vernon decried an "unnecessary eyesore" in their midst. A citizens' group threw a fit over the absence of plans to relocate those who would be put out of their homes. A delegation of fifty residents chartered a bus to protest the city's secrecy and arrogance to bureau officials in D.C.

It was too much for the mayor, Thomas D'Alesandro Jr. He asked planners to eyeball some of the older expressway proposals — and by now there were plenty to choose from — for alternatives that might spark less controversy. They received some unsolicited advice from Lewis Mumford, whose letter castigating the interstate's route through the parks west of Rosemont appeared in *Landscape Architecture*. "What is happening in your community is a classic case of the wanton damage now being done all over the United States for no good purpose," he squalled, fingering engineers and municipal officials "of bulldozer mind" who measured progress by "the amount of devastation that they can cause."

"If these engineers had the faintest insight into the art of city planning, they would know that long-distance highways should never enter a city's limits; that, on the contrary, they should bypass every large urban area, though offering a number of approaches."

Any other scheme could "only work damage to your city," he concluded, "of which the damage caused by the highway robbery of your park space would only be a small part of the total damage such a plan would finally work."

The city's planners were unswayed. They bought fifteen acres of land at Baltimore's western line, adjacent to one of the parks. The interstate's path through the middle of town might be in contention, officials explained, but its route on the west side, over by Rosemont, was settled.

16

A T THIS POINT, the patterns of settlement and movement that would define American life for the rest of the twentieth century had been fixed. The suburbs were booming, not only among homebuyers but among workers. City after city saw its downtown jobs flatline while openings exploded on the metropolitan fringe. Factories and warehouses sprawled on the cheaper land out there, and retailers were planting satellite stores amid their shifting customer base or abandoning downtown altogether.

These developments posed a real worry for cities jealous of their tax bases, as you might imagine, which is why the fifties saw so many push out their borders to ensnare surrounding bedroom communities. Another dilemma wasn't so easily solved. Mass transit worked only when its riders shared common destinations for work, entertainment, and shopping. Combine the suburbs' low-density housing with jobs scattered hither and yon, and no transit system — certainly not one on fixed rails, anyway — could do much to relieve dependence on the automobile, even if allowed to operate deep in the red.

A few cities, notably San Francisco and Washington, D.C., studied light rail or subway systems, regardless. Some others considered more radical fixes to their clogged streets. When utility officials in Fort Worth hired shopping mall pioneer Victor Gruen to rethink the city's downtown, he responded by banning cars altogether. Residents would drive to a beltway around the central business district, where they would park

in one of a half-dozen huge garages, none more than three or four minutes' walk from dead center, and hoof it the rest of the way to jobs or
stores. Electric shuttle cars would move those unable to walk, and de-
liveries would be made underground. Some streets "will be narrowed in
stretches so that they become malls," Gruen explained. "In other places,
streets will be widened into courts, and the rich colors of the paving,
the trees and the little pools in the central district will stand out like
jewels against the backdrop of the buildings surrounding them."

Sounded good, and got a lot of people excited. But many missed
the fine print. The garages would accommodate only enough cars to
carry half of the district's daily head count. The other half would ride
in on buses. In Fort Worth, which was already spread-eagled all over
the countryside, and in which only 17 percent of the population used
public transit, that wasn't likely to happen.

So municipal officials found themselves stuck. The shape of
the American city was changing, and the only form of transportation suited to this new shape was the very agent of the change.
And cars had become so multitudinous that only more and bigger
highways, it seemed, could keep the out-of-town exodus from becoming total.

Which is why the nation's highway men can be forgiven for feeling a
bit self-satisfied when they gathered outside Hartford, Connecticut, in
September 1957, at the first national summit on urban superhighways.
Saving the American metropolis was up to them, they believed, and
they had the expertise to accomplish the job. They came expecting that
view to predominate.

An ambush waited. The conference, titled "The New Highways:
Challenge to the Metropolitan Region," was held at the spanking-new
headquarters of the Connecticut General Life Insurance Company,
which had just moved its operation out of downtown Hartford to a
roomy modernist campus on 280 acres in suburban Bloomfield. It was
a cool, airy, classy place for a blooding.

Early speakers toed the highway line. Pyke Johnson, an old friend
of the Chief's and a longtime auto industry cheerleader, predicted that
the "already phenomenal pace of suburbanization will increase rather

than diminish," but that "first-class highway links between the suburbs and the downtown areas are sure to help the latter recapture some of their lost commercial and recreational appeal." Another lauded expressways as "our great new 'topographic' opportunity to give neighborhoods definition." Finally, Bert Tallamy told the conference that the interstates promised to be "probably the greatest single tool" for curing urban woes and offered "the chance of a century to make our cities sparkle brightly."

"Great care must be exercised," he acknowledged, "to make certain that urban areas will obtain the maximum amount of benefit from arterial highway construction." Even with such care, the highway community could rest assured that "there will develop forces opposed to it" — most of which, he predicted, eventually would come to recognize the genius of the new roads and their builders, and morph into supporters eager to "cut the ribbons and take the credit they do not deserve."

He did not have to wait long to meet the opposition; it showed up in the form of urban planners, who over the next two days made it clear that they did not regard the highway men as saviors. Rather, they called for a halt to urban highway building until the affected cities had time to plan for them in detail, something that virtually none had done. How could a state highway department know where to place an urban freeway, if the cities weren't sure themselves?

By and large, the criticism was firm but polite. "Past emphasis in highway planning may have been too much upon sound engineering features and too little on the overall picture," one planner suggested. The shortest distance between two points might satisfy motorists, but did it justify dissecting parks, fouling creeks, and casting neighborhoods in shadow? A housing activist took a harsher tack, objecting that the nation's highway program was too important to be "placed in the hands of highway engineers."

That was prelude to the conference's last speaker, who dispensed with any pretense of politeness and changed the whole tenor of the gathering: an eloquent, forceful, and very cranky Lewis Mumford.

• • •

Just a month before, Mumford had been all but branded a has-been by the *New Republic*, a magazine for which he'd written extensively. His latest book, the just-released *The Transformation of Man*, had been "hardly noticed." The conventional explanation for "this devastating reversal in esteem," the magazine said, was that "while Mumford's earlier and well-known writings on literature, architecture, and the urban scene had remarkably fresh interpretations, his latest books, concerned with morals, ideals and metaphysics, are . . . sermons on 'the condition of man' and 'the conduct of life.'"

But if Mumford did, in fact, teeter at the brink of irrelevance in August 1957, he took a decisive step back from the precipice on September 11. His remarks in Bloomfield were the first publicized attack on the year-old interstate program, and an opening salvo in what would come to be called the Freeway Revolt. They made Mumford a darling, to this day, of urban planners, anti-sprawl activists, and critics of the suburban lifestyle.

He went straight for the jugular on taking the stage. Tallamy and his colleagues lacked "the slightest notion of what they were doing," Mumford told the conference. Otherwise, "they would not appear as blithe and cocky over the way they were doing it." The interstate program was bound to bring destruction, not salvation, to the nation's cities. It had been founded "on a very insufficient study" of highways, rather than transportation — on "blunders of one-dimensional thinking" — and would benefit only the "fantastic and insolent chariots" that jammed the streets, "the second mistress that exists in every household right alongside the wife — the motor car." Want to save the cities? Forget about roads. The solution, Mumford said, lay in restoring a human scale to urban life, in "making it possible for the pedestrian to exist."

A choice was looming, for "either the motor car will drive us all out of the cities, or the cities will have to drive out the motor car." Americans should "apply our intelligence to the purposes of life," he said, concluding: "That means eventually we will put the motor car in its place. We will cast off the mistress and live with our wives instead."

It was a heck of a note on which to close a conference. The shocked highway community staggered from Bloomfield to lick its wounds, while Mumford recast the substance of his speech into an essay, "The Highway and the City," for *Architectural Record*. A half century later, it feels remarkably undated. "When the American people, through their Congress, voted a little while ago for a $26 billion highway program," it began, "the most charitable thing to assume about this action is that they hadn't the faintest notion of what they were doing. Within the next fifteen years they will doubtless find out; but by that time it will be too late to correct all the damage to our cities and our countryside, not least to the efficient organization of industry and transportation, that this ill-conceived and preposterously unbalanced program will have wrought."

His thesis stated, Mumford hacked away at the 1956 act, calling its "Defense Highway" label "specious, indeed flagrantly dishonest," and its urban freeways a sore on any town they touched: "The wide swathes of land devoted to cloverleaves, and even more complicated multi-level interchanges, to expressways . . . butcher up precious urban space in exactly the same way that freight yards and marshalling yards did when the railroads dumped their passengers and freight inside the city." They devoured not only open land, but real estate already occupied by people and homes. "Perhaps our age will be known to the future historian as the age of the bulldozer and the exterminator," he wrote, "and in many parts of the country the building of a highway has about the same result upon vegetation and human structures as the passage of a tornado or the blast of an atom bomb."

The hell of it was, all that disruption would do nothing to ease congestion. Here was a tool that "actually expands the evil it is meant to overcome," the piece argued, and which would continue doing so "until that terminal point when all the business and industry that originally gave rise to the congestion move out of the city, to escape strangulation, leaving a waste of expressways and garages behind them.

"This," Mumford declared, "is pyramid building with a vengeance: a tomb of concrete roads and ramps covering the dead corpse of a city."

Still bruised from the clubbing it received at the Hartford conference, the nation's highway community held another get-together at Syracuse University's Sagamore Center in October 1958. Mumford and his fellow critics were left off the guest list, which might explain why the five-day First National Conference on Highways and Urban Development felt like a love-in. Safe from the naysayers, highway men congratulated themselves on how well they cooperated, and they agreed with the city officials attending that they should work together at every stage of urban highway development.

They also agreed that roads should be part of a broader effort at city planning, and that they should keep the public apprised of what they had on the table. To help people understand why one plan might be stronger than the alternatives, they would make "a grand accounting of the costs and benefits," Pyke Johnson summarized. "Advantages and disadvantages of each alternative — in terms respectively of the highway user and the community — would be added up and evaluated."

That assumed, of course, that everything Americans loved or hated about their cities was quantifiable, that they measured the value of a park or river view, or the dispiriting advance of blight, in dollars and cents. The post-conference glow had not yet faded when the highway men received their first hard lesson that this wasn't so.

In San Francisco, state highway officials were at work on Interstate 480, a long-planned link between the Bay Bridge, which sprouted from the eastern waterfront, and the north shore's Golden Gate Bridge, which carried U.S. 101 across the mouth of San Francisco Bay. To highway engineers, I-480's route made obvious sense. The four-mile highway would hug the waterfront, which was jumbled with old piers and warehouses, but no homes, and skirt the business district, thereby serving commuters from both sides of town. In the interest of shrinking the interstate's footprint, the state opted to make it a double-decked "skyway."

Seeing a highway depicted on paper is one thing; beholding it finished, something else entirely. Too late, San Franciscans realized that they'd permitted a terrible blunder. In place of their waterfront — which, though partially blocked by low buildings, offered one of the most breathtaking urban vistas in the world, overlooking the shimmering bay and Alcatraz Island — they now saw an unadorned gray concrete barricade rising, at its peak, fifty-seven feet from the city's historic Embarcadero. It cast its surroundings in all-day twilight, severed downtown from the docks that had birthed it, and ran smack across the face of a beloved landmark, the Ferry Building, a gathering spot for generations and a survivor of the 1906 earthquake.

To tens of thousands of San Franciscans, the Embarcadero Freeway seemed less a highway than a vivisection. Petitions circulated. Protest groups bloomed. And the public's outrage was shared by the city fathers: on January 27, 1959, citing "the demolition of homes, the destruction of residential areas, the forced uprooting and relocation of individuals, families and business enterprises," the Board of Supervisors approved a resolution opposing seven of the ten freeways planned for the city, including the yet-unbuilt western two-thirds of I-480.

This meant refusing $280 million in Federal Aid money, an unthinkable act in the eyes of most municipal officials. It was a vote heard around the country. Not only did it effectively kill the state's ambitions for a lavish freeway grid through town, it reverberated with every American confronted by expressways he wasn't sure he wanted.

Highway officials predicted San Francisco would pay dearly for its stand. "It's the traffic which is the monstrosity, the traffic itself, not the freeway," as one former California highway commissioner said. "Building freeways is no different from building schools, a city hall, a hospital or other public buildings. It is the general public interest which must be served, and not the special interests of a few affected people."

The supervisors stood firm. The Embarcadero Freeway was left a stump, its westward flow abruptly halted near Telegraph Hill. The *San Francisco Chronicle* campaigned to have the completed mile and a half torn down, arguing that its "monstrous defects have so inescapably manifested themselves that they are now being inveighed against even by those who were shouting loudest for quick construction of the freeway," and denouncing its "corrosive effect" and "power to afflict the entire downtown area."

Mumford must have found grim satisfaction in these stirrings. At long last, he was leading a chorus. MIT professor John T. Howard told readers of the *American City* that if a highway "worsens the livability and efficiency of a metropolitan area rather than bettering it, that highway is a disservice to the community — even if it carries traffic to capacity, and all the traffic seems to want to go where it is carried."

Mumford might have written that himself. The mainstream press joined in. David Cort of *The Nation* decried "Chinese Walls," noting: "Every expressway excludes a number of people from what they love on the other side of the road." *Harper's* glumly observed: "The gasoline motor is making America a fit place for wheels to roll around in. Whether America will also be a satisfying place for human beings to live in, seems neither here nor there." Daniel Patrick Moynihan, a professor who would soon begin a long career as a United States senator, drew a bead on what he saw as a rush to build urban highways with a piece in the *Reporter* magazine. "In one metropolis after another, the plans have been thrown together and the bulldozers set to work," he wrote. "It is not true, as is sometimes alleged, that the sponsors of the interstate program ignored the consequences it would have in the cities. Nor did they simply acquiesce in them. They exulted in them."

Author John Keats's seminal 1958 critique of the automobile, *The Insolent Chariots,* went so far as to borrow its title from a phrase Mumford had coined at the Hartford conference. Mumford kept up his own attack in a November 1959 *New Yorker* article, "The Skyway's the Limit." His specific target was Robert Moses's Verrazano-Narrows Bridge between Staten Island and Brooklyn, but his observations applied to projects in Baltimore, San Francisco, any number of cities. The bridge would displace nearly eight thousand people in Brooklyn's Bay Ridge section, to say nothing "of the many other people whose lives or properties will be unfavorably affected by the elevated highway through their neighborhood," he wrote. "But what is Brooklyn to the highway engineer — except a place to go through quickly, at whatever necessary sacrifice of peace and amenity by its inhabitants?

"In the utopia that highway engineers have been busily bulldozing into existence, no precinct of the city and no part of the surrounding countryside are to remain inaccessible to automobile traffic on a large scale," he wrote. "As a formula for defacing the natural landscape and ruining what is left of our great cities, nothing could be more effective."

• • •

The most surprising critic of the new urban highways was the man who'd spurred their financing. It's hard to imagine how Dwight Eisenhower could have been unaware that the interstate system was designed to venture into cities, what with all the fuss in San Francisco, the controversies unfolding in Baltimore and other towns, and newspaper chatter on the paths of proposed freeways just blocks from the White House — not to mention that he'd signed the 1956 act and presumably read something about it beforehand.

But it wasn't until the spring of 1959, so the story goes, that the president got his first inkling that the highway system he'd envisioned differed in major respects from the one he would get. He was in the back of a limousine headed out of Washington for Camp David when the car bogged down in a highway construction snarl. Ike asked what was going on and learned that the highway in question was an interstate. This was far too close to Washington to comply with the president's notions of a largely rural, intercity system, an American take on the autobahns. Riled, Eisenhower demanded an explanation — and so, according to one school, discovered that "his" highway program wasn't.

Another version of his discovery process is less dramatic: Ike learned of urban interstates during a presentation by Harland Bartholomew, a St. Louis planner who'd served on the Chief's interregional highway committee and who was now involved in planning in the capital. Whatever the case, the president wasn't pleased. And so, at the same time that Blatnik launched his probe and Mumford's allies were poised to become an army, another major threat to the interstates blossomed within the executive branch.

In mid-June 1959, Eisenhower received a letter from his old friend and tolls advocate John S. Bragdon, suggesting they meet to discuss the "road situation." Now Ike's coordinator of public works planning, the retired major general had been exchanging letters with Bert Tallamy in recent months and related their back-and-forth to the president. "Mr. Tallamy agrees that the Interstate System is not designed to solve all the principal highway traffic problems of cities," he wrote, "but maintains it has always been the intention since the Interstate Highway System was conceived to extend those highways *into and through* as well as around metropolitan areas and cities."

Bragdon recommended the creation of a committee to revisit urban routing and other possible problems. He got it; Ike replied in early July that Bragdon was to undertake a "broad review of the Federal highway program" to ensure that its "policies, methods, and standards" were in sync with national objectives. Specifically, he and his committee were to eyeball the urban routes and drum up ways to ensure that highway officials worked in harmony with city planners. If they found that the interstates needed redirection, they were to suggest actions that would bring that about.

Bragdon apparently viewed this as license to rethink the whole program, down to its most fundamental assumptions, and he seized on the task like a pit bull on flank steak. He hired a full-time staff of nineteen and drew up a list of ideals he believed the system should meet. To start with, it should serve intercity traffic, not local; only beltways would be acceptable incursions into metro areas. The general also wondered whether Congress had been fully apprised of the system's urban character when it approved the 1956 act, and asked the administration to scour its files for documents that spoke to this "legislative intent." The answer: *Interregional Highways* had made it "perfectly clear" in 1944 "that the Interstate Highway System would penetrate the cities," and the wording of subsequent acts left no doubt that Congress had known what it was approving.

Maybe so, Bragdon responded, but the system OK'ed in 1944 had been enlarged by Public Roads; surely Congress never intended urban interstates in the numbers and sizes now contemplated. He convinced commerce secretary Frederick H. Mueller to suspend work on any planned city interstates until the bureau devised a way to incorporate them into formal urban planning efforts. Tallamy and the bureau were deeply unhappy at this. Bragdon was acting in opposition to the will of Congress. Every study on which the program was based had been explicit: the country's highway needs were sharpest in the cities. Congress had read those studies. Congress had seen the *Yellow Book*'s maps. Congress wanted urban routes.

The general was just hitting stride. In October 1959, he suggested a few of his own guidelines for urban routes. Outer beltways would get top priority. Inner beltways would have to be financed from regular Federal Aid money. Before the month was out, he'd decreed that the entire system should be scaled down; only with a reduction in mileage would it be possible to build a basic intercity system within the budget Congress had authorized in 1956.

Now the general's people started showing up in the bureau's field offices, amplifying the sense among longtime highway men that their most cherished program was under siege. They might have been even more alarmed had they realized that Bragdon and the president were reading from the same page. In a November "memorandum for the record," Bragdon wrote, after a meeting with Ike, that "the President confirmed the fact that his idea had always been that the transcontinental network for interstate and intercity travel and the Defense significances are paramount and that routing within cities is primarily the responsibility of the cities. The President was forceful on this point." Come December, an emboldened Bragdon wrote that the interstates should avoid centers of congestion and should never be larger than six lanes wide, and rarely more than four. A few weeks later, he resurrected the idea of using tolls to help meet the system's expenses.

The shape of the entire program was on the line when, on April 6, 1960, Eisenhower hosted a meeting on the committee's findings at the White House. Bragdon showed up with seventeen large easel charts, which an underling flipped at his signal; Tallamy spoke for the bureau. The adversaries emerged with varying accounts of what was said. In an interview decades later, Tallamy recalled that Bragdon was chugging through a lengthy presentation when he was interrupted by a wearying Ike, who gave the floor to the highway administrator. Tallamy "could see that the president was getting nervous about the time he was spending on this," so he jettisoned any formal remarks and instead whipped out a copy of the *Yellow Book*. This, he explained, was on every congressman's desk when the vote came in. He showed off several of its maps, the cities radiating thick black lines. The president, surprised, asked whether he was sure the book had been on every desk. Tallamy replied that he was as certain as he could be. Eisenhower snapped: The meeting's over, gentlemen. So ended the general's bid to reinvent the interstates.

Bragdon remembered the meeting differently, and unlike Tallamy — who was an old man by the time he related the story — he committed his version to paper just two days after the fact. He quoted the president as saying that he now realized that the promise of federal money in the cities, along with the *Yellow Book,* had sold the program to Congress. "He went on to say that the matter of running interstate routes through the congested parts of the cities was entirely against his original concept and wishes; that he never anticipated that the program would turn out this way," Bragdon reported. "He pointed out that when the Clay Committee Report was rendered, he had studied it carefully, and that he was certainly not aware of any concept of using the program to build up an extensive intra-city route network as part of the program he sponsored."

Tallamy "interjected that the interstate concept was nothing new — that it had been developed as far back as 1939. The President stated that, while that might be so, he had not heard of it and that his proposal for a national highway program was his own.

"In conclusion," Bragdon wrote, "he reiterated his disappointment over the way the program had been developed against his wishes, and that it had reached the point to where his hands were virtually tied."

Accepting that Eisenhower was ignorant of the highway program even as he stumped for it, it's difficult to fathom how he'd managed to remain oblivious in the years since. Yet if Bragdon is to be believed, here was the evidence, from Eisenhower himself. Here was Ike saying he knew nothing of the highway plans predating his arrival in the White House. Here he was, saying that he hadn't understood the bill he signed. Here he was, admitting that he'd been in the dark until just recently. Again, he wasn't much of a detail man.

Bragdon left the committee not long afterward for the Civil Aeronautics Board. His replacement filed a twelve-page report in January 1961, days before John F. Kennedy moved into the White House. Nothing came of it. But the general's work was not for naught.

His committee's consultants complained that the interstates were a "highway program rather than a transportation program" and couldn't possibly solve problems "much bigger than just highways." That view would gain widening favor in the coming years, and Bragdon's insistence that planning be an important part of highway conception, that the roads integrate well with their surroundings and with community needs, would very soon become law.

17

ONE LATE SUMMER dawn in 1981 I pulled off Interstate 44 at the exit for Conway, Missouri, and steered my MG Midget, a demonic assemblage of pot metal, bad wiring, and rust, into a Texaco station at the top of the ramp. My college girlfriend and I had been on the road from Los Angeles for three days, and I was feeling pretty cocky about having nursed the roadster across the desert and over the southern Rockies, what with its well-earned reputation for mechanical caprice; our destination, St. Louis, lay an easy four or five hours ahead.

McShane's Texaco was a big place, with a full garage and a café next door that advertised itself as "Home of the Little Round Pies." It hadn't opened for the day when I pulled up to the pumps; except for the lone Texaco cashier, the interchange was empty of life. I paid for my gas, fired up the MG, crossed back over the highway to the entrance ramp, and broke down.

Twenty minutes of pleading with the MG didn't restart it. Neither did a long witless stare under the hood, nor pushing the car down the ramp, jumping in, and popping the clutch; the engine sputtered for a moment but failed to catch. We left it on the shoulder and trudged back up to the Texaco, where we learned the mechanic wouldn't report to work for a couple of hours. So we sat on a curb ringing the station's parking lot, waiting. The sun rose in the sky. The temperature leaped. Before long, the gas station's concrete apron burned the skin. Cars and trucks and campers filed into the Texaco, filling the air with the smell of gas and the sound of the pumps' ringing bells, the shouts of vacationing families.

Eventually the station's full staff showed up and towed the MG onto the lot, where a young mechanic looked under the hood and made an announcement that I sincerely did not wish to hear: "I ain't never worked on one of these." He agreed to try his luck, however, and spent what remained of the morning at it, until he diagnosed the problem as a bad fuel pump and apologized that he couldn't find a replacement. I did what I had to do. I called for my mom, in St. Louis, to come get us.

That sentenced us to several additional hours in the parking lot. We were on high ground and from the curb had a fine view of pastureland sloping away to the east, thick copses of hardwoods, and farther off, the wooded hills and ridges of the Ozarks; no human activity, however, aside from the interstate, which issued hisses and jake-brake burps throughout the day. So we watched people in far more reliable vehicles roll up and down the ramps, stole into the café for brief respites from the heat, sampled the Little Round Pies, and fell into numb silence.

Years later I learned that the Little Round Pies were the invention of a café in Conway proper, back in the days when U.S. 66 was the principal route in southwest Missouri and ran through the settlement. The concoctions were a hit and earned Conway some small renown among the Mother Road's travelers. Had we broken down back then, our wait would have been far more tolerable. Pleasant, even: we would have been stranded in a community, among its people, rather than a long hike away on an outpost geared to momentary pause, to strangers.

But with the coming of the interstate, tourists and truckers didn't happen through Conway anymore. As the appetite for Little Round Pies had always been sharpest among folks passing through, in time the pies moved out to the interchange. The same went for the filling station. By 1981, pretty much all of Conway's commercial bustle, such as it was, lay out beyond the burg's edge, in a spot both heavily populated and oddly remote.

From where we sat the town proper was off to the east and out of sight. I'd driven that stretch of 44 a few times before my exile at

McShane's, and I've traveled it many times since, and still, I've never seen the place.

So it was for towns throughout the States. Mom-and-pop businesses on superseded U.S. highways watched their customers vanish as the interstates continued their crawl across the continent. As *Florida Trend* magazine would cry in 1965, the interstate system "diverts traffic away from former arteries of travel, drains the life's blood from established firms which are situated on the old highways and leaves them to die." Anyone visiting Quapaw, Oklahoma, a once-hale Route 66 stop-off bypassed by I-40, found a Main Street of vacant shops, closed service stations; a bankrupt motel, bought a few years before for $28,000, was now on the market for $5,000 and finding no takers. The owner of a gas station on U.S. 80 in east Texas lost 80 percent of his business immediately after I-20 opened nearby. A long stretch of the Lincoln Highway in Nebraska saw three-quarters of its traffic evaporate after I-80 opened a little to the south. Connecticut's neon-lined Berlin Turnpike, packed with traffic for years, lost nearly half of it when Interstate 91 opened, killing a regiment of small motels and marooning two full-service Howard Johnsons.

A great many towns, sharing Conway's fate, were both winners and losers in the new economy of high-speed travel. Income from passers-through didn't dry up, but it certainly left Main Street. The experience of Bertha Amick of Boonville, Missouri, was repeated a thousand times over. Amick was proprietor of the Kit Carson Motel, one of several businesses rendered superfluous when I-70 was built on the far side of town. She had to shutter fourteen of her twenty-two rooms. Her son Hugh bought 2½ acres of land out by I-70, where he put up the Atlasta Motel. His place was full every night.

Small-town shopping districts weren't just losing business to the exits, but to bigger towns suddenly made closer by the new highways' speed and convenience. Why shop for back-to-school clothes in Conway, when much bigger Lebanon was now half as far away as it had been, in terms of driving time? Why settle for the meager pickings in Eagle Rock, Virginia, when the malls of Roanoke were a quick jaunt down I-81?

Towns that had been bypassed decades before by the U.S. highway system now fell off the map altogether. Remember Lida, Nevada? It found itself some 165 straight-line miles from the nearest interstate. Few settlements are farther off the most beaten of beaten paths; today, Lida is 223.4 miles from the nearest Cracker Barrel.

Yes, for every place experiencing a gain in population and prosperity, it seemed, there was another to which the new roads carried hardship. The interstates eased the path of meat and produce from farm to market, but rights of way cost farmers and their spreads dearly, for each mile of interstate devoured 30 to 40 acres of ground; in Iowa alone, officials reckoned that their 710 miles of freeway would devour 26,000 acres of productive cropland, or more than forty square miles. And interstates didn't thread carefully among adjoining properties. They blundered through them, dividing farms, isolating pieces beyond four lanes of impenetrable concrete and rebar. A 1964 Kentucky State Highway Department study found fifty-four cases of "severance" — the department's term for splitting farm property — along eighteen miles of Interstate 64. The highway was sufficiently disruptive that in three out of four cases, farmers sold off the stray parcels; in one case, relatives whose properties had adjoined now had to drive seven and a half miles to reach each other's homes.

By the summer of 1962, about 12,500 miles of the system were open to traffic, and another 34 miles were opening, on average, every week. The economic impact of this effort was stunning. Each billion dollars spent on construction provided the equivalent of forty-eight thousand full-time jobs for a year and consumed an almost inconceivably vast pile of resources: sixteen million barrels of cement, more than half a million tons of steel, eighteen million pounds of explosives, 123 million gallons of petroleum products, and enough earth to bury New Jersey knee-deep. It also devoured seventy-six million tons of aggregate — so much aggregate, some in the business have surmised, that the United States could not mine enough rock to rebuild the interstates today.

The new highways were studies in sameness. AASHO and the bureau collaborated on a standard for virtually every feature of the highways — guardrails, rest stops, even the grass along their borders; on the medians, it was to be mowed to a height between three and eight inches, and on the shoulders, three to ten.

Turner took great pride that the system was "so uniform you can't tell what state you are in except as you look at the sign," that a driver from one part of the country would not confront "a totally different way of doing things" in another. Safe roads offered no surprises, required no sudden moves.

And indeed, the roads were far safer than practically any others in existence. A 1961 bureau study showed that the fatality rate on urban interstates was half that of conventional highways, and that an even bigger gap separated rural interstates from their predecessors — 3.3 deaths per 100 million miles traveled, versus 8.7. Overall, the system was about two and a half times as safe as the highways it replaced; its completion, "conservatively estimated," would save at least five thousand lives a year.*

Not everyone was so enamored of the system's unrelenting predictability. Critics had decried the sterile nature of high-speed roads since long before limited-access became a reality, since the very year that Benton MacKaye had proposed the townless highway. Phillips Russell of North Carolina's *Chapel Hill Weekly* wrote in 1930 that "as fast as improvements are perfected, highways constantly tend to become dull and uninteresting to travel over," lulling travelers into "a state of silent torpor, with no more animation than a box of hibernating terrapins."

The interstates' careful geometry amplified this effect. The system didn't rely on straightaways (or "tangents," as engineers call them) nearly as much as its detractors suggested, but even so, they're out there. One, on I-80 in Nebraska, stretches seventy-two miles, and plenty of others take a half hour or more to travel. Where the roads aren't straight, their curves are so gentle and banked so exactly that they go all but unnoticed; with rare exception, they cause no centrifugal pull, no sense, even momentary, of lateral movement.

Over time, the bureau came to view a gently undulating express-

---

* Cookie-cutter design made rational budgeting possible, too; after all, how could you estimate the relative needs of the states if their product varied?

way as an improvement on tangents, and it preached this view to its state partners. A well-executed curve in even relatively flat country might accomplish multiple goals — might save millions of dollars by swinging around a rise, rather than drilling through it; might look better, and be more interesting to drive, if it followed the land's contours, rather than defying them; and might help combat "highway hypnosis," a lethal daze that was said to descend on motorists who had too little to do behind the wheel. "Some drivers just fall asleep under the spell of the passing miles. Others are lulled into a trance, insensible to what is going on around them," *Changing Times* magazine warned. "'This one factor more than any other,' says the AAA, 'has accounted for most of the multiple-vehicle chain-reaction accidents we read about on super-highways.'"

Open-country bends not only kept a driver's hands busy, but they gave him features on which to focus his gaze, and thus instinctively stay on top of his speed; the same went for "vertical curves," dips and rises that relieved the monotony of an unchanging horizon and saved tons of money in fills and cuts. Like every aspect of the new roads, their wriggles were rigidly standardized. Not only did each maintain a prescribed minimum radius, but the point at which it met a tangent was softened with a "transitional curve," so that a driver experienced no kink in his smooth glide, no need to consciously move the wheel.

Of course, the critics were right about the downside to such safe and seamless motoring, though in fairness, travel had been moving toward monotony for a long time. A pilgrim of centuries past, on completing a day's walk across roadless terrain, would have had much to report about the country he'd traversed — the details of flora and fauna, the land's shape and character, the sounds and smells of village and field. He would have noticed the moss on tree bark, the conversation of a fast-moving stream, the lacework of afternoon light on the forest floor. He might have startled deer and bear, unalerted by his soft approach, or reveled in bird song.

A later traveler, riding horseback, might have spoken of the views he'd enjoyed, but they would have been limited views, next to the walker's. He would have moved at a faster clip, and thus missed the tiny details of his surroundings that only a leisurely pace revealed. Further on, a stagecoach passenger had an even tighter range of experience; he beheld landscape not only from a road's fixed path, but as a moving picture framed by his window, and his description of a long trip would likely dwell less on the scenery than on the discomforts of the stage, the bumps in the road, the passage itself. Trains erected a pane of glass between traveler and country, and further insulated him by boosting his speed.

But with the modern car on the modern freeway, the modern traveler was left with practically nothing to celebrate but the ever-briefer time he had to devote to getting from one place to another. He was sequestered not only from his setting, but from fellow passengers, if he so wished; he met strangers only when he pulled off the highway to gas up or grab a bite. He was insulated from sound, smells, and climate. The details of all that surrounded him were blurred by speed, too distant to make out, or too distracting to enjoy. Scenery was held at arm's length, beyond the well-manicured right of way; one drove through a piece of country, rather than becoming one with it. As John Steinbeck famously observed in 1962's *Travels with Charley: In Search of America*: "When we get these thruways across the whole country, as we will and must, it will be possible to drive from New York to California without seeing a single thing."

To Turner, ever-faithful to quantifiable results, the system's strengths were irrefutable, its flaws matters of opinion; he was far too busy to dwell on whether John Steinbeck enjoyed driving the interstates — or to read anything Steinbeck wrote, for that matter. He took an early bus to work, put in twelve to fourteen hours at the office, and, once back at the modest brick ranch he shared with Mable, changed and watched the evening news before dinner. Most nights, he had plans to attend an after-dinner meeting, either to speak about highways or as a member of his Masonic lodge; otherwise, he pulled out his briefcase and worked until 10:30 or 11:00 P.M.

Motorists seeking relief from the monotony of the drive found that the system's sameness wasn't limited to its right of way, for it wasn't but a handful of years before the mom-and-pop businesses that had moved out from Main Street were joined by national chains, and the mercantile knots at the exits soon seemed cut from a stencil. To this point, the conventional wisdom held that the best bet for a good roadside meal was a restaurant with long-haul trucks and police cruisers parked outside; now, restaurants waiting at the end of one ramp were not much different, if they were different at all, from those one exit back, or two exits, or ten, and they used a visual shorthand — logos, signature colors, the shape of roofs and other architectural details — to identify themselves. Filling-station chains did likewise, their outlets sharing designs as standard as the bureau's signage.

The aim of the companies responsible for the shift was standardization, providing the customer a predictable experience, no less than it was for Frank Turner. The first Holiday Inn had opened outside Memphis in 1952, a few months after a local homebuilder, Kemmons Wilson, packed his wife and five kids into the family station wagon for a drive to Washington, D.C., and found the lodging along the way tight, uncomfortable, and expensive. He incorporated the business in 1954 and franchised it in 1957; a year later, fifty Holiday Inns dotted the country, and a year after that, the number had doubled. By 1968, there were a thousand, and half were at the end of exit ramps.*

Howard Johnson enjoyed spectacular success as an interchange mainstay, as well. All but a dozen of the restaurants had shut down in response to gas rationing during World War II, but the company rebounded with a vengeance, its orange roofs spreading westward until they numbered more than nine hundred, better than half of them with a motel out back of the coffee shop. Turnpikes remained a HoJo

---

* Though the most familiar, Holiday Inn wasn't the first motel chain. In 1928, St. Louis–based Pierce Petroleum had attempted a network of roadside inns for travelers on the U.S. highways. The company operated gas stations at the time, as well as a few combination restaurant–gas station–bus terminals; the new venture seemed a natural progression. The first Pierce-Pennant Hotel opened in Springfield, Missouri, that July, and others followed in Columbia and Rolla and across the border in Oklahoma. But the motels — three or four stories tall, with garage parking and tasteful colonial-revival styling, down to their Currier and Ives prints — hemorrhaged cash, until Pierce came undone and sold all of its assets to Sinclair. That company ran the motels for a brief while until its losses halted the experiment.

specialty. A trip on the state-of-the-art superhighways of Maine, New Jersey, and Ohio, in addition to Pennsylvania, put travelers in close quarters with those trademark fried clams.

Old Man Stuckey raced to set up shop at remote interchanges to lure the full of bladder. Before long, he had 350 cookie-cutter outlets, each with predictably spotless bathrooms. And in time there appeared competitors even more precisely geared to the road-weary and time-starved. McDonald's had been around since 1940, when brothers Dick and Mac McDonald opened their first restaurant on U.S. 66 in San Bernardino, California, but the chain had expanded to only four lo-cations when, in 1954, milk shake machine salesman Ray Kroc con-vinced the brothers to grant him franchise rights. In ten years, he was drawing income from five hundred restaurants.

The same year Kroc got his start, the first Burger King — called Insta Burger King at the time — opened in Miami, its burgers and shakes priced at 18 cents apiece. One of its founders, James McLamore, had visited San Bernardino, as well, and, like Kroc, had been riveted by the McDonald brothers' simple menu and efficient service. And the broth-ers inspired yet another national chain. A Marine Corps veteran named Glen Bell ran a burger joint and later a taco stand in San Bernardino as the McDonalds perfected their system. He built the Mexican joint into a small chain and sold it to his partners — then repeated the process before launching Taco Bell in 1962.

Whataburgers popped up in Florida, Tennessee, and Texas. Carl's Jr. and In-N-Out Burgers sprouted in California. Dairy Queens and Burger Chefs and Roy Rogers outlets spread like the flu. Why? What was it about assembly-line food that drew customers by the millions? For starters, it was cheap: Burger King's Whopper cost 37 cents when it debuted in 1957, and a plain McDonald's hamburger, just 15.

But more than that, it answered a growing demand for speed and simplicity, as the auto cabin camps had decades before. A motorist making good time on the interstate wasn't inclined to squander his achievement with a fussy and time-gobbling sit-down meal, if he could slip in and out of a burger joint in fifteen minutes — or better yet, grab the goods and eat behind the wheel, while adding new miles to his tally.

And the chains' drive for efficient mass production mirrored a desire in the American public for predictable quality — for preferring the everyday but familiar to a surprise, good or bad. Sure, you could stray from the corridor in search of local flavor, and you might get lucky — might discover a diner with spectacular coffee, or a café serving Angus burgers big and juicy beyond description, or a small-town wayside famous for its Little Round Pies. Then again, you might get ptomaine poisoning.

And McDonald's coffee is pretty damn good. A Whopper isn't bad. Hardee's makes a creditable cinnamon roll. And they're right there, at the interchange. No need to hunt. They require barely a pause. Fast food and the interstates fed off each other. The highways provided the restaurants their customers; the restaurants, a service that kept the highways operating at maximum efficiency.

In a few odd places, an interchange escaped the chains. In fewer still, an exit — the actual interchange — became a destination in and of itself. One, near Dillon, South Carolina, grew into the grandest of interstate waysides.

Alan Schafer's place is dominated by a mammoth, neon-edged sombrero rising two hundred feet over Interstate 95 at its meeting with U.S. 301/501. Below, a sombrero-shaped restaurant serves steak. A ninety-seven-foot, sombrero-clad Colossus stands guard outside a gift shop, cars rolling between its legs. Motel guests swim in a pool enclosed by a sombrero-shaped solarium. Neon sombreros and cacti and rockets light the night. Supermarkets of fireworks and rubber whales and souvenir back scratchers abound.

Even the billboards fail to prepare you for South of the Border, and if you've driven 95 between Baltimore and Orlando, you know the billboards — yellow lettering and fluorescent sombreros on fields of black, their messages a mix of pun and guileless outburst. "Camp Weeth Pedro!" screams one, a half hour out. "Pedro's Weather Report: Chili Today, Hot Tamale," another advises. "You Never Sausage a Place!" promises a third, illustrated by a massive, three-dimensional kielbasa. For forty years or better, scores of them straddled the interstate, and as you neared the line separating the Carolinas they came ever faster, blotting out the roadside's pines and cedars, trumping drabber signs for cut-rate smokes and porno shops. In the past few years they've dwindled a bit in number, but at their height in the nineties, on one curve you could see eight of them at once.

Yet they understated the place. You see the sombrero tower first: curving steel legs, a glass elevator, the massive hat. Once off the interstate, you hit gas stations, arcades, restaurants — Pedro's Coffee Shop, Pedro's Pizza & Sub Shop, Pedro's Diner, the Sombrero, the Peddler Steak House, Pedro's Ice Cream Fiesta. In the stores (thirteen at last count) wait tiny Buddhas, lewd bowling towels, shot glasses, and key chains, all displayed under signs that push deals like carnival barkers. You want pig figurines? Here they are: pigs in baskets, in burlap sacks, playing cards. Want fireworks? The Border is among the nation's largest retailers of pyrotechnics, and some of the devices for sale are the size of trash cans. You can take your time browsing; roomy digs at the South of the Border Motor Hotel come with a carport. Twenty dirt-cheap honeymoon suites come equipped with headboard mirrors and Andre champagne.

South of the Border reckons that 112 million travelers have pulled into the place over the past sixty years, a figure that, if accurate, places the 350-acre spread among the nation's top tourist shrines. It happened by accident. In 1949, the adjoining North Carolina county voted itself dry and Schafer, the Miller beer distributor thereabouts, suddenly found himself long on stock and short of retailers. So he bought three acres on the state line, planted a pink eighteen-by-thirty-six-foot cinder-block shack there, and called it the South of the Border Beer Depot. Trade was brisk.

The name, however, didn't sit well with the state liquor folks. Schafer got them off his back by swapping "Beer Depot" for "Drive-In" and building a diner, its menu a short list of sandwiches. "Grilled cheese. Grilled ham. Peanut butter and jelly," he recalled when I visited with him years later. "That was the whole menu, except for soda and coffee — and beer, of course." So it may have stayed, a simple outlet for Miller beer, had a salesman not run out of cash one night in the early fifties, wandered into the diner, and pitched a deal: if Schafer gave him enough money to reach New York, he would hand over all of his samples. Schafer walked outside to the man's station wagon. It was filled with stuffed animals. Schafer bought them, "took about a five-times markup, and I put these animals on all the shelves," he said, "and in three weeks they were gone. And I said: *Jesus.*"

He put up a few billboards along U.S. 301/501, advertising his food and beer, and tourists showed up looking for shelter. The motel's first wing, forty rooms, opened in 1954. It did not have a vacancy for three years. By the time I-95 came through, the first big souvenir shop was open, and the original diner had grown into the Sombrero, a sit-down eatery with mock-cowhide booths and a sombrero-shaped salad bar.

In those early interstate years, Cadillacs and Lincolns crowded the parking lot, and Schafer strove to pamper his guests with bellhop service and a par-three golf course. The links eventually made way for a bustling back lot of warehouses and offices (under a mustard-colored water tower marked "S.O.B.") from which he directed a small empire of interconnected ventures. He remained the region's Miller and Heineken distributor and sold only those beers in his stores and restaurants; his Ace-Hi Advertising firm built all of South of the Border's billboards, which he wrote himself; and he owned a truck stop just up 301/501 that didn't make money but kept the Border's parking lots clear of big rigs, leaving room for tourists.

Just in case potential customers had missed the billboards — unlikely, but you couldn't be too careful — Schafer installed an enormous full-color, moving-image sign at the interstate's edge. Before he died of leukemia in 2001, its 24,576 bulbs had boosted his electric bill to about $110,000 a month.

When I had lunch at the Sombrero one afternoon, a carload of Mexicans — actual Mexicans — was seated a couple of tables away. They had trouble deciphering the menu and got little help from the wait staff. Nobody spoke Spanish.

18

BACK IN BALTIMORE, city officials searching for a way to kick-start their downtown's redevelopment announced that they'd found it in a gleaming black office complex called Charles Center, which in short order rose from the business district's southern edge. The project caused an immediate ripple in the city's plans for an east-west expressway. In July 1959, the *Sun* revealed that planners were secretly discussing a new I-70 route that swung south of downtown, instead of north — an alignment that spared Tyson Street and snuggled up to Charles Center.

This new secret plan routed the elevated freeway along the Inner Harbor's north shore, effectively sealing off downtown from the water, to meet north-south I-83 at an interchange built on or beside the harbor's docks. It promised to be Baltimore's version of the Embarcadero Freeway, a brutalist concrete veil over the city's most valuable asset, but that wasn't obvious at the time. Officialdom and the business community loved it. After all, it messed with nothing anyone cared about, at least anyone important. The Inner Harbor was a cesspool. And sure, east of the harbor the road would take out some houses, but they were old, in seedy riverside neighborhoods. No great loss.

When the planners' report, *Study for an East-West Expressway,* was formally released in January 1960, its language made plain its authors' driver-centric orientation. "Automobile driving along regular city streets is usually a rather dreary and dismal experience," it read.

"Driving on urban expressways is often stimulating and even exciting. Not only is there the pleasure of being able to proceed continuously and at good speeds through highly congested areas, but also expressways sometimes can provide the opportunity for interesting and even spectacular views of the city. . . . Expressways driving in many cases can be an exhilarating experience." It was mute on how the road might look to those not on it.

The city hired three local engineering firms to check the report's assumptions; it also encouraged them to weigh alternatives to the plan, and in so doing the engineers came on an idea they liked far more. So in October 1961, Baltimore found itself considering yet another new expressway proposal, this one the biggest and most extravagant yet. Dubbed "10-D," it called for I-70 to enter the city from the west via the two parks, slash through Rosemont, and cross most of west Baltimore along Franklin and Mulberry. Shy of downtown it would bend south and keep going in that direction past the Inner Harbor; eventually, it would meet I-95, coming up from Washington, and the two highways, merged into a single gargantuan stream, would snake eastward through a beloved landmark, Federal Hill, a dome of earth south of the harbor that offered the city's best views. From there, 70/95 would cross the narrowest point of the Inner Harbor's approach, its very neck, on a low-slung causeway. Interstate 83 would be extended southward to the same place, to meet 70/95 in a mixing bowl of ramps and flyovers built right out over the water. The sum would be a mammoth fourteen lanes wide and the signature feature for which Baltimore would become known the world over — as instantly recognizable, its straight-faced backers claimed, as the Golden Gate Bridge.

Granted, there were tradeoffs. The Inner Harbor would be cut off to anything but canoes and skiffs except in one spot, a 150-foot-wide opening tall enough for tugs and small sailboats. And east of the harbor, 10-D would, like the earlier plan, uproot folks from those purportedly seedy riverside neighborhoods. But next to what had come before, the route seemed positively light-handed; its residential victims would number under 4,800.

The business community swooned over it. The mayor backed it.

The city's public works director proclaimed it "the most advantageous route for the city." Again, the population disagreed. Nine white west side neighborhoods were up in arms over I-70's proposed course through the two parks—heavily forested, vine-tangled Leakin Park, one of the biggest pieces of urban wilderness in the East, and Gwynns Falls Park, a greenbelt straddling its namesake stream. Then there were the seedy neighborhoods east of the Inner Harbor. They were a quiltwork of Italian, Greek, and Polish enclaves, settled generations before, mostly working-class, fiercely house-proud. Their two-fisted residents didn't view themselves or their communities as expendable. One of those neighborhoods, Fells Point, was attracting more upscale defenders, who recognized its ragged eighteenth-century buildings as architectural treasures.

City Hall was aware of a mounting alarm in Rosemont, too, and along the Franklin-Mulberry corridor, but neither prompted much worry. Those neighborhoods were black.

Days before a public hearing on the plan, the city's public works director, Bernard Werner, announced that he wouldn't put up with any demonstrations. "You can't build an expressway without tearing down some homes," he said, in a variation on the old saw about omelets. "Somebody's going to have to be displaced no matter where we build it." He got a protest, all the same. For three hours, 1,300 angry Baltimoreans booed, heckled, and otherwise tormented 10-D's backers. The worst of it came when a spokesman for the engineering firms commented that "many of the neighborhoods affected have already been earmarked for slum clearance." As the *Sun* reported: "A chorus of boos greeted this remark, interspersed with shouts of 'Who says?' and 'My home's no slum.'"

When a spokesman for the Jaycees completed a short speech favoring the highway, city councilman William Bonnett, seated on the auditorium's stage, leaped to his feet, grabbed the microphone, and hollered that the speaker must be some suburbanite from Baltimore County. Again, from the *Sun:* "Mr. Werner struggled with Mr. Bonnett for possession of the microphone, but the determined councilman held on. 'About 15,000 people are going to be put out on the street because of this expressway. They are the people who ought to be heard, not those who live in the county," he said.

"With this, Mr. Werner finally regained the microphone and ordered Mr. Bonnett to his seat amid jeers and cries of 'Let him talk!' from the crowd."

George H. Fallon, Baltimore's big man in Congress, figured some such discord was unavoidable. "The fact that the road program has an impact on every American makes it the center of innumerable controversies," he told AASHO's annual meeting late in the year, no doubt thinking of his hometown. "You cannot avoid these controversies. You can prepare yourself for them, and you may be able to minimize controversy by telling your side of the story in a convincing manner, but you cannot eliminate the controversies."

The State Roads Commission was nonetheless stung by the fiery reception. It recommended no immediate action on the expressway's Inner Harbor leg and a quick start on the westernmost stretch, through the parks and Rosemont — what it called the "noncontroversial section."

A year after John Bragdon's report disappeared into the bureaucratic abyss, some of its central tenets resurfaced in a joint study conducted by the Commerce Department and the U.S Housing and Home Finance Agency. The subject was urban mass transportation, and this new document, released in March 1962, urged that American cities make their transportation plans "integral parts" of broader community planning, just as Bragdon had advocated. The joint report also recommended that the feds withhold transportation money from any city that failed to do so.

The suggestion came as the interstate system's urban legs moved from theory to designated corridors. In Atlanta, in Detroit, Cleveland, and Indianapolis, in the Boston area and Miami, homeowners, apartment dwellers, and businesses were finding that they were in the way, and more often than not, that they could do little about it. In most places, the men calling the shots were state highway engineers, unelected technocrats immune from voter anger, and they were armed with sheaves of technical studies and statistics and cost-benefit analyses that supported their positions. Public hearings were filled with words their audiences didn't understand.

Highway plans were almost always freestanding, disconnected from any vision for the city at large, including other forms of transportation. Pressure for a more comprehensive approach mounted quickly. In April 1962, John F. Kennedy borrowed from the joint report in his first message to Congress on transportation, placing the administration firmly behind the idea. In June, another conference of highway officials in Hershey, Pennsylvania, concluded that expressways "cannot be planned independently of the areas through which they pass." And in October, the Federal-Aid Highway Act of 1962 declared that as of 1965, the secretary of commerce would not approve "any program for projects in any urban area of more than fifty-thousand population unless he finds that such projects are based on a continuing comprehensive transportation planning process carried on cooperatively by states and local communities." Cooperative, comprehensive, continuing — the act's "3-C" requirement gave urban planners hope that highways might become tools for improving city life, rather than battering rams.

The new act notwithstanding, I-70's route through Baltimore's black neighborhoods seemed a foregone conclusion. By the middle of 1964, it was easy to pick out sections of the corridor. The stretch along Franklin and Mulberry streets, the one part of the proposed highway that had been included in every plan since the war, had fallen deep into blight, its occupants seeing no reason to maintain properties that were doomed. The decay had spilled into the adjacent blocks and was spreading; the future I-70, Baltimoreans noted bitterly, was killing neighborhoods even before the wrecking crews arrived.

That fall, state and federal officials signed off on 10-D. A young lawyer and city councilman, Tom Ward, urged his colleagues to cut the expressway from the city budget, calling the state roads boss "the people's enemy." The vote went against him, 22 to 1. Still, Ward was able to postpone the start of construction, first by insisting that the city's park board weigh in on the expressway's path, and later, by demanding that the planning commission review small adjustments to the route. The delays proved critical; they bought time for the opposition to organize.

The resistance in Baltimore was echoed all over America. In Nashville, I-40's planned path through black neighborhoods on the north side of town, a route that isolated one hundred blocks from the rest of the city and smashed through a long-established black commercial district, prompted those in the way to seek help from the NAACP's Legal Defense Fund, which started building a discrimination case against Tennessee's highway authorities. A few hours to the west, citizens stirred in Memphis, where the same interstate was to chew six lanes wide through Overton Park, a leafy preserve that included the city's zoo, a nine-hole golf course, and picnic grounds. Protest groups sprang up in Philadelphia, where a crosstown freeway threatened to sequester black neighborhoods, creating a Mason-Dixon Line of elevated concrete, and in Cambridge, Massachusetts, where state highway officials planned to thread an interstate between Harvard University and MIT and straight through a belt of middle-class homes.

In New Orleans, opposition swelled against plans for an elevated freeway that would skirt the famed French Quarter and carry its thundering traffic within view and earshot of Jackson Square and the country's oldest cathedral—a project that federal housing authorities judged would have a "severely deleterious impact" on the historic neighborhood, but which city and state officials pressed for, nonetheless.

When Baltimore held its first hearing on a condemnation ordinance for I-70, the first legal step to seizing land and clearing houses, the audience of 550 protesters was so boisterous that the councilman running the meeting walked out; the *Sun* reported that the session reflected all of the city's expressway plans: it ended "in shambles."

He rarely made it into the city's newspapers, but dig into the local history collections at the University of Baltimore, and Joe Wiles surfaces repeatedly. He was the quintessential background operator, a man whose community activism took quiet but persistent form, who put faith in persuasion and persistence over making a lot of noise. And now, under his leadership, the Rosemont Neighborhood Improvement Association turned its full attention to the expressway threat.

When homeowners in the Franklin-Mulberry corridor formed the Relocation Action Movement, or RAM, aiming to get a fair shake for families displaced by the expressway, Wiles and the Rosemont association joined it. That homes would be lost seemed a sure thing, but the group was outraged that in return the city offered nothing beyond fair market value; it was up to the displaced, most of them poor, to cover their own moving costs and to find replacement housing, which was sure to cost more than the homes from which they would be evicted.

That bum deal was aggravated by slack city housing inspections in the expressway's corridor. As the condition of properties slid, the market value of the surrounding neighborhood went with them, meaning that the sums the dispossessed would get for their places were shrinking fast. Within weeks, as the group's complaints resonated with Baltimoreans both within and outside the condemnation zones, RAM grew to hundreds strong.

Across town, another protest group mushroomed at the same time. Tom Ward and several well-heeled allies founded the Society for the Preservation of Federal Hill, Montgomery Street and Fells Point, dedicated to saving irreplaceable eighteenth- and nineteenth-century buildings in the city's southeastern neighborhoods. While tussling publicly with officials over the expressway's merits, the group quietly laid the groundwork to have the neighborhoods listed on the newly created National Register of Historic Places. Two upstart groups — one mostly black and poor, from west Baltimore, and the other white and better-off, and from the east — had joined separate battles in the same war.

Frank Turner and his colleagues in the Bureau of Public Roads witnessed the protests unfolding in city after city with dismay and frustration. Since early in its history, the bureau's reliance on technical expertise and isolation from politics had been the foundation of its strength. For more than forty years, its judgment as to where and how to build roads had been unquestioned. It had been entrusted by the

American people to foster an implied right—of mobility, of freedom to roam—and it had served that task and the people well. In 1966, Americans owned 57 percent of the world's passenger cars, drove 922 billion miles, made 92 percent of their intercity trips by road. Pleasure driving was considered the nation's top form of outdoor recreation.

Just imagine what a mess the place would be if the bureau hadn't known its stuff. But now, look—that work was vilified from coast to coast. *The Atlantic Monthly* made it sound like a bad thing that American highways occupied an area the size of West Virginia. Writers for the conservative *National Review* sniffed that expressways "had become the symbol of a complex and undisciplined society" and decided it was "high time for President Johnson or Secretary Udall to restrain their minions in the Bureau." Innumerable newspaper stories called the urban program into question, along with the agencies behind it.

Then there was Lewis Mumford, the Freeway Revolt's ideological Adam, who was in more of a rage than ever. In 1961 he'd published *The City in History: Its Origins, Its Transformations, and Its Prospects,* a 657-page masterpiece in which he'd described expressways as "funnels that help to blow the urban dust farther from the center, once the top soil of a common life has been removed." Many critics had judged it his finest work; the following year, it had won the National Book Award, and in 1964, Lyndon Johnson had awarded him the Presidential Medal of Freedom, the nation's highest civilian honor.

In "The American Way of Death," published in the *New York Review of Books* in April 1966, Mumford reprised his attack on "that religion for whose evidences of power and glory the American people, with eyes devoutly closed, are prepared to sacrifice some 59,000 lives every year, and to maim, often irreparably, some three million more." Most of the article, a review of Ralph Nader's *Unsafe at Any Speed,* was a diatribe against the automobile itself, which "could have made an invaluable contribution in creating a regional distribution of population" but instead accounted for some of the greatest crises facing city and countryside alike—"the nightmare of the air becoming toxic with poisonous exhausts, including the highly lethal carbon monoxide; of the water supply polluted with deadly lead from gasoline exhausts already half way to the danger point even in the Arctic wastes; the nightmare of diurnal mass commutation by car. . . ."

He reserved special scorn for the sterile monotony of the interstates:

> The same compulsory high speed, the same wide monotonous road, producing the same hypnotic drowsiness, the same air-conditioned climate in the car, the same Howard Johnsons, the same clutter of parking lots, the same motels. No matter how fast he travels or how far he goes, the motorist never actually leaves home: indeed no effort is spared to eliminate variety in the landscape, and to make famous beauty spots by mountain or sea into as close a counterpart of the familiar shopping center as the original landscape will permit. In short, automobility has turned out to be the most static form of mobility that the mind of man has yet devised.

Let that sort of talk get to you, and it could be pretty damn disheartening to work in the Bureau of Public Roads, to be any kind of highway man. Turner was especially bothered by the personal nature of some criticism. Lifelong public servants, men who had devoted their careers to their fellow citizens, to their communities, were being held up as heartless, single-minded bastards whose work ruined cities, left psychic and physical scars, and benefited an already fat consortium of oil, auto, and trucking companies. Turner decried the "nonsense" that "all highway people want to do is build highways. Just push 'em through, and to the devil with the consequences," as he put it to an interviewer. That the bureau had designed every mile of the interstates to "ravage a park; or to cut through a college campus; or to deliberately destroy a wilderness area or a fine trout stream," and to "remove tens of thousands of helpless homeowners and businessmen" with "no consideration except dollars being the yardstick."

If the taxpayers had an inkling of the thought that went into highway locations, Turner believed they wouldn't be so quick to denounce either the roads or their builders. He worked for the common good. "Highways, you know, are for people," he told the friendly *Highway User* magazine. "There is no reason for highways apart from people. Very simply, highways *are* people. Those who think they are a broom to sweep people aside simply don't know highways or how we think about them."

Urban interstates alone hadn't worked up the masses, he suspected. Something bigger was afoot — anti-highway sentiment was part of a series of tectonic shifts in American culture that dominated the TV news he watched with Mable every night. "We are in a period of change, of seething transition, when old values are under question everywhere," he wrote. "It is an age of hippies, of pot, of LSD, of dropouts, of teachers' strikes, of race riots, of looting. It is the period of the breakup of the home, the abandonment of morals, or at least the adoption of a different moral code than the one we knew and respected for centuries.

"In a time when even religion is questioned, then it is understandable that the value of the highway program should be questioned, too."

That didn't make the criticism sting any less, but it helped explain it, at least. Turner struggled to keep perspective, to not take the harsh rhetoric personally. Oftentimes, he succeeded. On days he didn't ride the bus he commuted into the district with his son Jim, who was impressed by how calmly his father could discuss attacks on the program. And by how open-minded the old man was: beginning in February 1967, when he was again promoted, Turner devoted many of his speeches and interviews to preaching empathy and an "enlightened view."

"We've heard a lot these past few years about human and social values," he told western state highway officials in an August 1967 speech. "And it's not just talk. If there ever was a time when roads were built only to move people and goods, that time is long gone."

In *Highway User* he almost sounded like a protester himself. "You cannot just ram a highway through a city area and say to the people, 'Oops, sorry! You'll just have to take yourselves and your businesses somewhere else. You know how it is — there's always some poor guy in the way,'" he told the magazine. "Let me tell you something else that we unfeeling highway people know, and some of us have discovered it the hard way. These people won't sit still for it. They'll fight."

Turner's new job was "director of Public Roads," which on paper seemed much the same post that Thomas MacDonald had left fourteen years before. But the bureau and its place in government were in the midst of change. In addition to overseeing the interstate program and riding herd on most of the rest of the Federal Aid system, Turner had spent months on a task force designing a new cabinet-level Department of Transportation, to which the bureau shifted in the spring of 1967. As part of the new setup, Public Roads became part of a new Federal Highway Administration. Turner speculated that this extra layer of supervision was prompted at least in part by the mushrooming crisis in the cities, by the perception that the interstate program's engineers had to be reined in. Whatever its genesis, the new DOT was the fourth-largest department in the government, with a budget of nearly $6 billion and more than ninety thousand employees, the bulk of both devoted to motor transport.

The new secretary was Alan S. Boyd, a Florida-born lawyer and past chairman of the Civil Aeronautics Board, whom President Lyndon Johnson called "the best-equipped man in this country" for "untangling, coordinating and building a national transportation system worthy of America." The new federal highway administrator, and Turner's direct boss, was Lowell K. Bridwell, a former reporter and columnist who, in a distinguished career with the Scripps-Howard newspaper chain, had made a specialty of transportation; among his long-running stories had been the Blatnik committee's investigations. Bridwell was an inspired choice; he was at once intimately familiar with the bureau's policies and beholden to none of them, a non-engineer who saw highways for their social effects as well as their traffic capacities. "We have learned how to build superior facilities for the fast, relatively safe, economic and convenient movement of people and goods by motor vehicle," he said. "But the way we go about planning, locating and designing [highways] is not good enough for today. It certainly isn't good enough for tomorrow."

"Highway planning," Bridwell asserted, "is not and cannot be a completely quantifiable process in which all elements can be . . . assigned numbers." A road's design might be a task strictly for engineers, he said, but the "planning and location of a highway facility involves many considerations other than engineering."

• • •

Sensing that Baltimore's highway program promised heartache to all involved, local architects convinced Maryland officials that I-70 would go down easier if the engineers designing the highway collaborated with experts from other professions — if they joined architects and planners to form a "Design Concept Team," aided by sociologists, economists, landscape architects, and other specialists. An interdisciplinary approach, they hoped, could transform an eyesore into "a major and lasting civic monument, like the Roman aqueducts."

The expressway's city and state bosses might have bought into just about any idea at that juncture, because the federal share of interstate spending carried a 1972 deadline, and the expressway was running late. Finishing in time meant evicting four thousand households in the coming couple of years, and somehow finding new homes for the dispossessed; demolishing not only houses but ninety businesses, seven churches, and eight acres of wharf; and relocating seventy miles of utility pipe and cable, all while building eighteen miles of highway and seventeen interchanges.

It took until early 1967 to hash out the team's particulars. It would comprise four partners, led by a Maryland engineering outfit and an international architectural firm. The team's leader and public face hailed from San Francisco: architect Nathaniel A. Owings, who in terms of his view of the automobile had much in common with Lewis Mumford. The interstate system, he wrote, had "raised more problems than it solved," had "cut through neighborhoods, parks and historic areas" in cities throughout the country. "Part of the tragedy," he added, "is that the cities themselves have rushed with a strange sense of urgency to cooperate in their own mutilation."

In exchange for $4.8 million, most of it supplied by the feds, the team was to blend the expressway, as best as it could, with Baltimore's "social, economic, and esthetic needs." It was a tall order. As *Sun* reporter and columnist James D. Dilts observed, "'Blending' a six- or eight-lane highway into the fabric of Baltimore is about as promising an assignment as 'blending' a buzz saw into a Persian rug."

By the summer of 1967, the resumé of one Stuart Wechsler, age twenty-five, white native of the Bronx, included sit-ins, rent strikes, picket

lines, several arrests and jail stays, a caning and kidnapping at the
hands of Florida bigots, and up-close views of several shotgun barrels, all in the service of the Congress of Racial Equality. He'd joined
the civil rights group while in college in New York, had agitated for its
causes there and in the Mid-Atlantic in the early part of the decade,
and had ventured into the South to register black voters. He'd been
down there for two years when CORE asked him to tackle a tougher
assignment: Baltimore.

The city was schizophrenic on matters of race in the mid-sixties.
Many of Baltimore's public gathering spots, including an amusement
park not far from Rosemont, had only recently been integrated. Its
neighborhoods and schools saw little mixing. Tensions between whites
and blacks often spiked. Wechsler was not long settled in CORE's offices in the Franklin-Mulberry corridor before he came to see the expressway as a racial issue — no way would it be aimed through a sta-
ble, middle-class neighborhood like Rosemont if the population were
white. It seemed a classic example of white men's roads going through
black men's homes.

So he responded eagerly to a call from RAM, asking for help in re-
sisting the planned buyouts in Rosemont and Franklin-Mulberry. In
early June 1967, the same month that the city approved a condemnation ordinance that enabled it to start snapping up houses, Wechsler
helped Joe Wiles and his compatriots organize a mass convergence
on City Hall to demand replacement value for doomed homes, rather
than the market price. The event brought RAM's first victory against
what Wechsler called "the city's Vietnam." The mayor, Theodore R.
McKeldin, vowed that he would go to Washington to ask for buyout
money. Come October, McKeldin made good on his promise, leading
a contingent of city officials, residents from Rosemont and Franklin-
Mulberry, Wechsler, and Wiles on a bus pilgrimage to the Federal
Highway Administration, where they met with Bridwell and Secretary
Boyd. The feds declared a moratorium on the taking of homes in
the I-70 corridor until the state authorized adequate replacement
payments.

An even bigger victory came in January 1968, when the Design

Concept Team judged the expressway's path through Rosemont so disruptive "that only a different road location could provide a reasonable solution." The team suggested shifting the alignment to the south and offered three variations on the idea. One followed U.S. 40's existing footprint along the neighborhood's southern edge, the path foreseen in the *Yellow Book;* it would cut the number of displaced Rosemont families by half. A second skirted Rosemont's west side and nicked a corner of Western Cemetery, the resting place of several thousand dead whites; it would take even fewer houses and save nearly $7 million over the original route. The third ran straight through the cemetery, at the expense of just 211 homes.

The report came less than two weeks after Baltimore was rent by a major civil disturbance in the wake of Martin Luther King's assassination; theoretically, at least, racial fence mending was a high priority.* But officials rejected the new choices, the state roads boss, Jerome B. Wolff, announcing that I-70 would run through Rosemont, like it or not. "I think we create more uproar by considering other routes," he explained to Joe Wiles. "We were reluctant to consider it in the first place. The route there is the final one."

Wiles was mystified by the decision. How could the city choose to uproot its living families, rather than move its dead, and to spend more money doing it? Such questions dominated talk at the dinner table, with Esther, among other members of RAM, and in May, Wiles took them to Transportation Secretary Boyd, in a characteristically respectful letter asserting that Rosemont was an upstanding place and that its people wanted to stay where they were.

A reply came from Frank Turner, and by any measure, it was disappointing. At a time when his speeches and published comments seemed to cast Turner as evolving toward a more thoughtful, inclu-

---

* The post-riot period wasn't a proud time for highway men in general. In D.C., surveyors ventured up fire-blackened Seventh Street, in Washington's Northwest, almost before the ashes had cooled. Their thinking: Property values were at an all-time low. Buy real estate now, and the taxpayer got a bargain. As the *New Republic* shrieked, any agency that "could think, for a moment, of cutting through the heart of an angry black community and across the campus of [traditionally black] Howard University is a measure of its understanding of urban social values and current modes of resistance."

sive approach to urban highway decisions, his letter to Wiles was a brush-off, in language of the sort that gives bureaucrats a bad name. "Alternate alignment considerations were studied, as you noted," he wrote, "and determination then made . . . that the team should concentrate their efforts in the original corridor toward development of a design solution which would contribute to the environment of the area and which would bring to bear the skill and the thinking of all planning disciplines so that the final design solution would reflect full public and private interest."

The *Sun* jumped on the letter. "What does one make of such official gobbledygook?" Jim Dilts wrote. "How, by any stretch of the imagination, can a highway that the Design Concept Team has shown will destroy Rosemont possibly 'contribute to the environment of the area'? Which area? What environment?"

Good questions, all. Turner had been making decisions without citizen interference for four decades, had sought consensus only with fellow engineers and small groups of community leaders — who, in his view (and it was by no means unique to him), "knew best" — and, it seems, simply didn't want or didn't know how to respond to someone outside the fold. It was one thing to encourage inclusion in the abstract, another to actually practice it.

Such treatment only fueled RAM's impression that its members had no hand in their fate. That summer, while busy denouncing "pavement plutocrats" and "concrete conquistadors," Wechsler decided the time was ripe to unite Baltimore's various anti-expressway forces under a single banner. At an all-day summit in early August, east-siders and west created a new umbrella organization incorporating some two dozen factions — RAM, neighborhood improvement groups, small anti-road cells, civil rights outfits, the League of Women Voters. They called it the Movement Against Destruction, or MAD.

Wechsler was elected its president and Wiles its vice president, and a young Legal Aid lawyer, Art Cohen, was recruited as its counsel. It was a motley union of people with little in common but what they simply called "the road," and its leaders well reflected the whole — Wechsler, the white community activist who hadn't finished college;

Wiles, the black family man; and Cohen, the product of a private boarding school, Oberlin College, and Yale Law.

The Design Concept Team remained troubled by the expressway's route through Rosemont and its enormous Inner Harbor crossing, and in August 1968 proposed another alternative. Why not bring the highway into town via the west-side parks, but then turn it south, around both Rosemont and the cemetery, and in a wider arc around downtown? And why not steer the highway onto the dock-lined peninsula that split the Patapsco River's middle and north branches, and cross the water on a bridge near Fort McHenry? Such a scheme would spare 1,400 homes slated for demolition, 500 of them in Rosemont.

City Hall listened; come December, the *Sun* reported that 10-D had been "all but abandoned." Almost thirty years into its quest for an east-west expressway, Baltimore was yet again embarking on a new plan; no one in the press or officialdom could even say, at this point, how many had come and gone before it. That same month, December 1968, Art Cohen took over MAD's presidency. Just before Christmas, he was the only "citizen" invited to a closed-door meeting at which the Design Concept Team walked the mayor through variations on its proposal. At the meeting's end, Mayor Thomas D'Alesandro III announced that Baltimore would pursue an option labeled "3-A," which would, indeed, cross the river on a high-rise bridge at Fort McHenry and spare Rosemont. But not Franklin-Mulberry; a spur, I-170, would drill east between those streets to downtown's west side. Neither would 3-A save the old neighborhoods along the water on the southeast side of town, which would be cleaved by a six-lane, elevated extension of I-83.

As Baltimore had come to expect, the decision didn't stick. The National Park Service objected that a double-decked, eight-lane bridge soaring 180 feet over the water would overshadow Fort McHenry, at which the tallest object was a 98-foot flagpole. No one, it seemed, had consulted with the people running the city's most historic site. And at about the same time, the Department of the Interior named Fells Point, the oldest of the imperiled southeastern neighborhoods, a

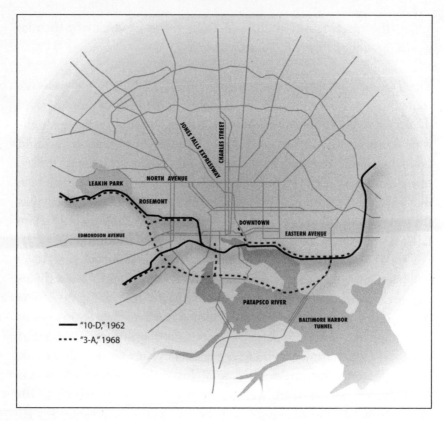

The Design Concept Team's 3-A proposal would have spared Baltimore's Inner Harbor, which has since become the city's showpiece. It would not have gone easy on the old waterfront communities southeast of downtown, however, or the black neighborhoods to the west.

National Historic District. No highway had ever been built through a place bearing the designation.

In early August 1969, the city and state held three public hearings on I-70's possible courses around Rosemont. They were packed, boisterous affairs, held in the auditorium of a local high school. Art Cohen arrived at the opening session to find whites seated on the auditorium's right side, blacks on the left — unusual in itself, as the city's races rarely convened in numbers. A white man stood and, speaking for many on his side of the room, complained that all four alternatives would drive the highway through Western Cemetery, sacred ground. At that, an older black man rose, said wait a minute — you're worried about dead people? I'm worried about losing my home. To which the white guy replied: You know, we face a common problem here, and the problem is this highway.

U.S. senator Barbara Mikulski, then a grass-roots hell-raiser on the east side of town and cofounder of a mostly blue-collar anti-highway cell called the Southeast Council Against the Road, was there with a contingent from Fells Point. She later recalled that the white speaker was a tugboat crewman and World War II veteran, and that he then turned to the black side of the room and said: "I'm going to reach out my hand to my brother veterans. We fought in one war. We're going to fight and win *this* war." He offered his hand to the leader of Rosemont's contingent. The auditorium burst into applause, and whites and blacks left their chairs and moved to the room's center.

It was a transformative moment. For the first time in the highway fight — and, a good many locals suspected, the first time in Baltimore's history — the city's people were united; a chorus of disconnected protests acquired a single, booming voice. From that point on, the hearings' speakers, black and white alike, rose to deliver the same message, over and over: Not only do we not want any of these alternatives, we don't want an expressway, any expressway. "You did one good thing," a woman speaker told the officials running the hearings. "You brought white and black together, and this is a beautiful thing."

So exhilarating was the sense of unity that when a Baltimorean read a declaration of war from the "Black Volunteer Liberation Army," promising the arrival of its "troops" if the highway men made good on their plans ("And believe you me," the speaker said, "they're not just jiving"), whites in the auditorium applauded as vigorously as the blacks.

Joe Wiles could celebrate the moment only so much. It had come too late for Franklin-Mulberry, which now was in such a ravaged state that its demolition, highway or no, was inevitable. And the unbuilt expressway had exacted a high toll on his own neighborhood. Having won replacement payments for their properties, nearly five hundred Rosemont homeowners in the original condemnation corridor had quit the place; their houses now stood empty, their lawns weed-choked, the streets littered with trash. The village in the city had so far kept the interstate at bay, but it was headed downhill, just the same.

19

OUT IN THE COUNTRYSIDE, gaps in the system's concrete continued to close despite daunting physical challenges. Two thousand miles west of Baltimore, I-70 nosed across Utah's San Rafael Swell, a seemingly unbridgeable succession of canyons and ridges that had never been breached by paved road; the story goes that when surveyors encountered a sheepherder in its backcountry and mentioned they planned to build a highway there, the man nearly collapsed from laughter. He and other doubters soon witnessed engineers make good on the plan and complete the biggest pioneer road project since the Alaska Highway.

A ways east, the Rockies presented one hurdle after another. The first was the Dakota Hogback, a towering ridge of sandstone and clay that marks the seam between the mountains and the Great Plains, just outside of Denver. Getting I-70 through it required a deep cut, which promised to defile a spectacular chunk of nature. But within the ridge, some luck waited; the bulldozers exposed stratified rock in a spectrum of pastels, studded with an array of fossil plants dating to the age of the dinosaurs — and so impressive was this window to the past that it became an accidental tourist attraction. Colorado highway authorities left the cut's stairstepped terraces in place so that visitors could reach the higher formations.

Another, bigger challenge loomed to the west, at Loveland Pass, where I-70 crossed the Continental Divide. For decades, drivers had topped the mountains' spine on skinny, switchbacking U.S. 6, a white-knuckle trip of 10 miles and thirty minutes. In the fall of 1963, crews started work on the first of two tubes forming the Strait Creek Tunnel, which would burrow through 1.7 miles of granite, talc, and clay, at the highest altitude — just over eleven thousand feet — of any such project in the world.

It would take nearly ten years to complete that two-lane tube, thanks to loose stone, disputes among engineers over how much ventilation it would need, a worker walkout (over a woman in the hole, considered bad luck among miners and tunnel diggers), and the normal difficulties that come with blasting and drilling through a rock of almost unimaginable size. At its height, the effort employed round-the-clock shifts, six days a week.

Lesser heights had to be scaled around the country: Snoqualmie Pass in Washington, chosen as I-90's passage through the Cascades; Sideling Hill in western Maryland, where crews would blast a notch for I-68 that is 340 feet deep and visible from miles off; the Great Smokies, through which I-40 wriggles, climbs, and falls from Tennessee to North Carolina.

And in California's Mojave Desert, halfway between sun-baked Barstow and Needles, there rose the Bristol Mountains, a jumble of granite and soft volcanic rock close to 3,900 feet high and smack in the path of I-40. For as long as travelers had braved the desert on wheels, they'd been unable to get beyond the Bristols without a lengthy detour. Both U.S. 66 and the Santa Fe Railway had swung far to the south and climbed 1,000 feet to end-run them. The railroad sorely wished for a straighter and flatter alignment, but the Santa Fe found that getting it required either a two-mile tunnel or cuts 500 feet deep. Either way, the price was too dear.

So the railroad called on the Atomic Energy Commission, which at the time was gung-ho about peacetime uses for nuclear power, with an audacious idea: How about nuking a hole through the mountains? Not long after, the California State Division of Highways received a call asking whether it might be interested in partnering on what was soon known as Project Carryall. You bet, it replied.

With that, a study group of engineers and scientists convened, and in the fall of 1963 its members agreed that the Bristols could be tamed with twenty-two carefully placed atomic bombs, each packing twenty to two hundred kilotons of explosive punch. Fired in two stages, the devices would vaporize sixty-eight million cubic yards of mountain, creating a chain of connected craters more than two miles long, as much as 340 feet deep, and 330 feet wide at the bottom — plenty big enough for twin railroad tracks and a full-size interstate. A twenty-third bomb would be used to blast a reservoir into the desert to collect runoff during storms. Odds were that it would never overflow, seeing as how it could have swallowed the Astrodome with room to spare.

All this excavation would take years to accomplish with the usual tools. The nuclear option would get it done in a flash and at a 36 percent discount. All the state need do after the explosions was to clean up, which wouldn't be too tough a job — little of the rubble would be more than two feet across. Sure, a few "rock missiles" might be lobbed about, and underground rumbles might crack the plaster or knock over knickknacks in Amboy, a town a few miles to the south, but all of the risks could be made manageable with a little more research.

Nowadays that seems a brashly optimistic claim, given that Project Carryall's bombs were to flex destructive muscle at least sixty times beefier than that deployed at Hiroshima and Nagasaki, combined. But the engineers promised that their confidence was well placed. "Based on present knowledge of the Carryall area," the highway official wrote, "safety hazards such as radioactivity, fallout, air blast, and ground shock have been evaluated and it has been concluded that there would be no hazard of such magnitude as to cause significant structural damage or endanger local inhabitants."

See, these would be "clean" nuclear explosions, which were touted as somehow safer than the standard, radiation-spewing variety. In fact, construction crews likely could spend a full shift in the new pass just four days after the blasts. Work could get started as soon as 1968. The highway could be carrying traffic the following summer. "The study group has concluded that this project is technically feasible," a

California highway official reported in 1964. "It can be done, and it can be done safely."

Well. You have to admire that can-do spirit. The parties had hatched this plan even as a nuclear test ban treaty was signed with the Soviets, but it remained in play for a couple of years, until California opted to carve out the alignment using slowpoke dynamite and bulldozers. That stretch of I-40 opened in 1973.

It was a break for Frank Turner that this nuclear option wasn't shared with the American public until many years later, because by the late sixties he was already fielding enough criticism over the interstate program's leaping price tag, which in 1965 stood at $46.8 billion, and just three years later at $56.5 billion — about double the initial "cost to completion" figures floated back in 1956. It would continue to bound, by another $12.25 billion in 1970 and $6 billion in 1972, would reach a whopping $90 billion in 1975 — and would keep going up from there.

Turner drew flak, too, over what had always been the program's greatest strength: safety. Two out of three fatal accidents on the interstates involved a single car going off the road, usually on the right side, and smacking into one or more fixed objects. Too often, the accidents would have been survivable, minus these roadside hazards — a lesson that Carl Fisher had learned during the disastrous opening races at Indy nearly sixty years before. And as it turned out, a good many of the obstacles had been put there by highway officials.

In 30 percent of these one-car wrecks, the first obstacle struck was a guardrail, a statistic that prompted bureau researchers to surmise that the rails themselves might be deadly. That jibed with the observations of one Joe Linko, a part-time TV repairman living in the Bronx, who cataloged and photographed the dangers he encountered while driving New York's interstates: guardrails with unbuffered ends that could skewer a car clean through; signs supported by unyielding steel legs; light standards just off the shoulder; exposed concrete culverts in drainage ditches, into which an errant car could too easily plow.

In 1967, Linko's pictures came to the attention of John Blatnik, who was still chairman of the House Special Subcommittee on the Federal-

Aid Highway Program. In testimony before the group, Linko raised good questions: Why was it that officials hung signs from massive steel brackets — bridges, really — even when overpasses were nearby? Why did the concrete foundations for utility poles jut above ground? Why did bridge abutments crowd the road? Why weren't sign supports designed to snap on impact? "It is sometimes difficult to determine where 'engineering shortcomings' end and 'common sense' begins," a sympathetic Blatnik observed, adding that the rapid pace of interstate construction was no excuse. "Does it take any longer to design for breakaway light poles and sign supports," he asked, "than for heavy-duty, rigid, non-yielding ones?"

Turner bristled at any implication that safety was not a top priority. "It is a fundamental consideration in everything we do," he said. "This is so elemental with us we have not separated safety out of the highway program as a single item. It is threaded through everything." No feature of the interstates had happened by chance. Why were signs so big? Because smaller signs were tougher to read, and thus a distraction — and a sign wouldn't be there in the first place if it were not imparting important, perhaps life-saving, information. Why were signposts so stout? Because they had to stand up to gales, lest the signboards they supported became windblown dangers.

Still, Linko's evidence was compelling. Safe as they were, the interstates could be made safer. Turner promised fixes, and they came. The breakaway signpost, soon required on all Federal Aid projects, was pioneered at the Texas Transportation Institute, the Chief's old outfit; a joint at the base gave way to sudden, massive blows, permitting the pole to swing away on a plastic hinge just below the sign's face. Metal guardrails acquired ends that corkscrewed into the ground or curved away from the road. Crash cushions — "impact attenuators," in engineering lingo — appeared at exits and around obstacles. Usually clustered barrels filled with sand or water, they weren't elegant, but they were a sight more forgiving than concrete or steel.

And state after state adopted the "Jersey barrier," a thirty-two-inch-tall concrete wall that could be poured in place or trucked to problem spots in eight-foot sections. Introduced in its namesake state in 1959, its sloping face was designed to deflect a sideswipe at highway speed. In theory, a car's tires would climb that slope before sheet metal made contact with concrete and would be gently steered by the angle back onto the pavement.

Those controversies were minor next to the continuing stink over urban interstates. Protest in the cities had become so endemic that in 1968 federal and state officials appointed a national version of Baltimore's Design Concept Team to devise formulas for happy coexistence between freeways and America's neighborhoods. Insofar as the beef in many cities, as in Baltimore, was over the mere *presence* of the roads more than the form they took, the effort was bound to fall short of all-out success. Even with that caveat, the commission's report, titled *The Freeway and the City,* was feeble: "The best arterial routes," one of its platitudes read, "are those that cause the least damage to existing communities and at the same time provide good traffic service at reasonable cost." Its key recommendation was that urban expressways be reduced in scale and softened with landscaped berms and swales and massed plantings. Bushes and piled dirt would have mollified neither MAD nor anti-freeway activists anywhere else.

Turner's boss searched for his own solution. Lowell Bridwell let it be known that he believed in "creative federalism," which he defined as giving local governments and citizens more say in decisions that previously had been the exclusive purview of highway officials; the feds, he said, were now willing to talk directly to highway protesters and broker compromises with the states.

New Orleans, where turmoil continued over I-310's close brush with the French Quarter, offered an early test of the policy. The feds "could have told the state not to worry about local protests; that it is none of our business," Bridwell said afterward. "Under the new approach we went down there, got a feel of the local situation and altered federal instructions to the state to facilitate a solution, which is on the way because federal people were willing to get their hands dirty trying to solve this problem."

The ultimate result: Bridwell would suspend federal funding for "an

Expressway Named Destruction," the press's nickname for the highway in New Orleans. Some state officials resented their federal partners' striving to play daddy, but the highway administrator rejected their complaints. It was his way or no highway. "What I'm trying to do is exercise some leadership in bringing [everyone] together," he said. "We have problems of a serious nature in at least twenty-five cities. If we don't step into these situations, the highway people are going to take a beating."

Creative federalism would also see Bridwell back-burner the Three Sisters Bridge, the most contentious piece of the freeway system planned for Washington, D.C. (later eliminated altogether from the interstate program), and fly to Nashville to try to hammer out an accord between road builders and local blacks.

Congress likewise amplified the public's voice in highway decisions in the Federal-Aid Highway Act of 1968.

Since 1956, state highway departments had been required to hold a public hearing (or at least provide the opportunity for one) before deciding to route a Federal Aid highway in or around a city, town, or village. In the program's early days, those hearings were often as not used to assuage towns up in arms over *not* getting an interstate.

The 1956 act had intended that officials use what they heard to ensure that they "considered the economic effects of such a location." The 1968 act swapped out that language for "economic and social effects of such a location, its impact on the environment, and its consistency with the goals and objectives of such urban planning as has been promulgated by the community." Instead of addressing people who worried the interstates would bypass them, the new hearings would solicit comments from those who worried they weren't far enough away.

This shift in orientation became public in October 1968, when the Federal Highway Administration published the regulations it planned to use to comply with the new act. They called for two public hearings, not one, on every Federal Aid project: the first a corridor hearing at which taxpayers could speak their minds on a highway's location, and the second a design hearing, at which they would have the chance to influence the project's size and style — whether it would be elevated, depressed, or built at street level, how it would be landscaped, that sort of thing.

To state officials, this guaranteed needless delay, and it was insulting, to boot. They knew how to conduct public hearings. They knew how to solicit citizen involvement. They didn't need the feds micromanaging every detail of a highway program that supposedly was led by the states. But they saved their real anger for another section of the new rules, with which Bridwell took creative federalism to an entirely new level. From now on, anyone unhappy with a state highway decision could appeal the matter directly to the feds, on any one of twenty-one grounds. Among them: that the state had failed to weigh neighborhood character, property values, natural or historical landmarks, conservation, or the displacement of households and businesses.

AASHO president John O. Morton found it "impossible to comprehend" how or why the feds would craft a regulation through which "the desires and needs of an overwhelming majority of the people . . . could be overridden by the action of a single individual, responsible or otherwise." He had a point; the grounds for appeal were so commonplace that every interstate project, every single one, was almost sure to be challenged. The program would drag on forever. It would never be finished.

Objectionable as the new rules were on practical grounds, it was the appeals process's implied refutation of the federal-state partnership that most left highway officials, in Morton's words, "confused, shocked and alarmed." It had never been a completely balanced relationship: AASHO and the states had always so relied on the bureau for research and technical expertise that the feds could influence a good many state initiatives as they took shape. But at no point in the long history of Federal Aid had Washington so minimized its partners.

AASHO executive director Alf Johnson, whose friendship with Frank Turner dated to the days when both worked on roads in Arkansas, blasted the "new people" in the Department of Transportation who seemed to "consider the highway program a federal program with the role of the state being subservient, or acting as an agent of the federal government." The feds wanted "to tell us how to do everything,"

Johnson complained, "even to the point of detailing how to handle debris or clean up after an accident." Some states, such as Texas, even talked about quitting the Federal Aid partnership outright. Why not? Washington already acted as if it were over.

All fifty states sent messages or emissaries to D.C. in opposition. Bridwell backed down. With just days remaining before Lyndon Johnson left the White House, he and Frank Turner signed off on a policy and procedure memo describing the new rules, and it did not include the appeals process.

Still, damage had been done to a pact in force for more than half a century.

The 1968 act amended the interstates in another lasting way: it lengthened the cap on their mileage from 41,000 miles to 42,500. An amendment tacked on additional miles, ultimately 500, for route modifications to the original system. Finally, the act authorized the secretary of transportation to label as interstates any completed state highway built to the system's standards that seemed a logical addition to the network; these additions were not counted against the mileage cap.

The mechanisms were now in place to enlarge the system past forty-six thousand miles. Congress would add another few hundred miles in the years to come, but conception of the interstates we know today was largely complete.

20

WITH RICHARD NIXON'S ascension to the presidency in 1969, the political appointees overseeing the highway program found themselves out of work. Into Alan Boyd's shoes as secretary of transportation stepped Massachusetts governor John A. Volpe, who'd been Ike's pick as interim federal highway administrator back in 1956. To take Lowell Bridwell's place, the new secretary named the senior-most engineer in federal employment, and a man with whom Volpe had worked thirteen years before: Frank Turner.

The quiet Texan's selection made sense to pretty much everyone. He was about to mark his fortieth anniversary at the bureau, and the projects he'd overseen since venturing north to Alaska were the most ambitious in the agency's history. *American Road Builder* called him "an excellent example of ability rising above politics," adding that "when the occasion called for the light of wisdom to shine through, then Frank Turner was sent for." *Engineering News-Record* called him "the old pro."

Outside of the industry, he remained largely unknown. To his few critics, those aware of his influence on the interstates and their advance — and on the ease with which Americans had come to own 101 million cars, in which they traveled more than a trillion miles a year — he made for a frustrating target; uninterested in power or publicity, and sincere in his Progressive Era beliefs that technical expertise, not politics, should drive decisions, Turner gave his detractors little to work with. Suggest that he understood numbers better than people, and he might agree. Call him a measurement-obsessed technocrat, and he might thank you. Label him a darling of the highway lobby, and he might quip, as he did to his boy Jim, "Son, I have one darling and I've had the same one for fifty years," or acknowledge, as he did at his March 1969 confirmation hearing before the Senate Public Works Committee, that yes, he did speak for the highway lobby — the 205 million people who used the nation's roads. "I believe it is a fairly powerful lobby, and I believe it is a lobby that you and I should be responsive to," he told the senators. "I believe that lobby is telling us they want an improved highway program. They want us to build not only more roads but to build better roads and make better utilization of the roads we do build."

That hearing forecast the issues that would challenge him in his new position. It was friendly — the committee's members had relied on Turner for technical background and straight answers for years, and his unanimous confirmation was never in doubt — but the freeway revolt in the cities figured prominently in the questions he fielded. He did his best to keep his testimony upbeat. Disputes, he said, were inevitable, part of the road-building process. "We have had several instances where we have had a very difficult problem determining a location to choose between, to make a Hobson's choice," he said. "We are going to have to do some damage, or surgery, and that does require some pain on somebody's part."*

Even so, the pieces in dispute totaled less than 150 miles, by his estimate, divided among sixteen cities. Four miles in Atlanta. Short stretches in Pittsburgh, Detroit, and Indianapolis, and another through upscale Shaker Heights, outside of Cleveland. A loop in Newark, several spurs and loops in New York, and a segment in Charleston, West Virginia. Nashville, where the noisy racial fight over I-40 raged on. The stretch through Overton Park in Memphis. The Boston area, already blighted by the ugly, invasive Central Artery, an elevated, six-

---

* He could have mentioned that he knew such pain — after all, he'd lost a piece of his house to one highway project, and his parents had lost all of theirs to another. He didn't bring it up, however.

lane evisceration that *Fortune* labeled "a road that seems to have committed all the possible sins." Several interstates in Washington, D.C., especially the extension of I-66 through suburban Arlington, not far from Turner's home, and across the Potomac into Georgetown. San Francisco, of course. And not least, Baltimore.

The thing to bear in mind, Turner stressed, was that these flash points were the exception, that while they had attracted buckets of ink, the vast majority of the program was proceeding quickly and smoothly. "Out of all of these miles of the system we actually have less than a half of one percent of the mileage that is involved in these questions of controversy," he said. "So on a relative basis, it is very small in extent, and the situations are not representative of the total problem, either in the urban areas or the total program that we are engaged in." Every week, he noted, almost twice the disputed mileage was put into service elsewhere, "and everybody rejoices."

All of which was true. The interstate system was two-thirds complete. Much of the long-distance mileage, the legs across the rural Midwest and the busy intercity highways of the East and West coasts, was carrying traffic. And as Turner testified, another 15 percent was "under construction at this moment, and most of the remainder is under engineering, right-of-way acquisition, or in the pipeline ready to go to contract and to actual construction."

But while the mileage in dispute was small, the affected percentage of the population was not. The freeway revolt involved major cities and millions of people. Try as he might to minimize it, the urban dilemma would not fade quietly away.

In fact, though it wasn't yet obvious, momentum was shifting to favor the protesters. In Baltimore, the historic designation for Fells Point complicated that stretch of the expressway immensely. To satisfy the preservationists, the highway men would eventually propose dismantling dozens of the neighborhood's old buildings brick by brick and reassembling them with the same care once the road was finished — a laughably expensive proposition. Money in general was becoming a major issue. The city and state had spent millions to buy properties that, with all the changes in routing, they did not now need — witness the hundreds of homes needlessly emptied in Rosemont — and during a dozen years of indecision and infighting the cost of the proposed interstates through town, once reckoned at about $200 million, had ballooned to well over a billion dollars. In a city of declining population, failing schools, aging water and sewer systems, and growing crime and poverty, the whole idea began to appear extravagant. It would take enormous political will to press on with the program.

Older cities around the country were beset with similar problems, and in each, as in Baltimore, that will was crumbling. A confluence of national trends was shifting the mood of the governed. Historic preservation was becoming a cause beyond the ranks of intelligentsia; Vietnam had created doubt that government knew what it was doing and had the people's best interests at heart; the civil rights movement had encouraged them to take their grievances to the streets and courts. And perhaps most important, the environmental movement had gained footing among a widening swath of America.

The cause had always had its soldiers, dating back to Henry David Thoreau and beyond, but environmentalism as a full-fledged mass movement had been around for only a few years, having been brought to life by ruinous oil spills, ever-worsening air and water pollution, and the 1962 publication of Rachel Carson's best-selling *Silent Spring*. Still considered one of the twentieth century's most important works of journalism, the book helped Americans redefine "environment" beyond "nature" or parkland; it was the setting for their every waking moment — the air they breathed, the water they drank, the soil in which they grew their food, the noise or smell or light of their surroundings; they need not journey to Yellowstone for it.

Silent Spring didn't mention the interstates, but its readers finished the book with a new framework for viewing the program. The environment was fragile, and the decisions that people made, singly and collectively, left marks. Some of them — such as the marks created by, say, crisscrossing the great outdoors with giant, elevated ribbons of concrete and steel — could be damn difficult to erase.

The bureau's first nod to environmentalism came soon after the book's appearance and seemed wonderfully green: states building Federal Aid projects had to certify they'd considered their possible effects on fish and wildlife. Actually, the rule was toothless, requiring only contemplation, rather than action, to protect animal life. Still, it was good public relations and didn't require the feds or their partners to change a single thing about the way they did business. A year after that, in 1964, the bureau had directed that when choosing road locations, highway officials consider all reasonable alignments, weighing the social, economic, and environmental effects of each. Again, this seemed to address the population's budding enthusiasm for the environmental cause without requiring hard action; asking engineers to consider unquantifiable effects next to quantifiable was bound to have a predictable outcome.

In the 1966 act that created the Department of Transportation, Congress had included a section that called on federal and state officials to safeguard the country's natural beauty. It also had ordered that the secretary of transportation not approve projects requiring "any land from a public park, recreation area, wildlife and waterfowl refuge, or historic site" unless "no feasible and prudent alternative" existed — in which case, the project had better include "all possible planning to minimize harm to such park." This, in fact, was to have major repercussions. But not right away; the act's wording was imprecise enough — what, exactly, does "feasible and prudent" mean? — that highway officials didn't feel the need to modify their procedures. Parklands remained a favored highway location.

So it would be fair to say that when Turner took office as federal highway administrator, environmental stewardship had not yet become part of the highway community's culture. As Richard Weingroff, the Federal Highway Administration's unofficial historian, puts it: "The elements of what today we think of as 'the environment' or 'ecosystem' were simply obstacles, like mountains or rivers, to be overcome with the best engineering skills and construction equipment available to the era."

But in the months before Turner's confirmation, another Senate committee — Interior and Insular Affairs, chaired by Henry "Scoop"

Jackson of Washington — had been hunting for ways to incorporate the country's growing passion for environmental protection into federal programs. Jackson's solution was a bill creating a national environmental policy, aimed at safeguarding the country's natural resources, and a three-member Council on Environmental Quality, reporting to the president, to "study and analyze environmental trends" with an eye toward their causes and their impacts on America's health and well-being.

In April 1969, a month after Turner's confirmation, one of Jackson's environmental advisers, Indiana University professor Lynton K. Caldwell, suggested that perhaps the president's office wasn't the place for the council, that the country might benefit more from an independent body empowered to review federal projects and programs — and arm-twist changes into them, if necessary — while they were still in the planning stage. The revised bill included just such an "action-forcing mechanism," as it was dubbed. Any federal agency contemplating a project that might affect the environment would have to craft a report on the nature of that impact, how it might be minimized or eliminated, and whether its irreducible effects were worth suffering — what we know today as an environmental impact statement. There lay the bill's real muscle, destined to forever transform the way government approached projects.

Nixon signed the National Environmental Policy Act into law on January 1, 1970. "What we really confront here," the president remarked to a few reporters and photographers who turned up for the signing, "is that in the highly industrialized, richest countries, we have the greatest danger. Because of our wealth we can afford the automobiles, we can afford all the things that pollute the air, pollute the water, and make this really a poisonous world in which to live."

Fitting that he should single out the motor vehicle, because by then the machine, along with the highways on which it traveled, was clearly producing a host of unhappy environmental byproducts. Smog had burned eyes and throats in Los Angeles since the forties; it had been so fierce at one point during World War II that the residents feared the Japanese had launched a chemical attack. Now, car and truck exhaust formed a dirty brown pall over even small cities. Noise, too, had become a pervasive hazard. Before the California State Division of Highways started experimenting with concrete noise barriers in the early seventies, the roar of truck traffic along San Jose's I-680 was akin to sticking your ear up to a garbage disposal. At its peak, it out-blasted a jackhammer.

Big roads played hell with drainage patterns and water quality. All that concrete encouraged flooding, and salts and oils carried in runoff poisoned nearby ponds and streams and fostered the growth of invasive weeds. Rural interstates presented insurmountable barriers to small mammals, turtles, and amphibians, one study concluding that a four-lane divided highway was as much a barrier to small creatures as a body of fresh water twice as wide. The slaughter of game by auto approached, and would soon exceed, that by hunting.

It was up to Turner to bring his agency into compliance with the new rules. For the first time, he and his colleagues were legally required to give "appropriate consideration" to "unquantified environmental amenities and values . . . along with economic and technical considerations." Just the same, Turner didn't regard the new act with any real urgency. He was among the last of the old-school technocrats, a man who viewed transportation as an essential government function and interstates as bargains — windfalls, really, if you assigned a dollar value to the time they saved the taxpayer, the lives they spared, the goods they carried; they were the only government activity, he was fond of saying, that repaid the taxpayer with interest. They more than compensated for whatever damage they caused.

Besides, Turner believed that the highway program was already hewing to a high environmental standard, and that it wouldn't be much changed by the law. "I want to make it clear that we in the highway program recognize our social responsibilities and are doing something about them," he said in a speech three weeks after the act took effect. Fourteen months later, he insisted that the highway program had been "quick to respond to these emerging concerns — not just with agreeable rhetoric but with meaningful action.

"We have not been constrained by blind adherence to a set of plans and specifications drawn up in 1956," he said. "On the contrary, we have approved some very significant change orders along the way. America has been changing these past fifteen years and so have we."

In truth, the agency abided by the letter of the new policy — in the first couple of years after its enactment, more than half of all the impact statements submitted to the Council on Environmental Quality came from the Federal Highway Administration — but not its spirit. When the nonprofit Center for Science in the Public Interest analyzed seventy-six of the agency's early impact statements, it found they "contain arguments rather than findings, opinions rather than studies, and generalities rather than facts." Most made no mention of mass-transit alternatives to highways, and one in three was mum on community disruption.

Against this backdrop, Baltimore's Road War moved to a new battlefield: wild, wooded, and honeysuckle-choked Leakin Park, at 1,300 acres the largest open space in town and the means by which I-70 was to enter the city from the west — and a portion of the expressway long considered a done deal. With the help of the Sierra Club, the preserve's neighbors organized the Volunteers Opposed to the Leakin Park Expressway (its acronym "VOLPE") to challenge the curving, two-and-a-half-mile road's "destruction of the only natural-area park in a major East Coast city."

They came armed. Interstate 40's routing through Memphis's Overton Park had prompted a citizens group there to press a suit against the city and Tennessee highway officials all the way to the Supreme Court, the crux of its argument being that the federal government had approved I-40's dissection of the city's most beautiful patch of green without establishing that there was no "feasible or prudent alternative" to the route, as required by the 1966 Department of Transportation Act. The government had held that in deciding whether alternatives were "prudent," it had to weigh the value of park preservation against the added costs of following a less direct highway route through homes and businesses — the sort of quantifiable, dollars-and-cents measures on which the highway community had always relied, and which had always trumped resistance in the past.

Not this time. In the spring of 1971, the Supreme Court had unanimously reversed the lower courts, finding that parks needed special protection because non-park highways were *always* more expensive; an interstate should thus avoid a park unless the disruption elsewhere would be truly extraordinary. The "very existence of the statutes," the justices ruled, "indicates that protection of parkland was to be given paramount importance."

Now VOLPE and its allies filed suit in federal court to block the Leakin Park route, their case styled as *VOLPE v. Volpe*. And as in Memphis, the court ruled that all work in the park should stop; only after officials held further hearings on the expressway's location and effects could it proceed. Joe Wiles spoke for many when he urged the city to junk the whole program: "Return the land already taken under condemnation to the local communities," he said, and leave it to them to figure out what to do with it.

Shouted out of Rosemont, priced out of Fells Point, and litigated to a standstill in Leakin Park, the city now faced the very real possibility that if it somehow got its expressway system built, its traffic would violate air-quality standards due to take effect in 1977. The Environmental Protection Agency said that to make the grade, Baltimore had to reduce its driving mileage by a fifth, and warned that the 3-A system's planned "intersection of three major interstate highways in the city's urban core area is inconsistent with this goal."

Early in 1973, MAD, now led by a fiery west Baltimore schoolteacher named Carolyn Tyson, retained a lawyer and sued in federal court to block the entire 3-A network, contending that it promised more destruction than benefit. Highway officials had not "given proper consideration to feasible and prudent alternatives" to the expressway's park leg, in the group's judgment, and had neither "made all possible efforts to minimize environmental damage" nor "based the system on the required coordinated transportation planning."

"At no time," the suit alleged, "has any hearing been held which allowed public consideration of . . . not building the 3-A system."

The court found for the highway, but by now the project's critics were so well organized and noisy, and its complications so varied and numerous, and the expense of sorting them out so extreme, that the

East-West Expressway — on which the city had been working steadily for thirty-five years, and on which a good many professionals had spent their entire careers — collapsed under its own weight.

The final blow came in 1977, when a proposal for the system's extension through Fells Point was sent to Maryland's state historic preservation officer, John N. Pearce, for his review and comment. Pearce wrote that it was so dreadful, and so defied fixing, that he could "only recommend that this road not be built as currently proposed."

The Road War was over.

21

- - - - - - - - - -

TWO YEARS INTO his tenure as federal highway administrator, Frank Turner was a man beleaguered; he'd spent his entire adult life with the bureau, had been rewarded for those decades of dedication and hard work with oversight of the entire nation's highway system, and now much of his work and his hopes for the future were coming undone.

Public opposition to urban interstates was so out of hand in so many places that in 1971, he was moved to write a memo to John Volpe, asking that the transportation secretary keep his "confidence in us" and characterizing the revolt as the "carpings of a few dedicated critics" who were "blinded by their desire to discredit" the program.

Such was the rhetoric the mild-mannered but heavily stressed Turner found himself throwing around with increasing frequency; in a 1972 speech he called freeway foes "misinformed persons, along with the zealots and dilettantes who regularly are opposed to anything for any reason, or even no reason at all."

That more urban mileage might not be the right answer for some places, Turner was willing to concede; he had come to that conclusion himself. But a good many of the program's critics insisted that fixed-rail transit was a viable substitute, with which he could not agree.

Turner was no foe of mass transit. He often spoke keenly of the need for it, of how no one mode of transportation could answer all of a city's needs. In fact, he was downright bullish on the idea — so long as it was provided by bus. Turner firmly believed that rail-based transit would not, could not, attract enough riders to justify the fortune it would cost to build, partly because it couldn't be adapted to changing travel patterns. Cities had changed since the days of the streetcar, were spread too far and wide for fixed-rail to take many people from where they were to where they wanted to go.

Buses, on the other hand, made excellent sense. Fifty or sixty could move as many people as three thousand cars, provide almost door-to-door service, and follow routes that could be adjusted as needed — and they piggybacked on an investment already in place, thus requiring no costly new infrastructure. By boosting the number of buses on the highways, you could actually reduce the need for more highways.

Like all his views, his enthusiasm for the bus was supported by research, by statistics. He could cite a 1962 study that showed that buses and subways moved people for about the same cost (3.2 cents per person per mile) but that buses were far, far cheaper to put into service. He could point to 1968 research that showed a single express lane devoted to buses could move the same number of commuters as four lanes of freeway. Of course, he had personal experience to draw from, as well, because he'd been riding the bus almost daily for as long as he'd worked in D.C. In the months after his confirmation, Turner directed the bureau's regional offices to be on the lookout for ways to use buses on metropolitan highways, backed bus transit studies in several cities, and opened many a meeting at bureau headquarters by asking: How many of you came by bus today?

And in September 1969 he'd helped launch an experiment in the D.C. suburbs that seemed to support his view that the lowly bus was the future of urban travel. With his encouragement, the Virginia Department of Transportation set aside new reversible lanes in the median of the Shirley Highway, as I-95 is called there, for buses alone. The lanes were a tremendous success; when the *Washington Post* staged a race between a bus and a car making the eleven-mile morning commute into the District, the bus won by thirty-two minutes, and soon the Shirley's bus commuters outnumbered their automotive counterparts. The experiment trimmed the highway's daily load by an estimated 3,140 vehicles and cut pollutants by 1,700 tons. Transit officials had to quadruple the bus fleet.

"Buses are the answer and the only answer," Turner said. When the Federal-Aid Highway Act of 1970 offered localities the cash to build dedicated busways, he'd been elated. "There is no doubt in my mind that a few years from now we will look back on this 1970 legislation as a landmark in the development of modern urban transit," he'd predicted, "just as we now look back on the Federal-Aid Highway Act of 1956, with its program for the interstate system, as a landmark in highway development."

He might have been a bit carried away. Still, Turner was onto a good idea and could not fathom why environmentalists, the press, and anti-highway activists didn't embrace the bus, or why they were so smitten with rail-based transit. The "infinite combinations of routings and schedules required by today's urban citizenry dictates that any transportation system must provide flexibility of route, destination and schedules," he said. "That's why fixed-route systems which are basically spoke lines attached to a downtown hub have such a hard time financing themselves in the fare box.

"And if they cannot support themselves at the fare box, then isn't this a good warning that they may be failing to provide that service which the customer wants?" For moving the poor, he figured "it would be cheaper to just issue them a car, or give them taxi coupons, like food stamps."

His favorite whipping boy became the Washington Metro, a cut-and-cover subway system that would initially cover ninety-eight miles and cost about $3 billion to build, an amount roughly equal to everything spent on the capital region's roads since the very beginning of white settlement there — and, incidentally, about $4,000 for every household. "What a huge capital expenditure to provide for the movement of about five percent of the transportation load within Washington's metropolitan area," he said. Just the annual interest on the debt "would buy about five thousand new buses every New Year's morning for the whole life of Metro."

Sensible though his position might have been, he was losing the argument. The harder he stumped for motor vehicle transportation, the more light rail and subways seemed to gather momentum. Worse, a growing chorus of critics, city officials, and members of Congress were arguing that fixed-rail transit should be financed with money from the Highway Trust Fund. Turner was almost religiously opposed to such a thing, believing that it was called a "trust" for a reason, that a sacred compact existed between Congress and the American motorist that fuel taxes would be used as promised, to build good roads. "I am a firm believer," he said, "in keeping a man's word."

If, despite his arguments, the people insisted on buying rail transit to solve their urban transportation problems, he could live with it; he wasn't opposed to a separate transit trust fund, even. But he could not abide building transit by stealing from the interstates. The other side argued that to earmark the trust fund strictly for highways, rather than transportation, shortchanged the taxpayer. It wasn't smart spending. Did it make sense, critics asked, to use taxes on what had become a societal vice to supply infrastructure encouraging that vice? If the same principles applied to the federal tax on alcohol, New York representative Jonathan Bingham reasoned, the income would be spent building bars.

While he fought these battles, Turner struggled to shepherd the agency's response to the National Environmental Policy Act, and he agonized over a piece of personal business that was the toughest problem of all. Back in 1962, when he'd received AASHO's Thomas MacDonald Award, Turner had given Mable much of the credit. "No man can earn this by himself," he'd said in a typically humble acceptance speech. "I am pleased to receive it in behalf of my wife, who is chief contributor to any achievements I have made, and the bureau with which I am associated."

But even then, it was clear that Mable was in decline. He and the children could trace her troubles back to the Philippines, recalled that her moods there had swung wide and deep and without warning, that she'd withdrawn into herself, become progressively timid. On some days, the thought of meeting people had consumed her with anxiety;

on a few, she'd been unable to leave the Quonset. Her social anxiety had mounted in the years after their return to the States. Her thinking grew foggy; her trepidation at leaving the house, paralyzing. With the children grown and gone her reliance on Turner had become all but total—so that as the interstates had spread across the land and his workload at the bureau had become crushing, he'd shouldered the added burden of caregiver.

Turner had promised the children that he would look after their mother until she died. By the opening months of 1972, it seemed the task might be beyond him. He could no longer leave Mable alone. When he was called out of town, he would contact a doctor friend who checked her into a local hospital for "tests." On one occasion when he tried to take her along to a meeting in Toronto, she became so confused and anxious on the way that he had to turn the car around. He faced the worst decision of his life: move his wife into an institution, or quit his job.

In a June 21, 1972, letter to John Volpe, Turner cited failing vision in his right eye for his decision. His letter to Richard Nixon of the same day offered no explanation at all. "After a little more than 43 years of continuous service in the Federal Highway Administration and its predecessor agencies, I desire to avail myself of the provisions of the Civil Service Retirement Act, with its special benefits available to June 30," he wrote. "It has been an unusual honor and personal privilege to have been able to serve a full career in the public service in an activity which I have felt was making a major contribution to a better America. It is with regret that I now take leave of the finest organization and most dedicated group of coworkers in Government."

Despite his long service, Turner was only sixty-three years old, which explains why news coverage of his choice invariably noted that he'd "unexpectedly" resigned. But aside from Mable's decline, the timing was probably right; the bureau's work was increasingly seen as a threat, rather than a public service. The highway community was losing its fights in the remaining holdout cities and was being second-guessed on decisions that Turner felt it alone possessed the expertise to make.

In March 1972, Volpe had come out in favor of breaking open the Highway Trust Fund for mass transit, proposing that an ever-greater share of the roughly $6 billion it generated each year be diverted from the interstates. The secretary's surprise move undercut Turner, who'd been so vocal against busting the trust; at best, he was made to look out of step with his own department, and at worst, an irrelevant dinosaur.

He was bothered, too, by the slow disintegration of the federal-state partnership. The bottom-up approach was fading; the Department of Transportation seemed bent on calling the shots, and he could see the day coming when the federal highway administrator would be little more than a middleman delivering orders to the states from a secretary strong on politics and weak in know-how. He didn't want to be around when the job came to that.

And really, he had little left to accomplish, anyway. The interstates were well on their way to completion and had delivered on much of their promise. They were fast; driving from New York to Los Angeles, which took an average of seventy-nine hours in 1956, now took just sixty-two, and that time was dropping every year. They were safe; when Turner joined the bureau in 1929, the fatality rate on American roads had been 16 deaths per 100 million miles traveled; now it was 5.5, despite a fourfold increase in the number of vehicles in service, and the rate on the interstates was just 2.52 and improving every year. The big roads were efficient, and convenient, and hardy. The highway program was bigger, in terms of the spending Turner oversaw, than the space program or atomic energy.

The president's reply, written the day after Turner packed up his office, saluted a career that "spanned more than years; it has helped bring to this nation an incomparable Interstate Highway System that continues to play a vital role in our development and prosperity.

"As an architect of the interstate system, you should feel a very special sense of pride in the fact that this, the largest public works program in world history, has been administered with uncompromising integrity and steadfast dedication to public trust," Nixon wrote. "This record fully merits the gratitude of all our fellow citizens, and, in their behalf as well as that of your many friends and colleagues throughout

Government, I want to express my deep appreciation for your service and my best wishes for the years ahead."

Turner stayed busy. He stumped for the protection of the trust fund as a director of The Road Information Program Inc., a mouthpiece for highway-related industries. He toured Virginia on behalf of another lobby group, the Highway Users Federation, to speak on "the arithmetic of transit." He was among the organizers of the No-Name Group, a small knot of leading transportation experts, most of them engineers, who met monthly over breakfast. He was one of the Road Gang, an informal lunch gathering of transportation officials. Its twice-monthly sessions were usually off the record, but a speech Turner delivered to the group in November 1972, in which he took on "self-appointed" highway critics who acted as if "they represent the public against those of us who've been in public service," was so popular that it was later reprinted in *American Road Builder* magazine, which received orders for twenty thousand extra copies.

Junior members of the highway community often drove out to Arlington to seek his counsel. The news they brought, and which he read in the papers, didn't always go down easy. As he'd feared, the trust fund was broken, first for the purchase of buses, in 1975, and for any kind of mass transit the year after; Turner would complain for the rest of his days that the decision gave systems like the Metro "a free ride." In the meantime, the Federal-Aid Highway Act of 1973 permitted the states and local governments to request permission to junk plans for as-yet-unbuilt urban interstates, and if they got the nod, to devote the unspent money to transit systems.

Turner had little idle time to stew. Mable rarely slept, took to wandering the house at all hours; Frank would be lucky to get a half hour's uninterrupted rest. For years he fed her, dressed and washed her, and watched his wife disappear before his eyes.

She died of heart failure in June 1982, a long ten years after his retirement, leaving Turner alone for the first time in his life. He stayed put in their house in Arlington, living simply; when his console TV crapped out, Turner bought a new model and set it on top of the old console.

He continued taking the bus, even took to riding the Metro once its lines reached the suburbs, though he still groused that it did "a good job for a few people."

On the infrequent occasions he backed the car out of the garage and steered onto one of his interstates, he stuck to the right lane. Frank Turner, the man who oversaw construction of the nation's high-speed superhighways, rarely topped fifty miles per hour.

In 1983, the Federal Highway Administration named a building at its research campus in McLean, Virginia, for Frank Turner. The entire facility, adjacent to the CIA's headquarters, was renamed the Turner-Fairbank Highway Research Center and thus paid tribute to two of the three men most responsible for the concept and construction of the interstates. It was probably the greatest honor that his old employer could have paid him, short of binding his name with the Chief's.

Turner's retirement continued to be an active one. At the 1984 gathering of state highway officials (who now called themselves "AASHTO," having added "transportation" to their name) he made what became known as the "Turner proposal" for a new design of heavy truck that would trim the load carried by each axle, thereby reducing road damage. The first interstates were more than a quarter century old now, and their use by tractor-trailers had far outpaced the bureau's forecasts; some especially busy routes were breaking down under the strain. Preserving the system required that the highway community "completely change directions by making vehicles that will fit our road system," he argued, "rather than continuing our efforts to make the highway fit any and all vehicles." A few years later, the problem still much on his mind, he suggested that the time had come to segregate trucks from automobile traffic on some interstates, to both preserve the auto lanes and relieve congestion. That idea had legs; more than twenty years later, it's still under study as a way to reduce maintenance expenses on parts of the system.

Construction proceeded, meanwhile, on the last few unfinished segments, most of them in cities or ecologically sensitive wilds. In June 1988, New Hampshire completed I-93, an alternating parkway and full-fledged interstate, through Franconia Notch in the White Mountains. For years, environmentalists had fretted that traffic vibrations in the deep pass might crumble the Old Man of the Mountain, a looming granite profile that was the subject of poetry and folklore, and so intertwined with the state's self-image that it was emblazoned on its license plates. The unique highway through the notch safeguarded the Old Man, which collapsed and tumbled down the mountain of its own accord in 2003.

Likewise, Colorado officials lavished attention on I-70's sinuous, 16-mile journey through Glenwood Canyon, 150 miles west of Denver, which carried the Colorado River between great limestone cliffs more than a thousand feet high. A road had passed through the canyon for generations — the earliest built specifically for autos dated to 1902 — but an interstate spooked just about everyone worried over the Glenwood's fragility. In 1968, when a study had concluded that the canyon was the only viable route, Colorado legislators had asked that the state's highway department aim for middle ground between the "'wonders of human engineering' and the 'wonders of nature.'"

With the help of citizen advisers, the department had delivered just that; with pioneering construction techniques, it built a tiered highway that rides thirty-nine bridges, traverses three tunnels, and hugs the rocky face of the canyon's north side. The canyon wasn't improved by this engineering marvel, but it wasn't ruined by it — and today the segment ranks among the most beautiful drives on any road, anywhere.

I-70's Glenwood Canyon leg was completed in 1992, making it one of the last original interstate segments opened to traffic. It was a good note on which to finish.

Drive into Baltimore today, and you'll find that the city's center is not crossed by an interstate highway. I-95 passes by to the south. With MAD's assent, it was built on the peninsula between the river's north and south branches, and crosses the water at Fort McHenry in a tunnel, rather than a high-rise bridge; at eight lanes wide, it was the biggest underwater tunnel in the world when it opened in November 1985. Interstate 83, the north-south Jones Falls Expressway, was never extended through downtown or the old neighborhoods to the south-east; it dumps its southbound traffic onto a wide boulevard, President Street, that ends in a traffic circle just east of the Inner Harbor.

As for I-70, it dead-ends at the city's western line, at the edge of Leakin Park. Its stump is occupied by a commuter parking lot, from which hiking trails diverge into woods; on weekends, the lot is crowded with cars fitted with bike racks and buses dropping off day hikers. A placard at the roadside commemorates the Baltimoreans who accomplished what the Rockies could not: blocking a highway that begins 2,153 miles to the west in Cove Fort, Utah.

Beyond the stump, just one short segment of the long-fought expressway did move from blueprint to concrete: a piece of the I-170 spur off the main line. Just shy of a mile and a half long, four lanes wide, and disconnected from any other freeway, it was built in anticipation that it would eventually connect to the 3-A network but was instead marooned when the rest of the highway was killed; it is, inevitably, the leg through ravaged Franklin-Mulberry.

Baltimoreans call it "the Ditch," or "the Highway to Nowhere." Both are apt descriptions. I drove it one Saturday afternoon in the summer of 2009, hunting around downtown's edge for its eastern end and, on finding it, descending the ramp from Franklin Street. I had the sense that I was traveling a Hollywood mockup, rather than an actual road. Sunk three stories below street level, its flanks sheer concrete walls, the highway took me speeding westward under ten overpasses and several interstate-style signs, and less than two minutes later launched me back to ground level just a little ways east of Rosemont. Invisible on the drive were the blocks north and south of the Ditch, among the most wretched in the city, where windblown fast-food wrappers bound among tall weeds, broken glass, and overturned shopping carts, and past the boarded windows and doors of derelict homes. The scene is sad testament to west Baltimore's agonizing decades in the path of the interstates, and to their lasting effects.

The Highway to Nowhere has been open for traffic since 1979. From time to time there's talk of filling it in, but the expense is such that it won't likely happen anytime soon. So this strange relic of the expressway fight endures, built to the highest state and federal standards, serving little useful purpose.

Joe Wiles, his daughters say, would shake his head when he drove past it. Would observe with quiet disapproval that homes had once stood in place of this bizarre, floating piece of an abandoned freeway system — not the city's best homes, by any means, but homes nonetheless, occupied by good people who simply didn't know how to fight the city's plans. Didn't know they *could* fight until it was too late. Who were targeted early, before the opposition gelled.

Never one to gloat, Wiles did not speak of the freeway struggle unless someone else brought it up, never reminisced about his quiet but persistent leadership of the Rosemont resistance. There was little time or reason to bask; Rosemont was still standing, but even so, the expressway had left it battered. The sense of community Wiles and his neighbors had worked so hard to build, the pride and cohesion, the willingness to work for the common good — all of that was gone. The shabbiness that the condemnation had ushered in lingered; although 425 of Rosemont's emptied homes were rehabbed and resold, the old spit-and-polish neighborhood did not return.

Not for lack of trying, however. Wiles continued to lead the improvement association, continued to write letters. He continued to devote meticulous attention to his yard and to help his older neighbors with theirs. After he retired from the arsenal, in 1979, he volunteered at the YMCA and his church.

In 1987, the neighborhood slipping despite his efforts, he and Esther finally moved out at their daughters' behest and into a retirement community a little west of Leakin Park in Baltimore County. Wiles petitioned the management to let him plant a garden and tended it as faithfully as he had the yard on Ellamont Street; he tended it right up to the first of his strokes, which eventually brought his death in November 1998.

In June 1996, Frank Turner was one of four "founding fathers of the interstate," along with Al Gore Sr., Hale Boggs, and Dwight Eisenhower, honored at a dinner hosted by Gore's son, then the vice president, to mark the system's fortieth anniversary. The meal and speeches took place under a tent in the Ellipse, the spot from which the army's 1919 motor convoy had departed Washington.

In truth, it was just the 1956 act's birthday; the men most responsible for the system's actual birth, the Chief and Herbert Fairbank, went unmentioned. But the dinner correctly recognized that the interstates had turned out to be more than fancy roads — that, often in ways unanticipated by their creators, they had been agents of far-reaching change and had reordered the American landscape. That we could thank the interstates for shrinking the distances between our cities, and the untidy growth of those cities beyond Lewis Mumford's worst nightmare; for the "Edge City" of shopping and office space springing up on beltways in any number of metropolitan areas, and the "big-box" stores that were fast becoming ubiquitous features of suburban interchanges.

They'd tamed rivers and bays, high plains and remote reaches of blackwater swamp where earlier roads dared not venture. You could set your cruise control (an automotive feature that would have been needless had the interstates not come along) and at seventy miles per hour, in climate-controlled comfort, summit the Sierra Nevada pass that claimed the Donner party.

The year after the Ellipse dinner, his health failing, Turner sold the Arlington house and went to live with his son Marvin's family in Goldsboro, North Carolina. He had developed cancer and, as he neared and passed ninety, a slowly progressing dementia; still, when in January 1999 the Transportation Research Board named him the first recipient of its Frank Turner Medal for Lifetime Achievement in Transportation, he made it to Washington. Speechmaking was beyond him by then. When he took the mike, Turner could muster just one sentence to summarize his life's work: "It's been fun."

In his lucid periods, it was plain that an engineer continued to lurk in his head. Later that year, he read of plans to rescue the Outer Banks' Cape Hatteras Lighthouse, which teetered at the ocean's edge on fast-eroding beach. He was fascinated by the notion that a twenty-story brick tower could be picked up and moved, and talked Marvin into taking him to see it.

No interstates link Goldsboro with the barrier islands; the trip, over undulating U.S. highway, took four hours. Turner slept most of the way. Once on Hatteras Island, Marvin found a place to park near the lighthouse, which had been jacked onto rollers that edged at a glacial pace across the sand, and Frank, thin and frail, got out and shuffled nearer. He studied the process intently for a few minutes.

"Well, I see how they did it," he told his son. "I think they're doing it right."

Then: "I'm ready to go home now."

22

- - - - - - - - - - - -

WHAT AMERICA GOT with its $130 billion investment in the interstate highway system can be summarized, for good and ill, in a summer's drive west across Tennessee on I-40. For the most part, it's a lovely trip, its demands minimal, the views inspiring. You descend from the mists of the Great Smokies into rolling pasture and cropland, pass distant towns and bisect a couple of small cities, watch the road's swells and declivities gradually flatten as you near the Mississippi. The unpocked asphalt invites high speed; the surface is smooth and steady, and meets tires with a quiet, unvarying hum. Tractor-trailers abound, but not so many that you feel hemmed in. Driving is close to effortless.

Between Nashville and Memphis lie the half-dozen interchanges serving the city of Jackson, among them Exit 82-A. Its ramp injects you onto southbound Highland Avenue and into a triple-canopy jungle of neon signage that for sheer ugliness, not to mention sensory overload, vies with the worst of the system's roughly fifteen thousand exits. You're surrounded by Waffle House, Taco Bell, Shoney's, Dairy Queen, Exxon, Pizza Hut, a Super 8 motel, Raceway Gas, LaQuinta Inn, an Executive Inn and Suites, and a Travelers Motel advertised with a flashing red neon arrow aimed at its roof. Strip-mall businesses hawk furniture, pet grooming, guitars; billboards and power lines fill the interchange's few visual blanks.

Sight unseen, in 2008 I booked a room at Exit 82-A's Ramada Limited, a minimalist concrete and cinder-block inn perched on a bluff on Highland Avenue's east side, just behind the Shoney's. It was an awful place, with stained walls and cheap, mustard-yellow bedspreads and an overpowering bouquet of spray air freshener, and to its disadvantage, it offered a commanding view of the surroundings. My second-floor window looked onto the Shoney's rooftop air conditioners and satellite dishes; farther away, beyond the immediate craze of lights and traffic and the expressway's rumbling blur of red and white, lay the mercantile glut served by Exit 82-B, along northbound Highland — strip malls, chain restaurants, big-box stores.

Jackson itself was a mile or two away. South on Highland, past the Old Hickory Mall and a mammoth hospital, a compact, red-brick downtown clustered around a dignified county courthouse. When I visited, a live band's country-rock covers were spilling onto a street busy with pedestrians, a good many of them, no doubt, students from Jackson's Union University.

But that Jackson was invisible from I-40, and most of my fellow boarders at the Ramada Limited would miss it. Their impressions of the place would begin and end with 82-A — with a gateway that advertised not what set Jackson apart, but what made it indistinguishable from a thousand other towns: a no man's land of out-of-town brands in hideous profusion, at what could be any exit, on any interstate, in any part of the country.

Thomas MacDonald and Herbert Fairbank didn't see it coming, but the system of interregional highways they envisioned is today a place unto itself, divorced from the territory through which it passes. With rare exception, a sense of place, of uniqueness, is undetectable from the off ramp. In place of a local barbecue joint, an exit in the Carolinas is likely to offer an Arby's or a Chik-fil-A. Southern greasy spoons are miles off the main line, shouldered aside by Waffle House and Cracker Barrel. The loathed hot-dog stand of the thirties has been replaced by McDonald's.

We patronize these cookie-cutter enterprises without hesitation, for they perform the same function as the highways along which they cluster: they offer a predictable experience, devoid of surprise, pleasant or otherwise. We know the McDonald's coffee is good, so why go elsewhere? We know a Wendy's salad will satisfy, so why take the time and effort to find a homegrown restaurant? We know that Hampton Inn has clean rooms, good beds, and free self-serve breakfasts, and more often than not a chain restaurant just a short walk across the parking lot, so why hassle with a locally owned inn that isn't a sure thing? Why venture to a bona fide Mexican restaurant, when there's Taco Bell — which is certainly fast and filling, if nothing else?

Interchanges have more in common with each other than any one of them has with wherever it happens to be. The twain have met; exit a California interstate, and you'll find what you left in Connecticut — and very little that you didn't leave in Connecticut. The interstates take a distillation of the broad American culture — a one-size-fits-all, lowest-common-denominator reading of who we are and what we want — wherever they go.

This may sound like a lament, and I suppose it is. But it's coming from one of the guilty. Faced with a cross-country drive, I'll almost always opt for the interstate, knowing that whatever I sacrifice in local flavor, in soul, I'll recoup in speed and safety. And at the end of a long day behind the wheel, I'm not much in the mood to reconnoiter a strange town in search of a decent mom-and-pop restaurant, if an Applebee's is aglow a few steps from my motel.

I know that such a journey offers only a distant view of the America through which I pass. But it's easy; and some days, many days, that counts.

For all of its flaws, which over the years have received no shortage of attention, the interstate system represents an epic achievement, which doesn't get nearly so much ink. In scale, for one thing. It includes fifty-five thousand bridges, all of them ambitious projects in their own right, some almost inconceivably so. The Monitor-Merrimac Memorial Bridge-Tunnel carrying I-664 over the James River's mouth at Hampton Roads, Virginia, is 4 miles long and includes two man-made islands, a 3.2-mile trestle that rises 45 feet above the river's surface, and 4,800-foot twin tunnels that dive 45 feet below. A causeway carrying I-10 across Louisiana's Atchafalaya Swamp tops 18 miles in length. Florida's 5.5-mile Sunshine Skyway Bridge soars 175 feet over Tampa Bay.

As engineers in Baltimore observed nearly fifty years ago, the interstates offer breathtaking vistas, particularly in America's cities. No views of Providence, Richmond, or Atlanta, of Dallas or Oklahoma City, top those from the elevated expressways skirting the business districts, and few skylines are as dramatic as that of St. Louis from I-70/64/55's Mississippi crossing, or of Pittsburgh from I-376.

The system's nearly forty-seven thousand miles represent the greatest single investment that the American people have made in public works. The most expensive single project in the interstates — not part of the original network at all, but a correction of its mistakes — is Boston's "Big Dig," a monumental array of tunnels and bridges that replaced the elevated and justly maligned Central Artery. I-93 now courses under the city's middle, at a cost — interest included — of about $22 billion. That's more than twice what it cost to build the Panama Canal, in today's dollars.

And we'll be pumping more money, a lot more money, into the network in the years to come — not so much to build new interstates as to maintain what we have. As Frank Turner observed in a 1986 speech, "Highways grow old and wear out at fairly predictable ages and life spans, and therefore must be replaced or restored."

Case in point: In March 2008 a highway inspector discovered a crack, six feet long and growing fast, in a concrete pillar supporting I-95 on its winding, elevated course through Philadelphia. The wound was so deep and wide that it exposed the concrete's rebar guts, and it so alarmed state engineers that they promptly shut down two miles of the East Coast's principal highway in both directions.

For two days, the eight-lane interstate's 184,000 daily users were detoured onto a couple of two-lane streets, a disruption so profound that the state urged travelers all through the East to find another route. Problem was, I-95 takes an awful lot of people where they want to go, and the alternate routes were ill equipped to handle the flood of cars and trucks that sought them out. The jams were titanic.

The interstates are showing their age, and not just in Philly. Like America's streets, highways, and bridges in general, the roads have fallen victim to creeping neglect and the pounding of traffic unimagined by their builders. Frank Turner saw the dilemma coming. "The highway system has to be continually improved and replaced every minute of every day, and that is a large project in itself," he observed in 1996. "There is a life to a mile of highway, about thirty to thirty-five years, I would say, and the average age of the interstates' miles is getting to the point where overloads, cracks and other deterioration are all really showing."

Even as he spoke those words, cash-strapped state governments were backing off the system's prescribed maintenance. They started letting cracks in concrete pavement go unpatched, and more time pass between resurfacings, and took to limiting the loads on weak bridges instead of overhauling or replacing them. They did this even as the demands placed on the system grew ever heavier. The interstates account for about 1 percent of the nation's road mileage but host a quarter of the nearly three trillion miles that Americans travel each year. More of the vehicles plying them are heavy trucks, which hammer bridges and pavements.

It isn't difficult to find examples of slipping state maintenance. In the summer of 2008 I drove east across Iowa on I-80 and found the highway's pavement smooth and unblemished; the moment I crossed the Mississippi into Illinois, I encountered a road so badly cratered and cracked that "lunar" is only minor hyperbole for its condition. The steering wheel jerked and the suspension thumped; I felt compelled to drop my speed to below the limit. Ironically, this wasn't far west of the AASHO Road Test, the last remaining track of which lay just off the highway's south shoulder.

Pretty much all of the interstates in Illinois are in rough shape. I can cite dozens of examples from other states, as well. I-95 from Philadelphia to Boston is potholed and debris-strewn. I-10 across Louisiana is a roller-coaster ride on buckled concrete. I-40 in Oklahoma, the midpoint of a major east-west trucking route, is disintegrating. All of Michigan's interstates are in rotten repair.

"We're in pretty bad shape, frankly," former AASHTO president Tom Warne told me. "We're neglecting a system in which we've invested a great amount. We've been lulled into thinking it's always going to be here, always going to function for us. And it won't."

One in four of the country's nearly six hundred thousand bridges is structurally deficient or obsolete. Most were designed to last fifty years. In 2008, they averaged forty-three years old. Most are on state and county routes and are subjected to relatively small loads. But not all — a fact brought into sharp focus on August 1, 2007, when an I-35W bridge in Minneapolis collapsed into the Mississippi at rush hour, taking thirteen lives and injuring hundreds. The accident resulted from a design flaw, not deterioration, but it came as a jolt, nonetheless. This wasn't some little country bridge. This was an *interstate*.

Bringing the system into full repair, and keeping it there, will cost us dearly. One federal study suggested that all levels of government should spend a combined $225 billion *a year* for the next fifty years to rehabilitate surface transportation. They're currently spending just 40 percent of that, in a country that does 96 percent of its traveling by car and truck.

What's at stake, ultimately, is a foundation of America's safety, economy, and mobility. And not making the fixes will wind up costing more. Left unaddressed, needed repairs balloon into needed reconstruction. "If we can get this work done now," said John Horsley, AASHTO's executive director, "it will cost one-third of what it'll cost if we put things off."

Mary E. Peters, secretary of transportation under George W. Bush, likened the need to pony up serious money for highways to "what you and I would do with our homes. We're not going to wait to fix the roof until it's open to the weather."

Compounding the challenge ahead is a slide in highway income. The Highway Trust Fund, shared among Federal Aid projects, mass transit, and a host of new uses since Frank Turner's retirement, remains largely dependent on the federal gasoline tax, and the nation's automotive mileage — and thus the gas it uses — has been falling since 2006. Part of the explanation for this decline is higher gas prices, which have curtailed the population's desire to roam. The fund's income also has been affected by more efficient cars, which though good for the environment have proved bad for roads — the cars cause as much wear as regular gas suckers but don't contribute as much to the kitty. In any event, in the fall of 2008, for the first time in decades, the fund needed an $8 billion infusion to stay in the black.

State highway officials thus are hunting for ways to do their jobs with less. One approach: Missouri transportation boss Pete K. Rahn reinvented the way his state planned and built highways, and found it's possible to both lower standards and preserve quality. Rahn's "Practical Design," which has been copied outright by two states and is being eyed by several others, aims "to not build perfect projects, but to build good projects that give you a good system," he told me, explaining: "The typical approach is to start a project with highest design standards, and you build as much to those standards as you can afford. Practical Design says start at the bottom of the standards and go up to meet the need, and when you meet the need, you stop."

Put another way: "We wanted to see if we were building Lincolns when Fords would do," Rahn said. On some projects, old and new approaches achieve identical standards. On others, the differences are likely to be invisible. A highway through mountains might have a thinner bed of concrete where it rests on bedrock, for instance. A worn road might be patched, rather than reconstructed.

In Pennsylvania, officials are beating the drum for "Smart Transportation," a program that calls on engineers to reexamine all of their assumptions about road building. "The old style was that if we had a road that was congested, we'd project the traffic out twenty-five years and add lanes to accommodate that future traffic," said Allen D. Biehler, the state's transportation secretary. "Well, guess what? We don't have enough money for that approach anymore."

Thus, when Pennsylvania couldn't afford a long-planned, $465 million freeway in the northern Philadelphia suburbs, Biehler sought a cheaper alternative—and found it after brainstorming with communities along the 8.4-mile route: a smaller and more leisurely parkway, bordered with lawns, trees, and bike trails, and costing less than half as much.

Another example, which I alluded to a few pages back: Along 750 miles of busy I-70 in the Midwest, engineers are studying whether dedicated truck lanes might improve safety and help highways last longer. Beefing up just the lanes that carry heavier vehicles could enable states and feds to spend less on those for cars alone.

Necessary though they might be, such programs don't come close to covering the gap between highway spending and need. "We've got a great asset that changed the way Americans live, but we have struggled almost from the time it was built to maintain that system," Missouri's Rahn said. "Ultimately, it will require an increase in resources."

Where will the money come from? One possible answer is to swap the gas tax for one based on miles driven, rather than fuel consumed — it promises to better reflect a motorist's actual use of, and wear on, the highways. An Oregon study showed that such a tax could be charged during fueling stops with minimal fuss. A computer chip in the car might communicate with the pump, say, to calculate how far you've driven since your last fill-up, and your tax could be assessed and collected on the spot. Fair as the idea seems, it raises some nettlesome privacy issues; not everyone is thrilled at the notion that Big Brother may have another means of tracking your movements.

Even more ambitious is "congestion pricing," which would require motorists to pay for the pleasure of using certain key routes according to market forces — more when demand is higher, less when the traffic's light. Such systems would rely on electronic devices carried aboard each vehicle, eliminating the hassle of tollbooths and enabling road officials to adjust rates by the quarter, the month, or even several times an hour.

Both strategies hold promise because they would be unaffected by advances in automotive technology, which over time will further erode income from the gas tax. Fuel efficiency is bound to improve by leaps in the coming years, as automakers react to the declining oil supply; before long, we'll be compelled to develop a wholesale replacement for gasoline.

We'd better hope we do, anyway. Because without alternative fuels, we may see the interstates morph from the world's biggest highway system into its biggest white elephant.

Men in the auto business have talked about the appeal of alternative fuels since before World War I, when the prospect of the world's running out of oil seemed preposterously remote. It should come as no surprise, blessed as he was with a nose for future profit, that among the enthusiastic seekers of a gasoline substitute was Carl Fisher.

In June 1914, Fisher, busy at the time with the Dixie Highway and Florida and a blizzard of side projects, was visited in Indianapolis by one John Andrews, an amateur inventor from McKeesport, Pennsylvania, and, in Fisher's estimation, a "poor, apparently ignorant Portuguese." Andrews told Fisher he had developed a water-based fuel that could be made for under 2 cents a gallon. "We put the material in an auto," Fisher wrote, "and it tested up in one case about twenty percent more mileage than a gallon of gasoline would give."

Fisher asked Andrews to return the following week for more extensive tests. In the meantime, he wrote his automotive buddies, among them Henry Joy and Roy Chapin, to offer them a piece of the action. "If they have the goods," he wrote, "and certainly the demonstration made today looks like they might have it, they have one of the most wonderful inventions that has ever been made, and certainly one that can be cashed in on for I don't know how many millions."

The next round of tests produced, in Fisher's words, "one of the most remarkable things that I have ever seen." In front of "a half dozen shrewd men to watch every move that was made," Andrews combined twenty-four gallons of water, about 4 cents' worth of naphthalene, and six ounces of unidentified liquid to distill five gallons of substitute fuel. They ran it through a six-cylinder Cole; it got better mileage than with regular gas. They put it into a six-cylinder National; not only did the car's mileage improve, but its top speed jumped from fifty-six miles per hour to sixty.

What were the mixture's secret ingredients? Andrews swore that they could be found in any grocery store, but beyond that, he wouldn't say; in fact, Fisher reported that when the "Portuguese" went to Washington to patent his invention, he purposely omitted a key ingredient out of fear his formula would be stolen, and was consequently sent packing by patent officials. Fisher was sympathetic. "It is only a few years ago," he noted, "that they refused to issue a patent to Wright for a flying machine." He sent his own patent attorney to McKeesport, and the man returned "just as bad a nut on the thing as I am," he wrote

Chapin, "and he is a level-headed man with a great deal of experience in fool inventions and fool ideas."

Fisher nonetheless practiced due diligence. Before opening his wallet he wanted to be sure that he could make the stuff in bulk, and solicited Joy and Chapin to share the cost of building a still. "This is purely a speculation," he warned them. "It may make a lot of money. It may be a big fake."

That fall, as automaker Howard C. Marmon built the still in Indianapolis, Fisher drew up a business model for what he called Zolene. His company would make stills of various sizes and license them to agents scattered around the country, who would have exclusive rights to the machinery and formula in their territories. The company would collect rent on the stills and a royalty on every gallon of Zolene sold. "Every test so far is satisfactory," he advised Chapin in mid-November. "We get two more miles per gallon from our fuel than [from] any other gasoline; we get from twenty to thirty degrees less heat; we get from ten to fifteen percent more power; and no smoke nor carbon — What more do you want?"

How embarrassing for Fisher, and frustrating for the rest of us, that it wasn't to be. His hired chemists couldn't decipher all of Zolene's secrets but found that it contained a substantial amount of benzene, making it too expensive to compete with run-of-the-mill gas. Still, it did seem to produce more power than standard fuel, which no one could explain, and it did leave an engine spotless.

"Andrews either continually uses chemicals of which we know nothing or some other means which none of us are able to catch, in order to make both ends meet," Fisher told Chapin. He put extra men on the task of watching Andrews at work; when the inventor realized he was under study, "he decided he wanted to go home," and an exasperated Fisher "told him to go ahead and go home, to Hell or wherever he wanted to go."

So ended their experiment. Fisher was deeply agitated by the experience, on which he blamed a flare-up of heart trouble that year. Not only had it wasted his money and time, it left him with tantalizing questions; as he wrote in a December letter, "The thing is not exactly a fake, Mr. Joy." Later, he reminded Chapin that Andrews's invention had worked — it just hadn't done so at an attractive price.

Fisher predicted that Andrews would attempt to peddle his invention elsewhere, and sure enough, in 1917 the inventor turned up at the Brooklyn Navy Yard to demonstrate Zolene in a motorboat. The yard's commanding officer was astonished and had him repeat the feat with salt water the following day. The boat's engine fired eagerly.

No sooner had he whetted the navy's appetite than John Andrews vanished. A reporter who followed him to McKeesport found his home in disarray and minus its occupant, and every attempt to track him down met with failure. Speculation about his fate circulated for years.

Not until a quarter century later did another reporter manage to locate him. Andrews insisted that he really had invented a fuel made from water. It had really worked. It involved no trickery.

But after so many years, he said, he had forgotten the formula.

Acknowledgments

THIS BOOK, like all books, is the offspring of a great many parents, and this one more than most. Its completion relied on a host of strangers who lent me their time, labor, and expertise with little expectation that they would benefit from the transaction.

I owe thanks, first, to Richard Weingroff, the Federal Highway Administration's unofficial historian and a font of data, wisdom, and encouragement. Richard has helped a legion of journalists and historians to untangle pieces of America's highway past over the years, but in helping me this generous man outdid himself. He arranged for my research at the Department of Transportation Library, dug up and shared obscure documents that settled small but important questions, and read the first draft of my manuscript — no small task, even without the one hundred typed pages of feedback he offered. In short, he made my project his own, and it is the better for it in countless ways, big and small.

I'm indebted to others who helped me ferret out the facts that form the story's bones. Valerie Coleman and her colleagues at Texas A&M's Cushing Memorial Library graciously put up with my rooting through the papers of Thomas MacDonald and Frank Turner. Michele Christian at the Iowa State University Archives helped me unearth the Chief's college past. Kevin Bailey at the Dwight David Eisenhower Presidential Library, Paul McCardell of the *Baltimore Sun,* and the folks at the National Archives at College Park, Maryland, put vital pieces of the past into my hands, as did the University of Michigan's Bentley Historical Library, Ames Historical Society, Poweshiek County Historical and Genealogical Society, and Fort Worth Public Library.

I have been lucky, over the past twenty-plus years, to count Robert Wojtowicz of Old Dominion University as my friend; that he happens to be Lewis Mumford's literary executor is pure providence. Robert guided me in my exploration of Mumford's life, supplied me with Mumford's books, and often picked up the check for lunch, to boot.

Many people with personal connections to the narrative shared their time, recollections, and mementos with me, among them the Chief's great-granddaughter, Lynda Weidinger; Frank Turner's daughter, Beverly Cooke, and sons Marvin and Millard "Jim" Turner; Joe Wiles's widow, Esther Wiles, and his daughters, Carmen Artis and Carole Gibson; Wiles's longtime neighbor, Mary Rosemond; Baltimoreans Art Cohen, Stu Wechsler, George Tyson, Jim Dilts, and Tom Ward; and Turner associates Kevin Heunue, Alan Pisarski, Tom Deen, Peter Koltnow, and Francis Francois. Mark Reutter and Andrew Giguere provided me with their research into Baltimore's Road Wars, enabling me to piggyback on their hard work.

My research required a lot of driving — about fifteen thousand miles' worth in the past couple of years — which would have been tough to pull off without the help of Anne Evans, April Cobb, and Michele Brady of Thrifty Inc. in Norfolk; Albert and Maritza Delarosa, Kenny and Barbara Rossen, and Mark Peterson and Greta Pratt, all of whom rode herd on my daughter while I was road-tripping; and Mike and Elizabeth Semel, old friends who offered me meals and a bed on my forays to D.C. My dad, E. V. Swift of Bedford, Texas, not only put me up on my trips to Texas but did some initial scouting for traces of Frank Turner's childhood.

At the *Virginian-Pilot,* my professional home for twenty-two years, Denis Finley, Maria Carrillo, and Lon Wagner engineered a leave of absence I needed to research the book, so earning my everlasting gratitude. Maria also read a chunk of early draft, as did former *Pilot* reporter Tom "The Pink Badger" Holden. A 2008 assignment from *Parade* provided me with much of the postscript, for which I have the diabolically talented Lamar Graham to thank. My brother, Kevin Swift of St. Louis, drew the fine-looking maps that accompany the text and remained in reasonably good humor throughout my edits.

I thank my agent, David Black, who always has my back, and whose unflagging efforts on my behalf made this book happen; Eamon Dolan, late of Houghton Mifflin, who first suggested I take on the project; and my editors at Houghton Mifflin Harcourt, Andrea Schulz and Tom Bouman, with whose guidance I've chiseled a mountain of facts into a svelte (relatively speaking) story.

Finally, I owe a lasting debt to the friends who helped keep me sane during the three years that I devoted to this beast, among them Mark Mobley, Mike D'Orso, Fred Kirsch, Rhett Walton, my parents, and Lilly Marlene Lindenberry Swift.

Special thanks go to my daughter, Saylor, who accompanied me on two epic navigations of the continent and a slew of shorter research trips, who saw her summers and spring breaks hijacked by my need to dig up more detail, who consequently knows more about the interstates than any teenager on the planet, and who has proved a festive traveling companion, just the same; and my smart, patient, and beautiful fiancée, Amy Walton, who every day thrills and inspires me, and with whom I look forward to traveling millions of miles of good road in the years to come.

Notes

Abbreviations

America's Highways: *America's Highways, 1776–1976* (Washington, DC: Federal Highway Administration, 1976).

Annals: *Annals of the American Academy of Political and Social Science* (journal).

Archives: Papers of the Bureau of Public Roads, National Archives II, College Park, MD.

Bentley: Papers of Henry Joy and Roy Chapin, Bentley Historical Library, University of Michigan, Ann Arbor.

DOT: Department of Transportation Library, Washington, DC.

ENR: *Engineering News-Record.*

FCT: Papers of Francis Cutler Turner, Cushing Memorial Library, Texas A&M University.

Fisher biographies: Jane Fisher, *Fabulous Hoosier: A Story of American Achievement* (New York: Robert M. McBride & Co., 1947); Mark Foster, *Castles in the Sand: The Life and Times of Carl Graham Fisher* (Gainesville: University of Florida Press, 2000); Jerry M. Fisher, *The Pacesetter: The Untold Story of Carl G. Fisher* (Fort Bragg, CA: Lost Coast Press, 1998).

History interviews: Transcripts of interviews that Francis Turner gave to researchers following his retirement from government service and included in FCT: January and February 1986 sessions with Darwin Stolzenbach for an AASHTO interstate history project; a March 21, 1988, session with John T. Greenwood for the Public Works Historical Society; a February 1988 session with Howard Rosen; and another session, interviewer unidentified, in the late 1980s.

ISU: Special collections, Parks Library, Iowa State University, Ames.

Langsdale: Papers associated with Baltimore's Road War among the special collections of Langsdale Library, University of Baltimore, among them those of the Relocation Action Movement, Movement Against Destruction, the Southeast Council Against the Road, and the Society for the Preservation of Federal Hill.

Mertz: "Origins of the Interstate," an unpublished manuscript prepared by longtime FHWA official W. Lee Mertz, available on the Web at http://www.fhwa.dot.gov/infrastructure/origin.htm.

NYT: *New York Times.*

Sun: The Baltimore "Sunpapers" — the *Sun* and the *Evening Sun.*

TAC: *The American City* (magazine).

THM: Papers of Thomas Harris MacDonald, Cushing Memorial Library, Texas A&M University.

US News: *U.S. News and World Report.*

Part I: Out of the Mud

page

12   Such was the world . . . : Fisher biographies.

14   And mixed with the mud . . . : Clay McShane, "Gelded Age Boston," *The New England Quarterly* 74, no. 2 (June 2001).
Crossing a street . . . : Martin Melosi, *Garbage in the Cities: Refuse, Reform and the Environment* (College Station: Texas A&M University Press, 1981); and James J. Flink, *The Automobile Age* (Cambridge, MA: MIT Press, 1988).

15   So it was that in October 1893 . . . : *America's Highways;* Mertz; Richard F. Weingroff, "Portrait of a General: General Roy Stone," http://www.fhwa.dot.gov/infrastructure/stone.cfm (accessed July 2, 2010).

16   Of Carl Fisher's many adventures . . . : Both the Jane Fisher and Mark Foster biographies declare that Carl Fisher and Barney Oldfield drove home from New York.

17   In fact, so few autoists . . . : Dayton Duncan and Ken Burns, *Horatio's Drive: America's First Road Trip* (New York: Alfred A. Knopf, 2003); and Axel Madsen, *The Deal Maker: How William C. Durant Made General Motors* (New York: John Wiley & Sons, 1999).

18   That October, automaker . . . : Roy Chapin's drive from Detroit to New York is often described as having taken nine days. I went with Chapin's own account, included in a telegram he sent to "Olds Motor Works" on November 5, 1901 (Bentley). See also "Motor Touring Influenced Campaign for Good Roads," *NYT,* January 10, 1926.

19   One of Fisher's favorite schemes . . . : Fisher biographies; *Horseless Age,* August 20, 1902.
Oldfield likened racing . . . : Bob Zeller, "Before There Was a 500," *Car and Driver,* May 2003.
Horseless Age numbered him . . . : *Horseless Age,* July 13, 1904.
It wasn't speed alone . . . : Fisher biographies; conflicting accounts of the accident are well documented at www.firstsuperspeedway.com/articles/category/49.

20   In 1904, an inventor . . . : Fisher biographies; Griffith Borgeson, *The Golden Age of the American Racing Car* (Warrendale, PA: SAE International, 1997).
Stuffing metal tanks . . . : Foster, *Castles in the Sand;* "Eleven Hurt in Explosion," *NYT,* June 7, 1908.

22 Rains continued to turn rural roads . . . : *NYT*, daily race coverage, February 2 to March 25, 1908.

23 The most common "improvement" . . . : Pyke Johnson and Herbert S. Fairbank, unpublished partial biography of Thomas H. MacDonald (FCT); Charles Livy Whittle, "Highway Construction in Massachusetts," *Popular Science*, May 1897; Nelson P. Lewis, "Modern City Roadways," *Popular Science*, March 1900; Charles M. Upham, "The Last Two Decades in Highway Design, Construction and Maintenance," *TAC*, September 1930; and Dan McNichol, *The Roads That Built America* (New York: Sterling Publishing Co., 2006).

24 At the end of 1909 . . . : Thomas MacDonald, "The History and Development of Road Building in the United States," a paper delivered before the American Society of Civil Engineers on October 6, 1926 (ISU).

25 In the fall of 1908 . . . : Fisher biographies; Zeller, "Before There Was a 500"; and *NYT* prerace coverage of February 8, July 11, and August 15, 1909.

26 A three-day extravaganza . . . : *Horseless Age*, August 25, 1909; "Two in Racing Auto Killed Before 10,000" and "Record Breaking Contests," *NYT*, August 20, 1909; "Three More Killed in Auto Carnival," *NYT*, August 22, 1909; and "Discusses Dangers of Track Racing," *NYT*, September 5, 1909.

27 A few days later, the county coroner . . . : "Blame for Auto Deaths," *NYT*, August 28, 1909; *Horseless Age*, September 8, 1909.
    Out-of-town criticism . . . : "Useless and Barbarous," editorial, *NYT*, August 21, 1909; "Condemns Speed Trials," *NYT*, August 27, 1909; "Protests Against Auto Track Racing," *NYT*, August 29, 1909; and "Slaughter as a Spectacle," editorial, *NYT*, August 30, 1909.
    Crews laid down 3.2 million bricks . . . : Zeller, "Before There Was a 500"; Borgeson, *The Golden Age of the American Racing Car*.

28 "Three of us drove out nine miles . . .": D. R. Lane and Gael Hoag, *The Lincoln Highway: The Story of a Crusade That Made Transportation History* (New York: Dodd, Mead & Co., 1935).

30 Alongside passenger cars came the first trucks . . . : "A Broad Road Plan Is Outlined," *NYT*, February 9, 1913; "Street Congestion Opens Motor Field," *NYT*, March 23, 1913; R. W. Hutchinson Jr., "Motorized Highway Commerce," *Scribner's*, February 1914.
    Then there was the question of health . . . : Hutchinson, "Motorized Highway Commerce."
    City and country alike . . . : "From 'Horseless Carriage' to Palace Motor Car: A Story of Twenty Years," *NYT*, January 12, 1913.

32 He laid out their findings . . . : Jerry M. Fisher, *The Pacesetter: The Untold Story of Carl G. Fisher* (Fort Bragg, CA: Lost Coast Press, 1998).

33 Four nights later . . . : Ibid.; Lane and Hoag, *The Lincoln Highway*; *NYT*, September 15, 1912.

34 Joy brought field expertise . . . : Henry Joy, "Transcontinental Trails: Their Development and What They Mean to This Country," *Scribner's*, February 1914.

35 Even so, Joy predicted . . . : "11 Days Across Continent," *NYT*, July 13, 1913.
    While Joy was on the road . . . : Fisher biographies; *NYT* stories of July 1, 12, 15, 21, and 23 and August 3, 1913.

36 The last seemed the most fitting . . . : Jerry Fisher, *The Pacesetter*. How bent on a direct route was Joy? President Woodrow Wilson requested in a June 19, 1914, letter that the highway swing through Washington, D.C. Joy refused the request (Bentley).

38 One such town was Jefferson . . . : *Jefferson Bee*, November 5, 1913; Richard Weingroff,

"The Lincoln Highway," http://www.fhwa.dot.gov/infrastructure/lincoln.cfm; Farwell T. Brown, *Ames in Word and Picture* (Ames, IA: Heuss Printing Inc., 1999).

The federal government's Office . . . : L. W. Archives Page, October 17, 1914, memo to the secretary of agriculture; Page, September 22, 1915, letter to U.S. Rep. T. W. Sims (Archives).

39 This approach had precedent . . . : Mertz; *America's Highways;* the Johnson-Fairbank manuscript; and Michael P. Conzen, "The National Road, or, a Landward Salient for a Potamic People," *Geographical Review* 88, no. 4 (October 1998).

40 Among the backers . . . : "Road Makers Organize," *Washington Post,* December 14, 1914; and George Coleman, "The Origin and Development of the American Association of State Highway Officials," *American Highways,* October 1939.

41 By its first anniversary . . . : A. R. Pardington, speech to the Pittsburgh Chamber of Commerce, reprinted in the *NYT* of April 5, 1914.

Farther west, little had changed . . . : Mark Twain, *Roughing It.*

That was the nature of the West . . . : *Lincoln Highway Official Guidebook* of 1915, reissued by the modern association. I bought my copy at Lincoln Highway Association (LHA) headquarters in Franklin Grove, IL.

A. L. Westgard, the AAA's field agent . . . : A. L. Westgard, "Motor Routes to the California Expositions," *Motor,* March 1915; Henry Joy, "Seeing America and the Lincoln Highway," *Scientific American,* January 1, 1916.

43 Others had attempted . . . : Fisher biographies.

And he envisioned an artery . . . : Ibid.; Claudette Stager and Martha Carver, eds., *Looking beyond the Highway: Dixie Roads and Culture* (Knoxville: University of Tennessee Press, 2006). For more on the proliferation of named trails, see Frederic L. Paxson, "The Highway Movement, 1916–1935," *American Historical Review* 51, no. 2 (January 1946).

45 Regardless of what labels . . . : Richard Weingroff, "Federal Aid Road Act of 1916: Building the Foundation," http://www.fhwa.dot.gov/infrastructure/rw96a.cfm; Mertz; *America's Highways;* L. W. Page, January 17, 1917, memo to the secretary of agriculture (Archives); February 16, 1953, BPR memo on highway history from Ed Margolin to Paul F. Royster (THM); L. W. Page, "One Year's Experience in the Federal Aid Road Law," speech delivered at AASHO's third annual meeting in December 1917 and reprinted in *Good Roads,* December 22, 1917 (THM).

46 Shortly after the Federal Aid Roads Act . . . : Transcript of the August 15, 1916, session (Archives).

48 And while its people might gush . . . : F. H. Trego, *Hints to Transcontinental Tourists Traveling on the Lincoln Highway,* originally published in 1914 and reissued by the modern-day LHA. Trego's advice on firearms was the conventional wisdom of early autoists — see "A Practical Automobile Touring Outfit," *Scientific American,* March 1, 1902, which advises: "You might also place a good six-shooter under your pillow. You will sleep just as well, and it might come in handy."

A State Department survey . . . : *Report of Joint Committee on Federal Aid of Post Roads* (House Doc. 1510, 63rd Congress, 3rd session).

The two sides might have smoothed . . . : *America's Highways;* Richard Weingroff, "Clearly Vicious as a Matter of Policy: The Fight Against Federal Aid," http://www.fhwa.dot.gov/infrastructure/hwyhist01.cfm; *ENR,* January 9, 1919, and January 1, 1920; and Thomas MacDonald, February 13, 1920, speech to the Road Builders Association in Louisville, KY (Mertz and THM papers).

50 A month after the Armistice . . . : Weingroff, "Clearly Vicious as a Matter of Policy";

America's Highways; and J. M. Goodell, report to BPR management chief J. E. Penny-backer about the conference (Archives).

52 He'd accomplished this . . . : Thomas MacDonald, "Iowa Roads and Their Future," *The Road-Maker,* February 1913.

The offer came just after . . . : MacDonald letter to George Coleman dated January 29, 1919.

53 The secretary took more than two months . . . : Houston note to MacDonald of January 18, 1919; MacDonald letter to Houston of January 9, 1919; and MacDonald letters to J. M. Goodell dated January 20 and 24, 1919 (all, THM).

"Tender you the position . . .": Houston telegram to MacDonald of March 17, 1919; Mac-Donald telegram in reply dated March 20, 1919; MacDonald letter to Coleman of March 24, 1919; Department of Agriculture press release of March 25, 1919 (all, THM); "New Roads Official Named," *Public Roads,* March 1919.

54 He didn't much discuss . . . : Johnson-Fairbank manuscript (FCT); Newton Fuessle, "Pulling Main Street Out of the Mud," *The Outlook,* August 16, 1922; undated question-naire for MacDonald's entry in the *National Cyclopaedia of American Biography* (New York: James T. White & Co.), completed by Caroline Fuller on MacDonald's behalf (THM).

MacDonald had been a typical Iowa teenager . . . : Johnson-Fairbank manuscript; E. L. Anderson, "Efforts of Thomas H. MacDonald Result in Our Modern Highways," *Iowa Engineer,* May 1935; William Atherton DuPuy, "MacDonald of Public Roads," *American Motorist,* October 1923; *Iowa State Gazeteer* (Dubuque: Iowa Directory Co., 1892); *WPA Guide to 1930s Iowa* (Ames: Iowa State University Press, 1986).

56 It turned out, though, that he was at home . . . : DuPuy, "MacDonald of Public Roads."

He arrived at Iowa State . . . : Bruce Seely, "Research, Engineering, and Science in Ameri-can Engineering Colleges: 1900–1960," *Technology and Culture* 34, no. 2 (April 1993); MacDonald transcript (THM); 1903–5 Iowa State College catalog (ISU).

Still in his thirties . . . : Anson Marston files (ISU); H. J. Gilkey, "Anson Marston: Builder of Engineering at Iowa State College," *Proceedings of the American Society of Civil Engi-neers* 55, no. 2 (February 1929).

They agreed on a two-pronged assignment . . . : MacDonald and Gaylord thesis (ISU). Gaylord went on to great success as a specialist in dredging and other marine projects; in 1912, he dug the Houston Ship Channel.

57 That spring, Iowa legislators . . . : "Uncle Sam's Hired Men Who Serve You," a Depart-ment of Agriculture news release dated May 16, 1921, supplied to me by MacDonald's great-granddaughter, Lynda Weidinger; William H. Thompson, *Transportation in Iowa: A Historical Summary* (Ames: Iowa Department of Transportation, 1989); and *Discover-ing Historic Iowa Transportation Milestones* (Ames: Iowa Department of Transportation, 1999). That last source also yielded Iowa's 1904 auto registration.

Marston must have been persuasive . . . : MacDonald letter of April 25, 1939, to Iowa State engineering dean T. R. Agg (THM).

58 Quietly, patiently . . . : Thompson, *Transportation in Iowa: A Historical Summary;* C. H. Claudy, "At His Nod Millions Move," *Motor Life,* June 1922; Mary Reynolds, "Brief Sketches of Interesting Western Road Builders," *Western Highways Builder,* October 1921; and William E. Lind, "Thomas H. MacDonald: A Study of the Career of an Engi-neer Administrator and His Influence on Public Roads in the United States, 1919–1953," a master's thesis prepared at American University in 1965.

In March 1907 . . . : "McDonald-Dunham," *Ames Times,* March 14, 1907; "Links That

Bind: The Fate of the Chained Five," *Ames Intelligencer*, March 14, 1907. Thomas Jr.'s November 21, 1907, birth was recorded in a single sentence in the *Times* of November 28, 1907; his birth certificate was not filed in the county courthouse in Nevada, Iowa, until January 1943.

59 "Iowa has an estimated mileage . . .": MacDonald, "Road Improvement and the Automobile Tax," *The Road-Maker,* November 1912.

60 "Seldom has there been such a swing . . .": "Nature Promotes Better Highways," *ENR*, April 3, 1919.
The *Des Moines Capital* . . . : Editorial, *Des Moines Capital,* March 26, 1919.
"Six months ago . . .": MacDonald letter of February 24, 1919, to J. M. Goodell (THM).
The *Des Moines Capital* . . . : Editorial, *Des Moines Capital,* March 26, 1919.

61 "I know it is not necessary . . .": MacDonald letter to Alabama state highway engineer W. S. Keller, April 24, 1919 (THM).
The nation's highways . . . : MacDonald letter of May 7, 1919, to Delaware state highway engineer Charles M. Upham (THM).
Among the warmest letters . . . : Henry Joy letter to MacDonald of April 2, 1919 (THM).
MacDonald replied . . . : MacDonald letter to Joy of April 24, 1919 (THM).

Part II: Connecting the Dots

65 Dwight Eisenhower enjoyed little promise . . . : Stephen E. Ambrose, *Eisenhower: Soldier and President* (New York: Simon & Schuster, 1991); James David Barber, *The Presidential Character* (Englewood Cliffs, NJ: Prentice Hall, 1992); and Richard Weingroff, "The Man Who Changed America," http://www.fhwa.dot.gov/publications/publicroads/03mar/05 .cfm.

66 The trucks had trundled . . . : Pete Davies, *American Road* (New York: Henry Holt and Co., 2002); Dwight D. Eisenhower, *At Ease: Stories I Tell to Friends* (New York: McGraw-Hill, 1988). My description of the convoy further relies on Eisenhower's after-action report, a lengthier report by army first lieutenant E. R. Jackson, and a program documenting a dinner held for the men in Sacramento, all available online from the Dwight D. Eisenhower Presidential Library and Museum at http://www.eisenhower.archives.gov.

69 The Townsend bill called for . . . : Weingroff, "Clearly Vicious as a Matter of Policy"; Mertz; *America's Highways;* and *ENR* articles of February 27, May 29, and June 12, 1919.
Good riddance to it . . . : Townsend 1920 Senate testimony (Archives); "Hearings to Begin on Townsend Highway Bill," *ENR*, April 22, 1920.
Its district engineers spent . . . : E. W. James, "Report of Operations for May 1919" (Archives); J. M. Goodell, January 23, 1919, letter to MacDonald (THM).

70 But the new boss was up . . . : DuPuy, "MacDonald of Public Roads."

71 His first memo . . . : Quoted in "The World's Greatest Roadbuilder," *Road News* (Australian Road Federation Ltd.), February–March 1963; and in Damian J. Kulash, "Professionalism and Politics," *Transportation Quarterly,* Spring 2000.
The latter were more important . . . : MacDonald speech published in *ENR*, December 11–18, 1919.

72 Other speeches followed . . . : Transcript of MacDonald speech to the U.S. Chamber of Commerce, April 29, 1920 (THM).
The importance of his topic . . . : *America's Highways.*

73 "Picture a pile . . .": MacDonald, "The Future of Road Building," *Curtis 1000*, April 1922.
It was pure MacDonald . . . : *ENR* briefs of April 21 and 28 and May 5 and 12, 1921.

The House approved . . . : "Revised Townsend Highway Bill Goes to Senate," *ENR*, August 18, 1921; "Senate Passes Amended Townsend Bill," *ENR,* August 25, 1921.

74 The Federal Highway Act of 1921 . . . : Mertz; conversations and e-mail exchanges with Richard Weingroff; Weingroff, "Clearly Vicious as a Matter of Policy"; and MacDonald and Herbert Fairbank, "Federal Aid as Road Building Policy: What Is It and What Has It Accomplished?" a paper prepared in April 1928 (DOT).

This wasn't necessarily recognized . . . : *NYT* brief on the House passage, November 2, 1921. On November 10 the paper devoted just a handful of lines to the president's signing the bill into law.

MacDonald, however, saw . . . : MacDonald, "Resume of Cooperative Road Improvement and Future Policies," speech (Archives).

76 The first step of the process . . . : *America's Highways;* Mertz; Turner history interviews; and the following documents from THM: a February 27, 1920, "memorandum for the secretary" in which MacDonald lays out the genesis of talks between the Bureau of Public Roads (BPR) and the War Department; remarks of agriculture secretary Edwin T. Meredith, February 11, 1920; a July 22, 1921, letter from war secretary John W. Weeks to the agriculture secretary; an October 14, 1922, letter from Weeks to the agriculture secretary, accompanying Weeks's submission of the Pershing Map; and a February 12, 1923, letter from MacDonald to BPR's district engineers, distributing the map.

77 James was to be . . . : *America's Highways;* James letter of February 21, 1967, to bureau historian Frederick W. Cron, reproduced at http://www.fhwa.dot.gov/infrastructure/ ewjames.cfm. The Arkansas financing mess was a pet cause of the *NYT* and enjoyed prominent play (usually front page and above the fold) in the paper's editions of March 26 and 29; April 2, 3, 10, and 18; May 8, 15, 16, 19, and 22; and June 7, 1921. James's role in the equipment scandal is summarized in "Trace Disposition of Road Equipment," *NYT,* August 3, 1921.

78 Now James and two other . . . : James letter to Cron.

As finally laid out . . . : MacDonald speech of June 4, 1923, at the dedication of the Zero Milestone, in the Ellipse in front of the White House (THM).

"This Roda serves . . .": Joseph Conley letter of August 7, 1918, typed on the letterhead of the Conley Hotel in Wendover (Archives).

79 If the bureau paid any notice . . . : Utah Governor Spry's role is documented in Henry Joy's February 18, 1927, letter to U.S. Sen. Tasker Oddie (Joy papers, Bentley).

But in September 1919 . . . : My account of the Wendover Road controversy was informed by documents preserved in the Lincoln Highway and Federal Aid-Utah files at the Archives: L. I. Hewes's letter to his Utah district engineer of October 18, 1921; "The Lincoln Highway," an editorial in the *Los Angeles Times,* February 1, 1922; "Nevada Urges Utah's Governor to Complete Lincoln Way," a news release containing an April 7, 1922, letter from Nevada officials to Utah governor Charles R. Mabey; Gael Hoag, June 8, 1922, report to the Lincoln Highway board; Hoag's July 25, 1922, report to the BPR on "Primary East and West Highways in Utah & Nevada"; undated BPR "Memorandum re Federal Aid Routes in Nevada"; Henry Joy letter to F. A. Seiberling of October 10, 1922; Warren G. Harding letter to Henry C. Wallace of October 25, 1922; Harding letter to Wallace of November 8, 1922; and "Are We to Have a Transcontinental Highway?" editorial, *Scientific American,* December 1922. I also relied on the Fisher biographies and Davies, *American Road.*

Newspapers throughout the West . . . : "Statement of Facts on Lincoln Highway," *Ely Daily Times,* February 3, 1922; editorial in the *Mountain Democrat* of El Dorado County, CA, quoted in "Broken Faith," editorial, *Salt Lake Citizen,* March 31, 1923.

80   In a May 1923 letter . . . : Wallace wire to Joy of June 4, 1923; Joy letter to Wallace of June 8, 1923; Wallace letter to Joy of June 28, 1923 (Archives).
     Joy and the rest . . . : Joy letter to Wallace of September 26, 1923.
81   Carl Fisher was too busy . . . : Fisher biographies.
     More than 200 . . . : Charles Pierce Burton, "America's Billion-Dollar Industry," *Harper's,* June 1922.
82   The first tentative step . . . : The LHA's efforts to build its "Ideal Section" are detailed in its survey results, titled "An Ideal Section: The Lincoln Highway" (Archives); "Minutes of Meetings of the Technical Advisory Committee of the Lincoln Highway Association, held at the Yale Club, New York City, on Friday and Saturday, December 18 and 19, 1920" (Archives); "Resolutions Passed by the Technical Committee" (Archives); "Plan Ideal Motor Road," *NYT,* January 2, 1921; and W. G. Thompson, "Design Features of Lincoln Highway 'Ideal Section,'" *ENR,* June 15, 1922.
83   Finally, its surface . . . : MacDonald's views on surfacing materials dominate his correspondence with the LHA from March 1920 to February 1921 (Archives); "Opposes Limiting Highways to One Material," *Highway Engineer and Contractor,* June 1921; "MacDonald Opposes One-Material Highways," *The Highway Magazine,* October 1921.
84   The stuff itself . . . : Earl Swift, "Rock of Ages," *(Norfolk) Virginian-Pilot,* December 16, 2007.
88   The following year, American factories . . . : Rudi Volti, "A Century of Automobility," *Technology and Culture* 37, no. 4 (October 1996); Fred C. Kelly, "How Many Can Buy Cars?" *NYT,* August 28, 1921; Earnest Elmo Calkins, "Virgin Territory for Motor Cars," *Atlantic Monthly,* March 1929; and Flink, *The Automobile Age.*
     Buyers demonstrated an eagerness . . . : "Huge Auto Outlay Seen as a Menace," *NYT,* April 22, 1925.
     In mid-1925 . . . : *NYT,* January 4, 1925.
     A year later, they stood . . . : Thomas MacDonald, "Highways in the Making, *TAC,* January 1928.
     The invention's costs . . . : "Automobile Fatalities Becoming One of Our Deadliest Scourges," *TAC,* September 1926.
89   Manhattan's streets . . . : "Start Parks and Stop Skyscrapers," *TAC,* September 1926.
     In 1928, the rate . . . : "About 1,000,000 Accidents and 27,500 Deaths from Motor Vehicles Last Year," *TAC,* July 1929.
     In 1929, when a new . . . : Brief, *TAC,* June 1930.
     "Our street systems will soon . . .": Daniel L. Turner, "Is There a Vicious Circle of Transit Development and City Congestion?" *TAC,* September 1926. See also "New Layout for City Urged by Planners," *NYT,* June 14, 1925.
     They spent ever-growing chunks . . . : John Chynoweth Burnham, "The Gasoline Tax and the Automobile Revolution," *The Mississippi Valley Historical Review* 48, no. 3 (December 1961).
     No wonder cars came . . . : "German Reichstag Member Analyzes American Motoring," *NYT,* October 18, 1925.
90   They started simply . . . : Warren James Belasco, *Americans on the Road: From Autocamp to Motel, 1910–1945* (Cambridge, MA: MIT Press, 1980).
91   "It is six in the afternoon . . .": James Agee, "The Great American Roadside," *Fortune,* September 1934.
92   Consider the travails . . . : Francis Turner letter to his parents, dated January 19, 1933, supplied to me by Turner's daughter, Beverly Cooke.
     In 1924, the Bureau . . . : *The Federal Aid Highway System Shown on a Map of the United*

States in 18 Sections (Washington, DC: Bureau of Public Roads, 1924).

The surest source . . . : The *Automobile Blue Book* is described by E. B. White in *Farewell to Model T/From Sea to Shining Sea* (New York: The Little Bookroom, 2003).

The trails were blazed . . . : Ezra L. Emery letter of November 12, 1923, to the U.S. Civil Service Commission (LHA file, Archives). Who, exactly, pioneered the auto trails' use of signature rings on telephone poles is unclear. As good a claim as any belongs to Emery, an early roads advocate in Wyoming.

93 "One well-known route . . .": "Highway Officials Ready to Adopt Uniform Markings," *NYT,* May 31, 1925.

AASHO followed the recommendation . . . : *America's Highways;* Mertz; the 1925 annual report of AASHO's executive secretary (Archives); "Nation and States Want Better Roads," *NYT,* March 1, 1925; and the James-Cron letter of February 21, 1967.

94 At the joint board's first . . . : Mertz; the James-Cron letter; Richard Weingroff, "From Names to Numbers," at http://www.fhwa.dot.gov/infrastructure/numbers.cfm; and "Uniform Motor Road Marking for Main National Highways," *NYT,* May 3, 1925.

Reconvened at the bureau's . . . : Mertz; Weingroff, "From Names to Numbers"; "Adopt National Road Signs," *NYT,* August 5, 1925; "Prepare to Designate 50,000 Miles of Road," *NYT,* August 6, 1925; and "Standard Signs Adopted for Federal Highways," *TAC,* October 1925.

The assignment was a tough one . . . : James's authorship of the numbered system and his meetings with Fletcher and Sargent are recounted in his Cron letter.

Privately, the association's . . . : Henry Joy letter to Austin Bement of June 29, 1927 (Bentley).

96 When the secretary . . . : "[J]ardine Approves New Roads System," *NYT,* November 20, 1925; and "75,884 Miles in National Roads," *NYT,* November 22, 1925.

Eastern highway officials . . . : "Too Many Roads as U.S. Highways," *NYT,* December 20, 1925; "Officials Plan Revision of United States Highways, *NYT,* December 27, 1925.

97 And the governor of Kentucky . . . : Mertz; Weingroff, "From Names to Numbers."

Henry Joy joked . . . : Joy letter of February 27, 1927, to Gael Hoag (Bentley).

98 They're sprinkled all over . . . : Richard E. Lingenfelter, *Death Valley and the Amargosa: A Land of Illusion* (Berkeley: University of California Press, 1986); notes from my visit to the town site in July 2006.

99 The Lincoln Highway's end . . . : The association's internal struggle over the road's final route in Utah and Nevada and its concurrent decision to disband are chronicled in letters filed in Henry Joy's papers at the Bentley.

100 At a busy intersection . . . : "A Safety Intersection on the Lincoln Highway," *TAC,* January 1930.

101 In September 1925 . . . : Fisher biographies; "Carl G. Fisher Buys on Montauk Point," *NYT,* September 22, 1925; "Florida Resorts Boom Long Island," *NYT,* January 10, 1926.

In February 1926 . . . : "Buys 10,000 Acres at Montauk Point," *NYT,* February 26, 1926.

102 But his opponent . . . : Robert A. Caro, *The Power Broker* (New York: Alfred A. Knopf, 1974).

But aside from a small plot . . . : "Development Work at Montauk Point," *NYT,* November 7, 1926.

Ah, but then came September 17 . . . : "75 Reported Dead in Miami; Hurricane Sweeps Coast; 2,000 Buildings in Ruins; $100,000,000 Damage in City," and "Miami Beach Under 3 Feet of Water," *NYT,* September 19, 1926; "Hurricane Rages 9 Hours" and "Realty Boom Area in Path of Storm," *NYT,* September 20, 1926; Fisher biographies.

103 Fisher hired a train . . . : "Realty Men Plan Florida Rebuilding," *NYT,* September 21, 1926; "Finds Relief Badly Needed," *NYT,* September 29, 1926.

104 Lo, the bypass movement . . . : The national conference recommendations are quoted in Harlean James, *Land Planning in the United States for the City, State and Nation* (New York: The Macmillan Co., 1926).

Five years later . . . : "By-Pass Highways," *TAC*, February 1929.

105 Desperate, city planners . . . : Daniel L. Turner, "The Detroit Super-Highway Project," *TAC*, April 1925; "Experts Advocate Super Highways," *NYT*, August 21, 1926; "Wider Roads for Traffic Relief," *NYT*, August 22, 1926; "Super-Highways Are Criticized," *NYT*, October 10, 1926; "Super-Highways," *NYT*, October 17, 1926; Roger L. Morrison, "Practical Means of Building Safety into Streets and Highways," *TAC*, November 1928; and Wyatt B. Brummitt, "The Superhighway," *TAC*, January 1929.

106 He belonged to a circle . . . : Lewis Mumford, *Sketches from Life: The Autobiography of Lewis Mumford* (New York: Beacon Books, 1983); Donald L. Miller, *Lewis Mumford: A Life* (New York: Weidenfeld & Nicholson, 1989); and Robert Wojtowicz, *Lewis Mumford and American Modernism* (Cambridge: Cambridge University Press, 1996).

The modern metropolis . . . : Flink, *The Automobile Age;* Kenneth T. Jackson, *Crabgrass Frontier* (Oxford: Oxford University Press, 1985); Sam Bass Warner Jr., *Streetcar Suburbs* (Cambridge, MA: Harvard University Press, 1962) and *The Urban Wilderness* (Berkeley: University of California Press, 1972).

107 What was needed . . . : Mumford, *Sketches from Life;* Miller, *Lewis Mumford: A Life.*

108 In 1924, MacKaye and company . . . : Ibid.

A small, one-family . . . : Display advertisement, *NYT* of May 2, 1926.

With the success of Sunnyside Gardens . . . : Mumford, *Sketches from Life;* Miller, *Lewis Mumford;* Wojtowicz, *Lewis Mumford and American Modernism.*

As the *American City* observed . . . : Henry M. Propper, "Construction Work Now Under Way on the 'Town for the Motor Age,'" *TAC*, October 1928.

109 MacKaye's *New Republic* piece . . . : MacKaye, "The Townless Highway," *The New Republic*, March 12, 1930; "Townless Highways," *TAC*, May 1930.

110 When journalist Walter Prichard Eaton . . . : Eaton, "Saving New England," *Atlantic Monthly*, May 1930. For more on the pox of roadside development, see "Highways for Your Mile-a-Minute Car," *Popular Science*, March 1932; and Jonathan Daniels, "The Smearing of U.S. 1," *The Nation*, June 21, 1941.

The roadside clutter . . . : Ray Lyman Wilbur radio address, published as "Must Our Fine Highways Be Bordered by Bewildering Signs, Tawdry Buildings, Weeds, Waste Paper and Old Cans?" in *TAC*, July 1929.

"They are not needed . . .": Walter E. Burton, "Beautiful Roadsides," *Scientific American*, July 1930.

It also coincided . . . : Edward M. Bassett, "The Freeway — A New Kind of Thoroughfare," *TAC*, February 1930. See also Weingroff, "Edward M. Bassett, the Man Who Gave Us 'Freeway,'" at http://www.fhwa.dot.gov/infrastructure/freeway.cfm.

While MacKaye labored . . . : Fritz Malcher, "Abolishing Street Traffic Intersections without Grade Separation: A Study of Highway Planning and Traffic Control to Meet the Needs of the Motor Age," *TAC*, September and October 1929; "The Steadyflow System," *TAC*, August 1930. See also Douglas Adams, "Norman Bel Geddes and Streamlined Spaces," *Journal of Architectural Education* 30, no. 1 (September 1976).

111 "Imagine a city . . .": Malcher, "A Traffic Planner Imagines a City," *TAC*, February 1931.

Malcher set out to fuse . . . : Malcher, "Express Highways Combined with the 'Steadyflow' System," *TAC*, January 1931.

McClintock had come to see . . . : "Unfit for Modern Motor Traffic," *Fortune*, August 1936; "Streamlining the Highways," *Popular Mechanics*, July 1939.

112   Right behind McClintock . . . : Robert Whitten, "Facilitating Traffic and Preventing Blight by Spacious Planning of Express Highways, *TAC,* August 1931.

      The same month . . . : MacKaye and Mumford, "Townless Highways for the Motorist," *Harper's,* August 1931.

113   Thomas MacDonald was beginning . . . : Transcript of 1971 interview of longtime bureau officer E. H. "Ted" Holmes by Michael Lash, provided to me by the FHWA's Richard Weingroff; and *America's Highways.*

114   The Bureau of Public Roads had been enthusiastic . . . : Bruce E. Seely, "The Scientific Mystique in Engineering: Highway Research at the Bureau of Public Roads, 1918–1940," *Technology and Culture* 25, no. 4 (October 1984). See also MacDonald, "Highway Transport — a Field for Engineers," *The Professional Engineer,* March 1922; MacDonald and Fairbank, "Federal Aid as a Road Building Policy: What Is It and What Has It Accomplished?"; and speeches MacDonald delivered to the New York Institute of Consulting Engineers on October 13, 1920, and the American Road Builders Association on February 9, 1921 (THM).

      MacDonald had been among . . . : MacDonald, "Thirtieth Anniversary of the Highway Research Board," an address delivered on January 10, 1951 (THM).

      In the wake of his victory . . . : Thomas MacDonald, "Highway Transport — A Field for Engineers," *Professional Engineer,* March 1922.

      The first such studies . . . : J. Gordon McKay, "Highway Transportation," *Annals* 116 (November 1924); Thomas MacDonald, "The Practical Application of Highway Transport Surveys to a State Highway System," address to 1930 AASHO annual meeting (THM); Mertz.

115   The Chief entrusted . . . : David C. Oliver, "In the Shadow of a Giant: H. S. Fairbank and Development of the Highway Planning Process," *Transportation Quarterly,* October 1991; D. C. Greer, "Presentation of First 'Thomas H. MacDonald Award' to Herbert S. Fairbank," *American Highways,* January 1958; and *America's Highways.*

      Now, while MacKaye and Mumford . . . : Mark H. Rose, *Interstate: Express Highway Politics, 1941–1956* (Lawrence, KS: Regents Press of Kansas, 1979); Thomas MacDonald, "Adjusting the Highway Viewpoint to 1932 Conditions," *Highway Engineer and Contractor,* February 1932; Mertz; and Weingroff, "Clearly Vicious as a Matter of Policy."

116   The surveys involved . . . : "The U.S. Highway System," *Fortune,* June 1941; MacDonald, "For Better Roads," *Scientific American,* June 1940; Oliver, "In the Shadow of a Giant"; Henry A. Wallace, "Great Southern Progress to Follow Road Survey," *Southern Highway Journal,* June 1937; Seely, "The Scientific Mystique in Engineering"; Mertz; and *America's Highways.*

119   Bess fell ill . . . : "Mrs. M'Donald Succumbs; Wife of Road Chief," *Washington Post,* August 7, 1935; 2009 interview with Lynda Weidinger.

      Besides Fairbank . . . : Joyce N. Ritter, "Thomas H. MacDonald and Charles D. Curtiss," *APWA Reporter,* October 1979; *America's Highways.*

      And there was Caroline . . . : Employment jacket of Caroline Fuller (Carrie Fuller in her early career at BPR), obtained through Richard Weingroff from the National Archives' personnel records depository in St. Louis.

120   He wandered for weeks . . . : MacDonald travel diaries (THM).

      In 1936 . . . : MacDonald travel diaries; Mertz.

      Even by today's standards . . . : Paul F. Griffin, "Blueprint for Autobahn, USA," *Scientific Monthly,* June 1954; and Edward Dimendberg, "The Will to Motorization: Cinema, Highways, and Modernity: For Wolf Donner, in Memoriam," *October* 73 (Summer 1995).

The Chief admired . . . : MacDonald's typed 1938 diary from the Eighth International Road Congress (THM).

121 But the Chief saw little . . . : MacDonald, "Contrasting United States and European Practices in Road Development," speech delivered December 5, 1938, at AASHO's annual meeting in Dallas (THM); MacDonald's testimony before the Senate Subcommittee on Banking and Currency on February 24, 1938 (transcript, THM).

Descended from highways . . . : Roger Shaw, "Mars Motors East," *Current History*, February 1939.

As *Time* pointed out . . . : "Hitler Hobby," *Time*, February 27, 1939.

Still, Hitler's highways . . . : "Memorandum on Super-Highways," National Highway Users Conference, February 19, 1938 (THM); MacDonald letter to Federal Emergency Relief Administration, October 24, 1934 (THM). The THM papers also include the proposals of various big thinkers inspired by the German highways — among them, the "U.S. Monumental Highway System" proposed by S. William Knoblock of Phoenix, the 1930 New York & New England Motorways project of Lester P. Barlow, and others.

122 Their meeting included . . . : The Chief's meeting with FDR was referred to in a February 7, 1938, morning press conference, a summary of which is part of THM. The president told reporters, the document says, that MacDonald "was coming in to see him today to discuss 'through national highways,' which are his 'favorite subject,' civil and military highway needs, and the problem of excess condemnation." Richard Weingroff places the meeting on the following day, based on press clippings.

123 As Fairbank put it . . . : Fairbank memo of March 5, 1938, to the Chief (THM).

Titled *Toll Roads and Free Roads* . . . : *Toll Roads and Free Roads* (House Doc. 272; 76th Congress, 1st session); a March 20, 1939, digest of the report prepared for the White House (THM); and H. E. Hilts, "Planning the Interregional Highway System," *Highway Research Board: Proceedings of the Twentieth Annual Meeting* (Washington, DC: HRB, 1940).

127 Among those praising . . . : Miller McClintock letter of May 5, 1939, to Pyke Johnson, copied to the Chief (Archives).

The man receiving . . . : Roland Marchand, "The Designers Go to the Fair II: Norman Bel Geddes, the General Motors 'Futurama,' and the Visit to the Factory Transformed," *Design Issues* 8, no. 2 (Spring 1992); Robert Coombs, "Norman Bel Geddes: Highways and Horizons," *Perspecta* 13 (1971); Paul Mason Fotsch, "The Building of a Superhighway Future at the New York World's Fair," *Cultural Critique* 48 (Spring 2001); "Tomorrow's America Modeled in 'Futurama,'" *Popular Mechanics*, July 1939; Dimendberg, "The Will to Motorization"; Douglas Adams, "Norman Bel Geddes and Streamlined Spaces."

You were then directed . . . : Quotes from the narration are from the Futurama script (THM).

128 Bel Geddes described . . . : Robert Coombs, "Norman Bel Geddes: Highways and Horizons"; Marchand, "The Designers Go to the Fair II."

129 They could step into a full-scale . . . : *Official Guide Book of the New York World's Fair 1939* (New York: Exposition Publications, 1939).

131 Among their critics . . . : "Rebuilding Our Cities: Parasitic Modes of Life Must Go, Lewis Mumford Argues," *Newsweek*, April 18, 1938; *Time*, April 18, 1938.

"Mr. Geddes is a great magician . . ": Mumford, "The Sky Line," *The New Yorker*, July 29, 1939.

The Chief wasn't impressed . . . : Mark S. Foster, *From Streetcar to Superhighway: American City Planners and Urban Transportation, 1900–1940* (Philadelphia: Temple University Press, 1981); conversations and e-mail exchanges with Richard Weingroff.

Perhaps sensitive . . . : Knudsen quoted in a July 20, 1938, GM news release. He reiterated the point in releases of April 19 and May 30, 1939 (THM).

132 When he was called on to speak . . . : MacDonald speech of November 2, 1939, at New York's Terrace Club (THM).

133 The state surveyed the line . . . : Mertz; "Speeders' Dream," *Newsweek,* May 6, 1940; "Railroadbed Highway," *Scientific American,* May 1940; undated pamphlet produced by the Pennsylvania Turnpike Commission (THM).

134 There was a catch . . . : Charles L. Dearing, "Turnpike Authorities in the United States," *Law and Contemporary Problems* 26, no. 4 (Autumn 1961).
    Ten thousand men . . . : "New Superhighway Tunnels the Alleghenies," *Popular Science,* September 1940; "Dream Drained," *Time,* October 4, 1937; "A Road to Match Today's Car," *Popular Mechanics,* March 1941; F. E. Wood and Paul F. Griffin, "Blueprint for Autobahn, USA," *Scientific Monthly,* June 1954.

135 He was bothered only by the toll . . . : "The Case Against Toll Roads," *TAC,* July 1947; MacDonald letter of April 22, 1947, to the *Manchester (NH) Sunday News,* made available to me by Richard Weingroff.

136 The company was a prototype . . . : Flink; John A. Jakle and Keith A. Sculle, *Fast Food: Roadside Restaurants in the Automobile Age* (Baltimore: Johns Hopkins University Press, 1999); and http://www.hojoland.com/.

137 Other chains sprouted . . . : Earl Swift, "Stuck on Stuckey's," (*Norfolk) Virginian-Pilot,* July 25, 2004.

140 That month, the president appointed . . . : MacDonald letter to FDR dated April 17, 1941 (Archives).
    The new panel . . . : Louis Ward Kemp, "Aesthetes and Engineers: The Occupational Ideology of Highway Design," *Technology and Culture* 27, no. 4 (October 1986).

141 It would span . . . : "Data on Proposed Report to the President Prepared by the Staff for Consideration by the National Interregional Highway Committee, Fourth Meeting" (Archives).
    Motorists on the interregional system . . . : *Interregional Highways* (House Doc. 379, 78th Congress, 2nd Session); conversations and e-mail exchanges with Richard Weingroff; Mertz; *America's Highways*; Rose, *Interstate: Express Highway Politics, 1941–1956*; Kemp, "Aesthetes and Engineers"; Oliver, "In the Shadow of a Giant"; H. E. Hilts, "Cooperation Is Essential in Building a National System of Interregional Highways," 1944 (Archives); "Chart Presentation of Design Standards Proposed in the Report on Interregional Highways," 1945 (Archives); "Report Explaining Recommended Standards for Interregional Highways," undated (Archives); V. T. Boughton, "Highways After the War," *Scientific American,* July 1944; Jean Ackermann, "You'll Like the Road Ahead," *Popular Science,* June 1944; Paul W. Kearney, "Iowa 'Roads Scholar' Plans for Postwar Highways to Put U.S. Back on Wheels," *Indianapolis Star,* June 25, 1944; and "Build Expressways Through Slum Areas," *TAC,* November 1951. The Chief's "We can't afford them" quote is from William Carter, "Roads Tomorrow," *Holiday,* March 1946.

143 Fairbank again did most, if not all . . . : *Interregional Highways*; Mertz; Carey Longmire, "Green Light Ahead," *Collier's,* December 29, 1945. That BPR intended the system to enter cities from the start is clear from its own documents. This refutes a stubborn myth about the interstates: that they were conceived as rural highways first and foremost, and that cities were added to win support from mayors and businessmen and, ultimately, the members of Congress who would supply the money to build them. Both *Toll Roads and Free Roads* and *Interregional Highways* devoted considerable attention to the system's urban stretches, and the Chief's first known reference to urban highway problems oc-

curred decades earlier, in his December 6, 1922, annual address to AASHO (Mertz); for the following three decades, he and Fairbank were unwavering in their push for urbanizing the federal highway program.

That warning was resounded . . . : Philip B. Fleming speech of December 1, 1943, to AASHO (THM).

144 FDR submitted the document . . . : "Message from the President," *Interregional Highways.*

The war effort had diverted . . . : Frederick Simpich, "U.S. Roads in War and Peace," *National Geographic,* December 1941.

In the two years before . . . : MacDonald, 1943 address to AASHO (THM).

They did so with little drama . . . : Transcript, MacDonald testimony to the House Subcommittee on Roads, which Richard Weingroff shared with me via e-mail.

145 As one Public Roads official put it . . . : R. E. Royall letter and report to Robinson Newcomb of April 11, 1949 (Archives).

America spent more . . . : "Our Transportation Mess," *Fortune,* November 1949.

146 "If we are successful . . .": MacDonald, *American Druggist,* July 1946.

The agency tried a number . . . : Mertz; *America's Highways;* Weingroff, "Designating the Urban Interstates," http://www.fhwa.dot.gov/infrastructure/fairbank.cfm; Kemp, "Aesthetes and Engineers." See also "Proceedings of the Urban Highway Design Conference," Washington, DC, February 13–17, 1950 (Archives).

"Each interviewer . . .": Weingroff, "Designating the Urban Interstates."

147 Some of the coming construction . . . : MacDonald, "The Case for Urban Expressways," *TAC,* June 1947.

MacDonald's boss, General Fleming . . . : Mertz; Rose, *Interstate: Express Highway Politics, 1941–1956;* Richard Weingroff, "The Man Who Loved Roads," http://www.fhwa.dot .gov/infrastructure/trumanpr.cfm.

148 That didn't, however, get them . . . : Mertz; Weingroff, "The Man Who Loved Roads."

Framing the interstates . . . : *Highway Needs of the National Defense* (House Doc. 249, 81st Congress, 1st Session); Frank Turner, "Highways and National Defense," *Military Engineer,* July–August 1971.

149 By the time they met . . . : Mertz.

Nothing happened . . . : "Highways in a Mess: No Answer in Sight," *Business Week,* September 16, 1950; "Rougher Roads Ahead," *US News,* September 7, 1951; "Highways Run Losing Race with Traffic," *Business Week,* December 8, 1951; and "Good Highways: When?" *US News,* March 28, 1952.

"On each such mile . . .": MacDonald's comment (originally delivered in a 1948 address) is quoted in "Highway Design and Safety," a paper prepared by the Automotive Safety Foundation for release on October 25, 1954 (FCT).

With no federal help . . . : Myron Stearns, "The Great Toll-Road Mirage," *Harper's,* October 1947; "Auto Speedway or Parkway?" *TAC,* July 1949; Karl Schriftgiesser, "Builders of the Great Thruway," *NYT Magazine,* December 17, 1950; "New Jersey Turnpike," *Fortune,* September 1951; "Ohio's Super-Highway," *Time,* June 16, 1952; and "The Concrete Canal," *Time,* July 5, 1954.

150 Metropolitan areas around . . . : "The San Diego Parkway," *TAC,* December 1947; "The Houston Expressway," *TAC,* November 1948; "Fort Worth Gets Expressway System," *TAC,* November 1949; "Kansas City Sees Expressways Preventing 1970 Traffic Jams," *TAC,* March 1952; "Kansas City's Downtown Story," *TAC,* April 1956; and "L.A.'s New Four-Level Intersection," *Fortune,* September 1951.

Truman had awarded him . . . : September 13, 1946, Federal Works Agency news release (THM); *American Highways,* October 1946.

Of even greater note . . . : Fuller's personnel file; 2009 interviews with Lynda Weidinger.
151 The Truman White House . . . : "Fitness, Not Years," editorial, *Fort Worth Star-Telegram,*
October 23, 1951.

Part III: The Crooked Straight, the Rough Places Plain

158 Buckner's thirteen-page response . . . : The report, complete with map, is available from
the Eisenhower Presidential Library and Museum.
159 But Eisenhower didn't know . . . : Eisenhower memo of February 4, 1953, to Gabriel
Hauge, *The Presidential Papers of Dwight David Eisenhower* XIV, Part 1, Chapter 1, Doc-
ument 20, available online at http://www.eisenhowermemorial.org/presidential-papers/
first-term/documents/20.cfm.
160 Exactly what was said . . . : Turner history interviews; Richard Weingroff, "Firing
Thomas H. MacDonald — Twice," http://www.fhwa.dot.gov/infrastructure/firing.cfm.
On paper, MacDonald's . . . : MacDonald letter of March 9, 1953, to Sinclair Weeks
(THM).
"I've just been fired . . .": Tom Lewis, *Divided Highways: Building the Interstate Highways,
Transforming American Life* (New York: Viking, 1997).
"Personally, I am awfully sorry . . .": Carl Vinson letter of March 27, 1953 (THM).
161 John A. Anderson . . . : Anderson letter of October 21, 1953 (THM).
Engineering News-Record saluted . . . : "The 'Chief' Retires," *ENR,* April 9, 1953.
On March 18 . . . : Commerce Department announcement of appointment (FCT); inter-
state history interviews; Mertz; du Pont letter of May 18, 1953, to the Chief (THM).
After finishing his last day . . . : The guest list for MacDonald's farewell dinner is included in his papers. Incidentally, it's been said that the Chief chose to travel to Texas by
train, but in a September 22, 1953, letter to Iowa roads boss Fred White, he wrote that he
"drove to Texas, stopping a few days at Hammond on route."
162 An old friend there . . . : Gibb Gilchrist's long recruitment of MacDonald is described in
the record of Texas A&M's Third Transportation Conference, on March 27, 1961; a copy
was supplied to me by Lynda Weidinger.
Even Herbert Fairbank . . . : Fairbank letter to MacDonald of May 2, 1953 (THM).
163 Nixon had more: The vice president's speech to the governors (usually labeled the
"Bolton Landing" address, after the conference center in which it occurred) is avail-
able in transcript form in the Archives. It's also discussed by Mertz, and by Weingroff in
"Clearly Vicious as a Matter of Policy."
165 It was only after a flurry . . . : Conversations with Richard Weingroff; "Resolutions
Adopted by the Governors' Conference, 46th Annual Meeting" (FCT). See also Edward
T. Folliard, "D.C. Road Parley of Governors Seen," *Washington Post and Times-Herald,*
July 14, 1954; and the "What's Going On" section of *Better Roads,* August 1954.
Over the following month . . . : Interagency Committee minutes (FCT).
Lucius Clay, hawk-nosed . . . : Richard Weingroff, "Lucius D. Clay: The President's Man,"
http://www.fhwa.dot.gov/infrastructure/Clay.cfm.
Even Eisenhower found him . . . : Ike diary entry of November 20, 1954, available at
http://www.eisenhowermemorial.org/presidential-papers/first-term/documents/1163
.cfm.
166 Even at gatherings . . . : My descriptions of Frank Turner's appearance, manner, and
place in highway history were informed by *America's Highways;* David C. Oliver, "In

Footsteps of a Giant: Francis C. Turner and Management of the Interstate," *Transportation Quarterly,* Spring 1994; Lewis Lord, "The Superhighway Superman," an essay included in "25 Shapers of the Modern Era," *US News,* December 27, 1999; Phil Patton, "Agents of Change," *American Heritage,* December 1994; Alan E. Pisarski, "The Frank Turner Story," and Bruce E. Seely, "Francis C. Turner, 'Father of the U.S. Interstate Highway System': An Historical Appreciation," *TR News,* March–April 2001; Bruce E. Seely, "Frank Turner: A Place in Transportation History," a paper presented at the Transportation Research Board annual meeting of January 11, 2000; Bill Wilson, "'Mr. Highways': A Legend Passes," *Roads & Bridges,* November 1999; and interviews with Turner colleagues and friends Alan Pisarski, Tom Deen, Peter Koltnow, Francis Francois, and Kevin Heunue.

It was an unadorned upbringing . . . : 2008 interviews with his daughter, Beverly Cooke, sons Marvin and Millard "Jim" Turner, and daughter-in-law Joann Turner; photos of the Powell Street house and the Turner children, provided to me by the family; Frank Turner, "Highways and Transit: A Partnership," speech delivered to the American Transit Association on October 6, 1971 (FCT). This section, and much of what follows about Turner, was also informed by the history interviews.

167 The highway engineering curriculum . . . : Texas A&M 1929 catalog; Donna Howell, "Turner Paved Road to Success," *Investor's Business Daily,* August 8, 2002.

The bureau's man impressed . . . : Thomas MacDonald letter to Turner of April 3, 1929; Turner reply of April 8, 1929 (both, FCT).

When he left . . . : A&M's reorientation to Texas Route 6 is described on a plaque on the campus's Jack K. Williams Administration Building.

168 A quarter century later . . . : Beverly Cooke interviews; reports of his various investigations (FCT).

"We would sit on the side . . .": History interviews.

In December 1930 . . . : Cooke interviews. Turner's yearbook is on file at the Fort Worth Public Library.

169 In the summer of 1933 . . . : History interviews, particularly that with Stolzenbach (FCT). The bosses took notice . . . : Turner personnel file (FCT).

170 An army of soldiers . . . : Heath Twichell, "Cut, Fill and Straighten: The Role of the Public Roads Administration in the Building of the Alaska Highway," *The Alaska Highway: Papers of the 40th Anniversary Symposium* (Vancouver: University of British Columbia Press, 1985); "The Alaska Highway" (Report No. 1705, 79th Congress, 2nd session); M. C. Sutherland-Brown, "The Alaska Highway in Canada — 10 Years Later," *Better Roads,* April 1956; and Harold W. Richardson, "Alcan — America's Glory Road," *ENR,* December 17 and 31, 1942, and January 14, 1943. Turner's assignment to the project is documented by a March 11, 1943, memo from Cap Curtiss to C. E. Swain (FCT).

It wasn't long before . . . : Turner memo of August 28, 1943, to J. L. Humbard (FCT); transcript, September 1, 1943, telephone exchange between army major W. H. Harvie and Public Roads' J. S. Bright (FCT); Humbard memo to the Chief of September 4, 1943 (FCT).

Three weeks later . . . : Humbard memo to Bright of September 13, 1943.

171 Few people called the camp . . . : History interviews.

The family's hut . . . : 2008 interviews with Turner's children.

And camp life . . . : Turner memo to the Chief of November 7, 1945 (FCT).

In December 1944 . . . : Interviews with Turner's children. Turner's weight and height are documented in his BPR medical records (FCT).

172   Frank Turner proved so . . . : Major Harvie letter to the Chief of July 24, 1944; Cap Cur-
tiss memo to C. E. Swain of July 31, 1944; Swain, August 1, 1944, memo to Curtiss; and
MacDonald, August 4, 1944, letter to Harvie (FCT).
By the end of the year . . . : Turner letter to R. E. Royall of November 23, 1944.
That winter, despite . . . : Turner memo to the Chief of March 27, 1945 (FCT).
The job finished . . . : Interviews with Turner's children.
He had to "rebuild . . .": Frank Turner, "Engineers Are Essential to Our Present-Day
Civilization," convocation speech delivered to Filipino student engineers on February
21, 1948, supplied to me by Beverly Cooke.

173   Turner recruited a force . . . : Turner's efforts to secure engineers, office space, and housing are described in a voluminous correspondence with BPR headquarters, and in meeting minutes of the Rehabilitation Agencies Committee in Manila (Archives). Beverly
Cooke supplied me with a map of Sea Frontier, the Quonset village; she and her brothers
provided me with a detailed picture of life there, as did Turner family friend Gay Wilkes
of Austin, Texas.
On or off duty . . . : Turner letter to the Chief of July 21, 1948; Turner memo of June 29,
1948, to the U.S. embassy (Archives).
In October 1948 . . . : Turner letter of October 29, 1948, to Isaias Fernando, the Philippines' director of public works (Archives).
In one of his son Jim's . . . : 2008 interview with Jim Turner.

174   Again, he excelled . . . : Letters and resolutions praising Turner's leadership are in the
FCT papers.
Beneath his diffident exterior . . . : Diaries of Frank and Jim Turner, supplied to me by
Beverly Cooke.

175   At about this point . . . : My account of the condemnation runs counter to that of several
histories, and to Frank Turner's own recollection in a number of interviews; all place the
incident years later, during the construction of I-35W through Fort Worth. As Turner
told it (some of the time, anyway), his mother asked whether he could stop the coming
highway, to which he supposedly replied: "I can but I won't."
    Good stuff, and probably in character—but fiction. The senior Turners lost their
house not to the interstate program but years before, at a point in their son's career when
he might have been able to stop or reroute a highway, but only in the Philippines. Texas
Highway Department records from May 1949 show that the Turners' Colvin property,
a corner double lot, lay in the right of way for the new North-South Expressway then
planned in Fort Worth. County assessment records show they sold the place to the city
on August 16, 1949.
    Their neighbors didn't sell until months later, so it's possible the Turners weren't out
of the house before Frank and family returned from overseas. If not, this scene must
have occurred—and Frank's children insist that it *did* take place—while he was on a
visit to the States. Whatever the case, the anecdote dates to this period.

177   Years later, Frank Turner . . . : Videotaped interview of Frank Turner for an in-house
FHWA television program, *Third Friday Report*. Richard Weingroff loaned me his cop-
ies of both the raw interview and the finished program, which aired on March 17, 1993.
Turner also described . . . : Lee Geistlinger, "First Person: Frank Turner," *Roads &
Bridges*, June 1996.

179   So it happened that the committee . . . : *Message from the President of the United States
Relative to a National Highway Program* (House Doc. 93, 84th Congress, 1st Session).
See also Mertz; Rose, *Interstate: Express Highway Politics, 1941–1956*; Richard Weingroff,

"Federal-Aid Highway Act of 1956: Creating the Interstate System," at http://www.fhwa
.dot.gov/publications/publicroads/96summer/p96su10.cfm; Seely, "Francis C. Turner:
Father of the U.S. Interstate Highway System"; "Coast to Coast on Four-Lane Highways,"
US News, January 21, 1955; "Sharp Curve Ahead?" *Newsweek,* January 24, 1955; "We've
Been Asked: About Financing Road Plan," *US News,* January 28, 1955; "More U.S. Aid,
but What Kind?" *Business Week,* February 26, 1955; Dero A. Saunders, "Those Expensive
Highways," *Fortune,* May 1955.

Successive drafts . . . : FCT papers.

180   Had Turner's contributions . . . : Du Pont letter to Turner of December 25, 1954 (FCT).

But as predicted . . . : "Here's Ike's Highway Plan," *US News,* March 4, 1955; Raymond
Moley, "The Clay Highway Plan," *Newsweek,* March 21, 1955; "Dead End for the U.S.
Highway," *Life,* May 30, 1955; and "A Well-Botched Job," *Time,* June 6, 1955.

The new chairman . . . : "Highway Plan Draws Both Cheers, Criticism," *ENR,* January
20, 1955.

Criticism bubbled up . . . : Weeks's criticism is contained in two pages of typed comment
he handed to du Pont at the White House on January 24, 1955, according to a handwrit-
ten notation on the document (FCT).

181   Byrd's testimony . . . : *Congressional Record.* Mertz quotes several passages.

Among Clay's defenders . . . : Automotive Safety Foundation daily congressional update
for March 22, 1955 (FCT).

Tall, bespectacled . . . : Conversations with Richard Weingroff; Weingroff, "Federal-Aid
Highway Act of 1956."

182   Du Pont hurried to his own office . . . : Pisarski, "The Frank Turner Story."

183   "Legislation to provide . . .": State of the Union, at http://www.eisenhower.archives.gov/
All_About_Ike/Speeches/Speeches.html.

Indeed, travel had jumped . . . : Thomas B. Dimmick, "Traffic and Travel Trends, 1955,"
Public Roads, December 1956.

Authorize the system . . . : Ike's budget message is available from the American Presidency Project, at http://www.presidency.ucsb.edu.

184   But much was happening . . . : Mertz; conversations and e-mail exchanges with Weingroff; Weingroff, "Federal-Aid Highway Act of 1956"; Rose, *Interstate: Express Highway
Politics, 1941–1956.*

The following week . . . : Ibid.; John Provan letter of March 24, 1983, outlining the fund's
chronology (FCT).

185   He'd eventually won a seat . . . : "Albert Gore Sr. Recalls Fight for Interstate Highway Bill,"
Bristol Herald-Courier, June 16, 1996.

186   Again, Treasury Secretary Humphrey . . . : Mertz; Weingroff, "Federal-Aid Highway Act
of 1956"; Rose, *Interstate: Express Highway Politics, 1941–1956.*

Eisenhower was back . . . : "Ike's Illness — the Political Meaning," *Newsweek,* June 18,
1956.

"Mr. Turner completed . . .": Performance review of May 2, 1956, covering Turner's activities from April 1955 to March 1956 (FCT). See also Bruce E. Seely, "Frank Turner and
the Interstate," *APWA Reporter,* June 2006.

Cap Curtiss, now the bureau's . . . : "No More Traffic Jams?" Q&A, *US News,* July 20,
1956.

Even before the final . . . : BPR "Experience and Qualifications Statement" of September
26, 1956 (FCT).

188   Turner later dismissed . . . : History interviews.

189 Big deal or no . . . : Mertz; conversations and e-mail exchanges with Richard Weingroff. See also "The National Highway Program — a Challenge to Cities," *TAC*, August 1956; and "How Freeways Will Break Traffic Bottlenecks of Big Cities," *US News*, September 14, 1956.

193 It didn't take long . . . : "They're Quickest on the Draw in the Highway-Building Program," *Business Week*, August 18, 1956; and "Road-Building Program Gets Off to a Flying Start," *Business Week*, August 25, 1956.
He decided it might goose . . . : Mertz; *America's Highways*.
That October, word came . . . : "In 13 Years . . . 50 Billions to Spend," *US News*, October 26, 1954.
The tall, mustachioed . . . : "New Yorker Heads U.S. Roads Program," *Washington Post and Times-Herald*, October 13, 1956.

194 For the interim . . . : Mertz; *America's Highways*.
As an official description . . . : BPR, "Experience and Qualifications Statement" for Turner, January 22, 1962.
As the first concrete . . . : "U.S. Sets Standards for New Highways," *NYT*, July 22, 1956; BPR Policy and Procedure Memorandum 20-4, August 10, 1956 (FCT).

195 One New Mexico official . . . : Robert Conradt, "Identify Interstate Highways with Letters," *Better Roads*, March 1957.

196 On the same day they unveiled . . . : "Adopt Interstate Sign and Numbering Plan," *Better Roads*, October 1957; "New Markers to Designate Routes," *NYT*, September 27, 1957.

197 AASHO was picky . . . : "Adopt Interstate Sign and Numbering Plan," *Better Roads*.
In March and April of 1955 . . . : "The Effect of Letter Width and Spacing on Night Legibility of Highway Signs," *Public Roads* 29, no. 1 (April 1956). See also Richard Weingroff, "Shields and Signs," at http://www.fhwa.dot.gov/infrastructure/50sheild.cfm.

198 It remained to standardize . . . : History interviews; Transportation Research Board, "Pavement Lessons Learned from the AASHO Road Test and Performance of the Interstate Highway System," *Transportation Research Circular* E-C118 (July 2007); "The AASHO Street and Highway Test — What It Didn't Say," *TAC*, July 1962; "World's Biggest Road Test Ends," *Business Week*, December 10, 1960.
Along the way . . . : "The AASHO Road Test," a technical Web article at http://training .ce.washington.edu/PGI/Modules/06_structural_design/aasho_road_test.htm.

199 He'd become well known . . . : Frank Tolbert, "Tolbert's Texas," *Dallas Morning News*, August 10, 1955.

200 He and Caroline Fuller . . . : Herbert Fairbank, "Posthumous Honor for 'Mister Public Roads,'" *Retirement Life*, December 1958.
They'd traveled a lot . . . : MacDonald letter of October 22, 1954, to Pyke Johnson (THM).
Suffering from an undisclosed ailment . . . : MacDonald letter of October 21, 1954, to Pyke Johnson (THM).
He'd been similarly upbeat . . . : MacDonald letter of April 5, 1957, to Gen. Franklin M. Kreml, director of Northwestern University's Transportation Center (THM).
The condition evidently . . . : Fairbank, "Posthumous Honor for 'Mister Public Roads'";
Pyke Johnson, ". . . and We Here Highly Resolve," *American Highways*, April 1957; "Tom McDonald," *Montezuma Republican*, April 11, 1957; and "Thos. MacDonald, U.S. Road Builder, Dies Here Suddenly," *Bryan Eagle*, August 8, 1957.
He and the casket . . . : Alf Johnson letter to AASHO members of April 11, 1957 (FCT); Gibb Gilchrist, April 30, 1957, letter to Caroline Fuller MacDonald (FCT).

201 The *Washington Post* wrote . . . : Editorial, *Washington Post*, April 16, 1957.

AASHO's Alf Johnson . . . : Johnson letter to AASHO members of April 11, 1957 (FCT). Fairbank delivered his tribute . . . : Richard Weingroff, "The Genie in the Bottle: The Interstate System and Urban Problems," http://www.fhwa.dot.gov/infrastructure/rwooc .cfm. Caroline stayed on in College Station with her sister after the Chief's death. When Jane died, Caroline moved in with the Chief's daughter, Margaret, in the suburbs of Orlando, Florida. In September 1986, she moved into the Florida Living Nursing Center in Apopka. She died there, aged one hundred, on May 1, 1989.

203 "We have progressed . . .": "Progress to Date," *Better Roads,* September 1957.

By the time the Clay Committee . . . : "Our Tangled Traffic," *Science Digest,* October 1955.

204 Cars gobbled vast stores . . . : Wilfred Owen, "Automotive Transport in the United States," *Annals* 320 (November 1958).

With the interstates still . . . : "Our Tangled Traffic," *Science Digest,* October 1955.

By one estimate . . . : "Congestion Costs New York City One Billion Yearly," *TAC,* February 1954.

Another forecast held . . . : "Our Tangled Traffic," *Science Digest,* October 1955. Rep. George A. Dondero, chair of the House Committee on Public Works, observed that buggies would be faster in a speech at AASHO's annual meeting, Seattle, November 1954 (FCT).

205 Born out of wedlock . . . : Lewis Mumford's childhood, discovery of Patrick Geddes, widening explorations of New York, and early writings are detailed in his autobiography, *Sketches from Life*; Miller, *Lewis Mumford: A Life*; and Wojtowicz, *Lewis Mumford and American Modernism.*

207 The turning point . . . : "Where the Great City Spread," *The New Yorker,* March 3, 1956. MacDonald noted Olmsted's grade-separation scheme years earlier — in a January 24, 1947, speech to the North Carolina Society of Engineers (THM).

The same year . . . : 2007–2009 conversations with Robert Wojtowicz.

208 An architectural detail . . . : Mumford, "Bauhaus — Two Restaurants and a Theatre," *The New Yorker,* December 31, 1938.

A proposed bridge . . . : Mumford, "Growing Pains: The New Museum," *The New Yorker,* June 3, 1939.

A Manhattan milk bar . . . : Mumford, "The Dead Past and the Dead Present," *The New Yorker,* March 23, 1940.

His "Sky Lines" . . . : "Form of Forms," *Time,* April 18, 1938.

He'd been taken, too . . . : Mumford, "Westward, Ho!" *The New Yorker,* February 25, 1939.

209 By 1947, Mumford was writing . . . : Wojtowicz, *Lewis Mumford and American Modernism.*

His magazine pieces . . . : *The New Yorker,* October 25 and November 15, 1947.

Moses's Stuyvesant Town . . . : Mumford, "Prefabricated Blight," *The New Yorker,* October 30, 1948.

Moses had responded . . . : Mumford and Robert Moses, "Stuyvesant Town Revisited," *The New Yorker,* November 27, 1948.

210 Moses devoted himself . . . : Mumford, "The Gentle Art of Overcrowding," *The New Yorker,* May 20, 1950.

One of his columns detoured . . . : Ad, *The New Yorker,* December 13, 1947.

In 1955, Mumford stepped up . . . : "The Roaring Traffic's Boom" ran in four installments in *The New Yorker:* March 19, April 2, April 16, and June 11, 1955.

213 By the late summer of 1957 . . . : "Is New Road Program Bogging Down?" *US News,* May 10, 1957.

Look magazine, while . . . : George Koether, "Roadblocks to New Highways," *Look*, October 29, 1957.

"Each step," he explained . . . : "Where Are Those Superhighways?" *Saturday Evening Post*, December 14, 1957.

214 But most Americans . . . : My passage on suburbanization was informed by Kenneth T. Jackson, *Crabgrass Frontier: The Suburbanization of the United States* (New York: Oxford University Press, 1985); Homer Hoyt, "The Changing Principles of Land Economics," Urban Land Institute Technical Bulletin 60 (1967); Carol A. O'Connor, "Sorting Out the Suburbs: Patterns of Land Use, Class, and Culture," and Michael H. Ebner, "Re-Reading Suburban America: Urban Population Deconcentration, 1810–1980," *American Quarterly* 37, no. 3 (1985); Peter Mieszkowski and Edwin S. Mills, "The Causes of Metropolitan Suburbanization," *Journal of Economic Perspectives* 7, no. 3 (Summer 1993); and "Why People Move Out of Cities," *US News*, August 10, 1956.

215 The new houses . . . : Herbert J. Gans, *The Levittowners: Ways of Life and Politics in a New Suburban Community* (New York: Vintage Books, 1967); James Howard Kunstler, *The Geography of Nowhere: The Rise and Decline of America's Man-Made Landscape* (New York: Touchstone, 1994).

A Virginia newspaper labeled . . . : Robert C. Smith, "The New Suburbia: Concept of a 'Mass Individualism,'" *Virginian-Pilot and Portsmouth Star*, July 10, 1955.

James W. Rouse, a Baltimore developer . . . : Edmund K. Faltermayer, "We Can Cope with the Coming Suburban Explosion," *Fortune*, September 1966.

All of which is to say . . . : Mumford, "Where the Great City Spreads," *The New Yorker*, March 3, 1956.

216 It wasn't just households . . . : "Shopping Centers Re-Studied," *ULI Technical Bulletin* 30 (February 1957).

A month after Southdale's debut . . . : "Too Many Shopping Centers?" *Business Week*, November 17, 1956.

217 But before long the circumferentials . . . : "Cities as Long as Highways — That's America of the Future," *US News*, April 5, 1957.

Harry Truman's once-rural hometown . . . : "I-70 Turns Towns into Cities," *Kansas City Times*, August 11, 1965.

And on the strength of three-bedroom . . . : *Architectural Forum*, January 1961.

Outside Louisville . . . : Simpson Lawson, "Interchanges Boost Value of Land, State Tells Court," *Louisville Courier Journal*, May 31, 1964.

In Robeson County . . . : Dick Brown, "Land Values Soar," *Raleigh News & Observer*, May 19, 1968.

218 Farther out in the country . . . : "Effect of Road Design on Property Values," *Better Roads*, May 1956; Claude C. Haren, "Rural Industrial Growth in the 1960s," *American Journal of Agricultural Economics* 52, no. 3 (August 1970).

Factories mushroomed beside I-80 . . . : Robert Evans, "New Industries Attracted by Keystone Shortway," *(Harrisburg, PA) Patriot-News*, March 15, 1964.

Chrysler cited the proximity . . . : "Transformation by Road," *Time*, October 15, 1965.

Interstate 35 spurred . . . : "How the Superhighways Are Changing America," *US News*, August 31, 1959.

Spartanburg, South Carolina, saw . . . : "Boom Is Riding South Along Interstate 85," *NYT*, July 8, 1966; see also Haren, "Rural Industrial Growth in the 1960s."

Mount Vernon, Illinois . . . : Paul Critchlow, "Sleepy Town Revives in Roar of Traffic," *Philadelphia Inquirer*, July 23, 1973.

219 Virginia's experience . . . : History interviews with Turner and Douglas Fugate, Virginia's former highway boss (FCT).

    If built on top . . . : Ibid. See also C. W. Enfield, "Right-of-Way Acquisition for the National Interstate System," *Better Roads*, June 1957.

220 The first scandal broke . . . : "Highwaymen at Work," *Life*, August 5, 1957; "Just Starting to Move," *Better Roads*, July 1957; "The Highway Billions," *Fortune*, September 1958; Fletcher Knebel, "Highway Robbery in Indiana," *Look*, December 10, 1957.

221 Before long, New Mexico . . . : "Program Suspended," *Better Roads*, January 1958.

    What with soaring . . . : "On Interstate Road Costs and Reimbursing States," *Better Roads*, February 1958.

    "Congressman after congressman . . .": Richard Weingroff, "Essential to the National Interest," *Public Roads* 69, no. 5 (March–April 2006).

    Blatnik and his eleven . . . : History interviews.

222 *Parade* followed suit . . . : Jack Anderson, "The Great Highway Robbery," *Parade*, February 4, 1962.

    In New Mexico, investigators . . . : Fletcher Knebel, "The Great Highway Scandals," *Look*, June 19, 1962; *Saturday Evening Post*, November 11, 1963. See also "Some 'Scandals' in the Roads Program," *US News*, May 13, 1963.

223 Much to Turner's chagrin . . . : History interviews; "$40 Billion Highway Program in Trouble," *US News*, March 7, 1960; Stanley Meisler, "Super-Graft on Superhighways," *The Nation*, April 1, 1961.

    A myth persists today . . . : History interviews.

224 Another piece of conventional . . . : Ibid.

Part IV: The Human Obstacle

229 One question confronting Moses . . . : James D. Dilts, "How Not to Run a Roadway," *Sun*, February 25, 1968; Mark Reutter, "The East-West Expressway," a master's thesis the Baltimore journalist produced in 1971, pieces of which he furnished to me; and Andrew M. Giguere, "'. . . and Never the Twain Shall Meet': Baltimore's East-West Expressway and the Construction of the 'Highway to Nowhere,'" a master's thesis completed by the Ohio University student in 2009.

    Some of the back alleys . . . : Frederick J. Kreller, *Sun*, October 20, 1944.

    But the slums . . . : "Artistic Freeway Urged by Experts," *Sun*, March 23, 1944; "Moses Group Favors Franklin Expressway," *Sun*, October 11, 1944; "Foes of Freeway Merge in Fight," *Sun*, March 19, 1945.

    Moses had little patience . . . : Reutter, "The East-West Expressway."

230 When the City Council . . . : "Building a Papier Mache Bridge from the Refuse of Citizen Crossfire on the East-West Expressway," *Sun*, April 26, 1972.

    Employment there had seen no growth . . . : "The Inner Harbor & City Hall Plaza," pamphlet, Greater Baltimore Committee and Committee for Downtown, 1965.

    "The arteries are clogged . . .": Herbert Fairbank speech to Advertising Club of Baltimore, November 13, 1946. Richard Weingroff supplied me with the text.

231 A few weeks later . . . : "Council Defeats Bill to Provide Plans for Part of Expressway," *Sun*, December 10, 1946.

    While all this excitement . . . : My passage on Joe Wiles's early life is based on interviews with his daughters, Carmen Artis and Carole Gibson.

232 Stuck in a succession . . . : Joe Wiles, letter of December 5, 1950, to Esther Wiles. She supplied me with a copy.

233 The Wiles family . . . : James M. Rubenstein and R. Ferguson, "The Impact of Relocation Activities on Baltimore," *Journal of Housing* 35, no. 10 (1978).

234 Yet Wiles saw . . . : Interviews with RNIA member Mary Rosemond, Artis, and Gibson.

235 The same went for Wiles's performance . . . : Artis and Gibson interviews.

The first came . . . : Artis interview; "Rosemont Unit Fights New Factory," *Baltimore Afro-American,* April 9, 1957; "Councilmen Pessimistic on Factory," *Baltimore Afro-American,* April 13, 1957.

At almost the same time . . . : Artis interview; RNIA papers (Langsdale).

Looking to avoid . . . : Susan West Montgomery, "Baltimore's Abbreviated Interstate System: The Consequence of Opposition, Legislation and Federal Intervention," a paper presented at the conference "Making Diversity Work: 250 Years of Baltimore History," November 15, 1996; Reutter, "The East-West Expressway"; "8-Lane Road Is Considered," *Sun,* November 1, 1956; "Project Basis for Stand on Road Plan," *Sun,* May 7, 1958; and James D. Dilts, "Changing City — 'We Must Destroy You to . . . ,'" *Sun,* August 4, 1968.

236 Its household income . . . : "The Battle Lines of Baltimore," *Innovation* 3 (July 1969).

237 Most outrageously . . . : Dilts, "How Not to Run a Roadway"; "Tyson Street Backers to See D'Alesandro Aides Today," *Sun,* October 3, 1956; "Planners Ease Tyson Street Blues," *Sun,* October 11, 1956; "Tyson Street Still in Danger Under New Highway Plan," *Sun,* July 18, 1957; "Tyson Street Plea Goes to Mayor," *Sun,* August 20, 1957; and "House Joins Fight to Save Tyson Street," *Sun,* February 27, 1958.

At first, the planners . . . : "Tyson Street Seen Doomed," *Sun,* July 19, 1957.

Property owners in Mount Vernon . . . : "Freeway Is Opposed," *Sun,* December 11, 1957. My description of the controversy also relied on Michael P. McCarthy, "Baltimore's Highway Wars Revisited," *Maryland Historical Magazine* 93, no. 2 (Summer 1998); "Group Opposes East-West Road," *Sun,* January 15, 1958; "Elevated Road Studied," *Sun,* February 20, 1958; "Dispute on Key Interchange Delays Expressway Plans," *Sun,* April 16, 1958; "Civic Groups Invited to Session," *Sun,* July 22, 1958; "Group Opposes Elevated East, West Road," *Sun,* October 22, 1958; and "Expressway Shift Urged," *Sun,* April 10, 1959.

238 "What is happening . . .": Lewis Mumford, letter, *Landscape Architecture,* December 1958.

The city's planners . . . : "City Buys 15 Acres for East-West Road," *Sun,* January 7, 1959.

239 When utility officials . . . : Francis Bello, "The City and the Car," *Fortune,* October 1957; "Downtown Traffic Cure," *Better Roads,* July 1957.

240 Early speakers toed . . . : Richard H. Parke, "Housing Is Linked to Road Planning," *NYT,* September 10, 1957; "The New Highways: Challenge to the Metropolitan Region," *Urban Land Institute Technical Bulletin* 31 (November 1957).

241 By and large . . . : "The New Highways"; William Yardley, "Warily, Connecticut Sets Its Agenda for New Roads," *NYT,* August 30, 2004.

242 Just a month before . . . : Van R. Halsey Jr., "Lewis Mumford's Golden Day," *New Republic,* August 12, 1957.

243 A half century later . . . : Lewis Mumford, "The Highway and the City," *Architectural Record,* April 1958.

Still bruised . . . : "Coordination," *Better Roads,* November 1958; E. H. "Ted" Holmes's March 2, 1969, speech to a Conference on Transportation and Community Values (FCT); and Richard Weingroff, "The Greatest Decade, 1956 to 1966," http://www.fhwa.dot.gov/infrastructure/50interstate.cfm.

244 In San Francisco . . . : "The Revolt Against Big-City Freeways," *US News,* January 1, 1962; Henry Ehrlich, "The Great Freeway Fight," *Look,* September 25, 1962; "Taming the Urban Freeway: New Principles for Fitting Highways and Cities Together," *Architectural Forum,* October 1963; David Hapgood, "The Highwaymen," *Washington Monthly,* March 1969; and Raymond A. Mohl, "The Interstates and the Cities: Highways, Housing and the Freeway Revolt," a research report for the Poverty and Race Research Action Council, 2002.

245 "It's the traffic . . .": Joe Allison, "Freeways — the Only Way," *San Francisco News Call Bulletin,* April 10, 1964.

The *San Francisco Chronicle* campaigned . . . : "A Move to Raze an Ugly Freeway," editorial, *San Francisco Chronicle,* August 29, 1962.

MIT professor John T. Howard . . . : "New View Points on Urban Transportation and Renewal," *TAC,* June 1957.

246 David Cort of *The Nation* . . . : David Cort, "Our Strangling Highways," *The Nation,* April 28, 1956.

Harper's glumly observed . . . : "Why Spoil the Adirondacks?" *Harper's,* October 1959.

Daniel Patrick Moynihan . . . : Daniel Patrick Moynihan, "New Roads and Urban Chaos," *The Reporter,* April 14, 1960.

Mumford kept up his own attack . . . : "The Skyway's the Limit," *The New Yorker,* November 14, 1959.

247 In mid-June 1959 . . . : My account of the Bragdon committee's activities is informed by Mertz.

248 He got it . . . : Eisenhower's letter, at http://www.fhwa.dot.gov/infrastructure/dde1959 .cfm.

249 The shape of the entire program . . . : Bragdon's account of the April 6, 1960, meeting is available at http://www.fhwa.dot.gov/infrastructure/bragdon2.cfm.

254 As *Florida Trend* magazine . . . : "Florida's Hosting Industry: Poised on the Threshold of Change," *Florida Trend,* June 1965. See also "The Great Uprooting," *Time,* March 24, 1958.

Anyone visiting Quapaw . . . : William E. Blundell, "Bypassed Business: New Interstate Roads Slash Tourist, Farm Trade in Some Towns," *Wall Street Journal,* September 19, 1962.

A long stretch of the Lincoln . . . : "Far Less Traffic on Hwy. 30," *Grand Island (NE) Independent,* August 4, 1970.

Connecticut's neon-lined . . . : "Where Business Longs for the Good Old Days," *Business Week,* April 9, 1964.

The experience of Bertha Amick . . . : Blundell, "Bypassed Business." See also "Who'll Get Helped or Hurt by Auto Freeways," *US News,* December 21, 1956.

255 Remember Lida, Nevada? . . . : Lida is not the settlement farthest from an interstate highway; that distinction belongs to Morgan, Montana, at U.S. 191's northern terminus, which is 191.4 miles removed from the system. But at more than 165 miles off, Lida's a haul, nonetheless. I found the nearest Cracker Barrel by plugging Lida's Zip Code into the restaurant chain's website, using the eatery's street address (in St. George, Utah) to get its map coordinates, then using a Web-based cartographic program to pinpoint the distance between the two.

The interstates eased the path . . . : "How the Superhighways Are Changing America," *US News,* August 31, 1959.

A 1964 Kentucky State . . . : "What Happens to Farms Divided by Super Roads?" *Louisville Courier-Journal,* February 2, 1964. See also "An Evaluation of Partial Taking of Property for Right-of-Way," *Public Roads* 33, no. 2 (June 1964).

The economic impact . . . : "Highway Construction: An Employment Generator," *Public Roads* 31, no. 7 (April 1961); "The Highway Billions," *Fortune,* September 1958.

It also devoured . . . : History interviews.

AASHO and the bureau . . . : AASHO, *Guide for Roadside Mowing,* 1962.

256 Turner took great pride . . . : History interviews.

A 1961 bureau study . . . : Charles W. Prisk, "Life-Saving Benefits of the Interstate System," *Public Roads* 31, no. 11 (December 1961).

Critics had decried . . . : Phillips Russell quoted in "Which — or Both?" *TAC,* June 1930.

Over time, the bureau . . . : Kemp, "Aesthetes and Engineers"; "Open Road," *Time,* April 12, 1963.

257 "Some drivers just fall asleep . . .": "How to Drive on a Superhighway — and How to Drive Away from It Alive," *Changing Times,* June 1956.

258 As John Steinbeck . . . : *Travels with Charley: In Search of America* (New York: Viking Press, 1962). For more rumination of that sort, see William R. Siddall, "Transportation and the Experience of Travel," *Geographical Review* 77, no. 3 (July 1987); Raymond Moley, "Highway Revolution — I," *Newsweek,* May 4, 1964; "Ode to the Road," *Time,* September 10, 1965; and Charles W. Morton, "Accent on Living," *Atlantic Monthly,* February 1956.

259 The first Holiday Inn . . . : John A. Jakle, Keith A. Sculle, and Jefferson S. Rogers, *The Motel in America* (Baltimore: Johns Hopkins University Press, 1996).

Howard Johnson enjoyed . . . : "Howard Johnson Tries a Little Harder," *Business Week,* September 29, 1973.

260 Old Man Stuckey . . . : Swift, "Stuck on Stuckey's."

And in time there appeared . . . : Jakle and Sculle, *Fast Food;* Don Babwin, "50 Years, Billions Sold," an Associated Press report carried in the *(Norfolk) Virginian-Pilot* of April 14, 2005. My discussion of fast-food joints was also informed by Erich Schlosser, *Fast Food Nation: The Dark Side of the All-American Meal* (New York: Houghton Mifflin, 2001).

But more than that . . . : "Turnpike Business Is Different," *Business Week,* September 6, 1952; Robert Lubar, "Interchange Ahead," *Fortune,* October 1958.

261 In a few odd places . . . : My passage on South of the Border is based on a two-day reporting visit in 1996, which I made as a staff writer for the *Virginian-Pilot.* I interviewed Alan Schafer in his windowless back-lot office; it featured a big board on which he kept track of the billboards and was decorated with his huge collection of antique beer serving trays. Schafer himself provided the history of the place. Not only did I witness the language barrier with which the passage concludes, but I also was present when some of my fellow SOB guests attempted to rent bathing suits from the front desk.

264 Back in Baltimore . . . : "The Inner Harbor & City Hall Plaza."

This new secret plan . . . : Edward C. Burks, "Expressway Rerouting Is Proposed," *Sun,* July 16, 1959; "Highway Shifts to Inner Harbor" and "Route Crossing Inner Harbor Is Advanced," *Sun,* October 28, 1959; James S. Keat, "New Route Urged for Expressway," *Sun,* January 31, 1960.

Officialdom and the business . . . : "Pratt Route Backed for Expressway," *Sun,* July 17, 1959; "Road Gains New Backing," *Sun,* July 18, 1959; "Werner, Goodman Support Expressway Shift to Pratt," *Sun,* July 22, 1959; and "Expressway Idea Better, Barnes Says," *Sun,* February 1, 1960.

"Automobile driving along . . .": Reutter, "The East-West Expressway."

265 The city hired three . . . : James S. Keat, "Study Scheduled for Expressway," *Sun,* April

24, 1960; "State Approves City Road Plan," *Sun*, February 12, 1961; and McCarthy, "Baltimore's Highway Wars Revisited."

So in October 1961 . . . : J. Anthony Lukas, "New Harbor Causeway Plan Given," *Sun*, October 12, 1961; Stephen E. Nordlinger, "Funk Approves Harbor Route for East-West Highway Across City," *Sun*, August 30, 1963; "Inner Harbor Road Favored," *Sun*, October 30, 1964; "Board Backs Leakin Park Road Route," *Sun*, January 13, 1965; Reutter, "The East-West Expressway"; McCarthy, "Baltimore's Highway Wars Revisited." See also Scott Kozel's excellent "Roads to the Future" website, at http://www.roadstothefuture.com.

266 The city's public works director . . . : J. Anthony Lukas, "Inner Harbor Route Given City Backing," *Sun*, March 22, 1962.

Days before a public hearing . . . : J. Anthony Lukas, "Route Hearing Warning Given," *Sun*, January 27, 1962.

He got a protest . . . : J. Anthony Lukas, "Irate Crowd Hits Planned Expressway," *Sun*, January 31, 1962; and Dilts, "How Not to Run a Roadway."

267 It recommended no immediate action . . . : James S. Keat, "Route Given for Freeway in Part Only," *Sun*, June 21, 1962.

The subject was urban mass . . . : Richard Weingroff, "The Battle of Its Life," *Public Roads*, May–June 2006; and Edward Weiner, *Urban Transportation Planning in the United States: An Historical Overview* (Washington, DC: U.S. Department of Transportation, 1997).

268 In April 1962, John F. Kennedy . . . : Ibid.

And in October . . . : Weiner, *Urban Transportation Planning in the United States*; Priscilla Dunhill, "Reconciling the Conflict of Highways and Cities," *The Reporter*, February 8, 1968; Thomas A. Morehouse, "The 1962 Highway Act: A Study in Artful Interpretation," *AIP Journal*, May 1969; and Weingroff, "The Battle of Its Life."

By the middle of 1964 . . . : Peter Marudas, "Expressway Indecision Causes Blight," *Sun*, March 27, 1964. See also "Specter of an Unbuilt Road," *Business Week*, May 2, 1970; and Anthony Downs, "Community Reaction to a New Transportation Corridor and the Effects of Relocation on the Community," *Relocation: Social and Economic Aspects* (Washington, DC: Highway Research Board, National Research Council, 1970).

A young lawyer . . . : "Ward Would Ban New Expressway," *Sun*, December 19, 1964; "Connector Opponents Seeking Its Removal," *Sun*, January 11, 1966; Reutter, "The East-West Expressway"; and telephone interviews with Ward in early 2009.

269 In Nashville, I-40's . . . : Helen Leavitt, *Superhighway-Superhoax* (New York: Doubleday & Co., 1970); "In the Path of Progress: Federal Highway Relocation Assurances," *Yale Law Journal* 82, no. 2 (December 1972).

A few hours to the west . . . : Daniel A. Farber, "Saving Overton Park: A Comment on Environmental Values," *University of Pennsylvania Law Review* 146, no. 5 (June 1998); John R. Porter, "Citizens to Preserve Overton Park Inc. v. Volpe: Environmental Law and the Scope of Judicial Review," *Stanford Law Review* 24, no. 6 (June 1972).

Protest groups sprang up . . . : Gordon Fellman, "Neighborhood Protest of an Urban Highway," *AIP Journal*, March 1969.

In New Orleans . . . : Lewis, *Divided Highways*; Russell Kirk, "From the Academy: The Bureau of Public Roads, Devastator," *National Review*, February 21, 1967; "The War over Urban Expressways," *Business Week*, March 11, 1967; "Halting the Highway Men," *Business Week*, July 19, 1969.

When Baltimore held . . . : Charles V. Flowers, "Expressway Hearing Ends in Shambles," *Sun*, July 21, 1965.

270 When homeowners . . . : Giguere, ". . . and Never the Twain Shall Meet"; James D. Dilts, "Expressway 'Victims' Fight Back," *Sun,* March 17, 1968.

That bum deal . . . : "Expressway Lag Rapped in Area Deterioration," *Sun,* March 9, 1967.

Across town . . . : Tom Ward interviews; Giguere, ". . . and Never the Twain Shall Meet"; John E. Woodruff, "East-West Expressway Due for Fight," *Sun,* February 14, 1967; Richard H. Levine, "Expressway Foes Clash with Backers," *Sun,* February 15, 1967.

It had been entrusted . . . : "We Drive Like Mad," *Tempe News,* March 4, 1967. The story quotes the bureau's claim that driving is the top form of outdoor recreation.

271 *The Atlantic Monthly* made it . . . : Norman Ritter, "Interstate 87," *Atlantic Monthly,* September 1967.

Writers for the conservative . . . : J. B. Jackson, "Abolish the Highways!" *National Review,* November 29, 1966; Kirk, "From the Academy."

In "The American Way . . .": Lewis Mumford, "The American Way of Death," *New York Review of Books,* April 28, 1966.

272 Turner decried the "nonsense" . . . : Cullison Cady, "Highways Are for People," *Highway User,* August 1966.

He worked for the common good: Ibid.

273 "We are in a period . . .": Transcript, Turner speech to AASHO's Committee on Administration, October 15, 1967 (FCT).

"We've heard a lot . . .": "Highway Goals for 1967–68," *Trucking Business,* August 1967.

In *Highway User* he . . . : Cady, "Highways Are for People."

274 Turner speculated that this . . . : History interviews. The same theory is aired in "Highway Juggernaut," *New Republic,* July 6, 1968.

The new secretary . . . : Robert B. Semple Jr., "Alan Boyd Named Transport Chief at Cabinet Level," *NYT,* November 7, 1966. See also Louis Dombrowski, "Boyd Seeks Transportation Balance," *Chicago Tribune,* March 8, 1968.

The new federal highway administrator . . . : John J. Hassett, "Two Will Fill Departing Whitton's Shoes," *Roads and Streets,* March 1967; and Dunhill, "Reconciling the Conflict of Highways and Cities."

"We have learned . . .": "Lowell Bridwell: Urban Highways Are the Big Challenge," *ENR,* March 21, 1968.

275 Sensing that Baltimore's . . . : Frank P. L. Somerville, "Architect Set for Road," *Sun,* October 26, 1966.

The expressway's city and state . . . : Michael Naver, "20 Years of Delays Peril Expressway Construction," *Sun,* March 19, 1965.

It took until early 1967 . . . : "Design Team Accepts Role," *Sun,* May 11, 1967; "Boyd Lauds 'Team' Idea," *Sun,* August 1, 1967; Wolf Von Eckardt, "New Freeway Theory Tested," *Washington Post,* September 24, 1967; "Team Approach Sets Pattern for Road Design," *ENR,* September 12, 1968; "Building Roads Without Disrupting the City," *Business Week,* November 18, 1967; Boyce L. Kendrick, "The Bumpy Road to a Better Highway," *AIA Journal,* February 1969; David Allison, "The Battle Lines of Baltimore," *Innovation,* July 1969; "How SOM Took On the Baltimore Road Gang," *Architectural Forum,* March 1969; "Biggest Snarl on City Highways," *Business Week,* October 18, 1969; Hapgood, "The Highwaymen."

It was a tall order . . . : Dilts, "Changing City — 'We Must Destroy You to. . . .'"

By the summer of 1967 . . . : Wechsler interviews.

276 So he responded . . . : Reutter, "The East-West Expressway"; Giguere, ". . . and Never the Twain Shall Meet"; Stephen J. Lynton, "Group to Oppose East-West Route," *Sun,* January

21, 1968; James D. Dilts, "The Changing City: Haunted Village," *Sun*, October 13, 1968; Dilts, "Expressway 'Victims' Fight Back."

In early June 1967 . . . : Reutter, "The East-West Expressway"; Adam Spiegel, "Mayor Vows Fight to Aid Relocated Home Owners," *Sun*, September 21, 1967.

Come October . . . : Dilts, "Haunted Village"; Jane L. Keidel, "Higher Prices for Doomed Homes Sought," *Sun*, October 4, 1967.

An even bigger victory . . . : Reutter, "The East-West Expressway"; Giguere, ". . . and Never the Twain Shall Meet."

277   But officials rejected . . . : Dilts, "Changing City — 'We Must Destroy You to. . . .'"

Such questions dominated . . . : Ibid.

A reply came from Frank . . . : Ibid.

278   The *Sun* jumped on the letter . . . Ibid.

That summer, while busy . . . : Wechsler interviews; Reutter, "The East-West Expressway"; Giguere, ". . . and Never the Twain Shall Meet"; "Mayor Meets Expressway Foes," *Sun*, August 15, 1968; Jane L. Keidel, "M.A.D.," *Sun*, August 30, 1968; and "New Civic Unit Criticizes Expressway Design Group," *Sun*, May 26, 1969.

Wechsler was elected . . . : Telephone interviews with Art Cohen in early 2009; Wechsler interviews.

279   The Design Concept Team remained . . . : "Southern Leg of East-West Expressway Is Proposed to Bypass Downtown Area," *Sun*, August 23, 1968; "Busting a Bottleneck," editorial, *Sun*, August 26, 1968; and Jane L. Keidel, "U.S. Aide Faults East-West Paths," *Sun*, December 13, 1968.

Just before Christmas . . . : Cohen interviews; David Runkel, "Preservationist Route Backed by Schaefer," *Sun*, December 16, 1968; "Expressway Choice," editorial, *Sun*, December 24, 1968; John B. O'Donnell Jr., "Mayor's Route Choice Averts Harbor Span, Bypasses Rosemont," *Sun*, December 24, 1968.

The National Park Service . . . : "Park Service Opposes High Span Near Fort," *Sun*, March 20, 1969; Joy Aschenbach, "Ft. McHenry in Battle Over Proposed Bridge," *Washington Star*, July 19, 1971.

280   In early August 1969 . . . : Cohen interviews; "Expressway Opponents Vilify Officials," *Sun*, August 7, 1969; "Rosemont Hearings," editorial, *Sun*, August 8, 1969; Jane L. Keidel, "An Expressway Bridges a Gulf Between People," *Sun*, August 17, 1969; Reutter, "The East-West Expressway"; and Giguere, ". . . and Never the Twain Shall Meet."

281   She later recalled . . . : U.S. Sen. Barbara Mikulski, speeches of December 15, 2006, and March 17, 2007 (transcripts supplied by the senator's office).

"You did one good thing . .": Keidel, "An Expressway Bridges a Gulf Between People."

So exhilarating . . . : "Negro Militants Vow War Against Rosemont Route," *Sun*, August 12, 1969; Keidel, "An Expressway Bridges a Gulf Between People."

282   The first was the Dakota . . . : John Volpe, essay in *Art Education* 23, no. 7 (October 1970). See also Cal Queal, "The Road That Goes Back 130 Million Years," *Denver Post*, June 29, 1969.

Another, bigger challenge . . . : "Continental Divide to Be Underpassed," *Dallas Morning News*, December 9, 1963; Jack Foster, "Pioneer Highway Tunnel Holed Through," *Denver Post*, December 4, 1964; Dick Thomas, "Divide Tunnel Dream Finally Coming True," *Rocky Mountain News*, September 27, 1970; Andy Roger, "Breakthrough," *Denver Post*, March 1, 1972; "Lady Engineer Given Task Atop Tunnel," *Denver Post*, November 14, 1972.

283   And in California's Mojave . . . : H. C. Prentice, "Application of Nuclear Explosives for a

Mountain Pass Highway and Railroad," *Engineering with Nuclear Explosives: Proceedings of the Third Plowshare Symposium,* April 21, 22, 23, 1964; J. G. Fry, R. A. Stane, and W. H. Crutchfield, "Preliminary Design Studies in a Nuclear Excavation — Project Carryall," and H. H. Zodtner, "Operations and Safety Problems Associated with a Nuclear Excavation Project," *HRB Record* 50 (1964).

285 Turner drew flak . . . : "Interstate System Accident Research," *Public Roads* 32, no. 11 (December 1963); "Fatal Collisions with Fixed Objects on Completed Sections of the Interstate Highway System, 1968," *Public Roads* 36, no. 1 (April 1970); and "Fatal Accidents on Completed Sections of the Interstate Highway System, 1968–70," *Public Roads* 36, no. 10 (October 1971).

That jibed with the observations . . . : Cullison Cady, "Highway Hazards," *Highway User,* August 1967.

286 "It is sometimes difficult . . .": Ibid.

"It is a fundamental . . .": Phyllis Dee Lovoca, "'We Have to Look at Both Sides,'" *Highway User,* September 1967. See also Turner's letter to the *Washington Post,* August 20, 1970, and the highway history interviews.

287 Turner's boss . . . : "Lowell Bridwell: Urban Highways Are the Big Challenge," *ENR,* March 21, 1968.

Congress likewise amplified . . . : Richard Weingroff, "Addressing the Quiet Crisis: Origins of the National Environmental Policy Act of 1969," at http://www.fhwa.dot.gov/highwayhistory/nepa/01.cfm#c; "Giving People a Voice on Highways," *Business Week,* December 14, 1968; John D. Morris, "Public Will Get a Voice on Roads," *NYT,* October 23, 1968.

289 To state officials . . . : Weingroff, "Addressing the Quiet Crisis"; and Ronald G. Shafer, "Volpe, Nominee for Transportation Post, Is Tilting with Agency on Highway Policy," *Wall Street Journal,* December 12, 1968.

291 *American Road Builder* called him . . . : Editorial, *American Road Builder,* March 1969.

Engineering News-Record called him . . . : "The Old Pro Speaks," *ENR,* May 15, 1969. See also "Francis Turner Sworn In as Federal Highway Administrator," *Transport Topics,* March 24, 1969.

292 Label him a darling . . . : Jim Turner interview. Turner's confirmation hearing is preserved, in transcript, as Serial No. 91-3, "Hearing Before the Committee on Public Works, United States Senate, 91st Congress" (FCT).

The Boston area, already . . . : "A Belt for Boston's Waist," *Fortune,* March 1966.

293 To satisfy the preservationists . . . : James D. Dilts, "Fells Point: A Dickensian Part of Baltimore Is Imperiled by the East-West Expressway," *Sun,* February 12, 1967; Edgar L. Jones, "That Road: Up Again from the Grave," *Sun,* August 28, 1970; and "Corridor May Claim 100 Fells Point Houses," *Sun,* December 18, 1970.

Money in general . . . : James D. Dilts, "Expressway: Now, It's Money," *Sun,* May 24, 1971.

294 The bureau's first nod . . . : Weingroff, "Addressing the Quiet Crisis"; Morehouse, "The 1962 Highway Act"; "Environmental Analysis and Reporting in Highway System Planning," *University of Pennsylvania Law Review* 121, no. 4 (April 1973); and the act, at http://ceq.hss.doe.gov/nepa/regs/nepa/nepaeqia.htm.

295 As Richard Weingroff . . . : 2009 e-mail exchanges with Weingroff.

296 In April 1969 . . . : Weingroff, "Addressing the Quiet Crisis."

Smog had burned eyes . . . : Chip Jacobs and William J. Kelly, *Smogtown: The Lung-Burning History of Pollution in Los Angeles* (New York: Overlook Press, 2008).

297 Big roads played hell . . . : Richard T. T. Forman and Lauren E. Alexander, "Roads and

Their Major Ecological Effects," *Annual Review of Ecology and Systematics* 29 (1998); Richard T. T. Forman and Robert D. Deblinger, "The Ecological Road-Effect of a Massachusetts Suburban Highway," *Conservation Biology* 14, no. 1 (February 2000).

Rural interstates presented . . . : D. J. Oxley, M. B. Fenton, and G. R. Carmody, "The Effects of Roads on Populations of Small Mammals," *Journal of Applied Ecology* 11, no. 1 (April 1974); Bill Thomas, "Those Other Traffic Victims," *Dodge News Magazine,* April 1972; and Ronald M. Kozel and Eugene D. Fleharty, "Movements of Rodents Across Roads," *Southwestern Naturalist* 24, no. 2 (July 31, 1979).

298 Against this backdrop . . . : James D. Dilts, "Expressway Design Hearing Is Tonight," *Sun,* May 25, 1971; James D. Dilts, "Hearing Held on Park Section of Highway," *Sun,* May 26, 1971; Edgar L. Jones, "Bulldozers at the Edge of a Rare Old Forest," *Sun,* September 24, 1971.

They came armed . . . : Farber, "Saving Overton Park"; Porter, "Citizens to Preserve Overton Park Inc. v. Volpe."

299 Now VOLPE and its allies . . . : "Conservationists Sue Officials to Keep I-70 out of Leakin, Gwynns Falls Parks," *Sun,* October 13, 1971; Isaac Rehert, "Leakin Park Expressway Given Its Day in Federal Court," *Sun,* January 25, 1972; James D. Dilts, "Judge Blocks Park Route for Road, Orders Hearing," *Sun,* June 9, 1972; "Court Upholds Leakin Route," *Sun,* January 10, 1973.

Joe Wiles spoke for many . . . : Reutter, "The East-West Expressway."

Early in 1973, MAD . . . : James D. Dilts, "Coalition Sues to Block 3-A Expressway Plan," *Sun,* April 1, 1973.

300 The final blow came . . . : Montgomery, "Baltimore's Abbreviated Interstate System."

301 Public opposition to urban . . . : Juan Cameron, "How the Interstate Changed the Face of the Nation," *Fortune,* July 1971.

Such was the rhetoric . . . : Fred Barnes, "Freeway Critics Come Under Fire," *Washington Evening Star,* June 1, 1972.

302 Buses, on the other hand . . . : Frank Turner, "The Bus in Your Future," *(Hackensack, NJ) Bergen Record,* February 22, 1971; Frank Turner, "Mass Transit: Rail or Bus?" *American Road Builder,* January–February 1973.

And in September 1969 . . . : "Insight: Francis C. Turner," *Washington Post Magazine,* February 3, 1986; Jack Eisen, "Express Bus Speeds Way to Old Slowdown," *Washington Post,* April 8, 1971; Fred Barnes, "Shirley Bus Boom Cuts Traffic," *Washington Star,* April 27, 1972.

The lanes were a tremendous . . . : Jack Eisen, "New Lane Puts Bus Far Ahead in 'Race,'" *Washington Post,* June 9, 1971.

303 "Buses are the answer . . .": Fred Brown, "U.S. Official Says Buses Solution to Transit Needs," *Denver Post,* May 26, 1971.

"There is no doubt in my mind . . .": Turner, "The Bus in Your Future."

The "infinite combinations . . .": Transcript, Turner speech to 90th annual meeting of the American Transit Association, Dallas, October 6, 1971 (FCT). For more on Turner's doubts about rail-based mass transit see Erich Blanchard, "New U.S. Roads Chief Says Subway Won't Cure Urban Ills," *Washington Post,* March 16, 1967; and Drew Marcks, "Mass Transit Overrated, Transportation Expert Says," *Baltimore News American,* October 5, 1973.

His favorite whipping boy . . . : Turner speech to the Road Gang, Washington, DC, November 1972. See also Turner, "A Quick Solution to Washington's Commuting Problem," *American Road Builder,* January 1974.

304 Turner was almost religiously . . . : "FHWA Chief Rips Proposals to 'Rob' Highway Trust Fund," *Transport Topics*, June 7, 1971.

"I am a firm believer . . .": Transcript, Turner confirmation hearing.

Back in 1962 . . . : *American Highways*, January 1963.

But even then . . . : 2008 interviews with Turner's children and with family friend Gay Wilkes.

305 In a June 21, 1972 . . . : Letter reproduced in *FHWA News*, October 27, 1972 (FCT).

His letter to Richard Nixon . . . : Ibid.

306 In March 1972 . . . : Jack Eisen, "Volpe Urges Use of Road Fund for Improving Mass Transit," *Washington Post*, March 15, 1972.

The president's reply . . . : *FHWA News*, October 27, 1972 (FCT).

307 He stumped for the protection . . . : FCT papers.

He toured Virginia . . . : Ibid.

He was among the organizers . . . : Ibid.; interviews with Alan Pisarski and Peter Koltnow.

Its twice-monthly . . . : Turner speech to the Road Gang, Washington, DC, November 1972.

As he'd feared . . . : "A Breach of Trust," editorial, *Dallas Morning News*, September 15, 1972; "Senate Takes Historic Step: Highway Funds for Transit," editorial, *Philadelphia Inquirer*, September 21, 1972; "Transit Breakthrough, . . ." editorial, *Washington Post*, September 21, 1972; and "Highway Trust Fund Takes Off in New Direction," *San Diego Union*, September 30, 1973. Turner's "free ride" quote is from Geistlinger, "First Person: Frank Turner."

308 Preserving the system . . . : Turner, "Looking Ahead from Milepost 1984 at the Federal-Aid Highway Program," *American Transportation Builder*, Winter 1985.

309 Likewise, Colorado officials . . . : "Pressure Renewed in I-70 Controversy," *Denver Post*, April 5, 1971; and R. A. Prosence and J. L. Haley, "Glenwood Canyon Interstate 70: A Preliminary Design Process That Worked," *Transportation Research Record* 757 (1980).

311 Never one to gloat . . . : Joe Wiles's late years were described by his daughters.

312 When he took the mike . . . : Interview with Beverly Cooke; Pisarski, "The Frank Turner Story."

Later that year . . . : Marvin Turner interview. Frank Turner died on October 2, 1999.

314 Between Nashville and Memphis . . . : I visited Jackson, Tennessee, during a road trip with my daughter, Saylor, in late June 2008.

317 The most expensive single . . . : http://www.boston.com/beyond_bigdig/; Seth Stern, "$14.6 Billion Later, Boston's Big Dig Wraps Up," *Christian Science Monitor*, December 19, 2003.

Case in point . . . : The bulk of my discussion of the system's disintegrating infrastructure, including all of the quotes but Frank Turner's, is from research I conducted for a *Parade* cover story published under my byline on March 8, 2009; some of the quotes made it into the magazine, some didn't. The Turner quote is from a March 4, 1986, speech he delivered to the New Jersey Alliance for Action (FCT).

321 Men in the auto business . . . : Correspondence between Fisher, Roy Chapin, and Henry Joy in the papers of the latter two men (Bentley).

Index

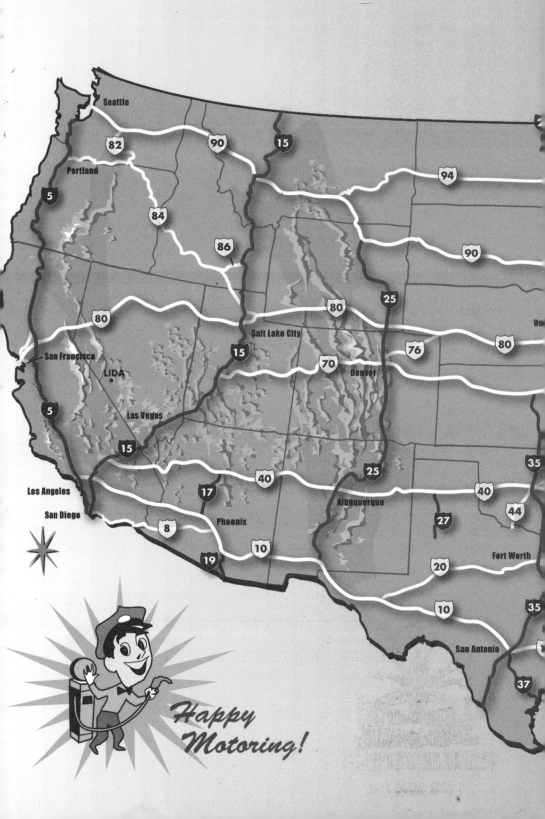